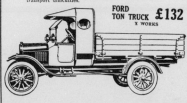

LETCHWORTH

The First Garden City

PRUDENS FUTURI

The Rotary Club of
Letchworth Garden City

PRESENTED TO D.G.
CHALMERS CURSLEY

It is always a great pleasure to welcome visitors
to our club in Letchworth Garden City. We hope
that you have enjoyed being with us and that you
will enjoy this book as a reminder of your visit

Bob Horgan

President

'Castle Corset' (Spirella), Fitzwater-Wray's 1923 cartoon. Cecil Hignett's imposing building (1912-20) towers above early Garden City buildings including 'The Cloisters', the Estate Offices, 'Homesgath', *The Skittles*, and a host of 'Bentley' bungalows.

LETCHWORTH

The First Garden City

MERVYN MILLER

PHILLIMORE

First Published in 1989 by
PHILLIMORE & CO. LTD
Shopwyke Manor Barn, Chichester, West Sussex

2nd edition, 2002

ISBN 1 86077 213 7

Printed and bound in Great Britain by
BUTLER & TANNER LTD
London and Frome

Contents

ST. JAMES'S PALACE

I am delighted to have the opportunity to congratulate Dr. Mervyn Miller on this revised history of Letchworth Garden City.

When Earl Grey proclaimed the foundation of the first Garden City at Letchworth in October, 1903, it was only five years since Ebenezer Howard had published his vision for a planned community, fusing the best of town and country living. With the help of an environmentally sensitive Master Plan, and the Arts and Crafts architecture of Barry Parker and Raymond Unwin, Letchworth set important planning standards for the twentieth century which remain highly relevant to us today.

In particular, Ebenezer Howard emphasized that residents should develop a positive commitment to their community. The creation of the Letchworth Garden City Heritage Foundation in 1995, with its charitable status and its obligation to apply the proceeds from the administration of the Letchworth Estate for the benefit of the community, is a present-day reflection of one of Howard's key principles. In January 1999, I visited Letchworth Garden City and saw for myself the remarkable transformation of the unique Spirella Building into modern offices which, nevertheless, retained intact its historic listed exterior and its marvellous ballroom. To me this project symbolized a willingness to invest in the regeneration of the first Garden City, as well as a model for others to follow.

My own experience of promoting a sustainable new community at Poundbury, on the outskirts of Dorchester, has given me an insight into some of the many challenges faced by community builders. It is remarkable that the first Garden City should have created a model which is still relevant a century later, and which remains capable of being updated to serve new needs. The Garden City continues to represent the antithesis of those many soulless housing estates which were developed in the mid-twentieth century, and which so tragically compromised and betrayed the principles of genuine community-building which Letchworth represented.

The forthcoming centenary of Letchworth represents a special occasion to recognize the contribution made by the first Garden City, and to reflect once more on the nature of planning and building which can properly reflect the needs and aspirations of the community as a whole. It is clear from this account of Letchworth Garden City that, despite the unprecedented changes in our way of life in the past century, its essential qualities continue to represent the enduring values of planning on a truly human scale. I hope that this message will not be lost on everyone concerned with community planning and "sustainable development" in Britain, and further afield.

To the original dedication to my son, Sam,
is added the memory of my mother,
Olive Miller, died 10 November 2001.

LIST OF ILLUSTRATIONS

Frontispiece 'Castle Corset'

LIST OF COLOUR ILLUSTRATIONS

ACKNOWLEDGEMENTS

The opportunity to revise this book after 13 years brought the task not only of bringing the story up to date, but also of addressing errors and omissions. In retracing my steps through the sources and archives noted at the end of this book, I have found that the story of Letchworth Garden City is even more remarkable than I originally supposed. The temptation to add length to my account of the sequence of events, from the publication of Ebenezer Howard's book in 1898, through the search for and purchase of a site, the excitement of the 'pioneer years', and the consolidation of a development that formed a model for community planning, had to be firmly held in check. I have added new material, where appropriate, however. I had seriously underplayed Lechworth's contribution to the Second World War, and the journey through the archives of the Letchworth Garden City Heritage Museum and the Hertfordshire Local History Collections at Letchworth Library, revealed the unstinting war effort, indomitable community spirit, and sacrifice of local servicemen and women.

The 1990s witnessed another transformation of the First Garden City's management and administrative structure. The Letchworth Garden City Heritage Foundation, established in 1995, is both a registered charity, and an entrepreneur in property development and management, with an obligation to distribute its operational surpluses for the benefit of the local community. In drafting its constitution, Howard's original concept was closely examined. The Foundation's immediate task was the regeneration of the town centre, which has brought physical and economic benefits, adding value to the fundamental asset of the First Garden City estate. In chronicling the activities of the Foundation, I am indebted to the co-operation and assistance of the Chairman, Peter Harkness; Director General, Stuart Kenny; and his colleagues, Director of Community Affairs, Allan Patterson; Director of Property, Marilyn Hands; and Director of Marketing and PR, Alan Howard, and his assistant, Christine Webb.

I am especially grateful to His Royal Highness, The Prince of Wales, for his Foreword to the book. Robert Lancaster, Curator of the First Garden City Heritage Museum; Ros Allwood, Curator of the Letchworth Museum; the staff of Letchworth Library, and Sue Flood, of Hertfordshire Archives and Local Studies, gave invaluable assistance, particularly over illustrations. William Heaton, of the Letchworth Garden City Society, lent material from his extensive postcard collection. Professor Takahito Saiki, of Kobe Design University Japan, spent a year in Letchworth in the 1990s, researching its development, and conducting a comprehensive aerial survey: I am indebted to him for two fine images, reproduced in the colour section. Professor Saiki also arranged for me to attend a remarkable conference, held in Tsukuba and Kobe in September 2001, at which the Garden City concept was analysed in detail. The Letchworth Garden City Heritage Foundation provided numerous illustrations of the refurbishment of Letchworth Garden City. Their generous underwriting of the colour printing has added substantially to the attractiveness of the book, and underscores the appeal of the Garden City, in art and architecture.

In producing the revised text, my secretary, Sheila Murray, worked tirelessly, integrating revisions, processing the new chapters, and co-ordinating old and new in the notes and bibliography. Eileen ten Hove coped gallantly with my chaotic index cards. The intervening period since the first edition has seen the death of many associated with the Garden City in its pioneer years, and with the promotion of planning history as an academic discipline. I should like to record my gratitude to the late Professor Gordon Cherry, for his initial encouragement to embark on my PhD study of Sir Raymond Unwin, and for his wise and kindly guidance over many years. During preparation of this revision, my mother, who always encouraged my work in the historical field, died: I have added her name to the original dedication to my son, Sam.

ILLUSTRATION ACKNOWLEDGEMENTS

The author wishes to thank the following for permission to reproduce illustrations: Margaret Bidwell, 60; *Comet Newspaper*, 128, 130; First Garden City Heritage Museum, Letchworth, 5, 11, 18, 23, 28, 29, 30, 32, 34, 35, 36, 43, 47, 48, 50, 53, 55, 60, 64, 66, 67, 68, 70, 71, 73, 74, 75, 77, 78, 79, 80, 81, 82, 83, 85, 86, 87, 88, 89, 90, 92, 93, 95, 96, 97, 98, 99, 100, 103, 104, 106, 109, 110, 111, 112, 113, 114, 116; William Heaton, 15, 16, 17, 19, 44, 45, 52, 72; Hertfordshire Archives and Local Studies, Hertford, 3, 4, 14; Hertfordshire Archives and Local Studies, Letchworth Library, 1940s end-papers, 115, 117, 118, 122, 123, 125, 126, 127; Joseph Rowntree Memorial Trust, 25; Letchworth Garden City Heritage Foundation, 131, 134, 135, 137, 138, 141, 142, 145, 146, 148, 149; Letchworth Museum and Art Gallery, North Hertfordshire Museums Service, 20, 21, 22; *North Herts Gazette*, 129; The late Mrs Barbara Barry Parker, 108; the remainder of the historic material is from the author's collection. Original drawings 56 and 145 by Mervyn Miller. Original photographs, 38, 41, 51, 54, 121, 124, 132, 133, 136, 139, 143, 144, 148 by Mervyn Miller.

The author wishes to thank the following for permission to reproduce colour plates: First Garden City Heritage Museum, Letchworth, VIII, XIV; Hertfordshire Archives and Local Studies, I; Letchworth Garden City Heritage Foundation, II, XXIII, XXVII, XXIX, XXX, XXXIII, XXXIV; Letchworth Garden City Heritage Foundation/BJP Photography, XXVIII; Letchworth Museum and Art Gallery, North Hertfordshire Museums Service, III, IV, V; Dr Takahito Saiki, XXXI, XXXII. The remaining colour photographs are by the author.

ONE

COKETOWN REBUKED

It [Coketown] was a town of red brick, or of brick that would have been red if the smoke and ashes had allowed it; but as matters stood it was a town of unnatural red and black like the painted face of a savage. It was a town of machinery and tall chimneys, out of which interminable serpents of smoke trailed themselves for ever and ever, and never got uncoiled. It had a black canal in it, and a river that ran purple with ill-smelling dye, and vast piles of buildings full of windows where there was a rattling and a trembling all day long, and where the piston of the steam-engine worked monotonously up and down like the head of an elephant in a state of melancholy madness. It contained several large streets all very like one another, and many small streets still more like one another, inhabited by people equally like one another, who all went in and out at the same hours, with the same sound upon the same pavements, to do the same work, and to whom every day was the same as yesterday and tomorrow, and every year the counterpart of the last and the next.

Charles Dickens, Hard Times (1856)

The Victorian industrial city elicited both praise and condemnation from many contemporary observers, not least the novelists and social analysts.[1] The work of Dickens was matched by that of Mrs Gaskell, who encapsulated the geographical and class division of society in the title *North and South.* Henry Mayhew was amongst the first to publish detailed observations of slum life, and the practice culminated in Charles Booth's massive *Life and Labour of the People in London*, in the last decade of the 19th century. The purpose of this chapter is to summarise the diverse reactions to urban environmental problems, of which such a keen social observer as Ebenezer Howard (1850-1928), the founder of the Garden City movement, would have been acutely aware. The context and the extent to which the Victorian city acted as catalyst will be discussed here, while more specific influences on Howard's concept will be described in Chapter Two.

The Health of Towns   The Victorian industrial city simultaneously represented both the triumph of economic progress and the tangible reflection of social and environmental consequences beyond the concern of *laissez faire* enterprise. Already, by 1801, 20 per cent of the population of England and Wales lived in towns with more than five thousand inhabitants, and by 1851 the proportion had grown to 54 per cent, rising to 72 per cent by 1891. In addition the population was growing rapidly and the largest cities and towns were attracting a great proportion of the increase, both by immigration and natural increase. London, with a population of 900,000 in 1801, expanded to 2,263,000 in 1851, reaching 3,900,000 in 1891. Important provincial cities rapidly expanded, primarily as a consequence of early industrialisation: in 1851 Liverpool had a population of 375,000; Manchester, 367,000; Birmingham, 232,000; Leeds, 172,000; Bristol, 137,000; Sheffield, 135,000; and Bradford, 105,000. The population of England and Wales doubled from 8,873,000 in 1801 to 17,927,000, and doubled yet again by 1911.

The local government structure, particularly during the early part of the century, was both ill-equipped and unwilling to regulate this massive urban expansion; between 1851 and 1911 rudimentary controls were introduced to alleviate some of the worst evils of slum housing, disease and overcrowding. Prior to 1830, a few towns established Improvement Commissions through private Acts of Parliament. The Liberal Reform government of the 1830s introduced rationalised Parliamentary constituencies and local government, laying the

1 Coketown personified – *Over London by Rail* – based on an etching by Gustave Doré (1832–83). The railway symbolised both the advance of the industrial revolution and the degradation of the urban environment.

foundations for civic pride, but much of this focused on the status of the city centres, and municipal aggrandisement.

National concern for public health arose following the widespread cholera epidemics of 1831-3, which claimed 32,000 victims, a further 62,000 in 1848-9, and a recurrence with 20,000 in 1853-4. Edwin Chadwick (1800-90), as Poor Law Commissioner, prepared reports on public health in the late 1830s, and a Select Committee on the Health of Towns reported in 1840.[2] In 1842 the Poor Law Commission reported on the Sanitary Conditions of the Labouring Classes. These reports identified the relationship between disease and polluted water supplies, arising from the lack of sewage and waste disposal facilities, and burial practices, and the contributory effect of overcrowded, particularly basement, housing was recorded.

Initially there was little government response. A Royal Commission, often known as the Health of Towns Commission, was appointed in 1843, to which Chadwick contributed significantly. A private propaganda organisation, the Health of Towns Association, was founded in 1844, and numbered Benjamin Disraeli among its supporters. The Metropolitan Association for Improving the Dwellings of the Industrious Classes (1841), and the Society for the Improvement of the Condition of the Labouring Classes (1844)[3] were constituted as charitable trusts, with articles of association limiting dividend to five per cent. They relied on altruistic investors, willing to accept a modest return for funding the construction and management of blocks of model tenements. In the 1860s the extensive work of the Improved Industrial Dwellings Company (1863), and the Peabody Trust (1862), coined the term 'five per cent philanthropy'. Between them the nine major Trusts had by 1905 housed 123,000; their limited dividend model was to prove a fruitful basis for Howard to expand as the development mechanism for his Garden City concept in the closing decade of the century.

Public Health Legislation 1848-75   Need for government intervention was underlined by the recurrence of cholera in 1848-9. Tentative efforts to control building standards had been reflected by local Building Acts, passed for 208 towns in England and Wales between 1800-45. The London Building Acts, first codified in 1774, had been extended and consolidated in the 1844 Metropolitan Building Act. However, a national perspective awaited passing of the 1848 Public Health Act. This was a landmark, in creating a central Board of Health, and empowering the formation of local Boards. The legislation controlled water supply and drainage, and introduced the passing of plans for buildings. A fundamental defect was its permissive adoption – by 1854 only 182 local Boards had been formed, but the pace quickened following the 1858 Local Government Act which extended powers to include constructional strength and stability, and space around buildings. Following the report of the Royal Commission on the Sanitary Administration of England (1869-71), the Local Government Board was established as the central government department with responsibility for public health, and, subsequently, housing and town planning. A further Public Health Act in 1872 established sanitary authorities with obligatory powers, measures consolidated in the Public Health Act of 1875. Model bye-laws followed two years later. The scene was set for the proliferation of the 'bye-law' suburb – healthier than the chaotic network of slum courts and alleys, but, to the aesthetically sensitive, a deadly reflection of unthinking conformity with prescribed standards, and further inducing the uncontrolled outward sprawl of the major urban areas.

Legislative concern extended to the closing of unfit housing from the 1860s. The Artizans' and Labourers' Dwellings Act of 1868, sponsored by William Torrens, aimed at introducing compulsory powers of demolition and repair, and building of replacement dwellings. In the event it was emasculated, but it highlighted the principle of the owner being publicly responsible for the condition of his property. The Home Secretary, R. A. Cross, promoted the Artizans' and Labourers' Dwellings Act, 1875, under which unhealthy areas could be cleared wholesale, and the land acquired for redevelopment by other bodies, including the housing trusts. There was, however, no obligation to re-house, and the legislation was sometimes used to enable lucrative commercial improvement, as with Corporation Street, Birmingham.

Practical Exemplars   Some industrialists were quick to learn the benefits, and subsequently advertising value, of model communities, housing a contented and productive workforce. Already in 1800, Robert Owen (1771-1858), a visionary industrialist whose name was to be linked with several Utopian schemes over the next three decades, was constructing housing for his workers at New Lanark,[4] a secluded valley 30 miles south-east of Glasgow. His stern moral proselytising was reflected in the dour rectitude of the community buildings, which today evoke the imagery of a closed society in which company domination of social life loomed large. Owen's *Report to the County of Lanark* (1820) advocated a series of agricultural and industrial villages, based upon unity and mutual co-operation, qualities which were to figure prominently in Howard's vision three quarters of a century later, but the notion of centralised control had, fortunately, disappeared. As will be discussed in Chapter Two, Howard's skill lay in tempering the extremism of Utopian concepts without sacrificing their essential principles.

By the 1860s a mainstream of model industrial villages had emerged which laid the foundation for further advances in the closing decades of the century. Freehold landowners could develop their estates largely as they wished, subject, as already noted, to few controls. In 1847, Colonel Edward Akroyd (1810-1887) began construction of housing at Copley, on the outskirts of Halifax in West Yorkshire.[5] Although back-to-back, the varied terraces, with mullioned windows and roof lines punctuated by gabled dormers, set a pattern for both local and more distant successors. Sir Titus Salt (1803-1876), a Bradford textile manufacturer who had made his fortune from alpaca, built a palatial complex of mills four miles north-west of the city, with housing to the south. Its name, 'Saltaire', combined its creator's name with the River Aire, on which a substantial park was laid out, next to the mills. Under construction from 1851-76, the village included varied terraces of housing in an Italianate style, a substantial

Institute, an imposing Church, and Almshouses for retired employees. The architects were Lockwood and Mawson. Not to be outdone, Akroyd founded a second village, Akroydon, on a hillside north of Halifax. Its main feature was an immense double quadrangle of Gothic-style housing, for which George Gilbert Scott (1811-78), one of the most eminent Victorian architects, acted as consultant. He also designed the impressive Gothic Revival All Souls church, nearby on Haley Hill. Akroyd's workforce considered their housing unduly like almshouses. Akroyd himself lived nearby. He aimed at merging social classes, an objective embraced by the Garden City movement, and particularly by Henrietta Barnett (1851-1936), at Hampstead Garden Suburb.

The Aesthetic Adventure   By the late 1880s, reaction against conventional Victorian values in the arts, architecture, and industry was manifested through the Arts and Crafts movement, influenced by the reforms in architecture and applied design advocated by John Ruskin (1819-1900) and William Morris (1834-96). Both had approached the shortcomings of the industrial society through their concern for the future of architecture and the arts, but they soon drew out the interdependence of aesthetics with social and economic factors.[6] Ruskin's prolific output of 'political economy' included passages which vividly anticipated the improved environment and integration of town and country advocated by the Garden City movement. Both Howard and, much later, Lewis Mumford selected the following quotation from Ruskin's *Sesame and the Lilies* for its figurative power in evoking the ideal settlement.

> Providing lodgments [for working people] means a great deal of vigorous legislation and cutting down of vested interests …; thorough sanitary and remedial action in the houses that we have, and then the building of more, strongly, beautiful in groups of limited extent … walled round so that there may be no wretched festering suburb anywhere, but clean and busy streets within, and the open country without, with a belt of beautiful garden and orchard around the walls, so that from any part of the city perfectly fresh air and grass and the sight of the horizon may be reachable in a few minutes walk. This is the final aim.[7]

Ruskin's imagery invokes Raymond Unwin's subsequent realisation of the built form of the Garden City. Morris perhaps provided a more strategic overview. In January 1884, lecturing in Leicester for the Socialist League, Morris hinted at the synthesis of social and environmental factors with which the Garden City movement, and subsequently town-planning, would be centrally concerned – 'honourable and fitting work', 'decency of surroundings'; and 'leisure'. 'Decency of surroundings' included

> 1. Good lodging; 2. Ample space; 3. General order and beauty. That is 1. Our houses must be well built, clean and healthy. 2. There must be abundant garden space in our towns, and our towns must not eat up the fields and natural features of the country. 3. Order and beauty means that not only our houses must be stoutly and properly built, but also that they be ornamented duly: that the fields be not only left for cultivation, but also that they be not spoilt by it any more than a garden is spoilt: no one for instance be allowed to cut down, for mere profit, trees whose loss would spoil a landscape: neither on any pretext should people be allowed to darken the daylight with smoke, to befoul rivers, or to degrade any spot of earth with squalid litter and brutal wasteful disorder.[8]

Rarely have the comprehensive goals in environmental planning been so succinctly and eloquently stated. Morris, of course, sought to attain such goals through revolution. Howard, who appears to have been indifferent to aesthetics, advocated 'the peaceful path', but could scarcely have been unaware of Morris's pronouncements. Raymond Unwin certainly was not, for in the early 1880s he joined the Socialist League as one of Morris's most active young acolytes. In the closing decades of the 19th century, Arts and Crafts began to appear, not only in individual houses, but also in model communities which directly influenced the built form of the Garden City.

Bedford Park, Port Sunlight and Bournville   Arts and Crafts architecture was first widely seen through the work of Philip Webb (1831-1915), who had designed the Red House for Morris himself in 1859-60, and more extensively through the buildings of Richard Norman Shaw (1831-1912). In the 1870s Shaw evolved richly eclectic architectural styles, one based on an Old English revival, another on country Queen Anne. This latter combined picturesque massing highlighted by the white painted sash, casement and bay windows, all three often mixed on the same building, with lively roof lines broken by numerous tall chimneys, and features such as gables enriched by tile hanging. The style formed the basis for Bedford Park, a middle-class suburb developed in west London from 1875 onwards, in which the street grid was purposefully fragmented to preserve mature trees, giving an informality and individuality to the grouping of houses designed by Shaw and others.[9] This visual harmony was disrupted in the late 1880s by a revolutionary tall white roughcast house, with stone mullioned windows, impudently commanding views across the village green. The architect was C.F.A. Voysey (1857-1941), one of the most influential of the younger Arts and Crafts followers, whose widely published designs for 'the smaller middle-class house' were to exert a profound influence over suburban and model Garden City housing, from the 1890s.

The 1890s witnessed the development of two of the most influential of the model industrial communities, which, in many respects, set environmental standards for the 20th century. They initiated a lineage, developed through the Garden City movement, Hampstead Garden Suburb, the pioneer 1909 Housing and Town Planning Act, and ultimately through local authority housing schemes prepared under the 1919 Housing Act. The begetters, W. H. Lever (1851-1925), and George Cadbury (1839-1922), both also assisted the Garden City movement during its crucial transition from theory to realisation.

Lever expanded a family grocery business into an industrial empire based upon Sunlight soap, brand leader by 1887 after only three years on the market. In 1888, he acquired a site on the west bank of the Mersey, between Birkenhead and Bromborough Pool, a pioneer model village built by Price's Patent Candle Company in 1853-8. North of his new factory he commenced construction of a model village named Port Sunlight in honour of his most profitable product.[10] Lever attended to its development with paternal pride, to realise 'a conveniently planned and healthy settlement laid out with all possible artistic thought on sound business lines'. He also built model housing at Thornton Hough, in the Wirral, around his newly acquired country house. Lever's architects, William Owen (1846-1910) and his son, Segar (b.1874), were among the leaders in the revival of the black and white Cheshire vernacular architecture. Their housing was strikingly individual, with elaborate, beautifully crafted, timber studwork above a stone base, a middle-class idealisation of working-class housing. This set the pattern for much of the development, although further consultants were employed, including London-based architects such as Ernest Newton (1856-1922) and Edwin Lutyens (1869-1944). The site of Port Sunlight, with its waterlogged channels, distorted the layout of housing quadrangles, but showed off picturesque grouping to advantage. Lever eschewed individual gardens in favour of open frontages, in which no individual shortcoming would spoil the corporate image. Allotments were provided in the inner quadrangles away from public view. Lever soon realised the publicity value of his settlement, which was regularly visited by leading politicians, and English and European royalty. The village was always, in effect, on parade, which created an uncomfortable impression of perpetual Sunday best. Lever had acquired a taste for town planning, and in 1909 endowed Liverpool University with a Chair in Civic Design. The following year a revised plan transformed Port Sunlight with Beaux-Arts formality. The creeks were infilled, creating vistas for formal set pieces such as the Lady Leverhulme Art Gallery.

Bournville was much less self-conscious, perhaps reflecting Cadbury's unassertive Quaker beliefs, which contrasted with Lever's loudly proclaimed non-conformist evangelism.[11] In 1879, Cadbury's chocolate factory moved five miles from the centre of Birmingham to benefit from the purer air of Bournbrook, near Selly Oak. Although advance housing for the works foremen was constructed, in a Victorian Italianate style, it was not until 1895 that development got fully under way, when Cadbury and his architect W. Alexander Harvey (1874-1951) began to plan a complete village. Harvey was influenced by Arts and Crafts architects, such as Voysey and M. H. Baillie Scott (1865-1945). His designs for informal terraces and semi-detached cottages rejected the more self-conscious artiness of Lever's village. The layout had affinity with Bedford Park, and community buildings and recreation areas were integrated, rather than standing out as formal set pieces.

Cadbury stressed the amenity, economic and recreative role of the individual garden, and plots were generously sized, allowing for a high proportion of a family's fruit and vegetables to be grown. Economy of construction, allied to the prevalent high quality of materials and craftsmanship, produced housing designs which influenced housing at New Earswick, Letchworth, and in the early London County Council cottage estates. In contrast to Port Sunlight, Cadbury made available up to half of the housing for non-Bournville employees, which promoted social integration and diminished the paternalistic character of the community.

Public Housing Initiatives   Isolated examples of local authority housing were built from the 1840s, but more general intervention was long delayed. The Royal Commission on the Housing of the Working Classes (1884-5), under the chairmanship of Sir Charles Dilke, and in which the Prince of Wales participated, received wide publicity. It revealed a situation in which street improvements had increased problems of overcrowded slum housing. As a Parliamentary Reporter, Howard would have been familiar with the findings. In 1892-4, he was official reporter of a Commission of Inquiry into Labour.[12] In 1888, Charles Booth began his monumental study of urban conditions, published as *Life and Labour of the People in London*, a 17-volume work which revealed overall that 35 per cent of the 900,000 population of East End London were in the three lowest classes of poverty. Later examination of the remaining districts confirmed that the findings were not restricted to the East End.

In 1888, the London County Council, the first of the metropolitan authorities, was created, with effect from 1 January 1889. Composed of an alliance of Liberals and Socialists, the L.C.C. pressed for improved housing legislation. In 1890, the Housing of the Working Classes Act consolidated existing measures, and added powers which enabled authorities to undertake housing for a demonstrated need, independent of their involvement in slum clearance.[13] A Housing Branch was created within the L.C.C. Architects Department, under W. E. Riley (1852-1937), which carried forward the pioneering work of the private trusts in its tenement estate at Boundary Street, Bethnal Green (1894-1900). A 1900 amendment to the legislation enabled local authorities to purchase land outside their own districts for housing schemes, and the L.C.C. acquired 39 acres at Totterdown Fields, Tooting, for their first cottage estate, soon followed by the much larger White Hart Lane, Tottenham scheme (1904-14).

The scene was set for the first 'Municipal Bournville', and this action was commended by Raymond Unwin at the first Garden City Association Conference, held in September 1901, appropriately hosted by Cadbury. The dawn of the 20th century appeared to herald a broad consensus on solutions to the housing problems created by the 19th. Although the underlying principles of the Garden City movement and concurrent moves towards improved housing and planning legislation were ultimately different, the imagery of the housing, drawn from Bournville and refined through the work of Unwin and the L.C.C. architects, was shared.

Two

An Ideal City Made Practicable

Ebenezer Howard (1850-1928)   Let Ebenezer Howard introduce himself:

> I was born on January 29th 1850, within the sound of Bow Bells in the City of London at 62
> Fore Street. My father's name was Ebenezer and he had several confectioners' shops round
> London. My mother was a farmer's daughter with good common sense, nothing brilliant about
> her … Fore Street has undergone many changes since 1850 but it is still one of those city streets
> where important looking warehouses stand cheek by jowl with confectioners and similar shops.[1]

The City of London had a Dickensian air during Howard's childhood. Ebenezer senior
was an absent-minded businessman. His lack of success possibly influenced his son's
advocacy that the Garden City company should undertake and regulate commercial activity.
Aged 4½, Howard witnessed the contrast between city and country life, when he was
sent away to a dame-school in Suffolk, and subsequently to Cheshunt, then a small
Hertfordshire coaching town, on the Cambridge Road. The latter left 'a latent memory
of fair landscapes and wholesome enjoyment would become active when long afterwards
the possibility arose of making a first Garden City in one of the choicest Counties in
England'.

Having completed his education at Stoke Hall, Ipswich, at 15, Howard joined Greaves and
Son, City Stockbrokers, as a clerk. He taught himself shorthand by taking down the sermons
of Dr Joseph Parker, of Poultry Chapel, a highly regarded non-conformist minister, who
stated that Howard's vocation would be as a preacher. The few surviving photographs of
Howard do give the impression of a rather muddling, slightly down at heel, yet defensively
respectable City clerk, of the type immortalised as Mr Pooter in George and Weedon
Grossmith's *Diary of a Nobody*. Yet Howard had a capacity for analytical thought and an
aptitude for unexpected, impulsive actions, both of which assisted his formulation and advocacy
of the Garden City concept.

American Adventure   In 1871, at the age of 21, possibly finding that both his intellectual
and spiritual non-conformity were too constrained by City life and work, Howard emigrated
to the United States with two companions. He travelled way out West, initially settling, for
two months, appropriately, in Howard County, Nebraska, as a homestead-farmer. He attrib-
uted his failure at this to the lack of co-operation from his companions and neighbours. On
his journey to Nebraska, crossing the River Missouri by ferry, Howard met Colonel William
Cody, alias 'Buffalo Bill'

> who was much interested in my rifle … of the Singer pattern … converted from an Enfield
> muzzle loader to a breech loader … I was much struck with his Winchester rifle … capable of
> firing 10 or 12 shots with one loading. [2]

The young Ebenezer survived the rigours of Western life – riding 30 miles in one day
without a saddle to obtain treatment for a septic hand at a military camp. After being given
a saddle for the return journey, and having quaffed 'a restorative which doubtless contained
whiskey', he galloped off 'in so cheerful a frame of mind', breaking his right stirrup, and was
promptly thrown off, happily unhurt. He retreated eastward to Chicago, Illinois, the hub of
the fast developing Mid-West, recovering from a disastrous fire, which had destroyed most
of the central business district in 1871. Howard worked for Ely, Burnham and Bartlett, law

2 Ebenezer Howard. The father of the Garden City greets readers of *Garden Cities of Tomorrow*.

stenographers until 1876, and became acquainted with Christian Science and Spiritualist circles after work, through Mrs Cora Richmond, a prominent Christian Science lecturer. The redevelopment of Chicago left its impact as he witnessed the growing American obsession with piling up increments in land values as the central business district was recreated in skyscraper form. Significantly, generous parks were also being laid out along the shore of Lake Michigan and the urban fringe, and Chicago was known as the Garden City of the mid-west. Its suburbs were growing rapidly. Twelve miles from the central 'loop', the great American landscape architect, F.L. Olmsted (1822-1903), had prepared a master plan for Riverside, one of the most prestigious suburban communities, with an informal layout, individual houses in generous plots, and landscaped parkway roads. Olmsted was, of course, best known for Central Park, New York, a lung of verdant landscape in mid-town Manhattan, a concept which was to be prominently featured in Howard's own Garden City diagrams.

Parliamentary Reporter Howard returned to England in 1876, although he subsequently revisited the U.S.A. to try to market his own improvements to the Remington Typewriter. A spare-time inventor, he worked on mechanical projects, culminating, towards the end of his life, in a complex shorthand typewriter. He joined the firm of Gurney and Son, official Parliamentary Reporters, and settled down to a career meticulously noting down details of lengthy debates, graduating to committees and government commissions. He was to reject Parliamentary procedure for bringing the Garden City to fruition. He was, nevertheless, impressed at the broad agreement on key problems such as housing and labour, but equally frustrated by the inability of Parliament to devise far-reaching and comprehensive solutions.

On 30 August 1879 he married Elizabeth Anne Bills, daughter of a Nuneaton innkeeper. The Howards honeymooned in Paris. 'Lizzie' proved to be an ideal partner, running a household on a slender income, supporting his activities, apparently unconcerned by the increasing domination of his extra-mural interests over family life. He joined the Zetetical Society, a debating club, which examined social and religious questions, and whose membership included the socialists Sidney Webb (1859-1947) and George Bernard Shaw (1856-1950), founder members of the Fabian Society in 1884. Howard spoke on Spiritualism in February 1880; the Society stimulated his broadening outlook.

Towards Utopia Howard's reading included early socialist writers. Although he never referred to Karl Marx, he was familiar with socialism through the writing of H.M. Hyndman, founder of the Social Democratic Federation. He also drew on the work of the anarchist Peter Kropotkin, who visited London in 1881, and discussed the merits of decentralised economic decision-making and self-government in his *Factories, Fields and Workshops*.[3] In 1883, Howard read Henry George's *Progress and Poverty* (1879), which examined the question of land reform, arguing that the artificially high values of city centre properties placed an undue financial burden upon the working class. A tax upon land values would help to recoup the value created by the community, which under free market conditions benefited landowners. This concept was to become one of the shibboleths of planning, and, to Howard, revealed the necessity of ensuring that land values increased by development were put into trust for communal benefit.

Howard acknowledged the influence of three distinct projects, from which he formed his own amalgam, 'A unique combination of proposals' which underpinned *Tomorrow: A Peaceful Path to Real Reform*, in which the Garden City concept was described in 1898. These were:

> (1) The proposals for an organised migratory movement of population of Edward Gibbon Wakefield and of Professor Alfred Marshall; (2) The system of land tenure first prepared by Thos. Spence [*sic*] and afterwards (though with an important modification) by Mr. Herbert Spencer; and (3) the model city of James Silk Buckingham.[4]

Wakefield had, in 1849, written of the necessity for overseas colonisation to be based upon a representative spectrum of society, rather than the social misfits who had been consigned to Australia, and Howard adapted the concept to the dispersal of population from the teeming industrial cities. Marshall was an eminent economist who had, in 1884, written of the desirability to decentralise population from central London to country estates and attract industries, to the mutual benefit of both the capital city and the new satellites. Thomas Spence, a late 18th-century radical from Newcastle-upon-Tyne, advocated parish ownership of land as a universal tenure, and his concept was revived by Hyndman in 1882. Howard wished to convey the rights to his model community after the purchase of the Garden City estate: he inherently distrusted nationalisation, which, to him, represented the substitution of one head ground landlord for another, without community accountability. Herbert Spencer, influential author of *Social Statistics*, had postulated that all men were equally entitled to use the earth, but could not work out an equitable system of compensating existing owners, which would also be remunerative to the community as a whole.

Howard credited a diverse group of philosophers and reformers with near discovery of the Garden City including Thomas More, Morris and Ruskin. Two Utopian community concepts were of significant importance in shaping the Garden City – James Silk Buckingham's *Victoria* (1849), and Dr Benjamin Ward Richardson's *Hygeia* (1876).[5] It was from the former that he drew most direct inspiration. Buckingham described his proposals in *National Evils and Practical Remedies*. A Model Town Association was to be formed by Act of Parliament and incorporated by Royal Charter. Development was to be wholly privately financed, however. A site of 10,000 acres (4,047 ha.) was to be purchased, on 1,000 acres (404.7 ha.) of which Victoria, a town of 10,000 inhabitants, would be constructed. Its layout was a square plan form, with major diagonal and radial avenues. The outer square contained 1,000 small houses, rented for £5 p.a.; the second, workshops; and larger houses, rented at £300 p.a., were located in the inner squares, together with public buildings. The whole settlement was to be illuminated by a central towering beacon. The development company managed the estate, retaining ownership of all buildings, and would also be the sole employer, operating a strict eight-hour day, providing free medical services, nurseries, public baths, kitchens and laundries. It would raise £3,000,000, in £20 shares, at least one to be held by every resident. £1,000,000 would be used to create industrial and agricultural enterprises, and dividends were to be limited to ten per cent. Howard was strongly influenced by Victoria, not least by its crisp finite form, which he transposed to circular geometry. He decided to attract industry to leased sites, believing that the development company might initially have insufficient financial resources for direct involvement. Buckingham's requirement for even the humblest resident to invest £20 in the community would have excluded those in greatest need of rehousing, and Howard dropped this. However, the partnership element was fundamental to the Co-Partnership movement, which subsequently built substantial amounts of housing at Letchworth, Hampstead Garden Suburb, and many model suburbs. Richardson's pamphlet *Hygeia or the City of Health* was based on his October 1875 lecture to the Social Science Congress in Brighton. He proposed a city with 100,000 population, 20,000 houses, built on a 4,000-acre (1,618 ha.) site, giving an average density of 25 persons per acre (61 p.p. ha.). The layout included three main tree-lined boulevards, below which ran an underground railway. Elaborate street cleansing mechanisms and houses built of glazed brick, with arches to permit maximum air circulation, would ensure a minimum mortality rate, the late 19th-century public health yardstick.

Both Buckingham and Richardson had taken their settlements out into the country and had proposed a self-contained built area in the centre of their estates. Agricultural enterprise figured prominently in Victoria, fusing town and country in functional symbiosis, while the countryside was to be brought into the streets of Hygeia. Howard was also well aware of the contribution to the urban park movement by Sir Joseph Paxton (1803-65),[6] and of the clean division between urban development and landscape found in parts of Bath and around Regents Park in London. The 1880s saw mounting agricultural depression, worsened by increasing imports of cheap cereals from America, as a consequence of Free Trade. Rural depopulation increased, swelling the urban population. As a counter-attraction, smallholding communities represented a significant theme in Utopian philosophy. In the 1840s a group of Chartist land colonies was begun by Fergus O'Connor (1794-1855), beginning at Heronsgate, near Chorleywood, Hertfordshire.[7] O'Connor overstretched his resources, his land company was declared illegal by a Commons Select Committee in 1848, and was compulsorily wound up in 1851. He died a broken man, but his settlements weathered the vicissitudes and served as models for the 'back to the land' movement of the late 19th century. Howard included smallholdings in his agricultural belt, which potentially assisted the integration of town and country more positively than the larger farms, and all would benefit from the accessibility of a ready market.

The Catalyst   An American Utopian novel by Edward Bellamy provoked Ebenezer Howard to formulate his own proposals. Published in 1888, *Looking Backward 2000-1887* described the transformation of Boston into a centralised consumer-oriented urban community, through technological advance and co-operation. The hero, Julian West, fell into a deep sleep on 30 May 1887, the public holiday for Decoration Day. He awoke on 30 September 2000, in the home of Dr Leete, who showed him a city transformed.

> At my feet lay a great city. Miles of broad streets shaded by trees and lined by fine buildings, for the most part not in continuous blocks, but in larger or smaller enclosures, stretched in every direction. Every quarter contained large open squares filled with trees, among which statues glistened and fountains flashed in the afternoon sun. Surely I had never seen this city nor one comparable to it before.[8]

Electrical power had created clean industry. A vast array of consumer goods was available, by credit card, from palatial showrooms, and purchases were delivered by pneumatic tube. The state was the sole employer, and held a monopoly over production and employment. Entertainment was available in every home through piped music, played around the clock in distant studios. Howard read the book at a sitting, initially carried away by its visionary eloquence and conviction.

> The next morning as I went up to the City from Stamford Hill I realised, as never before, the splendid possibilities of a new civilisation based on service to the community, and not on self-interest, at present the dominant motive. Then I determined to take such part as I could, however small it might be, in helping to bring a new civilisation into being.[9]

Howard underwrote the English publication of Bellamy's book, by taking 100 copies, largely given away to friends, and by compiling an index. Later, he would become sceptical about the centralised socialism that controlled every aspect of life in Bellamy's utopia. *Looking Backward* elicited a characteristically different response from William Morris, who shunned Bellamy's technocratic socialism, and retreated into medievalist guild socialism with *News From Nowhere* (1890), in which he described a communal society living in a federated network of villages, the poetic epitome of decentralisation.[10]

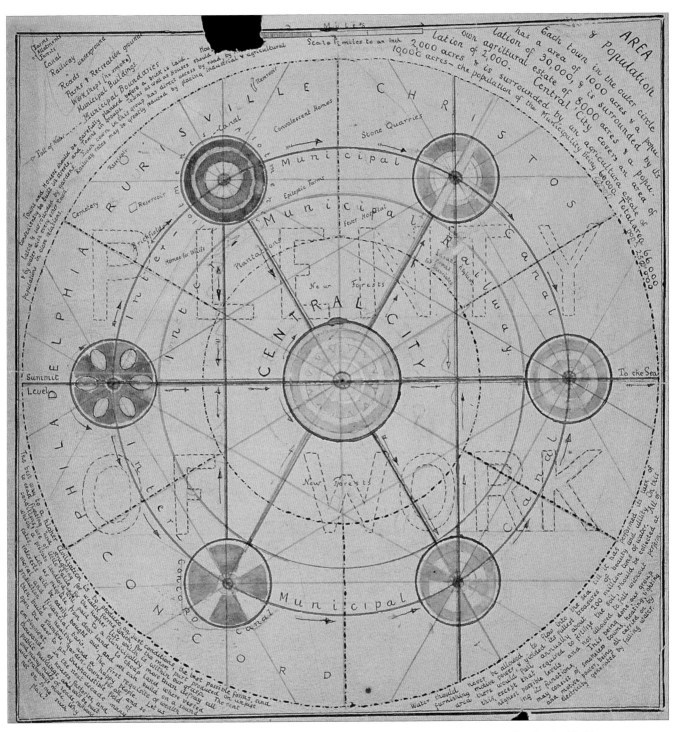

I A group of smokeless, slumless cities. Ebenezer Howard's hand-drawn diagram for the Social City cluster predates the publication of *Tomorrow*.

II 'From his Garden City friends.' Howard's portrait by Spenser Pryse was presented to him at a Dinner held in March 1912 at the Holborn Restaurant.

III William Ratcliffe (1870-1955), 'Manor Farm, Norton'. The farm was owned by Roger Parker, Barry's younger brother, who added a sleeping porch at the back, from which this view was painted.

IV Spencer Frederick Gore (1878-1914), 'The Road', 1912. This masterly image, by one of the leaders of the Camden Town Group, highlights the bright newness of the infant Garden City.

V Francis King (1905-2001), 'Letchworth Station – scene at dusk', 1950. The eerie half-light casts a sinister overtone on a familiar scene.

VI First Garden City Heritage Museum, built as the Parker and Unwin offices in 1907, seen in January 2002 after its re-thatching.

VII 'Howgills', Friends Meeting House, 1907, designed by Bennett and Bidwell, still evocative of the 'spirit of the place'.

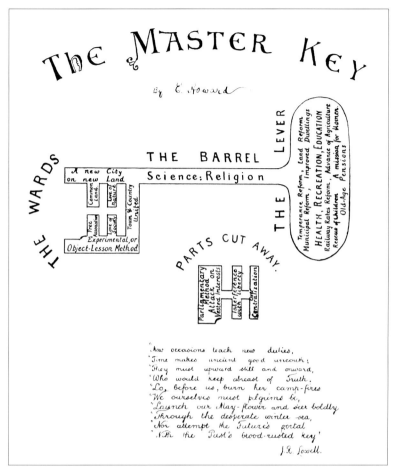

3 'The Master Key', Howard's unpublished sketch diagram, controversially cut away Parliamentary method as an obstacle to progress.

As the 1890s dawned Howard's concept took shape. Drafts and diagrams were discussed with family and friends. He was heartened by the evidence given by all parties, including the trades union leaders Ben Tillet and Tom Mann, to the Royal Commission on Labour (1892-4), at which he was the official reporter. Yet his distrust of government remained and he wrote a long chapter, 'The Master Key',[11] illustrated by a diagram in which he summarised the prerequisites for the new society, to be achieved through the 'experimental object-lesson method'. The key was to be fashioned by cutting away the redundant parts in order to fit and turn the lock – Howard cut away 'Parliamentary method', which he felt would support vested interests against social progress. He noted that 'it is in practice long after a majority are distinctly agreed on the passing of a measure that it at length emerges in a frequently mangled [*sic*] shape from this cumbrous piece of machinery'.[12]

In the event the chapter and diagram were omitted, though references to 'The Master Key' remain in Howard's introductory chapter to *Tomorrow*. Diagrams which were published were also modified[13] – the sketch of the 'Ward and Centre' of Garden City was originally embellished with land costings and the Biblical exhortation to 'go up and possess the land!'; this was struck through in pencil 'omit this'. The early 1890s were a period of social unrest, with Morris's Socialist League fragmenting into revolutionary anarchist groups. Evidently, Howard was persuaded that discretion would ultimately prove to be the better part of valour. Likewise, his land requirement for his prototype varied – Howard originally specified 9,000 acres (3,642 ha.), reduced to 6,000 (2,428 ha.) on publication. The name ranged through 'Unionville' and 'Rurisville' before the clarity of 'Garden City' was adopted. On the cluster diagrams showing 'the Social City', 'Christos', with possible overtones of blasphemy, disappeared in

4 Sketch of 'Ward and Centre'. The Biblical command, 'Go up and possess the land!' was omitted from the published version of *Tomorrow*.

favour of 'Gladstone', commemorating the Grand Old Man of Victorian politics, who died in 1898. Finally the manuscript was ready for publication. Swan Sonnenschein, of Paternoster Square, London, a firm noted for socialist literature including the English Edition of Marx's *Das Kapital*, issued the book in October 1898. *Tomorrow: A Peaceful Path to Real Reform* at last appeared in print.[14]

The Prototype Described　Howard described and illustrated his prototype with the precision of an inventor. He introduced the concept with chosen quotations from contemporary observers and illustrated it with 'The Three Magnets', one of the most famous of all planning diagrams succinctly summarising his physical, social and economic objectives. Over magnets representing 'Town', 'Country', and his new community, 'Town-Country', he superimposed the advantages and disadvantages of each. Terms such as 'Social Opportunity', 'Lack of Society', 'Gin Palaces', and 'Hands out of Work', have acquired Victorian overtones but do not obscure Howard's overall objective of combining the advantages of both town and country living and eliminating their disadvantages. If he achieved this ideal, the people would, given free choice and mobility, be drawn like iron filings to the strongest, the town-country magnet. With mounting enthusiasm he wrote

> Town and country *must be married, and out of this joyous union with spring a new hope, a new life, a new civilisation*. It is the purpose of the work to show how a first step can be taken in this direction by the construction of a town-country magnet; and I hope to convince the reader that this is practicable, here and now, and on principles which are the very soundest … from the ethical or the economic standpoint.[15]

The reader was asked to visualise the purchase of a 6,000-acre (2,428 ha.) estate, costing £240,000, or £40 per acre, an average for first-class rural land.[16] Capital would be raised by a development company, which would hold the estate in Trust 'first as a security for the

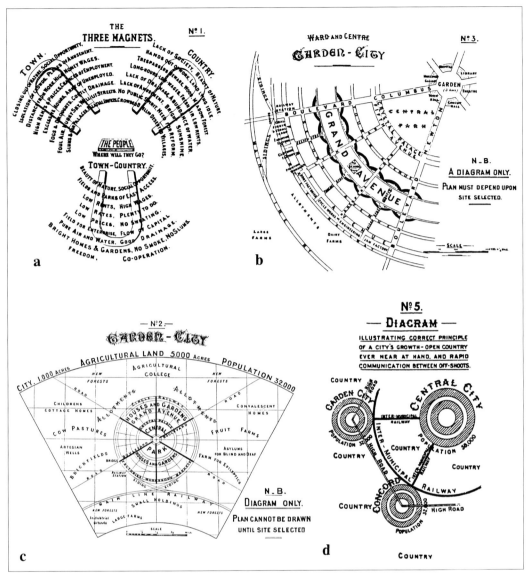

5 Iconography from *Garden Cities of Tomorrow*.
a. 'The Three Magnets', the most famous of Howard's diagrams, brilliantly summarised the key points of his advocacy of a 'joyous union' of town and country.
b. 'Ward and Centre' showed formal housing crescents along the Grand Avenue, and laid the basis for the concept of the neighbourhood unit.
c. 'The Garden City and Rural Belt' protected the green setting from development, yet suggested that it should serve the central settlement.
d. 'The Correct Principle of a City's Growth' diluted the message of the complete social city cluster of 1898.

debenture holders, and secondly … for the people of Garden City … which it is intended to build thereon'. Articles of association would limit the dividend to five per cent, with any surplus covenanted for community benefit. The proposal followed the traditional method of buying cheap land for development and, through periodic revaluations, raising additional capital to complete the scheme. Addition of the dividend limitation created five per cent philanthropy writ large. 1,000 acres (404.7 ha.) in the centre would be developed for the town area, in circular form, nearly ¾-mile radius. The Garden City would house 30,000 residents, with an additional 2,000 in the surrounding agricultural belt, which was to be preserved

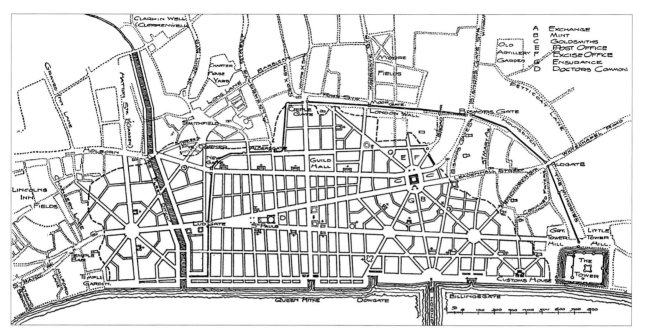

6 The Wren Plan for rebuilding the City of London, 1666. Wren's layout, with its combination of grid and radial roads, helped Unwin to formulate the layout for Letchworth. The resemblance between the area around 'The Exchange' and the centre of Letchworth is striking.

permanently from urban development. It would form a productive adjunct to the Garden City providing building materials, from brick earth or stone quarries depending on the geology of the chosen site. Smallholdings and allotments, hospitals and institutions, and facilities for recreation would be included. A main line railway would feed a circular loop serving the peripheral industrial belt. Through extensive use of electricity, a clean working environment would oust the dark satanic mills of Coketown.

The circular Garden City would be subdivided by six broad radial boulevards, each 120 feet wide, and named after the great historic figures, including Newton and Columbus, into wedge-shaped local wards, which anticipated the neighbourhood unit, one of the key community planning concepts of the 20th century.[17] Concentric circumferential avenues, numbered one to five, from the perimeter inwards, completed division into blocks, with cross roads named after such great literary figures or inventors as Milton and Shakespeare, Kelvin and Edison. Examination of *Tomorrow* reveals comparatively little detail of its built form or about housing provision. The major part of the latter was to be provided in 5,000 plots, with an average width of 20ft by 130ft depth, long narrow slices of land comparable with conventional bye-law terraced development. However, the built area was to be subdivided into two by a central circular Grand Avenue, shown flanked by curving sectoral crescents, suggestive of Regents Park, Hove or Bath. The Grand Avenue was to be 420ft wide, forming an internal green belt more than three miles long; a 115-acre park, within which would be six school sites, one for each ward, surrounded by playgrounds and gardens, with sites for churches and local community buildings. Reaching Fifth Avenue, a name immediately suggestive of the prestige development near Grand Central Station, New York, had residential development opposite an immense 'crystal palace', containing all commercial, shopping and exhibition facilities. Paxton's original Crystal Palace, wonder of the Victorian age at the Hyde Park Exhibition of 1851, had been rebuilt at Sydenham Hill, within sight of Howard's Dulwich home, on the southern outskirts of London. It long remained a popular cultural and exhibition centre. Howard extended the concept to include shops. His annotated copy of *Tomorrow* included photographs of the imposing Galleria Vittore

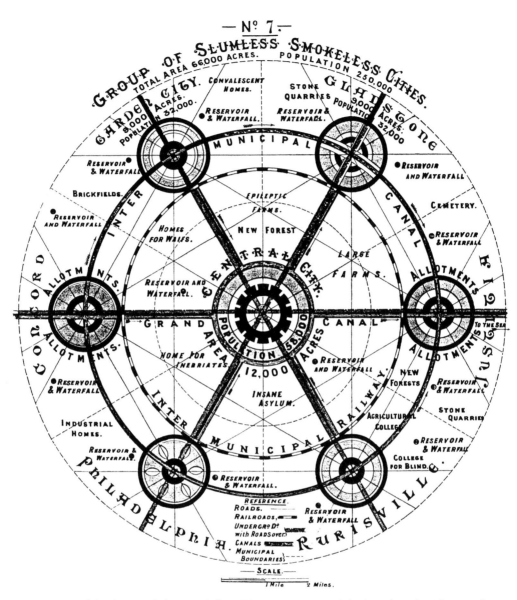

7 'A group of slumless, smokeless cities', from *Tomorrow*, represented the 'Social City', with a population of 250,000, analogous to Milton Keynes in the late 20th century.

Emmanuele in Milan (1865-67). William Moseley had proposed a 'Crystal Way', for London, in evidence to the Select Committee on Metropolitan Improvements in 1855.[18] Parallels with modern shopping malls are readily discernible, particularly that built at Central Milton Keynes in 1973-9. The crystal palace encircled a 145-acre (58 ha.) Central Park, with six major public buildings at the hub – museum and gallery; hospital; library; theatre; concert hall; and town hall. The overall character had a formality associated with Baroque plans such as Karlsruhe or L'Enfant's brilliant plan for Washington D.C. A network of main radial avenues running from a central square, with an imposing public building, was also to be found on Christopher Wren's 1666 plan for rebuilding the City of London. Howard sensibly warned that the final layout must depend upon the site selected. There was little suggestion, however, that the Garden City would consist predominantly of small houses, with little formal urban character.

The individual Garden City was only to be one element in the larger Social City cluster of six Garden Cities,[19] each of 32,000 population, around a larger 'Central City' of 58,000 population, all linked by inter-urban rapid transit and, in the original version, by canal. The federated Social City would have the benefit of a range of services and leisure activities available to a population of 250,000, without the congestion associated with a single town of that size. Howard stated that, as each Garden City approached completion, its development company would float a subsidiary to acquire a new site nearby, thus building up the overall complex. He did not describe the effect of bidding up the cost of the land through this process, but such was his confidence in his overall objective that he acquired the site for Welwyn Garden City as agricultural land a mere 15 years after the commencement of Letchworth.

The remaining chapters dealt with the revenue of the estate and its administration.[20] Howard envisaged that the whole of the revenue would be raised through his scheme of 'rate rents'. Fair rents from the land and property would, he believed, be more than sufficient to pay the interest on the purchase price of the estate; to provide a sinking fund to pay off the principal; and to construct and maintain all infrastructure normally provided by public authorities. After payment of limited dividends, he anticipated a large surplus for community purposes, which might even provide old age pensions or personal accident or health insurance. Individual leases would impose landlord covenants to apply the whole of the income to secure Howard's stated financial objectives. Administration of the city was to be by a Board of Management, to be elected by the tenants. Howard never formulated an entirely satisfactory control structure, and this was perhaps his greatest weakness. He shied away from the political role of the Board, although he provided details of every function of its administrative structure. While industry would be privately financed, and could range from the customary capitalist enterprises to co-operative ventures, shopping, together with varied social services, was described as 'pro-municipal undertakings', envisaged largely as non-profit making trusts. Howard also felt that housing could constitute such an activity, although he stated that the Company's finance might be overstretched if it attempted this from the outset,[21] thereby anticipating difficulties encountered in developing Letchworth. Other organisations such as building societies, co-operative societies, or even trade unions might enter the housing field. Finally, Howard reassured his readers that it was to be regarded as neither a communist nor a socialist experiment.[22] He was well aware of the many failures, which had beset earlier ideal communities, and of the controversy of emergent socialism, notwithstanding the success of the Fabian 'progressives' in the L.C.C. coalition. He had written his specification for a group of 'slumless, smokeless cities', and had described the prototype Garden City in detail.[23] He ensured that review copies of *Tomorrow: A Peaceful Path to Real Reform* were widely distributed after publication early in October 1898, and doubtless awaited public reaction with keen anticipation.

THREE

UTOPIA LIMITED

Mixed Reviews   Prophetically, Gilbert and Sullivan chose the title *Utopia Limited* for one of their last Savoy Operettas, produced in October 1893. Unusually for them, it was a comparative failure. The title was revived for a review heading for Howard's book. The catchpenny phrase aptly evokes the, perhaps, unlikely combination of an ideal community with a development company. In later years, with Letchworth and subsequently Welwyn underway, Howard and his followers possibly recalled the operetta's subtitle *The Flowers of Progress*, appropriately encapsulating the movement's internationally acclaimed achievements. Overall, the press was fair, if critical. *The Times* grandly pronounced 'the details of administration, taxation etc. work out to perfection, the only difficulty is to create such a city, but that is a small matter to Utopians'. Perhaps the unkindest comments came from *Fabian News*, which patronisingly concluded

> His [Howard's] plans would have been in time if they had been submitted to the Romans … we have got to make the best of our existing cities, and proposals for creating the new ones are about as useful as would be arrangements for protection against visits from Mr Wells' Martians.[1]

H.G. Wells (1866-1946), who had looked to the future through his vividly written science-fiction, was closely involved with the Fabian Society, whose secretary Edward Pease made the gratuitous reference. He was also scarcely complimentary about Howard's literary style. 'The author has read many learned and interesting writers and the extracts … are like plums in the unpalatable dough of his Utopian scheming', while Howard's diagrams were 'pretty coloured plans, nicely designed with a ruler and compass'. Considering that the prominent Fabians, Sidney Webb and Bernard Shaw, had been close to Howard in the Zetetical Society, this was a patronising dismissal. However, Wells relented sufficiently to become a vice-president of the Garden City Association within two years, while Shaw remained affectionate, if unable to resist directing the odd Shavian barb towards Howard.

Others were prepared to take Howard seriously. The *Manchester Guardian* felt that 'one or two model cities built under such auspices as to philanthropy and scientific modern ideas, as the Garden City … would be inspiring object lessons' and *Co-operative News* declared the concept 'a creative outlet for true co-operative enterprise', claiming that a 1d. levy per member per month for three years would purchase the freehold for the First Garden City.[2] Howard felt that its reception demonstrated that his scheme 'touches life at every point',[3] and that its broad potential appeal would endure.

The Path Forward   Shortly after publication, Howard began to lecture on 'an ideal city made practicable', first in December 1898 at Rectory Road Congregational Church, Stoke Newington, north London, then further afield to Glasgow and Manchester. By June 1899, sufficient interest had been generated to form the Garden City Association, with Fred Bishop of Tunbridge Wells as Chairman, and a barrister, F. W. Steere, who was also Secretary of the Land Nationalisation Society. The M.P. for Dundee, Sir John Leng, presided at the inaugural meeting held on 21 June. Howard began to attract public figures respected for their balanced views, which enhanced the credibility of the movement.

The Association's objects were

> To promote the discussion of the projects suggested by Mr Ebenezer Howard in *Tomorrow*, and ultimately to formulate a practicable scheme on the lines of that project.[4]

The minimum subscription was set at 1s. 0d. (5p) to attract a wide membership – perhaps Howard visualised thousands of co-operators committing their accrued monthly pennies, while 2s. 6d. (12.5p) bought the Association's full literature. With increasing publicity, Howard started the first press book, of a series forming a valuable record of the movement's pre-Letchworth 'Old Testament'. At a lecture in Hindhead, Surrey, Bernard Shaw wrote of 'Ebenezer the Garden City Geyser' [*sic*], concluding that 'I [Shaw] was the man who really understood … the geyser being a mere spring of benevolent mud'.[5] Howard marked up a London street guide to aid recruitment and three months later claimed membership from professionals, industrialists, Members of the L.C.C., and all political parties. Sectional Committees were convened to discuss land tenure, manufacturers and trade, labour, housing and public health, taxation, liquor, traffic, education, smoke abatement, and art. In May 1900 the Association resolved to form a limited company with £50,000 capital to be called Garden City Limited,[6] although two years were to elapse before the Garden City Pioneer Company was floated to search for a suitable site.

Eminent Recruits   In 1901 the Association's standing was assisted by the recruitment of two key, but different personalities. Howard learned that Ralph Neville, K.C. (1865-1930) had given full support to the Garden City project in an article in *Labour Co-partnership*.[7] He enlisted Neville who was unanimously elected as Chairman shortly after. A rising barrister, his involvement signalled that the Association was not lightly to be dismissed as a Utopian band of cranks. In April 1901, Thomas Adams (1870-1940), a young Scots surveyor with experience as a Liberal party agent and an interest in rural regeneration, was appointed Secretary of the Association.[8] His flair for publicity ensured regular reporting of the Association's activities. He encouraged George Cadbury, one of the Association's many Vice-Presidents, to host a national conference, held in Birmingham, at the Y.M.C.A. Hall, and in Bournville, on 21-22 September 1901.[9] This was the first of many, which spread the propaganda value of the Garden City concept, and its precursors, the model industrial communities. The conference represented a benchmark, both for the Garden City movement and the evolution of British Town Planning.

The Bournville Conference and its Successors   Neville and Earl Grey were joint Presidents of the Conference, whose objective was

> to consider the experiment of Mr Cadbury in moving their [*sic*] works to Bournville; the difficulties and advantages which attend the removal of works from large cities to new districts; how local districts … can co-operative with such movements … so that new towns may be established on land to be purchased for the community.[10]

A young architect from Derbyshire, Raymond Unwin moved the first resolution urging local authorities to make full use of the 1900 amendment to the Housing of the Working Classes Act 1890, and acquire outlying land for decentralised housing, to relieve inner-city overcrowding. This would be, he declared, a preliminary step 'until we can realise something in the nature of the Garden City proposal'.[11] There was a pointed contribution from Shaw, in the unlikely role of a St Pancras Borough Councillor, castigating his authority for conniving at illegal overcrowding and underground housing. F. Lee Ackerman (1878-1950), subsequently a leading advocate of Garden Cities in the United States, urged industrial decentralisation to 'areas … carefully planned so as to make adequate provision for the industrial and social needs of the people, especially with a view to securing for all time the advantages of town and country life'. Following an observation that the proposal appeared

Utopian, Howard emphasised its practicability if a wide range of industries could be attracted. The problem was of national scale, but should not, he stressed, await a government solution. He contended that the attending delegates represented 'sufficient power to start a Garden City'.

The next day, after a morning tour of Bournville, at the concluding session, Neville reiterated support of the Garden City's financial soundness, and three essential prerequisites:

1. The purchase, at agricultural prices, of land for a city;
2. The retention for the benefit of the community of the increased value of the land created by the community;
3. The permanent restriction of the area to be covered by buildings.[12]

The proceedings were enlivened by Shaw's imagining the discovery of a gold mine on the site, with the residents buying out the shareholders and retiring to Monte Carlo on the proceeds. Amid laughter he provided the answer to his rhetorical question:

> The answer is perfectly inevitable: that you must keep the unearned increment in the hands of the trustees … this notion that you are going to found a Garden City in order to make the inhabitants … the absolute proprietors would undoubtedly lead to this: if by an accident, owing to the development of industry, it became very valuable, you would enable the inhabitants to retire practically as landowners … sell their property … If you want to get this experiment through be prepared to meet that objective, and to show that your deed of trust does provide for that contingency.[13]

Shaw was not convinced by Neville's case, and corresponded with him at length after the Conference. As a committed Socialist, Shaw felt that capitalists would circumvent any restrictions on their activities. They were indispensable to the creation of Howard's Garden City, but could, equally, create their own, without his restrictions if they chose. They could afford to take the long view, and bind themselves through the five per cent limitation, which they would repudiate with alacrity once the potential return was worth fighting for. This proved to be the case during the take-over struggle almost sixty years later. Shaw had, almost casually, placed his finger on the flaw of the scheme, which was to prove almost fatal to the survival of Letchworth. For the present, however, doubts were silenced. Other papers[14] included Howard's 'Garden cities: manufacturers and labour' which gave examples of industrial mobility and a thumbnail description of the project, and two on housing. The first, by H. Clapham Lander (1869-1954), extolled the merits of co-operative housing – he would later design 'Homesgarth' (Sollershott Hall) co-operative flats at Letchworth. Unwin's 'On the building of houses in the Garden City' will be discussed later for its significance as a design brief for the Letchworth Master Plan.

The Conference attracted extensive publicity – no doubt in response to Adams's press releases. The Association's December 1901 Annual General Meeting was reported under the eye-catching by-line 'a five per cent model township'. Even critical comments could be turned to advantage – in January 1902 John Burns M.P. stated that garden cities would not solve London's housing problems. Adams immediately reiterated the prime objective 'to secure the unearned increment of the land' as being almost more important than providing low rent, low density housing to relieve inner congestion.[15] Early in March 1902, Adams represented the Association at a Manchester Co-operative Housing Conference on the theme of 'Municipal Bournvilles'. W.H. Lever, evidently not to be upstaged by the Cadburys, offered to host a Garden City Association Conference at Port Sunlight the following July. Between December 1901 and July 1902, membership of the Association increased from 520 to 1,300.[16] Howard revised his book for republication in a paper-covered shilling (5p) edition, under the title *Garden Cities of Tomorrow*, by which it would become universally known. This change of emphasis, from the 'real reform' of the original to the physical entity of the new community, was symbolised by Walter Crane's Pre-Raphaelite drawing of a medieval maiden holding aloft a model of a walled city. The

8 The 1902 re-issue of Howard's book, under the title *Garden Cities of Tomorrow* featured an attractive cover, drawn by the Socialist artist, Walter Crane.

drawing, used subsequently on the cover of the Association's journal *The Garden City*, almost unwittingly anticipated the take-over of the design image for the First Garden City by the Arts and Crafts movement.

The Garden City Pioneer Company On 2 June 1902, the Association convened a major meeting in London, which resolved to establish the Garden City Pioneer Company, with a working capital of £20,000, registered on 16 July 1902.[17] Its Articles of Association required acquisition of a site on which 'to lay out, construct, manage, and carry on any such Garden City'.

> The estate selected [is] to be carefully planned under the best expert advice, so that as the town grows, factories and workshops, the houses of the people, the parks and open spaces, schools, churches and other public buildings, may be placed in the most convenient position.[18]

Furthermore 'a broad belt of agricultural land around the town' would be placed 'under such restrictive covenants as may secure to the inhabitants the enjoyment for all time [of] the combined advantages of town and country life'. Town Planning in a readily identifiable form had virtually arrived.

Not unnaturally, Neville became Chairman, Howard, Managing Director, and the Board included George Cadbury, and T.H.W. Idris, a soft drinks manufacturer. Harold Clapham Lander, an architect who subsequently designed many buildings in Letchworth, including Howard's co-operative venture 'Homesgarth', was also a director. Cadbury had purchased 300 one pound shares, with an undertaking to increase his holding to 1,000, provided that the whole of the £20,000 was raised. Alfred Harmsworth, proprietor of *The Daily Mail*, provided support of up to £1,000, as did Lever. Neville subscribed £1,000, and Howard Pearsall, who subsequently made Letchworth his home, £120. The process was begun systematically. The Board formed a Site Sub-Committee, which drew up assessment criteria:

1. That the estate should consist of from 4,000 to 6,000 acres [1,618 to 2,428 ha.] of freehold land in a ring fence.
2. That it should have on or adjacent to it a main line of railway.
3. That there should if possible be means of water carriage.
4. That the estate should be capable of an economical drainage scheme.
5. That a completely satisfactory water supply should be available.
6. That it should be near to London or some other large centre of labour.[19]

Lists of major landowners were drawn up, by counties, and estate agents were contacted.[20] Due to a prevailing depression in agriculture, a wide range of estates was available, in all parts of the country. Investigations were conducted confidentially, to inhibit premature speculation.

Chartley Castle – the near miss   By early October 1902, Howard and Adams had formed favourable opinions of the 8,000-acre (3,237 ha.) Chartley Castle estate in Staffordshire, which fulfilled many of the conditions. As Chartley was to figure so prominently among the sites considered by the Pioneer Company over the next few months, it is appropriate to pause awhile to consider it further. The estate was owned by the Ferrers family, whose principal seat was at Staunton Harold, near Ashby-de-la-Zouch in Leicestershire. The family traced their origins to the time of Edward the Confessor, and had distinguished themselves in the armies of Edward III and Henry V.[21] Savallis Edward Shirley, 10th Earl of Ferrers (1847-1912) used Chartley mainly as a sporting estate. By the turn of the century he had amassed substantial debts, and was under pressure to reduce his obligations to one unnamed money lender to £100,000, an enormous sum, equivalent to at least £3 million a century later.[22]

The possibility of selling Chartley had been under consideration for several years. The hall had Elizabethan origins, although substantially rebuilt after a fire in the 1840s. It looked eastward to the Chartley Deer Park, with a ruined castle, built 1229 by Ranulph Blundeville, 4th Earl of Chester.[23] The surrounding, gently undulating countryside included 34 dairy farms, and the villages of Stowe-by-Chartley, Hixon, Drointon, Amerton and part of Weston-on-Trent. With the meets of the Meynell Hunt, plantations and coverts for breeding game birds, a well-stocked lake and fishing rights on the River Blythe to the east of the estate, it may have seemed ideal for the pursuits of a country gentleman, if not for a Garden City.

The estate lay midway between Stafford and Uttoxeter, remote from the industrial con-urbations of the West Midlands and the North Staffordshire potteries. Stafford, five miles from the south-west boundary of the estate, and eight from Stowe-by-Chartley, was still a modest country town, but had become an important railway junction, and a branch factory had been opened by Siemens, the German electrical firm. This prompted Howard to inves-tigate the potential for industrial development. The River Trent bordered the estate on the south-west, and the Trent and Mersey Canal ran northwards to Stoke. The main Stafford-shire Railway, which connected with the London and North Western Railway at Colwich, also served Stoke, connecting back to the LNWR route to Manchester via Macclesfield. A sleepy branch line of the Great Northern Railway ran from Stafford to Uttoxeter, diagonally across the estate, and it was claimed that, by changing at Stafford, connection could be made to London in 2½ hours, Birmingham in 1 hour and Manchester in 1¾ hours. While there was a likelihood that some industry would locate near Weston, this potentially conflicted with the amenity of the adjoining Ingestre Estate of Earl Shrewsbury.[24] It was recognised that the GNR line would require upgrading, and further light railways built, if development was not to be unduly lopsided.

Other sites entered the equation. By mid-November, estates at Althorne on the River Crouch in Essex, Wytham Abbey near Oxford and Ribblesford near Bewdley, Worcester-shire, were also under consideration. On 18 November, Adams drew up a list for Howard to investigate, which included 'Letchford Manor, Nr. Hitchin' [*sic*].[25] He also contacted Lord Salisbury, through Herbert Warren, the Solicitor to the Association, about an 1,800-acre estate at Wallington, Hertfordshire, a few miles east of Baldock. C. B. Purdom, recruited as a junior clerk to the office at 77, Chancery Lane in November 1902, witnessed growing confusion:

> Here was nothing short of chaos, and the office floor was covered with maps and offers of sites, extending from fifty acres to large estates, sent from all over the country. … How the work of investigation should be carried out nobody had an idea, despite innumerable reports by committees …, by Adams and by Howard.[26]

At the turn of the year there were conflicting reports. An army engineer, Captain W. Godsal, had been severely critical of Chartley, claiming that it possessed no suitable town centre site and that the most convenient areas for industry occupied the best quality agricultural land. Howard telegraphed to Unwin, requesting him to meet Adams at Stafford on 11 January 1903. Unwin's report was enthusiastic.[27] His description of the geology reflected his training as a mining engineer, noting potential sources of building stone and brick earth. He described the drainage pattern and the possibilities for water supply. He confirmed that the obvious location for industry at Weston in the south west of the estate would bring environmental conflicts but found that the estate centre around Chartley Hall would make a splendid residential district and a good public park. Adams broadly agreed with him and engaged an estate agent, Evans and Evans of Stafford, with a view to negotiation for a purchase option. It looked as if Chartley might be the final choice.

The Board disagreed, and further sites were considered. Unwin visited Kirklington near Newark upon Trent, and Grendon, north west of Atherstone, Warwickshire. Both were eliminated, although Grendon possessed excellent transport facilities. At the beginning of April 1903, Howard was present at a conference of industrialists held at the Pioneer Company's offices in Holborn (see also Chapter Eight). Ralph Neville chaired the proceedings. Locational and other criteria were discussed, with a preference for a site within 50 miles, or an hour's main-line train travel, of London. Howard cautiously referred to sites within an hour of other large centres of population, while T.H.W. Idris spoke of sites 'on the lines running north, as well as in reach of London'.[28] Howard revisited Stafford at the end of April 1903 and unilaterally negotiated an option to purchase Chartley for £285,000, subject to a further valuation.[29] Earl Ferrers's agents, John German and Sons, were clearly attempting to exact the maximum amount from the somewhat naïve Howard, as a subsequent valuation suggested £224,605, much to Ferrers's disappointment.[30] Within two months, however, Howard tactfully withdrew, informing the agents that 'matters have so advanced with regard to another site that there is no longer any possibility of our re-opening negotiations with regard to Chartley'.[31] The new site was none other than 'Letchford Manor, Nr Hitchin'. In December 1904, Walton and Lee advised that there was little likelihood of Chartley being sold as a whole for £250,000,[32] Ferrers's new objective. The estate was divided into 98 lots, beginning with the 'charming historical family mansion, Chartley Hall, its stabling, pleasure grounds and park. The auction took place at the *Swan Hotel*, Stafford, on 15 and 16 September 1904.[33] The pattern of life in Chartley remained undisturbed by its near selection as the site for the world's first Garden City.

… It's Near Hitchin   In one of his less performed plays, *John Bull's Other Island* (written in 1904), Shaw speculates on the possibility of Garden Cities being built in Ireland. The following exchange occurs. 'Have you heard of the Garden City?' 'D'you mane [mean] Heaven?' 'Heaven! No: It's near Hitchin'... (a copy of Howard's book is handed over) … 'you understand that … the circular construction – is only a suggestion'.[34] Indeed, the finally selected site was 'near Hitchin', and Hitchin took time to reconcile that fact. 'Letchford Manor' was not examined in detail until late Spring 1903. Still pressing the case for Chartley, Howard travelled to Hitchin, inspected the site, and discussed matters with Reginald Hine (1883-1949), the well known local solicitor and historian, who was frankly sceptical. Howard appeared as 'an insignificant little man who … did not appear to be worth many shillings'.[35] Hine's cynical opinions were characteristic of the citizens of 'Sleepy Hollow', who led a tranquil and prosperous life in the historic town.

It fell to Herbert Warren, the Pioneer Company's solicitor, who had purchased a country practice at Baldock, an historic coaching settlement on the Great North Road in north Hertfordshire, to appraise the potential of the Letchworth Manor land.[36] It lay between Hitchin and Baldock, largely south of the Great Northern Railway, whose Cambridge branch left the main tracks at Hitchin. A mile south of the railway a connecting road ran between Hitchin and Baldock. Centrally between the two, the presence of Letchworth was marked by a small Victorian estate cottage, with a post office in a Tudor house opposite. Letchworth Manor was only 1,014 acres (410 ha.), much too small by itself and, although Neville was

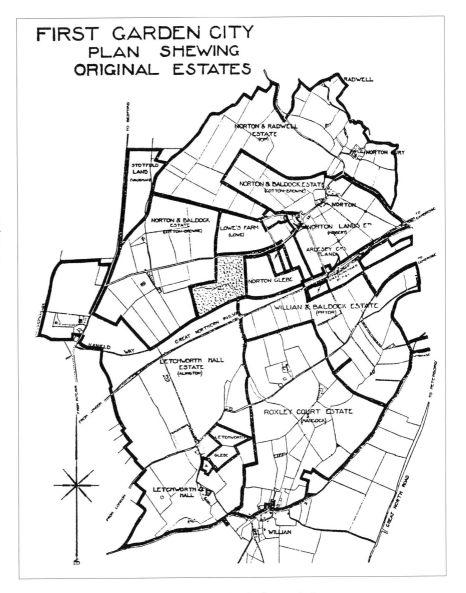

9 The original estates, 1903. Negotiation for the complex mosaic of landholdings demanded astute work by Herbert Warren and his clerk, James Brown.

favourably impressed, it was essential to obtain additional land. A much larger area was pieced together by Warren's clerk, James Brown, who was also the Baldock postmaster. The Roxley Court Estate at Willian, the Pryors' Willian and Baldock Estate, the Cotton-Brownes' Norton and Baldock Estate and the Pyms' Norton and Radwell Estate were the most important acquisitions, with several small inlying parcels, whose omission would seriously have impeded rational development. Altogether 15 owners were involved.[37] Most of the estates were acquired under nominees' names, with the assistance of the Hitchin solicitor, William Onslow Times.

Within a few weeks a site of 3,818 acres (1,545 ha.) had been assembled costing £155,587, an average of £40 15s. 0d. per acre, with a few expensive acres near Baldock as high as £101. The purchase was pressed through to enable notice to be given to any tenants whose leases were to be terminated before Michaelmas. On 24 July, the Pioneer Company convened its Engineering Committee to discuss obtaining a layout plan. The purchase of the Letchworth land did not satisfy everybody. Edward Cadbury wrote to Howard that he had supposed a site would be obtained at £20 an acre in one of the neglected areas of England. He had not expected the company to develop 'a suburb to a thriving town and important junction, such

BOARD OF DIRECTORS
FIRST GARDEN CITY LIMITED.

The Hon. Mr. Justice Neville, whose portrait occupies the central space has been compelled, by reason of his appointment to be one of his Majesty's Judges, to retire from his position as a Director, and the Chairmanship of the Board of Directors of First Garden City Limited. He still retains his interest in the scheme and will continue to act as Chairman of the Council of the Garden City Association.

10 The Board of Directors of First Garden City Ltd. Ralph Neville, centre, is surrounded by his colleagues, including Ebenezer Howard, immediately to the right.

as Hitchin'.[38] The location was kept secret, although Adams wrote to inform Barry Parker and Raymond Unwin.[39]

First Garden City Ltd First Garden City Ltd was registered at Somerset House on 1 September 1903, with an authorised share capital of £300,000.[40] Membership of the Board virtually remained unchanged from the Pioneer Company, with the addition of W. H. Lever and H. B. Harris. The first £80,000 capital was sought, divided into £5 ordinary shares with dividend restricted to five per cent. Investment was to be sporadic and slow: directors and their friends undertook to find the first £40,000. Although £100,692 had been subscribed at the end of the first year's operation in September 1904, the total had only risen to £181,026 ten years later. With £93,934 mortgaged on the freehold of the land, development was inevitably piecemeal and cautious.[41]

Nevertheless the prospectus confidently proclaimed that the Company would 'not only promote a great social improvement, but provide for those who could afford to wait an investment which will prove a sound one'.[42] It was claimed that the Garden City represented the means of solving both urban overcrowding and rural depopulation. The location, '35 miles out of London', was 'admirably adapted for the purpose of industrial and residential development ... traversed not only by important highways, but ... by the Great Northern Railway from London to Cambridge ... [which is] prepared to give the Company facilities for starting the scheme and has consented to erect a temporary station at once.' The major part of the estate would be preserved from development, which would stimulate agriculture and provide a ready market for the existing farmers. The first issue of shares would finance part payment for the land and preliminary work including the layout plan. The Company hoped to issue the remainder of the shares within six months. Howard had not proved a very able Managing Director and, sensing that his uncommercial attitude might inhibit raising capital, the new Company restricted his role to publicity and promotion, lecturing and writing. He was, however, 'to give special attention to the work of the first designing of the town'.[43]

The Unveiling of the Estate 'I think Mr Ebenezer Howard is greatly to be congratulated upon the fact that within five short years his visionary hopes for tomorrow have become the almost fulfilled realisation of today ... The fortunate community living on this estate will rejoice in the knowledge that the unearned increment which may result from the rents of a population of 30,000 souls will not go to enrich any individual landowner, but will be spent in such a way as will tend to refine the lives, enoble the characters and exalt the minds of all who reside on the estate.'[44] Thus spake the 4th Earl Grey (1851-1917), Lord Lieutenant of Northumberland,[45] noble patron of the Garden City movement, as he declared the

11 Old Letchworth: Letchworth corner post office, the cottage in which Raymond Unwin and Robert Bennett made the first sketch plan for Letchworth. In the 1920s the house was reconstructed as 'Scudamore'.

12 Old Letchworth: Hall Farm Cottages, Letchworth Lane. The timber-framed and brick cottages survive but the elm thicket has long since been felled, due to Dutch Elm disease.

Letchworth estate open on Friday 9 October 1903. A marquee had been erected behind the fine Tudor farmhouse used as the Letchworth post office, south of the Hitchin-Baldock road. The ceremony took place in the pouring rain. C. B. Purdom (1883-1965), who had joined the association as assistant accountant in November 1902, wrote, 'How it did rain! and how thick everyone was covered in mud! My recollection of that day is being soaked and muddy, for many visitors wanted to see as much of the estate as possible, which was very little'.[46] Purdom became seriously ill and spent several months convalescing. One thousand guests took lunch in the marquees and the hardiest later made forays into the undisturbed pastures of the estate. It had also rained two days previously when Ralph Neville, Ebenezer Howard and Thomas Adams had hosted a gathering of 250 representatives of the nation's press. Most appropriately the road leading to the site, now Letchworth cricket ground, was later named 'Muddy Lane'. The mud was to be an essential part of the Garden City experience at both Letchworth and Welwyn. So little money was available for surfacing the roads that mud remained an abiding memory. F. W. Rogers, pioneer, printer and journalist, summed up the feeling of the earliest residents:

> When you've tramped the Garden City and shuffled round the globe,
> From China to the point where Howard stood.
> You will find, as he then found, that no other slice of ground,
> On this sphere has such a plenteous stock of mud.[47]

Four

'LETCHFORD MANOR'

A Sense of History Any green-field site in England is bound to have deep historical associations. After the opening of the Letchworth Museum in 1920, Reginald Hine, the Hitchin lawyer and local historian, wrote: 'A praiseworthy and laudable project to build a museum when as yet you have nothing to put in it but yourselves.'[1] Hine's tongue was firmly in cheek; he recognised that even the most liberated residents possessed a sense of history:

> ... you can see the modernists in garden city, who at one time proposed to found a society for the complete obliteration of the past ... satisfying their starving souls ... by digging for Roman and British remains in their own astonishingly prolific soil.[2]

There was indeed a great deal of history to be discovered, and this began with those hardy mortals who made muddy forays into the rain-soaked garden city site on 9 October 1903, following the map helpfully provided by the *Financial Standard*. The site was divided into three parishes, of which Letchworth, straggling along the sunken lane south of the Hitchin to Baldock road, was the smallest. In the extreme south was Willian, nestling in a hollow at the end of a minor lane leading westward from the Great North Road. In the north Norton stood on a hillside looking east towards Baldock, a mile away. Letchworth Hall, the three historic churches, the vernacular cottages and a dozen farmsteads were a modest legacy of a long history of settlement, which began with prehistoric encampments along the historic Icknield Way which curved into the site from Willbury Hill, an ancient encampment facing westwards over the Bedford plain.

Some visitors arrived at the Great Northern Railway's (GNR) temporary halt, built out of railway sleepers, located in the middle of nowhere in a cutting a few hundred yards west of the present Letchworth station. They picked their way across a muddy field to what is now Spring Road, which led southwards towards Letchworth corner on the Hitchin to Baldock road. Most preferred to leave the train at Hitchin and took a cab, or climbed briskly along the Cambridge Road. After the ceremonies, the recommended route led down into Old Letchworth, towards Willian, then back to the Baldock Road, eastwards to Pixmore Farm, north along Dunhams Lane, crossing the railway, and along what is now Green Lane to Norton. Here the adventurous pushed onwards to visit Norton Mill and Radwell. They returned along Wilbury Road, skirting the north flank of Norton Common, to Standalone Farm and Willbury Hill with its Roman camp, then back along Icknield Way to the station with its strategically located tea marquee. It was an eight-mile trek.

Topography and Geology The site of Letchworth is comparatively level, between 200 and 300 ft. above sea level.[3] To the south-east of the estate the Weston Hills rise almost to 500ft., and are part of the Hertfordshire Downs, linking the Chiltern Scarp to the East Anglian heights. Extensive views are commanded by Jack's Hill on the old Great North Road and Lannock Hill on the Weston road. West of the estate the land drops away to Hitchin, 'sleepy hollow'. To the north-west of Letchworth the low-lying Bedford Plain stretches away to the distant pine-clad greensand ridge, running from Woburn Park to Sandy. The outcropping of hard rock at the foot of the hills creates springs at Baldock, which forms the River Ivel, the north-east boundary of the Letchworth estate, with mills at Blackhorse Farm and Nortonbury. The Pix brook through the centre of Letchworth rises near Letchworth Gate and flows northwards, turning west through Norton Common, and

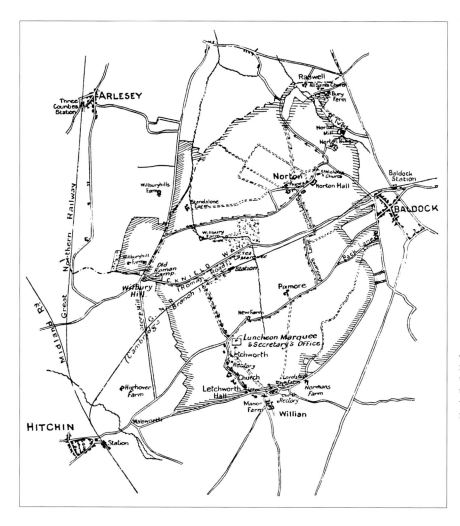

13 The route map for opening day. The recommended route took in all the existing tracks and lanes which were later incorporated into Unwin's layout.

north again through Standalone, to join the Hiz, and eventually the Ivel at Henlow Grange. It formed a marshy area along Rushby Mead, known as Pix Moor, the origin of Pixmore Way, and was later culverted through Howard Park.

Geologically, the local strata are the chalk, gault clay and greensand. The beds are part of the Cretaceous system, laid down over a 40-million year period from 110 million years ago on the slowly sinking floor of a shallow sea. The earliest beds, the Lower Greensand, 150ft.-thick outcrop near Shefford, lie five miles north-west of Letchworth. The gault clay is 200ft. thick, containing an Upper Greensand bed with phosphate nodules known as coprolite, dug for fertilizer in the 19th century. The gault clay was extensively worked at Arlesey, three miles north-west of Letchworth, for making the distinctive yellow grey 'Arlesey White' bricks. The chalk marl outcrops near Arlesey and was used for cement manufacture. Above this the Toft lower chalk was worked at Arlesey pit for building stone similar to Totternhoe clunch from Dunstable.

The 300ft. thick middle chalk underlies Letchworth and is a compact white rock, with a few flints, and the upper chalk outcrops at Jack's Hill. At the end of the Cretaceous period, the strata were uplifted to form dry land. Later disturbances folded the rock into the gentle concave syncline of the London basin causing the chalk to outcrop as the Chiltern scarp. One million years ago, the Great Ice Age formed glaciers which moved slowly south, depositing accumulated detritus or earth and rock fragments – patches of gravel and boulder clay. There were four distinct periods of glaciation, with deposits from as far afield as the Pennines, Wales and Scandinavia.

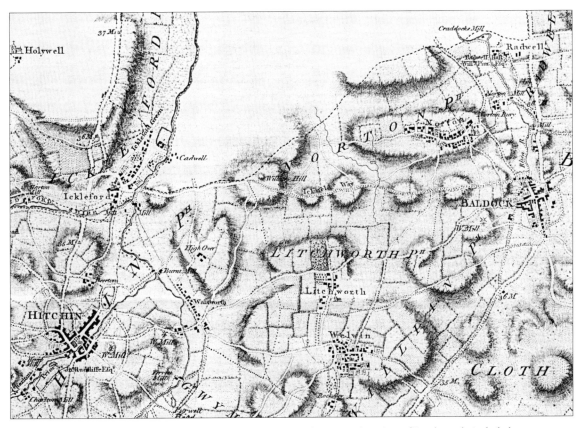

14 The historic setting: Dury and Andrews' map (1782). The regional setting of Letchworth included the historic market towns of Hitchin and Baldock while Willian village was shown as 'Welwin' on this fine 18th century map.

Norton Common now forms the least disturbed habitat in the Garden City. Uncultivated and ungrazed areas soon became covered by hawthorn scrub, and larger trees developed to form a natural woodland. Ponds and streams silted as marshland. Near to Icknield Way are old oak, ash, maple trees, hawthorn, blackthorn and elder, with wild clematis and lesser celandines. The elms along Letchworth Lane and around Norton succumbed to Dutch Elm disease in 1974. A plantation of Scots pines at Willbury Hill forms a local landmark, as do the horse-chestnuts by Letchworth Hall. The three old oaks on the northern fringe of Town Square were a decisive factor in its location. The preservation of existing landscape features, the generous planting of new species and extensive gardens have fostered a rich wildlife presence. Moles, shrews and hedgehogs are common, with less frequent sightings of foxes and badgers. Although the black squirrel was native to Norton Common, it has virtually been ousted by its grey compatriot, which reached the district about 1940.

Early Settlement The area had a long record of settlement.[4] Mesolithic man may have settled beside Lake Hitchin at 7500 B.C., and the Neolithic inhabitants of the district made tracks across the chalk downlands, bringing trade and supplies along what was to become Icknield Way, one of the principal pre-Roman routes, leading from the Norfolk coast to Salisbury Plain. Evidence of Neolithic occupation was found in Blackhorse Road when the extension to the industrial estate was laid out in 1960. Five pits, each dug ten feet deep for flint extraction, contained an antler pick, an ox shoulder plate and Neolithic flints including arrowheads and scrapers, with a radio carbon date of 1880 B.C. Late Neolithic beaker pottery of *c.*1640 B.C. has also been found. In the subsequent Bronze Age the Icknield Way maintained

15 The tiny 12th-century St Mary's church, only 60 ft. long internally, reflected the small size and remoteness of Letchworth Manor.

its importance. Willbury Hill was part of an Iron-Age hill fort, with only its southern part remaining – two Iron-Age brooches have been excavated, together with some pottery and many Roman remains.

According to Caesar, the inhabitants of southern England included the Belgae who had migrated from Belgian Gaul, first to plunder then to settle. Caesar's reconnaissance took place 55-54 B.C., and he brought Cassivellaunus, chief of the Catuvellauni, to heel at his capital, Wheathampstead, 15 miles south of Letchworth. The main Roman invasion under Claudius in A.D. 43 had a major impact on Hertfordshire, and the Catuvellauni were a major obstacle to Roman victory. Verulamium, on the outskirts of the more recent St Albans, was the major regional city, with Baldock, a settlement of local importance, on the site of a native British community, and an important Roman cemetery was discovered at Walls Field in 1925. Following the departure of the Romans the area went through turbulent periods, but the expansion of Mercia brought more permanent settlement — Offa, best known for his activities on the Welsh marches, built a house at Offley in 758, and consistent rural settlement of the Letchworth area dates from that period. The Blackhorse Road excavations of 1960 revealed a Saxon cemetery, with a skeleton buried with the remains of the spear which killed him still embedded in his shoulder (see page 34).[5] Further excavations west of Green Lane in 1988-9 were to reveal more of the significance of the burial ground.

Lecha Weorthig   'Lecha Weorthig', the farm by the rivulet or 'Lecworde' or 'Lycceweorth', probably began as a small settlement along a wooded track, which still remains as Letchworth Lane.[6] The Manor, centred on Letchworth Hall, was in existence by the time of the Domesday survey in 1086.

> William also holds LETCHWORTH from Robert. It answers for 10 hides. Land for 7 ploughs. In lordship 2. 9 villagers with a priest have 5 ploughs. 2 Freemen with 1½ hides; 4 cottagers; 1 slave. Meadow for ½ a plough; pasture for the livestock; woodland, 100 pigs. Total value £6; when acquired £7; before 1066 £8. Godwin of Souberie, a thane of King Edward's, held this manor; he could sell. 3 Freemen, his men, had 2 hides and 3 virgates; they could sell.

Robert Gernon, an Essex Baron had his major seat at Stanstead Mountfichet. He fortified the Letchworth Manor and Church, and the arms of the Montfichets are in the east window. It was c.1130-35 that St Mary's church was rebuilt; of flint, a two-cell structure with a nave, the smallest in Hertfordshire, and a lower chancel, no tower, but only a small bell-turret. Located off Letchworth Lane, its setting still serenely reflects its early remoteness.

16 Letchworth Hall, seen here in the early 1930s, dates from the 15th and 16th centuries, but has been greatly enlarged. In 1904 it became a hotel and welcomed its first guests that Christmas.

In the reign of Edward I the Manor passed into the possession of the Knights Templar, received as a gift from Richard de Montfichet, one of the 25 Barons appointed to enforce the Magna Carta of 1215. The Knights Templar refounded Baldock and prospered until the dissolution of their Order in 1312, when Letchworth Manor passed to the Knights of St John of Jerusalem, the Knights Hospitaller. In the reign of Henry VI it was acquired by Thomas Barrington, Sheriff of Hertford and Essex, who held it until the reign of Henry VIII. The Hanchets bought the estate and the smaller Manor of Nevells, but quickly disposed of them to Thomas Snagge in 1547. His 11-year-old grandson, also named Thomas, had a distinguished career – Member of Parliament for Bedfordshire in 1571, Attorney General for 1577, Speaker of the House of Commons in 1588. His eldest son was knighted by James I in 1603 and later sold the Manor to Sir Roland Lytton of Knebworth. There is evidence that Letchworth was neglected in the 16th century, both before and after the Reformation and in 1552 the Church Commissioners reported of poverty, both in the vestments and plate of the church, and in the maintenance of the chantry priest, by only 28s. 6d. in tithes.

The Lyttons embarked upon a comprehensive remodelling of Letchworth Hall, the first of many which resulted in an amalgam of building from the 15th to the late 20th centuries. Some portions of 15th-century work remain, but the major surviving early fabric is of 17th-century date, a notable example of Jacobean architecture, but modest compared with Knebworth or North Mymms, let alone Hatfield. The porch and galleried great hall survive, together with several fireplaces. The Lyttons retained the Manor through the turbulent 17th and 18th centuries with Parliamentary leaders, including John Hampden, being entertained at the Hall. The Hitchin to Cambridge Road became a turnpike, but Letchworth remained a remote backwater.

The Lyttons sold the Manor in 1796 to John Williamson, a Baldock baker. The Hall was downgraded to a farmhouse and after Williamson's death in 1830 remained empty until his grandson, the Reverend John Alington, came to live at the Hall. Alington had a long running feud with his rector and, after having been banned from taking services in the Church, held his own inimitable form of worship in the Hall. Congregations included tramps, gypsies and 'all the whores of Hertfordshire', accompanied by music and dancing, with generous helpings of beer and brandy. Alington also embellished the Hall in an overscaled Victorian-Jacobean style, adding the west tower. He died in 1863, characteristically after tossing back a half tumbler of brandy. The estate returned to a quiet oblivion until its purchase by the Garden City Pioneer Company in 1903.

Weligas   Barely half a mile away lay Willian, 'Weligas' or 'Willen', the Manor of the Willows, partly owned by the Manor of Weston at the time of Domesday. After the Conquest it

17   The pastoral charm of Willian village, with its pond and *The Fox Inn*, is evident in this fine pre-1914 view.

passed to Robert de Pontcardon, whose name is commemorated in the later constructed Punchardon Hall. There were prolonged disputes over the ownership of Willian during the 12th and 13th centuries, until 1243, when Henry III granted the Manor to Paul Peyvre, for the rent of one sparrow hawk per year. All Saints church, Willian was an ambitious structure. Although a 12th-century doorway remains, much of the fabric dates from the 14th and, significantly, 15th centuries, the latter showing evidence of the work of Hitchin masons. The interior contains the remains of the 15th-century rood screen and the chancel seats have poppy head decoration of the same date. The patronage of the living remained with the Manor until 1384, and the first vicar was appointed in 1400. Near to the church was a small timber-framed cottage, the Old Vicarage, which, although much extended in the early 20th century, still shows the character of a medieval clergy house.

The last Peyvre died in 1429 and his daughter married into the Broughton family, who thus inherited the Willian estate. The village passed through a stormy period during the Reformation and part of the Manor passed to the Crown. In the 17th century the village settled down to prosperity and in 1617 the rector, John Chapman, reported 'there is none in the Parish of Wilyen that be of requisite age, that have not received the Sacrament of the Lord's Supper at Easter last'. The next owners, the Wilsons, reconstructed Punchardon Hall, a fine late Tudor house, notable for its clustered shafted chimneys. During the Civil War, in 1644, the vicar, Richard Way, a Royalist, was replaced by a Puritan, Isaac Bedford, who was to become a non-conformist minister in 1660. The village grew steadily and prospered. Towards the end of the 17th century, Brays Manor and half of Willian Manor were sold to Sir John Dimsdale, whose family retained ownership until 1867. In the 18th century, Thomas Dimsdale, who was ennobled by the Russian monarchy for the introduction of smallpox inoculation, reunited the two halves of the estate. By 1825 the population of Willian was 269.

After 1867 came Charles Frederick Hancock, a self-made businessman from London, who set about rebuilding Willian as a model estate village. His architect, Owen Jones (1809-74), was better known for his comprehensive analysis of decorative design and his display rooms of exotic decor at the 1851 Great Exhibition. For Hancock he designed distinctive blocks of white-rendered cottages with modern drainage, set in generous gardens. Their character anticipated Garden City cottages built 40 years later. Hancock also rebuilt the public house *The Willian Arms* (now *The Fox*) in a well-mannered Italianate style, which looks particularly

18   In 1908 Norton Common already served as an adventure playground for young explorers.

well across Willian Pond. In 1872 a school was built at a cost of £820 which also served Letchworth, and three years later a Free Library was started. Hancock considerably enlarged Roxley Court which, in 1903, was let to the Dowager Countess of Lindsey. By the time a fête was held in July 1903 to celebrate the marriage of her daughter, Captain Mortimer Hancock had sold a large part of the estate to the Garden City Pioneer Company. In many respects Willian remained a model village within a Garden City after 1903.

Nortun   Norton village dates from the Saxon era. In 795 Offa of Mercia granted it to the Monastery of St Alban. The ownership was reiterated in 1007, by Ethelred II defining its boundaries between Wiligbyrig (Wilbury), Stodfald (Stotfold) and Readanwylles (Radwell).

19   Norton village is of Saxon origin, and prospered as a farming community from the 17th century. The attractive thatched cottages survive, but the pond and elms fronting Manor Farm have long disappeared.

20 The Saxon, whose skeleton was found in Blackhorse Road, had been speared to death.

The Domesday survey recorded that Norton was 'terra ecclesia sancti albani' on the north edge of 'Heorotfordscir in Bradewatre hundred [Broadwater]'. Most of the land was under the plough with no woodland to support swine and worth £16 per year, 'A priest and a Frenchman with 14 villagers have 7 ploughs. 5 cottagers; 1 slave. 2 mills at l6s; meadow for 2 ploughs; pasture for the livestock.' The Church of St Nicholas was rebuilt in the late 11th century and dedicated in 1119. A Norman chancel arch survives but the church was greatly altered in the 15th and in the early 19th centuries. The diocese of St Albans held the village until the dissolution of the monasteries – the monks may not have been good landlords for the men of Norton joined the Peasants Revolt of 1381.

After the dissolution, the crown commandeered monastic estates. Henry VIII granted the Manor to Sir Richard Williams, alias Cromwell, ancestor of Oliver Cromwell. He disposed of it to his bailiff, John Bowles of Wallington, in 1542. The status of the church fell and in 1586 the examiner of the archdeacon of St Albans found the vicar, Thomas Longley

ignorant in the Latin tongue and not able to decline a noun substantive or to discern parts of speech. And further to be unable to answer easy questions in the grounds of faith and religion, or to allege aptly any scripture for proof of any article of religion.

His successor, John Pratt, from Great St Bartholomew in London, certainly did not tolerate slackness, for he sent an order of penance to a local farmer George Clarke 'for appointing his servants to work in removing hay from a stack on a Tuesday in Easter week last'. In the 17th century Norton became a prosperous farming community; Manor Farm, Norton Grange Farm, Paynes Farm, Norton Bury and Standalone Farm gave testimony to the growing wealth of farmers and landowners. In the Civil War, in 1643, a skirmish between Cavaliers and Roundheads near Wilberry Croft and, later, a case of witchcraft against John Palmer, who was found guilty of contracts with the devil, ruffled the rural calm. In 1662 Norton Manor was acquired by William Pym and remained in his family until 1903. The Enclosure Act of 1796 changed matters. In 1798 Norton's enclosure award was made, and three broad fields were measured and divided up and planted with hedges. Pasture was allocated on the common in proportion to land held in the parish. In the mid-19th century there was a serious outbreak of cholera near to Baldock at Norton End. Many cottages in this area were demolished in 1850 when the railway was built from Hitchin to Cambridge, via Royston. Public health problems re-appeared, only a few months before the estate was acquired by First Garden City Ltd., when the drinking water in Norton End was found to contain 14 per cent sewage.

'Rodenhanger' In May 1988 initial trench-ing for housing construction east of Green Lane, south of Norton, revealed archaeological features, excavated between July and

VIII 'Health of the Country – Comforts of the Town', poster issued *c*.1925 by First Garden City Ltd., showing 'Scudamore', Letchworth Corner.

IX 158 Wilbury Road, the most radical of the 1905 Cheap Cottages.

X 102 Wilbury Road, designed by Barry Parker in 1909 for his brother Stanley, photographed in 1988.

XI 29 Norton Way North, designed by M. H. Baillie Scott in 1906.

XII 34 and 36 South View, 1912, designed by Courtenay Crickmer.

XIII 'Sappho', photographed in 1988 while she still held sway over the Charles Ball Memorial Gardens.

XIV 'Foursquare our City', banner made *c.*1909 by Edmund Hunter, on a theme from Henry Bryan Binns's poem 'The City'.

XV 'Ploughmen's Cottages', Paddock Close, 1905, designed by Geoffry Lucas for First Garden City Ltd.

XVI 19–25 Lytton Avenue, 1907, designed by Courtenay Crickmer for Letchworth Cottages and Buildings Ltd.

XVII 34–40 Rushby Mead, 1911, designed by Bennett and Bidwell for Howard Cottage Society, photographed in 1988.

XVIII Meadow Way Green flats, 1916, designed by Courtenay Crickmer for Howard Cottage Society.

21 'Rodenhanger' excavations, 1988: rescue archaeology in advance of new housing development east of Green Lane.

November.[7] Nearby, as noted above, excavations in 1960, when Blackhorse Road was constructed, had revealed an Anglo-Saxon burial ground. This may have served the settlement unearthed in 1988, when traces of 23 cellars cut into the chalk were discovered, of which 16 appeared to be related to buildings, arranged in a linear pattern suggesting an east-west street. Few artefacts were found – sherds of pottery, fragments of bone and glass, and a piece of a decorated ring. The settlement was hitherto unknown. However, a deed of Ethelred II, of 1007, and Domesday Book mentioned 'Rodenhanger', 'wooded slope by the road', the latter possibly referring to the Icknield Way a few hundred yards south. Rodenhanger had been given to St Albans Abbey by Offa, along with Norton, but was repossessed by powerful nobles, before eventually being returned to the abbey by Leofric. The boundaries were confirmed in Ethelred's Charter; but only one dwelling seems to have existed in the settlement by that time. The excavations were assisted by the developers, McLean Homes and Bryant Homes, English Heritage, Letchworth Garden City Corporation and Hertfordshire County Council, and were carried out by G. R. Burleigh, K. J. Mathews and A. J. Platell of North Herts Museums Field Archaeology section. A successful public open day was held before the development began in earnest.

Museum pieces Finds of prehistoric objects were common from the inception of the Garden City. The Estate Forester, F. J. Cole, was an amateur archaeologist, but many remains were casually treated, and their location poorly recorded. The idea of a museum at Howard Hall was considered, but the first tangible action was the formation of the Garden City Naturalists' Society in April 1908. Its collection of cases of birds was exhibited at 'The Skittles' until funds could be raised to start a permanent museum, aided by a legacy of £200. Barry Parker designed the Georgian-style Museum flanking Town Square, and the ground floor was opened in October 1914. That July, William Percival Westell had been elected Secretary of the Society, and was curator of the Letchworth Museum until his death in 1943. In May 1920 Earl Lytton opened the completed museum, which was taken over by the Letchworth U.D.C. in 1926, with the collection transferred to the Council in 1939. Through Westell's formidable energy the museum was one of the pioneers of a schools' service, now greatly expanded. The Garden City movement was only included after 1945, and the museum mounted a special exhibition for the Golden Jubilee of Letchworth in 1953. The creation of the First Garden City Heritage Museum 20 years later allowed the Letchworth Museum to concentrate upon the archaeology and natural history of the region, and to display collections of paintings by local artists such as William Ratcliffe, interspersed with travelling exhibitions. A North Herts Archaeological Society was formed in 1960, encouraged by the curator of the museum, John Moss (Eccardt), who was responsible for the Blackhorse Road excavations.

22 W. P. Westell and museum visitors, *c.*1932. The curator explains about the Roman settlement nearby at Baldock.

What's in a name? After dropping 'Rurisville' as a name for his ideal settlement, Howard had opted for the clear but distinctly uncharismatic 'Garden City'. Acquisition of the Letchworth estate raised the pressing question of a name. Early publicity used 'Garden City', but the location was often made synonymous with either Hitchin or Baldock. The movement aspired to develop further 'Garden Cities', so the generic name alone was not entirely appropriate. A distinctive identity was required. In August 1904, a plebiscite was held among shareholders and residents.[8] The alternatives included 'Garden City'; 'Letchworth', both alone and with 'Garden City' in parenthesis; 'Wellworth', a truly awful conflation of 'Willian', 'Willbury' and 'Letchworth'; 'Homesworth'; and 'Alseopolis'. This last rectified the mixed derivation of 'Rurisville' with pure Ancient Greek. The concept of the Platonic Ideal of a democratic city appealed to supporters of the movement, but 'Alseopolis' had a distinctly mid-western American twang, incongruous in Hertfordshire. Common sense, or at least a common denominator, prevailed and 'Letchworth (Garden City)' was chosen. The appendage quickly disappeared and Letchworth predominated; in 1919, when the second Garden City adopted the name Welwyn Garden City to distinguish it from the nearby historic town of Welwyn, many forgot that Letchworth was the precursor. Consequently, with the approach of the centenary in 2003, the Letchworth Garden City Heritage Foundation embarked on a campaign to restore the full name, Letchworth Garden City, without the parenthesis so that there could be no future mistakes about the significance of Howard's first 'object lesson'. In June 1999, Railtrack officially renamed the station 'Letchworth Garden City', and in all signage, destination boards and computer screens. The Post Office was distinctly cool about the name change, and it remains to be seen whether its successor, Consignia, will be more co-operative. The Foundation opened a petition, which by winter 2001 had attracted over 1,000 signatures. North Hertfordshire District Council endorsed the proposal, which was also backed by the Divisional M.P., Oliver Heald.

The naming of streets and districts presented an opportunity to commemorate progress or literary achievement, following Howard's model. However, the visitor will look in vain for 'Boulevard Newton', 'Shakespeare Road', 'Edison Street'. The prosaic but locationally precise 'Fifth Avenue' had to await development of the Business Park over 80 years later. In practice, street names followed local historical features,[9] particularly field names from the tithe map, upon which the Hitchin historian Reginald Hine advised, or local worthies, including the lords of the three manors. Thus, the creators of the Garden City generally had to wait a long time for commemoration. Howard himself was the exception – during his lifetime, on

31 May 1905, representatives from the Worshipful Company of Gardeners named the open space east of Norton Way 'Howard Park' in his honour. Nearby, the small public hall was named in memory of Howard's first wife Elizabeth, who had died in the late autumn of 1904. Howard Drive and Howard's Wood followed in the 1950s. As first Chairman of the Garden City Association, Ralph Neville Q.C. was commemorated in 1930, 12 years after his death, when the new bridge over the railway was named Neville's Bridge. Thomas Adams, secretary of the Association and subsequently Estate Manager at Letchworth, has not so far been honoured, but his successor, W.H. Gaunt, lent his name to Gaunt's Way on the post-1945 Grange Estate. In 1982 two culs-de-sac on the new Fearnhill residential estate north of Sollershott West were named Parker Close and Unwin Close.

Several of the existing names were retained; Dunhams Lane and Green Lane, for example. Letchworth Lane was formalised as a name for the deep sunken historic track leading down from Letchworth corner to Letchworth Hall. Other names related to existing farms – Pixmore was widely used pre-1914, whilst the nearby Jackmans Plantation gave its name to Jackmans Place in 1919, and ultimately the much larger Jackmans Estate. Across Letchworth Gate, the connecting road to the Great North Road opened in 1931, the Lordship and Manor Farm Estates (1970-8) took their names from farms of the former Willian Manor. Field names were particularly popular; Birds Hill and Bowershott, for example; Campers Avenue, Field and Walk derived from Camps Piece, an 1839 field name. Croft Lane was named from a list of Norton landholders after the Enclosure Acts, and Glebe Road from the Glebe Fields. Leys Avenue also used a former field name and 'The Leys', shown nearby on early plans, was renamed Gernon Road to avoid confusion. Rushby Mead was also a field name, and its line followed the gentle curve of the wandering bed of the Pix Brook.

The historic location of Letchworth in the Broadwater Hundred, the largest in the county, was marked by the designation of Broadwater Avenue in 1910, originally medievalised as Bradewatre, in succession to the distinctly suburban Acacia Road shown on a 1905 layout plan. Norton had later been hived off into the Cashio Hundred, which was commemorated by Cashio Lane. Icknield Way retained its historic name verbatim, but Wilbury Road to the north of Norton Common, named after Willbury Fort, was mis-spelled by the omission of the second 'l'. The same in reverse occurred, with the addition of a second 'l' to Allington Lane, named after the colourful Alingtons of Letchworth Hall, whilst in 1972 'Chapmans' on the Manor Farm Estate, named after the founder of a Norton Charity, became 'Chaomans', through a typing error and the name stuck. Local worthies and families were extensively commemorated: Souberie Avenue after Godwin of Souberie, 11th-century holder of Letchworth Manor; Gernon Road after the Gernons, Norman holders of the Manor; Barrington Road after the lords of the Manor from 1400-1537; and Lytton Avenue, their 17th- and 18th-century successors. Nevells Road, a 1908 substitute for 'Exhibition Road', marked a smaller manor, while Sir Richard Williams, alias Cromwell, who handled the disposal of Norton Manor for Henry VIII, was marked by Cromwell Green and Cromwell Road. The Dimsdales of Willian gave their name to Dimsdale Place off Ridge Avenue, built 1915, but the name disappeared when it was redeveloped as Holmdale barely 50 years later.

Some names were created with no apparent local connection. Eastholm and Westholm, with their Arts and Crafts overtones, were used for early cottage society housing groups, and the names were repeated, with the addition of Midholm, at Hampstead Garden Suburb. Eastcheap and the stillborn Westcheap were brought in to suggest the bustle of a central shopping area, with nearby Commerce Avenue, now Commerce Way, more overt in its mercantile imagery. Broadway was adopted for the main axial road in 1908, succeeding the more prosaic 'Main Avenue'. The first major road to be built, Norton Way with its link southwards along Willian Way, was shown as 'North Road' on some early plans, originating from a proposal to divert the Great North Road, through Baldock, and through the margins of Letchworth town centre. The Garden City had a merciful escape from the chaos which would have ensued had this suggestion been adopted.

Five

The Layout Plan

The First Designing of the Town   Once the land options had been confirmed, it was imperative to obtain a layout without delay, and to begin development to convince sceptics that Howard's ideal city was being made practicable.[1] On 17 July 1903, in reply to Barry Parker, Adams guardedly wrote, 'I think we owe it to you and to Mr Unwin to tell you where the First Garden City will be. We have decided on about 4,000 acres near Hitchin … please keep the matter absolutely private as there is still the possibility of an accident whilst the legal formalities are incomplete … We are not yet taking up the question of expert advice on architectural subjects, and note that when we do we shall have the benefit of your help'.[2] A week later the Pioneer Company convened an Engineering Committee consisting of Howard, H .D. Pearsall and H. B. Harris. It was resolved that H. Howard Humphreys, a Westminster surveyor, should make a preliminary report,[3] with a map to indicate the position of main roads, site for the railway station and sidings to serve the industrial area. Humphreys later took spot levels and prepared a full contour survey. In August, G. R. Strachan was asked to report on sources of water supply: both he and Humphreys recommended the construction of a reservoir in the Weston Hills, three miles to the east. Humphreys advocated construction of a station 1¾ miles west of Baldock, overlooking Norton Common and the valley of the Pix brook, along which he envisaged that the main north-south connecting road, ultimately Norton Way, should run. The sector between the Pix and the railway, a rounded plateau, would provide an ideal site for the town centre and this subsequently influenced Unwin's layout. Humphreys felt that factory sites would best be placed to the leeward of the town, notwithstanding Howard's advocacy of improved technology and electricity. By August Unwin had twice visited the estate and the Committee asked for his report. Regrettably this does not appear to have survived.

The Engineering Committee began to have other ideas about architectural advice. Although Unwin's involvement was discussed in October, no positive decision was taken. The Committee consulted the architectural section of the Garden City Association,[4] led by H. Clapham Lander, who recommended Richard Norman Shaw, W.R. Lethaby and Halsey Ricardo. Shaw (1831-1912), the foremost architect of his generation, had in the 1870s popularised the eclectic 'Queen Anne' style through his involvement with Bedford Park Garden Suburb. Lethaby (1857-1931) had trained in Shaw's office, and became a leader of the Arts and Crafts movement and a founder of the Art Workers Guild. He was better known as a theorist and teacher than as a practitioner. Ricardo (1854-1928) had had a varied career ranging from Arts and Crafts houses to the Calcutta railway station. In October 1903, Herbert Warren was asked to consult Aston Webb (1849-1930), R.I.B.A. President, one of the leading architects of Edwardian Pomp and Circumstance, and best known for the Baroque splendour of the Royal Naval College at Dartmouth and his proposals for The Mall and the Victoria Memorial facing Buckingham Palace.[5] Both Webb and Shaw appear to have declined; had one or other become involved it is an intriguing speculation as to what form the First Garden City might have taken.

On 20 October 1903, Pearsall, Howard and Lever interviewed prospective consultants.[6] Lethaby and Ricardo requested further clarification of the brief. Lever replied that the Board required the best plan with the least trouble. Pearsall asked them to participate in a limited competition, and also asked for advice on assessment! Parker was called in and Howard queried him about Unwin's experience as an *engineer*. Pearsall asked how long it would take to prepare a plan: Parker replied that a week to ten days on site would be sufficient and a finished plan could be ready within five weeks. The Committee also suggested a £50 payment to each architect, with a premium of £200 for the best plan. The Board approved these arrangements on 29 October. A third plan, unrecorded in the minutes, was prepared by Thomas Geoffry Lucas (1872-1947), a Hitchin architect,[7] in collaboration with Sidney White Cranfield (1870-1961). After serving articles with the Hitchin architect, Walter Millard, Lucas had worked for a succession of prominent London architects, including William Flockhart, Leonard Stokes and W. Curtis Green, before commencing independent practice in 1896. He probably met Cranfield through the office of E. W. Mountford, with whom he collaborated on the winning entry for the Hitchin Town Hall competition in 1899. The press also tried to visualise development of the estate by hiring artists to give a bird's eye view of a slice through Howard's circular diagrams. At least one unsolicited entry was submitted to the Garden City Association, while A. R. Sennett, an engineer, prepared and published a massive two-volume work on Garden Cities,[8] which included his layout for Letchworth, on a hexagonal grid resembling a giant honeycomb.

Barry Parker and Raymond Unwin: 'The Artistic …and the Practical' Barry Parker (1867-1947) and Raymond Unwin (1863-1940) were pioneers of both Garden City architecture and town planning.[9] Although they settled in the south-east, they were born in northern England, which influenced their design philosophy. The Parker and Unwin families were related by marriage, and the ties became stronger when Unwin married Parker's sister, Ethel, in 1893.

Barry Parker was born in Chesterfield in 1867. His father, Robert Parker, prospered as manager of a local bank, and in the 1880s the family moved to Buxton, a fashionable spa, largely developed by the Dukes of Devonshire. In the mid-1880s Barry and his sister developed close friendship with their half-cousin Raymond Unwin, then working in Manchester. His enthusiasm for socialism elicited deep suspicion from the Parker *paterfamilias*. Barry Parker was educated at a private art school in Derby, taking examinations in decorative design at the South Kensington College. In 1889 he was articled to G. Faulkner Armitage (1849-1937), a northern Arts and Crafts architect whose richly eclectic designs for country houses included textiles, furniture and even wrought ironwork from the smithy at his Altrincham studio.[10] Such a total approach was characteristic of the Arts and Crafts movement and, subsequently, of modernism, and was a technique whereby the realm of design ultimately extended from the individual object to the regional plan, largely through the efforts of Parker and Unwin themselves. Parker was Clerk of Works on several of Armitage's buildings. In 1891, Robert Parker purchased a large plot in the Park Ring, Buxton's fashionable suburb laid out by Sir Joseph Paxton (1801-65), famed as the designer of the Crystal Palace for the Great Exhibition of 1851, but also gardener to the Duke of Devonshire, the landowner. Barry Parker designed three houses for his father. The largest, 'Moorlands', completed in 1894, became the family home.

Although Raymond Unwin had been born near Rotherham, his formative years were spent in Oxford. His father, a minor businessman, had sold up and took a degree at Balliol College, an unusual undertaking for a middle-aged family man in the 1870s. Unwin was educated at Magdalen College School, and was offered a scholarship to read Divinity. He had become deeply concerned with social issues and consulted Canon Samuel Augustus Barnett (1844-1913), then recruiting students for Toynbee Hall, the first University settlement in East London. On learning that Unwin was more deeply concerned by man's unhappiness than his wickedness, Barnett advised against the Church as a vocation. Over twenty years later Barnett's wife, Henrietta, commissioned Unwin to plan Hampstead Garden Suburb. Unwin became a secular evangelist, drawn inexorably towards socialism. The built form of Oxford also exerted its influence: its collegiate quadrangles became a model for Unwin's designs for cooperative housing. Lectures by Ruskin and Morris were a potent formative experience. Many years later

23 The Parker and Unwin families at Buxton, *c.*1898. Raymond Unwin stands in the back row at the extreme left, and Barry Parker at the extreme right. Parker's parents are seated in the wicker chairs, whilst in front, to the right, sits Ethel Unwin (née Parker) with the young Edward Unwin, already clad in flannel smock and sandals.

Unwin recalled

> One who was privileged to hear the beautiful voice of John Ruskin declaiming against the degradation of *laissez faire* theories of life, to know William Morris and his work ... could hardly fail to follow after the ideals of a more ordered form of society, and a better planned environment for it, than that which he saw around him in the 'seventies and 'eighties.[11]

In 1884 he returned northwards to enter an engineering apprentice at the Staveley Coal and Iron Company, a rapidly expanding combine of mines and foundries, based at Barrow Hill, near Chesterfield. In 1885, Unwin moved to Manchester and, as Secretary of the local branch of Morris's Socialist League, wrote long polemical articles for the League's newspaper, *Commonweal*. He spoke on street corners for the League and the Labour Church. He became a companion of the Socialist philosopher Edward Carpenter (1844-1929), who had formed a rural commune at Millthorpe near Sheffield, and whose prescription for the 'simple life' as '... healthy, democratic, vegetarian'[12] was taken up by Unwin and, later, by the Garden City pioneers. In 1887 Unwin returned to Staveley, as an engineer. His duties also involved the development of mining townships, and design of schools, chapels and churches. In 1894 he collaborated with Parker over St Andrew's church, Barrow Hill, their first joint work. The previous year, after a long courtship, obstructed by hostility from her father, he had married Ethel Parker. In the early 1890s, in a letter to his bride-to-be, Unwin wrote that

> Barry seems to think that we might join up someday and set up as architects, he [Parker] doing the artistic part and me [Unwin] the practical.[13]

In 1896, the Unwins moved to the Lodge by the Beeches, outside Chapel-en-le-Frith, Derbyshire. Raymond Unwin commuted daily by train to Buxton, to work with Barry Parker. The partnership lasted until 1914, shortly before Unwin joined the Local Government Board and began a distinguished Civil Service career.

'Concerning the coming revolution in domestic architecture'   The firm's first commissions were middle-class houses, influenced by published work of Voysey and Baillie Scott, and overlaid with the richly eclectic Northern Arts and Crafts style.[14] 'The Shanty', Marple (1895-7); 'Woodcote', Church Stretton (1896-7); 'Greenmoor', Carlisle Road, Buxton

(1898-1900); and 'Chetwynd', Northwood, Staffordshire (1899-1902), showed a progressively simplified form, with growing confidence in handling interior space, and integration of fittings and furnishings into a total domestic environment. Such work did not satisfy Unwin's objective to attain the social purpose inherent in the Arts and Crafts movement. In 1895, under Unwin's influence, Parker had sketched 'An Artisan's Living Room', later published in *The Art of Building a Home* (1901), a collection of essays and designs which impressed Ebenezer Howard.[15] In the late 1890s Unwin designed an urban quadrangle of co-operative housing, with shared common rooms and restaurant, anticipating 'Homesgarth' at Letchworth, promoted by Howard in 1911, and designed by Clapham Lander. He also sketched an idealised village green for a rural co-operative community, with housing groups facing southwards over open countryside – a prophesy of Westholm Green at Letchworth. Unwin wrote of eliminating the 'festering suburb', interposed between town and country, contrasted with the self-contained organic nature of rural communities:

> The village was the expression of a small corporate life in which all the different units were personally in touch with each other, conscious of and frankly accepting their relations ... it is this crystallisation of the elements in a village in accordance with a definitely organised life of mutual relations ... which gives the appearance of being an organic whole, the home of a community, to what would otherwise be a mere conglomeration of buildings. We cannot of course put back the hands of time ... the relationships of feudalism have gone, and democracy has yet to evolve some definite relationships of its own ... we could, if we really desired it, even now so arrange a new building site ... that it should have some little of the charm of the old village.[16]

Despite evoking the future imagery of the Garden City, theory had outstripped practice. By 1901, only three Parker and Unwin-designed working-class cottages had been built. The most significant, a semi-detached pair in Cunnery Road, Church Stretton (1900-01), had roughcast walls, a hipped roof and a central gable, and served as a prototype for the first cottages at New Earswick and Letchworth. It was Unwin's writing on housing design that carried authority. He emerged from provincial obscurity through his ability to be in the right place at the right time. Autumn 1901-Spring 1902 witnessed publication of *The Art of Building a Home* and his Fabian Society Tract, *Cottage Plans and Common Sense*. He appeared at the Garden City Association Conference in Bournville, and gave several key lectures in London. In September 1901, the *Daily Mail* reported his advocacy of democracy in design under the by-line 'Concerning the coming revolution in domestic architecture'. The revolution was closer at hand than even Unwin supposed.

Towards Community Design   Early on, Unwin conceived the idea of a broad, overall framework to give a sense of form to urban development, and he described this with conviction in his Garden City Conference paper of September 1901. The title 'On the Building of Houses in the Garden City' became a peg upon which he hung a 'design brief' which strikingly anticipated features of the Letchworth plan. Notwithstanding enthusiasm for the village as a community ideal, Unwin warned against over self conscious informality and advocated 'that beauty and orderly design for the creation of which alone power had been given to us', hinting at the formality of a renaissance plan. The layout was to be

> arranged in conformity with the land ... sites for our civil, religious and recreative public buildings ... have been determined, dominating the city. Wide avenues or roads must be planned to lead off from these sites in all directions, so that glimpses of the open country beyond shall be obtained from all parts ... and vistas leading up to the finest buildings shall greet the visitor from every direction ... In the arrangement of the space to be denoted to dwellings ... a complete acceptance of natural conditions must be combined with some definite design. No weak compound of town and country, composed of meandering suburban roads, lined with semi-detached villas, set each in a scrap of garden, will ever deserve the name of 'Garden City'.

WEDNESDAY, SEPTEMBER 18, 1901.

Interior of a £200 house for an artisan. On the ground floor all the usual stifling little rooms are thrown into one, thus creating a very spacious and airy apartment.

A £500 specimen of the new artistic dwellings, which are to combine a Ruskinian beauty and simplicity with special comforts and convenience.

24 'The artisan's living room' (originally sketched in 1895 by Barry Parker), and a '£500 artistic dwelling', as published in *The Daily Mail* on 18 September 1901, under the headline 'concerning the coming revolution in domestic architecture'.

Through co-operation the whole would attain still greater value than the sum of its parts:

> splendidly attractive as the Garden City scheme is ... because it presents to us ... a clean slate to work upon; it is yet more attractive ... because it promises to call together a community inspired with some ideal of what their city should be ... which will have in its life something more worthy to be expressed in its architecture than mere self-centred independence and churlish disregard of others, which have stamped their character on our modern towns.[17]

Enlightened bye-laws and regulations would control development, possibly through an advisory committee who would, as a last resort, possess 'an absolute veto on monstrosities'.

In eight pages, Unwin had defined key elements – a broad overall plan, detailed design standards, aesthetic control exercised by committees – which marked the transition from the Victorian reform tradition to modern environmental management, exercised in the public interest, which underlay town planning. His detailed ideas on housing design were developed through lectures to the Fabian Society and the Workmen's National Housing Council in November 1901. Fabian Tract 109, *Cottage Plans and Common Sense*, published 1902, contained a rational approach to housing design and layout techniques, to be used at New Earswick and Letchworth. Unwin balanced individual and communal aspects, working first principles of 'shelter, comfort, privacy', defining general criteria and specific standards. Housing had to be freed from the Victorian bye-law straitjacket. Sunlight was a key agent, to be 'insisted upon as an absolute essential, second only to air space ... every house should turn its face to the sun whence come light, sweetness. and health'.[18] He defined accommodation standards, 930 sq. ft. for a three-bedroomed house of 18 ft. 9 in. frontage. The living room, which included the stairs, was 195 sq. ft., with, in a few cases, a 126 sq. ft. parlour. The principal bedroom was 147 sq. ft., with two of 100 sq. ft. each, and a very small bathroom. These standards were adopted at New Earswick, Letchworth and Hampstead Garden Suburb, finally becoming national statutory requirements, largely through Unwin's advocacy. The plans showed built-in furniture to ensure space for all family activities. The exterior, for the moment, used a closed quadrangle form. Subsequently, at New Earswick and Letchworth, short informal terraces predominated, enlivened by gables and projections, derived from the Church Stretton cottages. In 1902 Parker and Unwin prepared a plan for housing at Starbeck, on the outskirts of Harrogate, Yorkshire.[19] It showed 'chequerboard' siting of semi-detached cottages, with picturesque gables and dormers, a

25 Western Terrace, New Earswick. These cottages, developed from those designed for Church Stretton in Shropshire, represented the theme around which complex variant housing plans were woven.

determined break away from the monotony of bye-law terraces. 'Cottages near a town' was exhibited at the Northern Artworkers Guild in Manchester in 1903 – an indication of the fusion of the Arts and Crafts and Garden City movements in the emergent discipline of town planning.

At the 1901 Garden City Association Conference, one of the delegates was Benjamin Seebohm Rowntree (1871-1954), younger son of Joseph Rowntree, the Quaker chocolate manufacturer, who had recently rebuilt his factory on the northern outskirts of York. Unwin's meeting with Rowntree brought the commission for New Earswick, a valuable testing ground for housing design and layout.[20] Unwin's 1902 layout indicated development of a flat, 150-acre (61 ha.) tract, a mile north of the Rowntree works, bisected by the north-south Haxby road, and bounded on the east by the meandering River Foss. The Haxby road was generator for an irregular street grid. Western Terrace and Poplar Grove were underway in 1902-3, and about 26 cottages had been completed by December 1904 when the Joseph Rowntree Village Trust was formed. The varied designs were simplified as costs rose. On 30 October 1903, a residents' group met Seebohm Rowntree, Barry Parker and Raymond Unwin, and criticised the 'back to front' arrangement of houses in Poplar Grove, which brought the outside closet door into public view, an expedient adopted to enable the main living areas to receive sunlight. This was avoided at Letchworth, but another dislike, the open-plan living room with stairs rising from it, was to recur there. New Earswick was a valuable testing ground and, although only a small part was under way before Unwin prepared the Letchworth layout, its influence was felt in early housing design and layout for the First Garden City. In May 1905, Unwin designed the Folk Hall for New Earswick, which closely resembled the Mrs. Howard Memorial Hall at Letchworth.

'That the Plan be issued as the Company's Plan'   Preparation of the master plan for the new Garden City at Letchworth was divided between the Buxton Office and Letchworth. Parker and Unwin employed about six assistants and a secretary. Smooth running of the scattered domestic projects and the building of New Earswick required skilled management. Unwin, with his industrial experience, was more effective, but neither he nor Parker was a harsh taskmaster. Robert Bennett (1878-1956), Wilson Bidwell (1877-1954)[21] and Cecil Hignett (1879-1960)[22] achieved successful independence at Letchworth. A more obscure assistant, Bowland Brockman Moffat (1880-1925), was clearly impressed by Unwin's 'quickness in grasping new ideas' as 'the Garden City scheme speedily took shape'. He found it

> A unique experience … quite out of the general range of architectural knowledge … and valuable in helping one to regard architecture not as appertaining merely to isolated buildings, but as controlling whole towns and masses in one scheme.[23]

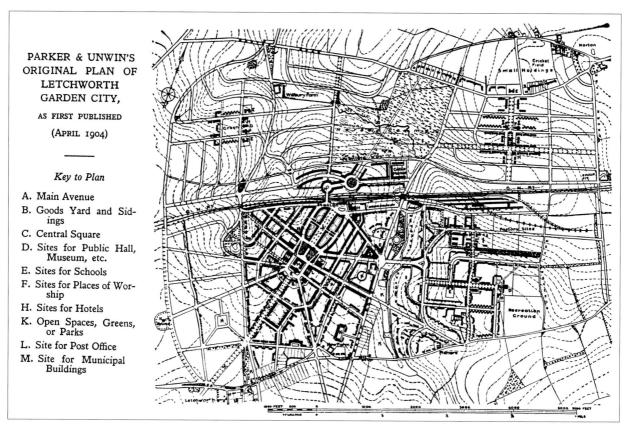

PARKER & UNWIN'S
ORIGINAL PLAN OF
LETCHWORTH
GARDEN CITY,

AS FIRST PUBLISHED

(APRIL 1904)

Key to Plan

A. Main Avenue
B. Goods Yard and Sidings
C. Central Square
D. Sites for Public Hall, Museum, etc.
E. Sites for Schools
F. Sites for Places of Worship
H. Sites for Hotels
K. Open Spaces, Greens, or Parks
L. Site for Post Office
M. Site for Municipal Buildings

26 'The Company's Plan'. Parker and Unwin's winning layout, as first published. Although detail, particularly in the outlying areas, was modified, this plan endured as the overall master plan for the First Garden City.

Unwin and Bennett set off for Letchworth, lodging in the post office at Letchworth corner, spending their days tramping over the estate and evenings sketching overlays on Humphreys's survey. The position of the town centre was fixed and a natural feature helped Unwin to clinch matters.

> The three old Oak trees which stood out solitary in the central town area were very helpful in fixing exactly the main axis line … I often remember, with a feeling of gratitude to them, the day when they suggested to me the exact position, and Mr Bennett and I were able to begin to lay the plan down on paper.[24]

The final drawings were completed in Buxton in December 1903, with the Parkers' dining table commandeered for the preparation of a large-scale layout.

The Board assembled on 7 January 1904. Ricardo and Unwin had explained their plans to the Engineering Committee shortly before. The final selection was left open until after a site meeting. On 28 January, the Engineering Committee met and compared the layouts with the requirements of the Great Northern Railway. They cautiously recommended acceptance of the Parker and Unwin plan. The Board concurred and instructed Adams

> To write to Mr Unwin for lithograph copies of his plan … and request … that he modify his plan in accordance with the Railway Company's plan … and also to inform him that his plan has been accepted, but only provisionally.[25]

On 11 February 1904 the waiting was over. The Board finally resolved 'that the plan be issued as the Company's Plan'.[26] There would be modifications and compromises, and Unwin found that Adams had his own ideas about the layout. For the present, however, efforts were

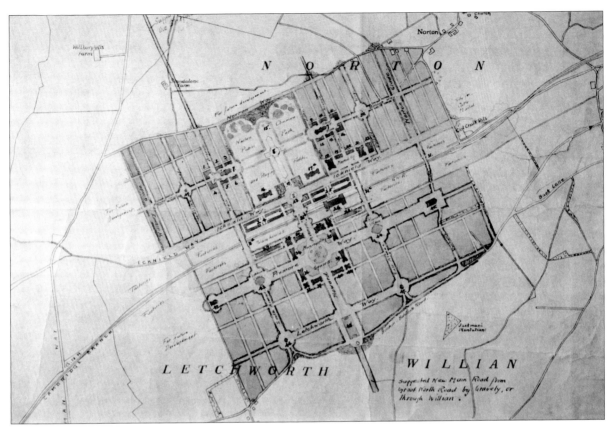

27 The Letchworth master plan by Geoffry Lucas and Sidney Cranfield, 1903. Another grid layout, with Norton Common reworked as an elaborate public park.

directed towards the public launch in April, at a *soirée* in London's Grafton Galleries, where printed copies of the plan were distributed to shareholders and guests.

The three alternative layouts all reflected a formality derived from the geometrical precision of Howard's original diagrams.[27] The Lucas and Cranfield plan was, perhaps, the least satisfactory, although it had the merit of compactness, being about 1.5 miles square, symmetrically disposed north and south of the railway, between the Wilbury road on the north, and the Hitchin-Baldock road on the south. It was basically a grid layout imposed arbitrarily over the undulating landscape, emphasising the division of the site by the railway, with twin factory belts running through the centre of the estate on both sides of the tracks. Norton Common to the north was to be transformed into an elaborate, rather Victorian park, with a central ornamental canal. A grand boulevard, appropriately to be named 'Howard Avenue' ran southwards to a vast *piazza* at the town centre, bordered by public buildings. Smaller, outer squares were designated 'College Place', 'School Place' and 'Market Square'. Quadrangles were shown for most of the housing, but there was also a suggestion that 'large private residences' would be developed south of the Hitchin road, anticipating The Glade.

The Lethaby and Ricardo plan also had several questionable elements. The industrial area was located to the north-west of the town, with sidings and a goods yard branching from the main tracks on the town edge. The first impression of the town from the railway approach via Hitchin and from the open terrain north of Willbury Camp would have been industrial, and difficult to screen with planting. The town area was compact, with a clear street grid overlaid with major diagonals. Their report stressed that 'the city should not have the appearance of an overgrown village', the antithesis in some respects of Unwin's plan, as implemented. A mile-long major axis

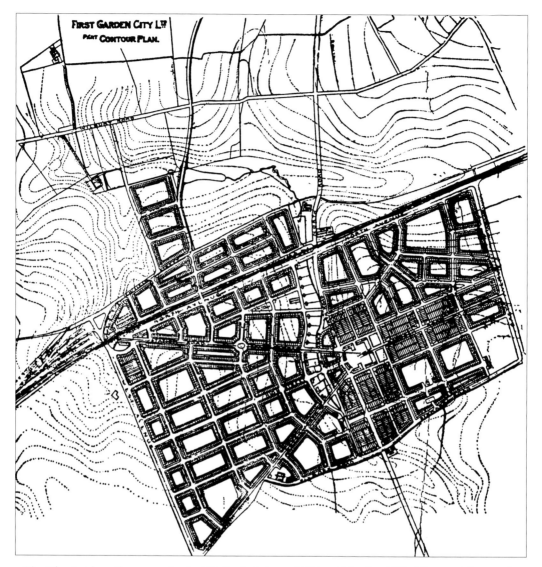

28 The Letchworth master plan by W. R. Lethaby and Halsey Ricardo, 1903. Thomas Adams and, later, C. B. Purdom expressed a preference for its compact formality.

led eastward from the station, towards the town centre, an impressive concept, which would have been seriously weakened by undulating contours. The town centre was to be located on rising ground east of the Pix valley, close to the present location of the Hillshott School. Housing quadrangles predominated, with inner allotments as at Port Sunlight, and impersonal undivided strips of lawn and garden, planted and kept trim '[aiming] at efficiency, lastingness [*sic*] and ordinary pleasantness rather than … picturesqueness'. Adams was impressed, and later wrote that the plan's compactness would have made early development more viable.

Unwin's plan[28] contained a blend of formal and natural elements and fitted the character of the site better than its competitors. At a casual glance, it seemed an exercise in formal geometry, with carefully regulated major and minor axes, but these fitted the contours with effortless ease. The railway, the existing Wilbury to Norton road, the old Icknield Way and the Hitchin to Baldock road were given their due weight as east-west routes. Existing lanes such as Letchworth Lane, Spring Road and Dunhams Lane already provided fragmentary north-south communication. Unwin incorporated Humphreys's recommended north-south road skirting Norton Common, and running west of the Pix valley, south of the railway. This became Norton Way, one of the first major roads to be built. The main axis, now Broadway, ran at an angle from the Hitchin Road, through the area reserved for the Town Square (now J. F. Kennedy Gardens), to intersect the railway at the site reserved for the permanent station. Beyond, it was projected through The Quadrant, and ran as a broad walk across Norton Common, north of Icknield Way. Both sides of Broadway, between Town Square and the station, were sweeping curved roads, recalling the line of Oxford High Street, one of Unwin's favourite historical examples. From Town Square, minor axes radiated in a web-like pattern, providing open vistas of countryside from within, and glimpses of the intended group of public buildings in the centre, to visitors approaching the town, fulfilling Unwin's objectives from his Bournville paper. Minor roads created a modified grid layout which closely resembled the area surrounding the Exchange on Sir Christopher Wren's plan for rebuilding the City of London, prepared in 1666 after the Great Fire, one of the few major precedents for this type of layout.

Unwin took a justifiable pride in preserving most of the existing trees and hedgerows,[29] and this was highlighted by the more informal treatment of the outlying areas. The Pix valley represented a logical break east of the town centre, although two of the minor axes, Hillshott and Pixmore Way, were thrust across. The upper slopes of Pixmore were to be developed for working-class housing, informally grouped as at New Earswick, with a defined neighbourhood centre. Detail was subsequently modified but guiding principles remained. The factory area was zoned as a broad belt north and south of the railway, but was concealed from the town centre by a bluff, for which Unwin designed the Birds Hill/Ridge Road housing scheme. North of Icknield Way the Norton Glebe lands were to be developed as a further neighbourhood, and the field boundaries and hedgerows were incorporated in the modified grid layout. During implementation Unwin reduced the number of east-west roads, in accordance with his principle that the cost saved would justify better housing and larger gardens. This theme became the keynote of *Nothing Gained by Overcrowding*, published in 1912 by the Garden Cities and Town Planning Association. Norton Common was largely preserved in its natural state, but Unwin attempted to bring the major axis of the plan to it by a civic design sequence of a broad crescent and two interconnecting circuses. The name, The Quadrant, recalled the Buxton address, where Parker and Unwin opened their offices. The axial line of The Quadrant remains, but the area was radically replanned to include Exhibition Road (now Nevells Road) to accommodate the 1905 Cheap Cottages Exhibition. Adams felt that the axial line across the Common would make a convenient road. Unwin flatly disagreed stating

> We do not need more than a wide handsome walk … A broad grass glade … with perhaps a narrow paved way … would carry forward the axial line of the town and provide … a short cut for pedestrians, the extra distance for vehicle traffic … would be very slight.[30]

The area north-west of the town centre contained another proposed neighbourhood centre, but in the early 1930s the plan was radically altered by Parker to create the bold axial line of the present Bedford Road. Likewise in the south-west there was little development beyond Spring Road until the early 1920s, with the exception of Sollershott West. The individual elements were largely integrated by Unwin's strong geometrical framework, tempered by his regard for natural features. At a functional level, influenced by German practice, he developed the principles of land use and density zoning, with definition of town centre, commercial and industrial areas, varied residential districts forming the overall town area, beyond which agricultural uses, corresponding to a modern green belt, would predominate. The plan provided a transition from Howard's diagrammatic idealism to 20th-century town planning.

Promoting and Controlling Development On 23 March 1904, Parker and Unwin were appointed Consulting Architects to First Garden City Ltd., to oversee building and to exercise design control. This role brought its frustrations from the beginning. 'Alpha Cottages', built by local contractors, were indifferently designed, provoking Unwin to write to Howard stressing the importance of high standards. In July 1904 Adams advertised for the appointment of an independent consultant at £200 a year, which attracted 150 applications. Unwin passionately defended his position:

> People are expecting that the Garden City will be a more interesting and beautiful place than an ordinary new building suburb, … The general effect … may yet be made or marred by the way in which the plan is carried out in detail … [and] will depend not only on the detail of the roads, but on the planning of buildings, and their arrangement on the plots, and the treatment of corner sites; … it seems to me very important to make suggestions to builders.[31]

Although the Directors compiled a shortlist, the Board eventually reaffirmed the appointment of Parker and Unwin at £200 per annum, plus expenses. Subsequently Unwin dealt with layout matters, until his partnership with Parker ended in May 1914. Parker undertook detailed design control, following Unwin's move to Hampstead in May 1906, and remained sole consultant architect to First Garden City Ltd from 1914 to 1943. The degree of control fluctuated according to the magnitude or urgency of the proposed development, and expediency often seemed to triumph. C.B. Purdom, initially an accountant in the Estate Office, witnessed the conflicting opinions and the triumph of the 'practical men', anxious lest they deter potential developers.[32]

Unwin also pressed for the adoption of building regulations. The Hitchin Rural District Council was generally permissive and, while experimental methods and materials were unlikely to be vetoed, thus permitting the Cheap Cottages Exhibition of 1905, there was no guarantee of sound construction. Unwin believed that construction and aesthetics were inseparable, as evident from his draft building regulations, dated June 1904.

> *General Suggestions and Instructions Regarding Buildings Other Than Factories on The Garden City Estate*
>
> The Directors of First Garden City Limited are convinced that the high standard of beauty, which they desire to attain in Garden City, can only result from simple, straightforward buildings and from the use of good and harmonious materials. They desire as far as possible to discourage useless ornamentation, and to secure that buildings shall be suitably designed for their purpose and position.[33]

Unwin included building area standards, building lines and grouping, aspect and prospect, the use of hedges to define boundaries and submission of materials for approval – many of the points earlier included in *Cottage Plans and Common Sense*. The building regulations, published in 1905, were largely successful in practice. Welsh slate, reminiscent of bye-law terraces, was largely vetoed in favour of tiles. Bricks presented a problem, for Unwin found the local yellow-grey gault Arlesey whites drab, and insisted on their being pebble-dashed or colour washed over. However, the more expensive red facing bricks were permitted, and widely used in the town centre. The regulations included differential zoning of densities and land uses, following German practice. Residential density control was related to building cost, ranging from four per acre for houses costing above £500, to 12 per acre for those below £200. The smallest cottages had to include a living room of 144 sq. ft. Detailed constructional standards, ventilation and drainage were also covered by the regulations. Although most developers complied, Unwin was sometimes overruled. One of the earliest infringers was Halsey Ricardo who defiantly built Elm Tree House, in Letchworth Lane, and an identical house on Hitchin Road in Arlesey whites, not the red facings shown on the plans. The Building Committee, with Edward Cadbury in the Chair, received Unwin's report but took no action. At the same meeting Unwin also lost out over his objections to a bungalow designed by a local builder, Mr Beckley.[34] These skirmishes led Purdom to conclude that 'If the client was sufficiently determined he could put up much what he liked, as the buildings in the town bear witness'.[35] It was overstatement, for the domestic architecture of Letchworth was one of its strengths, and attained a maturity and homogeneity, aided by good materials and generous tree planting and landscaping.

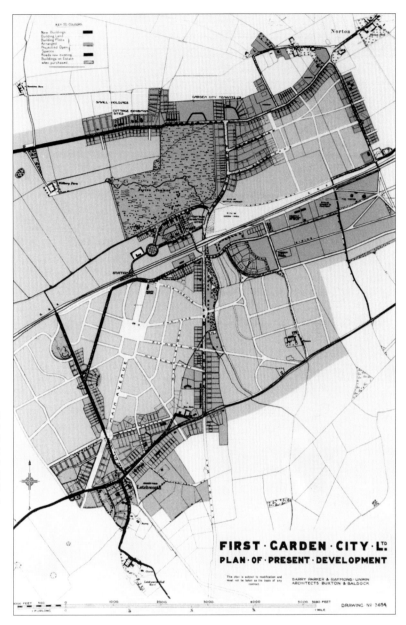

29 Plan of Present Development, 1906. Many of the roads on the layout plan were destined to remain on paper for many years. The darker tone indicates roads built by Spring 1906, along which housing plots have been laid out.

Garden City in the Making Development of Letchworth was heavily dependent upon infrastructure – public utilities, roads and transport facilities.[36] The estate had the advantage of the railway, but few made-up roads apart from the Hitchin to Baldock road, and no public utilities. Well water and cesspits were unsuitable for town development. Provision of adequate services for a town with an ultimate population of 30,000 was an enormous task for a private company with little capital, the extension of whose borrowing power was dependent upon a rolling programme of development to enhance the value of its basic asset. The Garden City had, above all, emphasised a healthy form of development in contrast to the Victorian industrial city, and there could be no compromise over public health.

In February 1904 G.R. Strachan prepared a water supply scheme.[37] Springs outcropped at Norton Bury Farm on the north of the estate, where the Chiltern chalk gave way to gault and greensand. A 16-inch diameter bore hole was sunk 220 ft. below Baldock Road and tested up to 6,000 gallons per hour, and a 250,000-gallon reservoir was constructed in the

30 The London unemployed outside 'The Sheds', 1905. Although the road builders departed after a single winter, 'The Sheds' endured to become the Cheap Cottages Exhibition Centre, the first infants' school, and the first factory for Spirella.

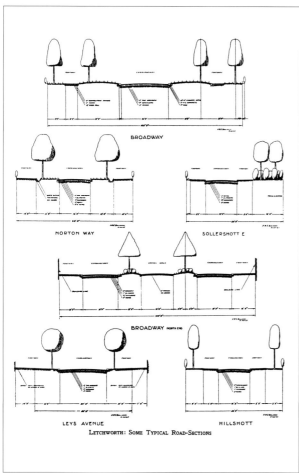

31 Typical road sections showing landscaping. The use of tree-planted grass margins helped to give the impression of *Rus in Urbe* on all Garden City roads.

Weston Hills above Baldock, which was also served. In 1907 the facilities were duplicated. Between 1905 and 1913 consumption rose from 10 million to 85 million gallons, and the water mains from five miles' length in 1905 to 21 miles in 1913. Capacity was increased by a new 500,000-gallon reservoir. Up to September 1912, £26,183 had been spent on water supply, with £7,000 towards a new bore hole to improve capacity. Strachan also designed the sewerage scheme. A temporary sewage farm, north of the railway in the Bedford Road area, provided a gravitation disposal system until 1923, when the newly created Letchworth Urban District Council built a new treatment plant allied to separate drainage system, off the Stotfold road. Factories had to undertake to treat noxious waste before passing it into the sewers. Construction of the system proceeded with the roads at a pre-1913 cost of £18,000, providing 15¾ miles of sewers. By 1924, 21 miles had been laid by F.G.C. Ltd.

Many roads were destined to exist only on paper for a long period.[38] In March 1904 the Board resolved to construct 'North Road' (Norton Way South) from the Baldock road to the Great Northern Railway. Its width was to be 60ft. between fences, with a 16ft. carriageway, flanked by 12ft. greenswards and 10 ft. paths.[39] The construction of Station Road, with a 45ft. reservation followed. Varied treatments of the highway reservation,

32 The temporary wooden station, built by the Great Northern Railway in 1905, which took the first commuters to and from London, and brought thousands of day trippers to the Cheap Cottages Exhibition.

with tree-lined greenswards and pathways, helped to create the Garden City character. In the winter of 1904-5 unemployed labourers from the East End of London dug out roads and sewer trenches. They were housed in a group of sheds erected north of the railway, subsequently used for the 1905 Cheap Cottages Exhibition, as the first primary school, and as a temporary factory for Spirella.

'Main Avenue' (Broadway) was completed as far as the multiple junction with Spring Road and the Sollershotts, where one of the first purpose-built traffic roundabouts was constructed and named 'Sollershott Circus'.[40] This was opened with ceremony in 1910, and many of the waiting cars overheated in the summer sun. It was many years before Letchworth drivers became accustomed to the discipline of clockwise circulation. Broadway had a 100 ft. reservation, with a 27 ft. carriageway and broad but asymmetrical greenswards, the wider one originally intended to accommodate a tramway to Hitchin. The remainder of Broadway to Town Square was made up in the 1920s after long years as an informal cinder path. In order to join the two sections of Norton Way, a major road bridge was constructed in 1913 beneath the railway embankment, to supersede the old 'cattle creep', in the early years the

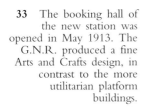

33 The booking hall of the new station was opened in May 1913. The G.N.R. produced a fine Arts and Crafts design, in contrast to the more utilitarian platform buildings.

only direct route between Norton Common and the town centre. The cost of the new bridge was shared between F.G.C. Ltd., the Great Northern Railway, the Hertfordshire County Council and the Hitchin Rural District Council. At the other end of the scale narrow lightly-paved roads and culs-de-sac were used in residential areas, and the subsequent widespread use of the motor car has caused problems. The length of new roads rose from 5¼ miles in 1905, to 11½ in 1913, and 18 in 1924. F.G.C. Ltd. constructed the major lengths, but Hitchin R.D.C. made up Green Lane and part of Works Road in 1908. In 1911 the County Council took over substantial lengths for maintenance at public expense, and in 1919 the Letchworth U.D.C. began building estate and other roads.

The Great Northern Railway branch line from Hitchin to Cambridge was an important asset, indicated by the concern to meet First Garden City Ltd.'s requirements. The halt, provided for the estate opening in 1903, was replaced by a more imposing temporary station in April 1905, under the control of Letchworth's first station master, Richard Thacker. The service included fast Cambridge to King's Cross trains which took 50 minutes for the 34-mile journey from Letchworth.[41] A horse omnibus to Hitchin provided connections for the main line to and from the north, and the Midland Railway branch to Bedford. The G.N.R. acquired 24½ acres for a permanent station site to the east, and for a goods yard beyond the Norton Way bridge. Purdom and others criticised the separation of the passenger and goods facilities, but this avoided major severance of the town centre. The permanent station was opened on 17 May 1913, the same day as the new Norton Way bridge. The platforms, designed as islands to allow additional lines to be laid, were capped with traditional canopies and fretted valances of the standard G.N.R. pattern. By contrast, the Booking Hall, above the cutting, facing Station Place, entered into the spirit of the Arts and Crafts movement with its rich red brickwork, tiled roof and leaded bay windows.

Howard had stressed the necessity to capitalise on technological advance, but gas was given priority over electricity.[42] Construction of the gasworks, initially to produce six million cu.ft. coal gas annually, began early in 1905, south of the railway on Works Road, with sidings for delivery of coking coal. Gasholders and retort houses had to be increased in size almost immediately, with nine miles of mains laid, 1906-7, and an increase in demand from five million cu.ft. to 12 million. By 1912, the demand was 50 million cu.ft. The scattered form of development, compared with industrial towns meant, however, that the consumption per mile of mains was much lower, and relatively less profitable. The Company was a subsidiary of F.G.C. Ltd. It initially provided metering and gas stoves free, which boosted domestic demand. Many cottages remained gas-lit until the 1940s, with gas street lighting from distinctive Parker and Unwin designed copper lanterns. The First World War boosted demand, which reached 118 million cu. ft. by 1924, with 22 miles of mains.

Electricity supply commenced in 1907,[43] with a 500-volt direct current system, supplied from a generator in Works Road. Initially, supply was restricted to the industrial area, with half-mile mains and a modest 44,017 units consumed in 1908. In 1909 a cable was run to serve the Picture Palace in Eastcheap, and mains gradually spread to the residential areas. Generating capacity was substantially increased in 1910 and again in 1912. Consumption reached 513,286 units in 1913 from five miles of mains. Expansion was rapid during the First World War and the generators were increased in 1915, 1916 and 1921. The peak wartime demand was reached in 1919 when 8,911,800 units were consumed; by 1924 this had dropped to 3,432,000 units, with 20 miles of mains.

The provision and rapid expansion of infrastructure was itself evidence of the successful implementation of the Garden City project. The plan and public utilities, however, were both to be regarded as a framework for others to develop. As Howard pragmatically stated:

> The Company does not propose to build the town: its aim is to provide a well formed skeleton – and it asks others to clothe that skeleton – the ground plan which has been very carefully prepared, … with beautiful houses, churches, public buildings, well designed factories and convenient shops.[44]

Six

GARDEN CITY HOMES

'I am Alpha' On 26 November 1903 First Garden City Ltd. convened a Building Committee, even before the layout plan had been resolved.[1] One of the directors, H.B. Harris, undertook to obtain details of four-roomed homes costing £135. In January 1904 the Committee agreed to build up to 20 cottages, based on Bournville plans, along Baldock Road adjoining New Farm. The local builders, Picton and Hope, took the lease, and submitted their plans for Unwin's scrutiny in April. Construction of 'Alpha Cottages', a semi-detached pair and a group of four (Nos 22-32 Baldock Road), was soon under way. On 7 July 1904, Miss Elizabeth H. Revill moved into No. 1 'Alpha Cottages', the first resident of a purpose-built house in Letchworth Garden City. Within a few weeks, the Collinses, Janeways, Furmstons, and Watts moved in. The latter family followed their furniture up Hitchin Hill on a railway dray only to find that the painters had downed tools before finishing the job. They dossed down on the floor to begin their new life in the Garden City.[2]

That summer a few more pioneers, including Howard, Parker and Unwin, moved to the estate. Unwin lodged in Baldock, until his house in Letchworth Lane was completed, half of a semi-detached pair, built jointly with the Howard Pearsalls. 'Laneside' and 'Crabby Corner' (both now 'Arunside') rejected conventional symmetry for an informal, subtle composition, which expressed differing internal layouts. The building read almost as single storey, its dominant roof punctuated by varied dormers, and surmounted by tall Yeoman Tudor chimneys. The whitewashed roughcast walls were enlivened by shadows from the overhanging eaves and projecting bays. It was, essentially, an enlargement of the grouped cottages of New Earswick. The Unwins' home became a focus for the pioneers' community life. Parker and

34 Alpha Cottages, 1904. The workmen from Picton and Hope pose on wooden scaffolding in front of the nearly completed block of four.

35 Raymond Unwin's sitting room in 'Laneside'. The attributes of the simple life are here in abundance - bare limewashed brickwork and ceiling joists, an exposed brick inglenook fireplace with copper hood, bare boarded floors, a heavy settle, and elegantly proportioned rush-seated Clissett chairs.

36 Raymond Unwin lived in 'Laneside' from 1904 to 1906, when he left for Hampstead Garden Suburb. Newly married, Barry Parker moved into the other half, 'Crabby Corner', seen here, and added the sleeping tower, at the right, in 1914.

37 Garden City in the making – market gardening near the Cheap Cottages Exhibition. This view emphasises the relative isolation of early groups of houses and the raw appearance of the streets before the newly-planted trees matured.

Unwin also designed a somewhat similar group of four houses, built on Norton Way South (now numbered 355-361) for Ebenezer Howard, who lived at No. 359 until 1911. Thomas Adams leased Punchardon Hall, Willian, a fine 16th-century house. It was essential, however, to attract more extensive residential and industrial development, to ensure the viability of the infant Garden City.

The 1905 Cheap Cottages Exhibition   In the early 1900s the depressed agricultural wages, of 14s. 0d.-16s. 0d. per week, seriously inhibited provision of sound dwellings on an economic basis. J. St Loe Strachey, editor of *The County Gentleman*, took up the cause of the £150 cottage in October 1904, when he wrote of the necessity to demonstrate new constructional techniques. That November, Thomas Adams gained Board approval to offer a site at a peppercorn rent, to be developed for a Cheap Cottages Exhibition, to be opened the following summer.[3]

Although a high population of agricultural workers was never envisaged, Adams grasped the project's publicity value, and the bonus of the subsequent availability of the permanent exhibits to house industrial workers. The chosen site, predominantly the area between Icknield Way and the railway, disrupted Unwin's projected civic design, but The Quadrant extends the axial line of the town centre to Norton Common, an appropriately rural backdrop. One plot backed onto its eastern flank, and several more along Wilbury Road faced it. A small estate of 22 houses was developed in Birds Hill, close to the industrial area, while First Garden City Ltd. entered their 'Ploughmen's Cottages' in Paddock Close, off Norton Way South. 124 dwellings were built, with the emphasis on the detached cottage, rather than the group. A £100 prize was offered for the best £150 cottage with living room, scullery and three bedrooms. Other classes involved pairs of five-roomed cottages, groups of three or four, and the best cottage for £35 per room. Special prizes were also offered for the 'Cheapest Cottage', the 'Best Wooden Cottage' and the 'Best Concrete Cottage'. Unwin was warned against over-zealous control, for the Board ruled that 'Architects [are] not to be interfered with as regards details or matters of taste by [the] consulting architect'.

The Exhibition was opened by the Duke of Devonshire on 25 July 1905. The event was a great public success with over 60,000 visitors (some estimates even totalled 80,000), many

38 No. 4 Cross Street, The Concrete Machinery Company won first prize in 1905 for the best concrete cottage for this entry, built of concrete blocks manufactured on site.

39 No. 221 Icknield Way, Bennett and Bidwell, newly independent from Parker and Unwin, designed this charming black-boarded cottage which was awarded second prize in its class in 1905.

travelling by the 3s. 5d. cheap day returns from King's Cross. Near the station, the sheds, built the previous autumn as a hostel for unemployed labourers from London, were adapted as a restaurant and gallery. Many exhibits were furnished by London stores, and some incorporated novel kitchen gadgetry and patent folding baths. Press verdicts were mixed, with many cottages seen as better suited to middle-class 'week-enders' than to agricultural workers. Purdom, writing in 1913, was dismissive:

> there can be no question that the exhibition, while it gave the place a tremendous advertisement, did no little harm. It set a rage for cheapness from which Garden City has hardly yet recovered, it gave the town the character of a village of tiny weekend cottages not very well built: its curiosities of planning, construction and material, which had nothing in common with the objects of the town, gave the place a name for cranky buildings … It will be a happy day for Letchworth when the exhibition is forgotten and all its consequences are destroyed.[4]

Although his interest in building technology was aroused, Unwin's verdict was also reserved:

> Many a £150 cottage is an excessively dear cottage. It is necessary to emphasise this because it is one of the curses of our times that this idea of cheapness … acquires an artificial and altogether misleading meaning … we may be quite certain that we are on the wrong track … if we do not build them [cottages] well.[5]

Most of the exhibits have survived the major part of their 99-year span, some are 'listed' buildings, and all are located within the Letchworth Conservation Area. In several, traditional appearance concealed experimental construction, and a few were truly revolutionary. Exhibition Road (Nevells Road) was the centre of the Exhibition. Nos. 206 and 208, built by Bournville Village Trust, architect H. Bedford Tylor, were inferior to the standard prevailing in that pioneer model village. No. 212 'The Stone House', built of concrete blocks, with a 'Canadian Style' projecting porch, was designed by Robert Bennett and Wilson Bidwell, former assistants of Parker and Unwin. No. 216, by the Barrow Construction Company, architect William Moss Settle, used a pre-fabricated system of grooved oak posts and concrete slabs, exposed externally but later rendered over to inhibit damp penetration. Nos. 218 and 220 Nevells Road, set diagonally across the corner into Cross Street, and designed by

H. S. Barrett and C. H. Driver, were economy versions of C.F.A. Voysey's design idiom, with their roughcast buttresses and chimneys. No. 4 Cross Street, designed by Gilbert Wilson Fraser (1874-1954) for the Concrete Machinery Co. of Liverpool, won the prize for the Best Concrete Cottage. It was built from blocks made on site by a portable machine with a capacity of 150 per day. Nos. 13, 15 and 17, on the opposite side, were exhibited by Potter and Co. and won the First Prize in Class II. Although conventional in appearance, the walls were steel framed, with roughcast over expanded metal lathing.

The exhibits on Icknield Way ranged from rather basic structures such as No. 211, by John McManus, Iron Building Manufacturer, to No. 245, designed by Oswald Partridge Milne (1881-1968), a vernacular revival cottage with overhanging jettied front. No. 217, a solidly built roughcast cottage, won First Prize in Class I. It was designed by Percy Bond Houfton (d.1926), a Chesterfield architect responsible for progressive colliery villages in Derbyshire and Yorkshire. No. 221, at the junction with The Quadrant, won Second Prize; it was a timber framed cottage, designed by Bennett and Bidwell. The grouped cottage Prize was awarded to the 'Ploughmen's Cottages' at Paddock Close, designed by Geoffry Lucas.

Nos. 7/7A Norton Way North, 'Elmwood Cottages', were designed by Mackay Hugh Baillie Scott (1865-1945).[6] Their cost of £420 eliminated them from serious consideration; Scott considered such materialism irrelevant and wrote in the Exhibition Catalogue that: 'the Cottage should be the dream come true, the result of infinite pains, and whether it pays five or six per cent is quite a secondary matter'. This 'new-old' design, based on the

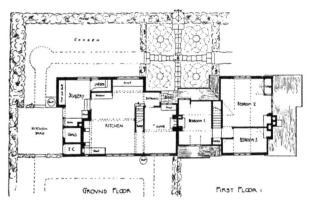

40 'Elmwood Cottages', Nos 7/7A Norton Way North, by M. H. Baillie Scott. This entry proved one of the most influential in creating the vernacular imagery of the Garden City cottage.

revival of the medieval hall house, with genuine timber framed construction in part, received wide acclaim. The sophisticated open-plan interior had a single living space divided by a handsome elm staircase, and a recessed inglenook fireplace containing the kitchen range. The roof, of reclaimed tiles complete with moss, originally swept low over a scullery, set impractically a few steps below the main floor level, later raised, spoiling the exterior by flat-roofed extensions. Eastholm Green at the junction of Norton Road and Wilbury Road was developed by Garden City Tenants, a branch of the Co-Partnership Tenants Housing Society. The plain grouped houses appear mainly to have been designed by Parker and Unwin. Wilbury Road led westwards, marking the northern limits of the infant Garden City. Nos. 150-156, used mansard roofs to economise on brick external walls. They were designed by W. Clough of Ringwood, Hampshire, and supervised on site by his young nephew Clough Williams-Ellis

41 The Round House, No. 140 Wilbury Road, was possibly the most radical of the 1905 Cheap Cottages, with its concrete panel construction. It survived until 1987.

(1883-1978).[7] Further west, No. 126, an almost puritanically simple cottage designed by A. Randall Wells (1887-1942), won First Prize in Class IV, and later became C. B. Purdom's home.

The two most revolutionary exhibits, Nos. 140 and 158 Wilbury Road, both pioneered prefabricated reinforced concrete technology. No. 140 'The Round House', designed by Robert Lemprière Hesketh (1850-1937) and Walter Stokes for Cubitts, the London contractors, was the most radical of the exhibits. It had a 16-sided plan, made up from heavy panels fixed to a prefabricated frame. Its form was derived from a logical consideration of the material and methods of construction. It was claimed that work above foundation level could be completed in three days. The rooms were awkwardly shaped, like wedges of cheese. The cottage survived in an overgrown and deteriorated state, although still inhabited, until 1987 when, regrettably, the panels disintegrated whilst the building was being taken apart for re-erection at the Standalone Farm Centre.

No. 158 Wilbury Road was designed by John Alexander Brodie (1858-1934), City Engineer of Liverpool, who pioneered a prefabricated reinforced concrete system for model flats.[8] The panels were cast in a quarry near Liverpool, complete with joinery, with clinker ash from the city incinerator used in the mix. The constructional principle was that of a dovetailed box, and the 15 panels were dispatched to Letchworth on railway wagons. Visually the cottage still surprises with its smooth white walls and flat roof – the opposite of the Arts and Crafts picturesqueness of many of the exhibits. It appears remarkably modern, but the sinuous curve of the roof parapet, the boldly projecting cornice with its mildly classical brackets, a classical string course masking the joint between ground- and first-floor panels and the small paned windows, all confirm the early 20th-century date. The cottage was enthusiastically written up by Georges Benoit-Lévy (1880-c.1960), leader of the French Garden City movement, in his book, *La Cité Jardin*.[9] It appeared to influence the remarkable, unbuilt, *Cité Industrielle*, 1904-18, designed by the Lyons architect Tony Garnier (1869-1948), and, through him, the experimental concrete houses of Le Corbusier (1887-1965).

The novelty of the 1905 Cheap Cottages Exhibition was followed up at Letchworth and elsewhere. A second exhibition was held at Letchworth in 1907, under the auspices of the National Housing Reform Council.[10] The urban cottage area had an Unwin layout, which provided a demonstration of town planning. The site included parts of Lytton Avenue (then

Middle Street), Gernon Road (then The Leys) and Pixmore Way. The associated rural homesteads, south of the Baldock Road, have been encroached upon by ribbon development. Overall design standards in 1907 were higher than in 1905. Many awards were won by Courtenay Crickmer (1879-1971),[11] a London architect who had moved to Letchworth. The Exhibition had become one amongst many and failed to attract large numbers of visitors. Shortly afterwards, the *Daily Mail* began to champion house design, and in 1910 sponsored the first Ideal Home Exhibition, and subsequently in 1921 a model village at Welwyn Garden City, Howard's second creation.

Co-Partnership Cottages Housing Societies, registered under the Industrial and Provident Societies Act, 1893, carried on the tradition of 'five per cent philanthropy' and at the turn of the century began to develop suburban sites in London. Tenants were required to become investors, inevitably attracting skilled artisans rather than labourers. Ealing Tenants Ltd., pioneers of co-partnership, began development at Brentham in April 1901.[12] They contributed the rather utilitarian No. 221 Icknield Way to the 1905 Cheap Cottages Exhibition. Their activities spawned a national body, the Co-Partnership Tenants Housing Society, chaired by Henry Vivian, M.P. (1886-1930), founder of the movement. The Co-Partners' offshoots, Garden City Tenants Ltd. and Hampstead Tenants Ltd., played a key role in the housing development at both

42 The panel system of No. 158 Wilbury Road. *Top*: withdrawing the panels from the moulds; *centre*: trial erection; *bottom*: loaded on railway wagons for the journey to Letchworth. J. M. Brodie's system does not appear to have been used for any other cottages apart from the Letchworth entry.

43 Nos. 7-17 Lytton Avenue, designed by Courtenay Crickmer, were prizewinners in the 1907 Exhibition. The statue of 'Sappho' can be seen front centre.

44 'Westholm', designed by Parker and Unwin, in 1906, was built by Garden City Tenants, and was based on Unwin's diagram of an idealised village green, published in *The Art of Building a Home* (1901).

45 Birds Hill housing, by Parker and Unwin, 1907. The designs with their multiple gables and dormers proved too expensive for labourers to rent.

Letchworth and Hampstead Garden Suburb, particularly under the design and layout consultancy of Parker and Unwin.[13]

Each of their Letchworth estates advanced the techniques of site layout and housing design. The first Eastholm (1905-6) was partly completed for the Cheap Cottages Exhibition, and showed little attempt to group the individual units into corporate entity. The most striking houses were the angled corner pair, turning in from Wilbury Road. The houses faced an attractive green, later cut through to form Eastern Way, access to the post-1945 Grange Estate. Westholm, begun 1906, north of Wilbury Road, closely followed Unwin's idealised village greens from *The Art of Building a Home* (1901).[14] It fitted the topography well, with its open-ended green, commanding views of Norton Common, flanked on three sides by groups of two, four and five cottages. Their multiple gables and dormers were similar to cottages in Station Road, New Earswick. Block ends were emphasised with projecting parlour cottages. 'Westholm' and its successor, 'Birds Hill' (1906), created a kit of parts, capable of variations to fit particular site conditions and orientation. 'Birds Hill' marked an important stage in the evolution of site planning, with a cul-de-sac to enable development in depth, in addition to a village green, a playground, and retention of a tree-planted 'buffer zone' to separate the housing from the adjoining industrial area. The commanding site above Birds Hill, and the rising curve of Ridge Road, presented the opportunity to develop an effective sequence of street pictures. This reflected Unwin's enthusiasm for groupings advocated by the Austrian urban planner Camillo Sitte (1843-1903), whose book, *Town Planning According to Artistic Principles*, he had avidly read shortly after completing the Letchworth layout. Unwin was fast becoming an international authority on housing, and his Letchworth estates were featured in his 1906 R.I.B.A. International Congress Paper, 'The Planning of the Residential Districts of Towns'.[15]

The house plans were divided into parlour and non-parlour types, subsequently an important distinction in local authority housing for many years. Unwin favoured large living rooms to eliminate compartmented social convention. The parlour remained an enduring status symbol distinguishing artisan from labourer. Rents ranged from 4s. 6d. (22½p) per week for a two-bedroom non-parlour cottage to 8s. 5d. (42p) for three- and four-bedroom parlour cottages. These sums provoked controversy in *The Garden City* magazine, where it was claimed, with some justice, that the cottages were extravagantly constructed and excluded the poorer labourers, who rented rooms in the back streets of Hitchin and Baldock and walked to work. Unwin refuted his critics, both on the detailed costings, and by claiming that a wage rise of 9d. (4p) per week for the unskilled labourer would solve the difficulty:

> for if Garden City stands for anything surely it stands for this: a decent home and garden for every family that come here. That is the irreducible minimum. Let that go and we fail utterly. And if we succeed utterly what then? A beautiful home in a beautiful garden and a beautiful city for all.[16]

Astutely, he prepared designs for simpler, cheaper cottages and set out the prerequisites for economy in design:

> If cottages are to be built cheaply they must be built in groups; thorough organisation of the building operations must be secured; a sufficient number must be built, to effect the great economies which arise … and a thoroughly economical plan … must be adopted. It is very important to standardise the various parts … Too much care cannot be taken in designing … doors … and windows, so that they may be pleasantly proportioned … Where groups of cottages must be kept absolutely simple, good results will depend largely on the arrangement of them. Here as in so many cases our forefathers have shown us the way … they knew full well that a degree of simplicity in design which would be wearisome if spread out in a long straight row may be extremely pleasant when the buildings are grouped round a square of green.[17]

A few of the simpler cottages were included in the ambitious Pixmore Estate, which Garden City Tenants built 1907-9, a pioneer neighbourhood unit with institute and recreational

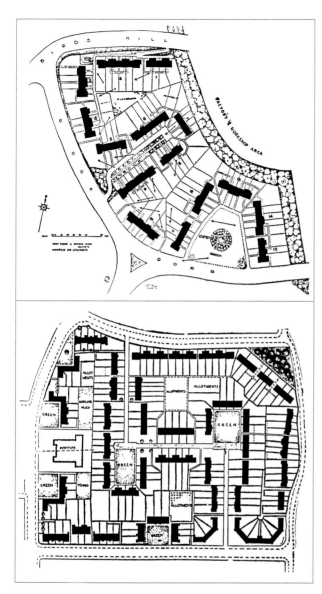

46 The layout of Birds Hill, 1906 (*top*) incorporates a village green and a cul-de-sac. The existing plantation was retained as a buffer between housing and the industrial estate. Pixmore, 1907-9 (*bottom*) reached the scale of a self-contained neighbourhood, complete with its own institute, now the Hillshott School.

facilities. The site area was 16.35 acres (6.6 ha.), and the 164 houses, mainly in groups of four, gave an overall density of 10 per acre, 12 per acre net (30 per ha.), excluding roads, the institute and recreation space. The layout was intended to minimise highway cost in relation to houses served, a principle which Unwin generalised in *Nothing Gained by Overcrowding*, his brilliant critique of 'bye-law' development with its extravagant area of paved streets and back alleys.[18] At Pixmore, Unwin was almost too successful in serving the centre of the block by a single narrow access road, latterly choked with parked cars, unthinkable the time of construction.

By 1907 Letchworth had begun to develop a significant industrial base, which increased the housing requirement. Industrialists might build: in 1907, J. M. Dent, the publishers, built 24 cottages for their key workers in 'Temple Gardens' off Green Lane. Overall, industrialists willing to provide housing as a matter of course were absent. First Garden City Ltd. began a more direct role in housing provision. In 1907 Letchworth Cottages and Buildings Ltd. was formed as its subsidiary. By 1911, it had constructed nearly 200 cottages, many costing under £150 each, with simple but visually effective designs by Parker, following Unwin's principles for standardisation. The Common View groups brought the roof down to incorporate the bedroom windows in broad catslide dormers. A simple tiled porch identified the individual house within the block. The self-conscious picturesqueness of some early designs was superseded by the recreation of the innate fitness for purpose of the vernacular cottage.

The original local authority for the Letchworth Estate, the Hitchin Rural District Council, was able to raise loans from the Public Works Loan Board to cover the full cost of cottage building, with repayment spread over 60-80 years, more favourable terms than available to cottage societies, who could raise only two thirds of the building cost, with a maximum 40 years' repayment. Letchworth Garden City had little voice in local government, even after March 1908 when it became a unified Parish Council, a non-executive body. Through its urging, in 1912, Hitchin R.D.C. at last built four cottages on Icknield Way, followed by more extensive construction under the wartime conditions of 1915-16.

The Howard Cottage Society In August 1911 the Howard Cottage Society was formed to take advantage of more generous loan terms offered to housing societies under the 1909

47 Cottages in Common View costing £120 each, built by Letchworth Cottages and Buildings Ltd. in 1909-10, designed by Parker and Unwin.

Housing and Town Planning Act.[19] Among its shareholders was George Bernard Shaw, who assisted the work of several cottage societies. Ebenezer Howard, after whom the Society was named, was a Director, and the Chairman, Howard Pearsall, had long been interested in working-class housing. The office was in Pearsall's home, 'Glaed Hame', and in 1912 Frederic Osborn (1885-1978) was recruited as Executive Secretary.

Development of housing along Rushby Mead, facing Howard Park, began in 1911. The overall layout by Unwin was a masterpiece of informal design, through which he reworked his early admiration of village groupings in terms of his more recently acquired analytical approach. The road followed the old course of the Pix brook. Great care was taken to preserve existing hedges, and to vary siting to avoid monotony. The work of several architects blended together unobtrusively. Southwards from Birds Hill, the first two blocks were set back from the road behind long gardens, with a short return block at right angles followed by a frontage block. These were designed by Bennett and Bidwell, subsequently prolific and skilful housing designers. Rushby Walk was a pioneer cul-de-sac, flanked by two blocks by Parker and Unwin and two by Crickmer. The southern section of Rushby Mead incorporated an 'L' form space, giving an effective focus to the view from Hillshott. Materials throughout were restricted to roughcast brick walls, with red tiled roofs punctuated by gables and dormers, occasionally with an infill of black weatherboarding or tilehanging. Features such as string courses, lightly curved dripmoulds or the boldly projecting timber cornices of the bay windows were indicative of the great care taken over detail. The original colour scheme of cream roughcast and green woodwork has been retained creating an overall harmony, and an environmental quality not often subsequently achieved in mass housing.

The Society built further cottages in Ridge Road and Broughton Hill and by the outbreak of the First World War had completed 300 at costs ranging from £150 to £220, and rents from 5s. 6d. to 8s. 6d. There were two main types, both three-bedroomed, but some incorporated a small parlour in addition to living room and scullery. All included a fixed bath and were gas-lit. Osborn became a man of all trades, consulting Howard, checking tenders and accounts for new cottages, allocating tenancies and collecting rents, becoming almost a social worker, answering complaints, and making suggestions for design improvements to the architects. Howard provided Osborn with detailed grumbles to sort out!

48   Rushby Mead, a landmark in housing design, by the Howard Cottage Society, built in 1911. Layout by Raymond Unwin, cottages left and centre designed by Bennett and Bidwell.

> Now one of the Ewarts men … who went into one in the Rushby Mead complains bitterly of his garden being overrun by dogs and I do hope something … will be done and done speedily to protect him. He and his son are very fond of gardening.

> Wood complains that his sitting room is draughty because of the stairs going straight out of it. He would very much like a door. Also he would like a dresser. Are they not absolutely reasonable complaints? I think they are.[20]

The generous gardens were widely appreciated and Osborn organised a competition in which a week rent-free was offered as the prize for the best garden on each estate. Letchworth gardens soon became famous for their productivity.

The fame of the Howard Cottage Society spread, with correspondence from Canada and the U.S.A. and from Pavel Mizhuev, the Russian expert on Garden Cities. The outbreak of war in 1914 and the subsequent influx of Belgian refugees increased pressure for new housing. A new 100-cottage estate to the west of the town centre, around Campers Road, was soon nicknamed 'Little Belgium'. Osborn worked virtually single-handed to supervise construction, using the pre-war designs, but at times he even designed new cottages himself when site conditions demanded. Post-1919 housing provision shifted emphasis to the local authority sector, due to more generous exchequer subsidies, but the Howard Cottage Society and its contemporaries in the voluntary sector continued to build in Letchworth, as will be discussed below in Chapter Nine.

Co-operative Living   What had become of the vision of co-operative quadrangles, advocated by Unwin and Howard?[21] With their emphasis on communal facilities these would have provided a radically different form of working-class housing. Howard remained loyal to the

49 'Homesgarth (Sollershott Hall), promoted by Howard in 1911, designed by H. Clapham Lander. 'Homesgarth' originally provided communal facilities, including a residents' club, in the three-storey central block which served a partly-completed rear quadrangle of flats.

concept. In 1906 his 'suggestion' for co-operative housing was published both in *The Garden City* and the *Daily Mail*. He leased a four-acre site near the corner of Spring Road and Sollershott East, and raised finance by £10 mortgage debentures with 4 per cent interest, totalling about £5,000 in 1911, when the partly completed 'Homesgarth' was opened. The scheme, designed by Harold Clapham Lander (1868-1955), aimed at providing co-operative living for professional people. The 32 dwellings, grouped around a spacious quadrangle, were service flats, with meals from a central kitchen, available either in the individual apartments or the communal dining room. The most prominent element was the three-storey block containing the communal rooms, facing Sollershott Circus, dominated by a central gabled portion flanked by towers capped with elegant concave profiled copper roofs with elongated finials, suggesting the influence of Voysey. The flats behind, linked by a glazed canopy, were of a more domestic scale. Regrettably, the frontage was later cluttered with outbuildings and garages, and the quadrangle was disrupted by new three-storey flat-roofed flats added in the 1960s. The communal facilities were gradually closed and converted into additional flats. In the 1920s the name was changed to Sollershott Hall. Howard was resident until 1920, when he left for Welwyn Garden City. He had exactly fitted his own description of the intended tenants: 'One of those numerous folk of the middle-class who have a hard struggle for existence on a meagre income … those who require domestic help, but can very ill afford it'. In conjunction with the Howard Cottage Society, Miss Pym promoted the development of co-operative flats for single business women. Courtenay Crickmer designed the first phase of Meadow Way Green. Construction was delayed by discussions with the Public Works Loan Board as to whether the housing was defined as 'working-class'. The Society insisted that the income limit should be £160 per annum, much higher than the prevailing average. The first phase opened in 1916, and a second block, south of Meadow Way, was completed in 1925. Post-war inflation in building costs had taken its toll, as the design was more utilitarian than on the original block.

A Who's Who of Domestic Architecture The residential areas of Letchworth were widely recognised as a clear demonstration of the success of new density and layout standards.[22] The aesthetic control process curbed the exuberance of speculative builders, without imposing uniformity. Tree-lined roads such as Norton Way South attained a pleasant ensemble.

50 Arts and Crafts fundamentalism in No. 102 Wilbury Road, built in 1909 for Barry Parker's brother, Stanley.

Letchworth was notable for many progressively designed pre-1914 houses; after the First World War costs escalated and designs were simplified, with, in many instances, little difference between Garden City housing and suburban development elsewhere.

The domestic work of Parker and Unwin was naturally extensive, with design themes already noted in their grouped housing, mirroring the range of domestic design illustrated in their *Daily Mail* article of 1901, 'Concerning the Coming Revolution in Domestic Architecture'. The designs indicated that Parker, in charge of the Letchworth office, was willing to give assistants an opportunity to develop individuality. Parker himself, newly-married, moved into 'Crabby Corner' in 1906, shortly before Unwin's departure for Hampstead Garden Suburb. In 1914, with a growing family, Parker added a three-storey wing, with playroom, sitting room and sleeping porch beneath a tall, hipped roof, reminiscent of Bavarian hill towns. Both he and Unwin were enthusiasts for the historic vernacular architecture of middle Europe.[23]

The small middle-class house, costing £500-£750, gave scope for a wide range of designs. One of the most attractive, 'Briarside' (now 'Netherton'), Hitchin Road, 1905, belonged to a series based on a square plan form, with 45-degree splays and diagonals giving the entrance hall, inglenook and corner bay a spatial complexity, emphasised externally by the boldly hipped, near-pyramidal roof. Two semi-detached pairs in Green Lane, Nos 14 and 16, and 22 and 24, 1904-5, had ingenious cruciform plans set at 45 degrees to the road. A large square studio, originally open to the rafter roof, was the major element of 'The Den' (now 'The White Cottage'), built in Croft Lane in 1906 for the artist, Charles Fox. The plan consisted of interlocking squares defining the inglenook, kitchen and bathroom, with the generating module expressed in the recessed porch. The soft lines of the thatched roof, thrown casually like a blanket over the building, concealed the discipline of the plan. By contrast, houses built in 1908-10 were statements of elemental simplicity, a fulfilment of Parker's youthful manifesto for 'plain, simple and ungarnished homes'.[24] They shared roughcast walls, with leaded casement windows set directly into concrete mullions. Internal finishes were puritanical; limewashed brick walls, exposed joists and rafters, elm plank doors with wooden Norfolk latches and blacksmith-made wrought-iron hinges, and boldly detailed fireplaces. No. 102 Wilbury Road was built in 1909 for Barry Parker's younger craftsman brother, Stanley, who designed and made his own furniture, complementing the ascetic interiors. All non-essentials were eliminated in the manner later advocated by reforming modernists, but on the basis of craft technology, and without losing the traditional image of the home. 'Treetops', No. 12 Cashio Lane, 1910, combined simplicity of detail with a sophisticated open plan based on an interlocking square grid. The living room projected outwards to gain views and aspect. Its square

51 'Glaed Hame', 1906. This imposing house was built for Howard Pearsall, the Fabian and Director of F.G.C. Ltd. The sleeping porch (now demolished) was added in 1920.

central area was defined by exposed posts and beams, with the inglenook balanced by a dining recess, and the bay projecting into the garden, corresponded to the entrance from the recessed front porch, flanked by larger squares containing den and kitchen. A richly concentrated spatial pattern was generated, and the linear emphasis of post and beam in counterpoint with the bare walls suggested Japanese influence. A square grid also underlay grouped housing at the junction of Field Lane and Sollershott East, built in 1910. Six houses, each with a square modular plan, formed twin blocks with low-hipped roofs, and deep overhanging flared out eaves. Tall brick chimneystacks with angled tiled offsets framed the point where Field Lane sliced through the group.

The larger houses related earlier designs from Derbyshire: 'The Coppice', 1905, and 'Glaed Hame', 1906, both in Pasture Road, were developed from the plan of 'Greenmoor', Buxton, 1898. Howard Pearsall commissioned 'Glaed Hame', an unusually large house for Letchworth. The garden front, with three exposed studwork gables, mullioned windows, and elaborate chimneys veered towards Stockbroker Tudor, concealing a progressive plan with interconnecting hall, sitting and dining rooms, capable of use as one large space, or subdivision into separate rooms by sliding and folding doors. A sleeping porch, with a flat concrete roof was added in the 1920s; it was demolished in the 1970s, when the house was extended. 'St Brighids', Sollershott West, 1908, was built for Edmund Hunter, the textile designer. The house was a variation on the popular Edwardian 'butterfly' plan, designed to attract maximum sunlight to the living rooms. The plan had complex 45-degree splays. Parker provided the initial sketches, and a gifted assistant, Samuel Pointon Taylor (b.1884), worked up the details. The central hall, an irregular hexagon, led to the living room, which had a half-octagonal bay and angled fireplace, boldly detailed with a conical copper hood and an exposed concrete lintel.

Parker and Unwin worked in Baldock until 1907, when the Letchworth offices were opened in Norton Way South, backing onto the attractive wooded glade of the Pix valley. Parker designed the building, and indicated a mirror image extension to house Unwin's drawing office and private suite, never built due to his remaining in Hampstead Garden Suburb. Cecil Hignett (1879-1960)[25] prepared the technical drawings. The choice of the romantic thatched hall house as its model, emphasised the domestic quality of the building,

Specimen of Reed Thatching, done on Architects' Offices, Garden City.

52 Parker and Unwin offices. No. 296 Norton Way South (now the First Garden City Heritage Museum), 1907. For the Norton Way offices, Parker chose the romantic model of a thatched hall house. The thatcher proudly used the job to promote his business.

but the planning was another example of a square grid. The open hall became the drawing office, lit by concrete mullioned windows, open to the roof which was spanned by an enormous timber baulk, its outward thrust taken externally by a sloping buttress. The solar, at higher level, became Parker's private office, with a discreet squint, through which he could observe the goings-on in the drawing office. The centrepiece of the room was an arched inglenook fireplace, with copper hood, comparable to many in the practice's houses. The

large cruciform concrete mullioned north light window had stained glass inserts of 'The Four Seasons', by Heasman, a craftsman from Harpenden. Externally the building fitted unobtrusively into its bosky setting, while the garden reflected the design principles of Gertrude Jekyll. Parker added a two-storey south wing in 1937 when the building became his home, and it was further extended in 1973 to form the First Garden City Heritage Museum.

Several of Parker and Unwin's assistants achieved independent practice: one of their assistants wrote, 'a new job was always given to one assistant entirely – he prepared the sketch plans and so on to the last detail and then settling up'.[26] Robert Bennett (1878-1956) had been an articled pupil from 1898-1902, and Wilson Bidwell (1877-1944) had joined the firm in 1902. Shortly after moving to Baldock, they set up an independent office.[27] They were both excellent designers of individual and grouped housing. Examples of their cottage work have been noted above. Among

53 The Drawing Office, *c*.1910. Assistants, including Cecil Hignett and Samuel Pointon-Taylor, work to produce yet more designs for Garden City housing.

54 Designed by Bennett and Bidwell, 'Carfax' , No. 501 Broadway. This house, on an angled site at the junction of Broadway and Sollershott West, featured exposed timber studwork in the re-entrant between the main wings.

the individual designs were 'The Croft', Nos. 16 and 18 Baldock Road, 1906, the latter being Bennett's first Garden City home, and 'The Cottage', No. 7 Willian Way, 1909, was the Bidwell family home. Bidwell admired the work of Baillie Scott, whose influence is notable in the handling of the bold gables facing Willian Way, and in the organisation of the open plan, with its interconnecting living spaces. The use of plain, high quality materials with natural finishes, the folding doors to subdivide or open up the living areas, and the reworking of traditional inglenook fireplaces, created a practical, inherently elegant, domestic environment. 'Carfax', No. 501 Broadway, 1909, was a major house on the triangular site on the corner of Sollershott West and Broadway. The central gable with exposed beams, between the two terminating principal wings of the plan, gave the appearance of a 'butterfly' plan. The major living hall was given extra height, pushing the bedroom above well into the roof. Robert Bennett built 'Hall Barn', The Glade, for himself in 1923, one of the last major Arts and Crafts houses to be designed with complete conviction. Bennett adapted the 'butterfly' plan but reversed it so that the house ran along the slope rather than embracing it. It was, unusually, built with an integral garage, with a loft above for Bennett's carpentry. The joinery details were of an excellent standard, the staircase balustrading being influenced by the work of Ernest Gimson and Sidney Barnsley. Smaller fireplaces were influenced by Lutyens's brickwork at 'Daneshill', Old Basing but the living room inglenook was pure Letchworth, almost a room within a room, with a vast copper hood gleaming in the firelight. Shortly afterwards, the firm began to design the varied houses, in styles ranging from Queen Anne to Tudor, which graced the eastern side of the newly made-up run of Broadway from Sollershott Circus to Town Square.

Cecil Hignett (1878-1960) achieved independence in 1909. He had worked for Edgar Wood (1860-1935), a leader of the Northern Arts and Crafts movement.[28] Wood used progressive forms including flat roofs, and advanced materials such as concrete. Wood's only house in the south-east, 'Dalny Veed' near Royston, was built in 1907. Hignett appears to have been involved with the grid planning of several of Parker and Unwin's houses. He remained in Derbyshire to close down the Buxton office, then, July 1906, headed for Letchworth. Traipsing through the mud, he eventually found 'Laneside'. Ethel Unwin opened the door and bade him remove his boots, 'I walked into the living-room where there was a nice warm fire, to be greeted by Raymond Unwin – in my socks – I had arrived'.[29] Hignett's home, 'The Three Gables', Croft Lane, was built in 1907, while he was working on the technical drawings for Parker's offices. Significantly, both buildings were thatched. The house was designed for open-air living and its central entrance hall led into a recessed porch fitted

55 'Arana', Hitchin Road, 1908. Designed by Courtenay Crickmer, this fine house features his trademark 'M' double gable.

with a settle. The thatched roof was brought down to the height of the ground-floor window heads on the side facing the lane, and the building only appeared as two-storeyed from the garden, where a central gable with a half hip dominated the elevation. The outer 'two gables' were little more than eyebrow dormers. The living room turned towards the garden with only small windows towards the corners on the north. This allowed Hignett to accommodate a handsome antique dresser, a family heirloom. All joinery was individually detailed, and the front door contained a delightful stained glass insert of swirling fish. 'Croft Corner', 1911, was a larger version of 'The Three Gables', diagonally set across the corner of Croft Lane and Cashio Lane. He also designed Nos. 102-110 Common View, 1910, for Letchworth Cottages and Buildings Ltd., pantile-roofed terraces, enlivened by header-brick patterned diaper work between the first-floor windows. Hignett's later houses included characteristic three-bay designs, in brick, sometimes with tile-hanging, such as Nos. 7, 9 and 11 South View, 1923. In 1935, the most imposing of his Letchworth houses appeared, 'Dolphin House' in Garth Road, built for Major Chater-Lea, whose factory in Icknield Way he had designed in 1928. His major industrial buildings are discussed below in Chapter Eight.

Courtenay Crickmer (1879-1971)[30] was the most important Letchworth architect outside the Parker and Unwin circle. He built a pair of modest, competent houses on Baldock Road in 1904-5, Nos. 15 and 17, and moved into one of them. 'Crossways', Hitchin Road, 1906, one of his best early houses, was dominated by an 'M' gable with exposed vertical studding. This design was simplified for 'Arana', 1908, on the north side of Hitchin Road. The brick ground floor contrasted effectively with the rendered first floor, creating a 'skirt and blouse' effect, and the plain gables made the dominance of the 'M' form the more effective. The plan strung the principal rooms along the south front, with interconnecting drawing and dining rooms, an arrangement elaborated in 'Dean Row', Pasture Road, 1910, a substantial brick and stone house. Crickmer's best work included grouped houses and cottages. At the junction of Sollershott East and South View a dominant block was built in 1911 by Town Planning and Garden City Estates Ltd, Nos. 32-38 Sollershott East and No. 47 South View. The dominant centre gatehouse had a brick gable incorporating traditional tumbled-in brickwork, and flanked by twin octagonal shafted chimneys. Although some of the long front gardens have, regrettably, been spoilt by intrusive parking spaces, the group remains one of the finest in Letchworth. Around the corner in South View, Nos. 34 and 36 were a semi-detached assembly of two of Crickmer's First Prize

56 'Tanglewood', No. 17 Sollershott West, 1907, by M. H. Baillie Scott. This house, with its open-plan interior including a 50 ft. living room, is one of Scott's finest designs for the 'smaller middle-class house'.

cottages in the 1911 Gidea Park Competition. Externally the stairs occupied distinctive narrow gabled turrets forming a transition between the single- and two-storey parts. Crickmer repeated this design on many sites in Letchworth and elsewhere. Nos. 41-43 South View and three similar groups in Spring Road, built 1922-6, show a post-1919 economy version of the same design, simplified with metal casements substituted for the leaded lights of the original.

Harold Clapham Lander (1868-1955) designed Nos. 35 and 37 Baldock Road in 1905. These wide frontage, semi-detached houses, with roughcast walls and prominent gabled tiled roofs, were among the best early Letchworth houses, clearly influenced by Voysey. 'Abendheim', No. 302 Norton Way South, 1911, an endearingly eccentric house, was modelled on a Bavarian chalet, but executed so well as to disarm criticism. The building formed an effective feature on the corner of Pixmore Way and Norton Way South. First floor corner balconies with dark stained slatted balustrades nestled beneath the overhanging eaves and all windows were shuttered. A tile-canopied gateway completed the picture. Allen Foxley (1869-1955) was more restrained. Nos. 3 and 5 Norton Way North had a rectangular plan, and wide frontage. The rear elevation was divided by an irregular sequence of brick pilasters containing the windows within a grid, a visually effective design. No. 508 Broadway, 1912, was the best of Foxley's Letchworth houses, a design which reflected classical inclinations. The pilaster treatment was emphasised by the use of contrasting grey and red brickwork, while the roof's end gables were treated as pediments. On the south elevation, prominently visible from Broadway, Foxley ran a central chimney, picking up the drawing room and principal bedroom flues, through the pediment, with an arched attic window in the centre of the chimney breast. Above the roof ridge, the flues were connected by an arch. Foxley must have known of the games played with such details by Lutyens. At the rear of the house was an impressive two-storey veranda and sleeping balcony, now regrettably demolished.

M.H. Baillie Scott[31] was the most distinguished of the 'outsiders'. He had commenced practice in the 1890s in the Isle of Man and gained prominence with his articles on the 'smaller middle class house', published in 'The Studio', and his prize-winning scheme for 'An art lover's house', sponsored by Alexander Koch, a German publisher. Scott had moved to Bedford in 1901, close at hand when the development of Letchworth began. Apart from his influential entry in the 1905 Cheap Cottages Exhibition, 'Elmwood Cottages', Nos.7 and 7A Norton Way North, discussed above, he received four more Letchworth commissions. Each showed his characteristic emphasis on picturesque massing, sometimes bordering on idiosyncrasy, as with No. 29 Norton Way North, 1906, where he brought the eaves of the almost pyramidal hipped roof to within two feet of ground level to the right of the studwork entrance feature. Such a capricious feature could only be achieved by sinking the scullery floor, almost a ship's galley, 18 inches below the ground-floor level. 'Spring Wood', Spring Road, 1906, was built for a local artist, Edward Docker, and incorporated a two-storey studio within an open-plan ground floor. The house faced southwards over a generous garden, and was placed at right angles to the road. 'Tanglewood', No. 17 Sollershott West, 1907, was one of Scott's best small houses. The studio and sitting room formed a single space 36 feet long. The fireplace and bay window were defined by exposed principal beams, effectively breaking the overall room down into functionally distinct areas. The exterior was clearly derived from the medieval vernacular, especially the immaculately detailed central section with its structural timber studwork, within which were placed leaded casement windows and the front door. The contrasting garden elevation incorporated an 'M' gable. Scott repeated the design, with variations, at Biddenham, north west of Bedford. 'Corrie Wood', Hitchin Road, 1908, was the last and most sophisticated of Scott's Letchworth houses. The principal living rooms were ranged across the south front, with a large living area, incorporating a slightly raised dining recess, parlour and garden room, with a total length of 42 feet. Externally the house originally had an overall pyramidal form, emphasised by the sweeping hips of the roof, in places with eaves only two feet above ground level, and an 'M' gable dominating the garden front. The bedrooms were broken up by the irregularities of the roof, and the building was lengthened in 1923, and subsequently further extended, losing some of the original compactness of form. Charles Harrison Townsend (1851-1928) was acclaimed for his distinctive Whitechapel Art Gallery, 1897-1901, and Horniman Museum, 1899-1901, Forest Hill, London, both of which had strong Art Nouveau influences. He also designed many small houses. 'The Glade', 1906, is a sound example of an Edwardian house, if without any special flair. A. Randall Wells (1877-1942) was one of the fundamentalists of the Arts and Crafts movement, and modelled his work on vernacular architecture, especially evident in his Cheap Cottages entry, No. 126 Wilbury Road. A larger, more self-conscious version was built at No.1 Norton Road in 1906-7. A third Wells house, 'Yoxford', No. 3 Cashio Lane, 1906, was rather swamped by 1922 alterations designed by Cecil Hignett. William Curtis Green (1875-1960) began as a designer of small houses, but ultimately branched out into lucrative commercial practice. No. 109 Wilbury Road, 1909, a good example of his early work, was a variant on the popular 'butterfly' plan, turning its living areas southwards towards Norton Common.

Reputation Building Although the architect had been brought into much greater prominence, most houses in Letchworth were designed by their builders, under the control of Parker and Unwin as consultants.[32] Within a few years many firms were active.[33] Picton and Hope, already noted as builders of 'Alpha Cottages', used this fact for many years in their advertisements. They also built the 'sheds' in Exhibition Road, and several of the 1905 Cheap cottages. Beckley and Turpie built some of the smallholdings cottages for the 1907 Exhibition. J. F. Bentley was both a contractor and an entrepreneur, involved with the Picture Palace, and extensively constructing his 'Palace Gem' bungalow, remarkable value at £175, in the Meads and Common View. Some builders became prominent local figures.

J.T. Openshaw founded his firm in 1905, and built many of the best known Letchworth public buildings, including the Post Office, the Girls Club and the Free Church. Among his housing, the three blocks of 'Silver Birch Cottages' in Station Road, 1905-7, were commissioned from Parker and Unwin and were closely related in design to the Westholm groups. Their layout, at a slight angle, gave interest to an otherwise rather monotonous street.[34] Openshaw also constructed much of the Birds Hill Estate. He became a member of the Parish Council and later of the U.D.C. Charles Ball, another firm of high repute, operated principally as civil engineering contractors, constructing many of the highways in Letchworth.

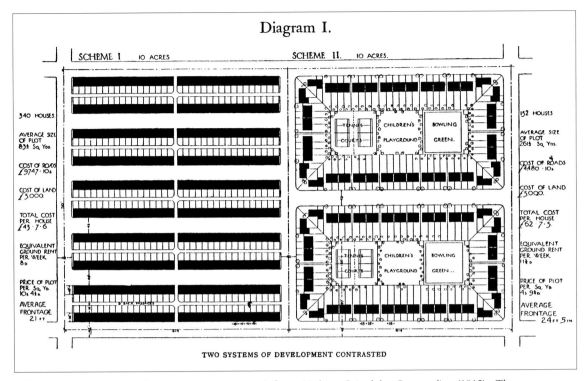

57 The two systems of development contrasted from *Nothing Gained by Overcrowding* (1912). The contrast between the harsh urban terraces and hard paved streets and alleys, and the loose-knit Garden City development with its communal facilities underlined the desirability of the new standards but underplayed the fact that, unless land could be obtained at agricultural rates, the more widely-spread development was inevitably more expensive.

With the rapid development of housing both for sale and private rental, estate agents flourished. Before professional standards were rigidly codified, they sometimes doubled as architects. Edgar John Simmons (1874-1938) was an auctioneer, estate agent and man of all work. He even designed the remodelling of the 'Picture Palace' in Eastcheap in 1924, and cinemas in Hertford and Barnet in the 1930s. He designed one of the earliest shop and office developments in Letchworth town centre, 'The Colonnade', and later remodelled three Tudor cottages on Baldock Road to become 'Scudamore', notable for its elaborate shafted chimney stacks and exposed timber studwork. The house featured on posters issued by F.G.C. Ltd., and was Simmons's home. His local rivals, Underwood and Kent, were only in business for a few years. Like Simmons, Underwood designed one of the town's best known houses – 'Melverley', Pixmore Way, basically a 'butterfly' plan set diagonally against the road frontage, with an infill between the wings containing a polygonal galleried hall. Gables and dormers proliferated, with exposed studwork, a stone entrance porch and red brickwork ground floor, looking like a stray piece of Victorian Cheshire revival architecture relocated in the Garden City. Another estate agent, T. Clarence Howard, was Ebenezer Howard's nephew. He moved to Letchworth in 1905, and began work as a rent collector, from No. 10 Station Road, becoming a tax collector during the First World War. Joan Howard, daughter of his first marriage, was the first baby girl born in the infant Garden City.

Nothing Gained by Overcrowding   Reform of domestic architecture, promoted by the Arts and Crafts movement, was internationally publicised from the 1890s. Such was the acclaim that the Prussian government appointed an ambassador, Hermann Muthesius, to prepare a comprehensive report, *Das Englische Haus (The English House)*, published in 1904. Although Muthesius did not include any Garden City examples, this was rectified by his

The Garden City Method of Development.

FRONT GARDENS TO HOUSES UNDER TOWN PLANNING.

The By-Law Method of Development.

ORDINARY SUBURBAN VILLAS, SHOWING AMOUNT OF SPACE FOR FRONT GARDEN.

58 The Garden City and Bye-Law housing compared: from *Nothing Gained by Overcrowding* (1912). The verdant front gardens in Hampstead Garden Suburb (*top*) are contrasted with the hard urban character of North London Bye-Law housing (*bottom*). Unwin and the Garden City movement relied heavily on such propaganda to create the political climate for the acceptance of new housing standards in 1919.

successors Bernard Kampffmeyer and Berlepsch Valendas, who visited Letchworth and Hampstead Garden Suburb in the early 1900s. Georges Benoit-Lévy was an early French visitor who systematically described early development. The influence of Letchworth and the Garden City movement was soon felt throughout Europe, and further afield.[34]

Unwin and others began to press for legislation to bring the new residential standards into more general use. The Housing and Town Planning Act, 1909, enabled local authorities to regulate suburban development to garden city layout and density standards.[35] Among the first schemes to be prepared, Ruislip Northwood, involved Thomas Adams as the first Principal Planning Inspector at the Local Government Board, and Unwin acting as consultant to the principal land owner, King's College, Cambridge. Hampstead Garden Suburb, developed from 1907 onwards with a master plan by Unwin and much excellent co-partnership housing in the 'Artizans' Quarter', was widely emulated. However, C. B. Purdom, and other fundamentalists of the movement, felt that suburban town planning 'weakened the good wine of the Garden City' – an ironic simile for a teetotaller to use. In 1909, Unwin put together a textbook, which became a classic.[36] *Town Planning in Practice* contained a comprehensive review of historic towns, and also analysed the design of residential development, the basis of most early town planning schemes. Unwin drew lessons from Letchworth and Hampstead, claiming that the famous '12 to the acre' standard literally sprang from grass roots level:

> Twelve houses to the net acre of building land, excluding all roads, has been proved to be about the right number to give gardens of sufficient size of commercial value to the tenants – large enough that is, to be worth cultivating seriously for the sake of the profits, and not too large to be worked by an ordinary labourer and his family. This figure … has now been fairly well tested … at Bournville, at Earswick, at the Garden City at Letchworth, at Hampstead and many other places.[38]

Unwin argued that the value of food produced in the gardens helped to offset higher rent levels for the lower density housing. He extended this argument, albeit at times with some dubious reasoning, to a general theory of site design, published by the Garden Cities and Town Planning Association in 1912 as *Nothing Gained by Overcrowding*.[39] He contrasted alternative block development plans, showing urban terraces with their compulsory 'bye-law' hard paved streets and alleys, and the lower density Garden City development with much cheaper roads, and communal bock centres. Cheaper suburban land would bring the benefits of larger gardens, and allotments and playgrounds. The concept was developed from the housing quadrangles of Port Sunlight and Unwin's own early theoretical schemes. Contrasting pairs of photographs juxtaposing the gloom of terraced development with the verdure of Hampstead Garden Suburb underlined the message.

A public career for Unwin was, perhaps, inevitable and in December 1914 he became Principal Inspector for Town Planning at the Local Government Board, following Adams's departure for Canada. Initially he held planning inquiries into schemes prepared under the 1909 legislation. However, in 1915, he was seconded to the Ministry of Munitions to advise on the development of housing for munition workers in remote areas.[40] An ambitious plan for development at Gretna and Eastriggs north of the Solway Firth was prepared, and Crickmer acted as the site architect. The Gretna development has claims to have been the first state-assisted new town. In addition, the Ministry of Reconstruction was giving careful consideration to housing standards after the war. It was already evident that rising construction costs would seriously inhibit the private sector, and even housing societies, from providing adequate working-class housing. Unwin worked closely as an unofficial colleague of Seebohm Rowntree, who sat on the housing panel. The panel recommended that an ambitious programme of state-aided housing should be commenced immediately after the war. To develop the detail, a major housing investigation was chaired by Sir John Tudor Walters. Witnesses included Crickmer, fresh from his experience at Gretna, W. J. Swain, the Clerk of Works from New Earswick, and representatives of bodies such as the National Housing and Town Planning Council. The Tudor Walters *Report*, published in 1918, bears hallmarks of being largely written by Unwin. It pressed for a massive state-subsidised housing programme, with standards based on Garden City practice. The post-Armistice commitment by David Lloyd George to 'Homes for Heroes', was enacted through the Housing Act 1919, which also established the Ministry of Health with responsibility for housing and public health.[41] Christopher Addison became the first Minister, and Unwin was appointed Chief Housing Architect. The initial generous subsidy restricted the local authority loss on housing to 1d. (0.4p) rate; an inducement to fulfil the statutory duty to provide working-class housing. There was an unpromising start as construction costs soared in the period of post-war scarcity – the cost of a three-bedroomed house rose from £350 in 1914 to £900 in 1920, reaching a peak of £1,050 early the following year. The generous subsidies were soon terminated and housing became a sensitive political issue. Nevertheless, an important principle had been accepted and, with it, the Garden City as the physical model. Unwin must have been pleased to see the newly created Letchworth Urban District Council among the first to build, and their housing role will be described later.

SEVEN

THE SPIRIT OF THE PLACE

The Arcadians   The years 1904-14 were a Golden Age of Garden City life, perhaps already fading as war broke out and shattered illusions. While the community was little larger than a village, all pioneer residents shared a common experience, exciting if beset by minor hardships. Accounts by A. W. Brunt, C. B. Purdom, Charles Lee and Ethel Henderson all attest to the feeling of a new beginning and of a community-spirit binding individuals together.[1] A century after the initiation of Letchworth Garden City, there are no survivors who remember the pioneer decade, but the early buildings and circumstantial, personal memoirs form a starting point from which to reconstruct the quality of pioneer life. Buildings alone are imperfect landmarks. Reginald Hine, the Hitchin lawyer and historian, posed rhetorical questions:

> But what shall it profit a city to gain all these adjuncts of town planning and fail to acquire a soul? And what city can possess a soul unless it be inhabited by honourable men?[2]

This chapter will be concerned with the soul of Letchworth, personified as the *genius loci*, the 'spirit of the place' in the Garden City pantomimes, and with the personalities that shaped the distinctive pioneer lifestyle. A note of caution must be sounded, however. The most articulate of the pioneers were almost universally middle-class, the successors of the Utopianists of earlier centuries.

Despite attempts to break down class barriers with receptions for newcomers, distinctions remained. Mabel Barry Parker, who actively promoted social harmony, unwittingly referred to divisions between residents north and south of the railway tracks as *The Left Bank* and *Champs Elysées* respectively.[3] This division ran through many aspects of Garden City life, particularly the 'Improving' lectures and the temperance question. Description of the Arcadian lifestyle needs to be tempered by realisation that it was enjoyed by a minority. Nevertheless, tangible environmental benefits accrued to all, reflected in the dry vital statistics of public health, and more generally in a sense of community well-being. The camaraderie was enduring, too. In February 1934, a pioneer meeting was held in Icknield Halls, Eastcheap, attended by those who had been resident in Letchworth before December 1908. Group photographs were taken and signatures were recorded in a Pioneers Book, and later worked into a circular cloth radiating from Howard's posthumously reproduced autograph. By the time of the Golden Jubilee in 1953, the pioneers' nostalgia conjured up Letchworth as a 'City of Dreams', as in an account by Dorothea Hunter, widow of Edmund Hunter, the handloom weaver. The Garden City

> drew together a community fired with the desire that the 'dreams' should be faithfully embodied; and unity of purpose was undoubtedly strengthened by the fact that in most cases home and work had one centre. Their enthusiasm was reflected in the ... endless hot debates, the many lectures, the welcoming of newcomers by the residents' union, ... the Mayday processions and the dancing children; and the delightful pantomimes.
>
>   Later, as the population grew, the people were less pioneer, less young, life was more like that of a normal town, but gardens were in full flower. Letchworth was fulfilling its purpose. It has shown a new way in which industry can live healthily. Ebenezer's vision has been brought to earth.[4]

The Simple Life   Pre-1914 Letchworth gained a reputation for smocks, sandals and, in the context of prevailing conventional moral standards, scandals. Though rational dress, associated with late 19th-century free-thinking, was a minority cult, it was identified with plain

59 The young pioneers, Edward and Peggy Unwin, *c.*1906. Wearing woollens, tweeds and sandals, hand-made by George Adams from Derbyshire, these two children typify the spirit of adventure during the early development of Letchworth. Their father Raymond Unwin prepared the layout plan for Letchworth Garden City.

living and a high moral tone. Raymond Unwin's daughter, Peggy, recalled the discomfort of Ruskin flannel, hand woven in the Isle of Man, and the use of horn-handled cutlery at the family table to consume the vegetarian fare.[5] The Socialist philosopher Edward Carpenter (1844-1929), a close friend of Unwin's, had spread the vogue for the simple life,[6] assisted by George Adams (1857-1910), craftsman and sandal maker at Carpenter's Derbyshire commune at Millthorpe, who moved to Letchworth. Smocks were worn by few, but widely publicised, not least in Letchworth itself, which appears to have relished its cranky reputation. Hats and gloves were widely discarded by Garden City folk. The Cheap Cottages Exhibitions attracted mass visitors to Letchworth, and therein lay the persistent theme of 'scandalising' the bourgeoisie.

Louis Weirter, brother-in-law of Thomas Adams, published many cartoons in *The Citizen*. His targets included F.G.C. Ltd., and the new Letchworth Parish Council. One of the best, 'What some people think of us', published 1908, took the theme of shocking the outsiders. The cartoon showed day-trippers, dressed in their Sunday-best, bemused as if in a human zoo. 'Daddy! I want to see them feed!' shouted a child in front of a table spread with 'nuts for the bald headed nut-peckers'. The family was directed to the 'non-tox-pub' (*The Skittles*),

60 & 61   The Arcadians. (*left*) Through a Garden City window: Mrs Wilson Bidwell. The photograph was taken by her architect husband, at 7 Willian Way, the family home which he also designed. (*right*) Smock and sandals: Andrew Muir. Rational dress was adopted by the followers of Edward Carpenter of Millthorpe, Derbyshire, and his sandal maker, George Adams, moved to Letchworth.

the 'Single Life Hotel' (*Simple Life*). In the foreground were three prominent local figures, described in the doggerel caption:

> Our architect is harmless quite,
> *Un'win*some, too, at present,
> Our di-Rector ap-*Pears all* smiles,
> Our Agent, *Gaunt* — but pleasant.

Raymond Unwin sat at his drawing board, clothed in smock and sandals, photographed by Clutterbuck clad in 'flat 'at' and leopard skin. To the right, Howard Pearsall dug his luxuriant cabbage patch, fed through Dr. Poore's patent drainage system with the effluent of his own home, while Walter Gaunt, Estate Manager, hopefully hawked 'Garden City plots to let'. A 1909 painting by Horace Taylor, 'The Garden Citizens of the future', showed an immaculately dressed couple—she with a huge broad brimmed Gainsborough hat, and he resplendent in top hat and morning dress, confronted by naked children, a bearded man digging a manure heap, a poet reciting to an 'earth mother' figure, and two women striking 'aesthetic' poses. 'Are you intense?' ran the caption from one of George du Maurier's most famous *Punch* cartoons from the aesthetic '80s. That cult lingered on in the First Garden City. With roseate hue of hindsight exaggeration crept in. Could

Charles Lee, co-author of the Garden City pantomimes, really have known 'Frederic Farmer—typical Garden Citizen', who wore knickerbockers and sandals, dabbled in art, and was a vegetarian Theosophist? Could he have kept two tortoises, polished with the best Lucca oil, and burned joss sticks beneath Madame Blavatsky's portrait?[7]

George Orwell, who later moved to Wallington, a few miles beyond Baldock, included Letchworth among his targets in *The Road to Wigan Pier* (1937). He equated the presence of 'every fruit juice drinker, nudist, sandal wearer, sex-maniac, Quaker, nature cure quack, pacifist and feminist in England' with the popular failure of Socialism.[8] It undoubtedly made good copy. The vegetarians founded *The Simple Life Hotel* in Leys Avenue, which included a food reform restaurant and health food store. Vegetarian banquets became regular social events into the 1930s and beyond. Open-air living became popular, and sleeping porches were added to several homes. Possibly the best known was Barry Parker's three-storey extension to his home, 'Crabby Corner' in Letchworth Lane. Esperanto, the universal language, quickly found favour. Howard, with his inventive turn of mind, commended its study, and was almost detained in Paris shortly after the outbreak of the First World War, where he was attending an international Esperanto conference.

CARTOON No. 3.— WHAT SOME PEOPLE THINK OF US.

Two German ladies, who visited Letchworth last week, said on leaving : –" We are awfully disappointed in one thing : we were assured before coming that the people at Garden City were only half clothed, and that they all went bare-headed and wore sandals, and we have not seen one person of that sort ! "

It really is too bad of folks
    To come expecting something eerie,
We are just ordinary souls,
    The right-side up, not "tapsalteerie."

Our architect is harmless quite,
    Un' winsome, too, at present,
Our di-*Rector* ap-*Pears all* smiles,
    Our Agent, *Gaunt*—but pleasant.

62 'What some people think of us', Louis Weirter, 1909. The Garden City soon earned a reputation for the eccentric behaviour of its middle-class 'simple lifers' with their cult religions, vegetarianism, Esperanto, smocks and sandals. Raymond Unwin, Walter Gaunt and Howard Pearsall are all the subject of gentle satire in this cartoon published in *The Citizen*.

63 'The Garden Citizens of Tomorrow', Horace Taylor, *c*.1910. Aesthetic poses, back-to-the-land principles, and free expression amongst children, shock visitors from London.

64 *The Skittles Inn* (*The Settlement*), built 1907. A fine Parker and Unwin design, the exposed studwork also shows the influence of Baillie Scott. The fitted settles under the covered porch were a pleasant meeting area on summer nights.

Temperance: a local option   Howard had described Temperance Reform as a 'local option', and suggested regulation rather than abolition of alcohol.[9] F.G.C. Ltd. acquired *The Three Horseshoes* at Norton and *The Fox* at Willian, leased them to the Peoples' Refreshment House Association, and continued to permit them to sell alcohol. *The Three Horseshoes* at Willian belonged to a local brewery. All were over a mile from the town centre.

Demand for a town centre public house increased as the population rose to 4,300 in 1907. A poll was taken in June 1907 on the question of opening a licensed public house, near the station. There were 631 noes, 544 ayes, majority against 87. Further polls were taken in 1908 – 89 majority against, and 1912 – 596 majority against.[10] The latter poll was organised by the Letchworth Parish Council. These were, unusually, conducted on the basis of universal suffrage for adult residents: it was held, by disappointed men, that the women's vote had prevented the opening of new alcohol-licensed premises. Edward Cadbury and Aneurin Williams founded *The Skittles Inn* (The Settlement), in Exhibition Road (Nevells Road), which opened on 8 March 1907. 'The Liberty, Hall of the Letchworth Worker', it offered 'fellowship, rest and recreation, good meals and an extensive variety of beverages all non-alcoholic.' The building was one of the most successful Parker and Unwin designs, a series of gabled roofs, some with exposed timber studwork, and an open porch or 'stoep', with fitted settles, facing westwards to the track from to 'cattle creep' and Station Road. A long low offshoot housed the skittle alley. The interior with its inglenooks and exposed roof trusses lent itself to congenial pastimes. Tantalisingly prominent was a green-tiled bar counter, over which Cadbury's drinking chocolate and 'Cydrax', a non-alcoholic apple wine, were dispensed. *The Skittles* became notorious as 'The pub with no beer', a 'Blackcurrant Julep kind of pub' indeed, renowned for its affable host, W. G. 'Bill' Furmston (1869-1950),[11] who claimed a varied clientèle from tramps to millionaires. Many were spectators, however. One hundred and fifty sightseers once spent 2d. between them. *The Skittles* became a meeting place for trade unions, local clubs, and housed the nucleus of the Letchworth Museum, with cases of stuffed birds ranged round the principal room. In 1923, *The Skittles* was reconstituted as *The Settlement*, an adult education centre. It had been hoped to build new premises designed by Barry Parker on the north side of Leys Avenue, opposite Howard Park. However, in 1924 commercial premises north of Station Place were leased and *The People's House* was opened. Bill Furmston, caricatured as 'Friar Boniface' in Fitzwater-Wray's *Sir Gadabout*, continued to run a somewhat barn-like restaurant.

In 1920 a further poll showed a narrow 65 majority against a public house. Sensing capitulation, the opponents countered with a vigorous campaign. It was calculated that the

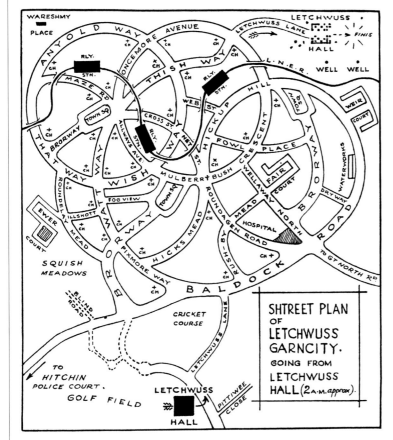

THE PEOPLE'S HOUSE **BEER IS BEST**
GINGER

Friar Boniface weeps over Licence in High Places

65 'Temperance – a local option'. *Top right*, advertisement for *The Skittles*, *c.*1910. The Cadbury sponsorship perhaps coincidentally resulted in a brisk demand for Bournville chocolate. *Below right*, W. G. Furmston (Friar Boniface), 1935. 'Old Bill' acquired his nickname as a result of Fitzwater-Wray's 1923 'Sir Gadabout' saga. Despite his emphasis on healthy eating he was a heavy smoker! *Left*: 'The Drunkard's Map', 1935. The granting of a licence to Letchworth Hall saddened many of the teetotallers and the map reproduced in the 1935 Civic Week programme predicted dire consequences.

Letchworth residents spent £20,000 a year on alcohol, compared with £90,000 in a town of similar population with public houses, so there were rich pickings at stake. A second poll showed 1,532 for, 2,149 against, majority against 617. In 1930 another poll produced a close result. Meanwhile licences had been granted to the Conservative and Unionist clubs, and to the golf club; in 1935 *Letchworth Hall Hotel* received a licence. Friar Boniface was not amused! *Hullabaloo*, the Civic Week programme, helpfully published a 'drunkards map' upon which all roads inexorably returned to 'Letchwuss Hall'.

Churches and Creeds   Acquisition of the Garden City Estate marked a watershed in the religious life of the area.[12] The Rev. W. Walls retired from St Mary Letchworth in 1905, and long incumbencies drew to a close in Norton and Willian. The Rev. George Pierson succeeded to the living in 1842, retaining it until 1910, by when he had become 'not only the father, but the grandfather of his people. And his daughter, a trained nurse, came to be looked upon as their mother'.[13] At Willian, the incumbency of the Hon. and Rev. Lewis

66 The Free Church's first building, 1905. Looking like a colonial mission room, the Free Church was first extended in 1908-9, by Parker and Unwin, before being replaced by Parker's excellent classical design of 1923.

William Denman lasted 48 years.

> An old rowing Blue, something of a poet, a gracious preacher, a good Hebrew scholar, a man of noble appearance … 'his was an absolute monarchy'. Whenever he noticed a Willian woman neglecting to curtsy to him on the road he would read her a lecture on the spot.[14]

Such feudal attitudes became a thing of the past as the Garden City gathered momentum. The new Rector of Letchworth, the Rev. F.N. Heazell, was acutely conscious of the remoteness of his church from the town, and founded the Mission Church of St Michael and All Angels, Norton Way South, dedicated on 22 February 1908, a small red brick basilica designed by Crickmer. It was envisaged that the Established Church would eventually find a permanent home in the central buildings of Town Square, and St Michael's was rebuilt there in 1968. Heazell was succeeded by the Rev. G.K. Olivier, whose son, Laurence Olivier, the eminent actor, grew up in the Garden City. All Saints, Willian, built a Mission Hall in 1917, on the acute angled site between Pixmore Way and Baldock Road, and construction of a 'Victory' church, St Paul's, began in 1919. Designed by Arthur Heron Ryan-Tenison (1861-1930), in Gothic style, an imposing fragment was consecrated in 1924. In 1915 Norton parish opened a church hall on Norton Way North to serve the Glebe housing area, and the site frontage was developed for the modern St George's church in 1963.

Many pioneers were agnostic. Unwin's home 'Laneside' became an early focus for community life, beginning on Whit Monday 1905 with a 'United Religious Meeting'. Services were conducted by Joseph Wicksteed, and later by the Rev. J. Bruce Wallace, a charismatic Ulster Scots Congregational Minister, who had served at the Canning Town settlement.[15] Wallace later formed the 'Alpha Union', a fundamentalist group with Christian Socialist sympathies, to develop an international non-sectarian federation which recognised a spiritual basis for universal harmony. The Sunday Evening Meeting at 'Howard Hall', in which Wicksteed, C. B. Purdom and A. W. Brunt were involved, also became a regular feature of spiritual life. Purdom had conducted the first non-conformist meeting at Abbis Collins's home in 'Alpha Cottages' in December 1904. Later meetings were held at Letchworth Hall. A committee was formed, chaired by Thomas Adams, with A. E. Stark as Secretary, and including the local builder J. T. Openshaw. £49 3s. 9d. was raised to begin construction of a hall which cost £300. On 17 October 1905, 'The Free Church', Gernon Road, opened a simple building with buttressed roughcast walls and a tiled roof, twice extended by Parker and Unwin. The first permanent pastor, the Rev. R.W. Jackson, was appointed on 18 September 1907, and remained for 10 years. In 1923-4 a new church was built alongside – a bold classical design, on a Greek cross plan, with red brick walls,

67 Based on 'Briggflatts', Yorkshire, 'Howgills', The Friends Meeting House, 1907, was designed by Bennett and Bidwell. Wilson Bidwell took this photograph of its finely crafted, serene interior.

a stone portico and a green slate roof. The building was designed by Barry Parker, and built by J. T. Openshaw.

The Methodists built two Letchworth churches. The Primitive Methodists with James Brown, who had negotiated the options of the Letchworth land, as secretary, built their handsome red brick classical-style church on Broadway, and it opened in August 1914. It closed in 1937 and, after use as a lecture hall, was demolished in 1967 for an extension to the Letchworth Technical College (later North Herts College). The Wesleyans chose a site on the south-west corner of Pixmore Way and Norton Way South and built a Gothic-style church, designed by George T. Baines (1852-1934) and his son, Reginald Palmer Baines, which also opened in 1914. The Roman Catholics began worship in 'Astley Cottage' on Baldock Road, home of Bernard Newdigate, manager of the Arden Press. The Rev. Adrian Fortescue (1874-1923) administered the Sacrament in the 'sheds' on 30 November 1907, and shortly afterwards Charles Sydney Spooner (1862-1938) designed the church of St Hugh of Lincoln, Pixmore Way.[16] A simple brick structure, it was embellished with Arts and Crafts fittings. Fortescue was a well-loved priest, a linguist and a respected figure in the social life of the town. C. B. Purdom, a convert to Catholicism, was the first to be married at St Hugh's, in 1912. Quakerism flourished in Hertfordshire, notwithstanding persecution – in 1660 over 94 Quakers were taken out of their meeting houses, mainly from Hertford and Baldock. In 1668, George Fox 'was moved of the Lord God' to visit Hertfordshire and set up monthly Meetings. In 1669, at Norton, a 'conventicle of Quakers' followed John Crooke, a former Justice of the Peace, 'and now a grand seducer and disturber of ye peace'.[17] In 1907, Juliet Reckitt, daughter of a Hull industrialist, sponsored the building of 'Howgills', the Friends Meeting House in South View. Designed by Bennett and Bidwell, it was an excellent example of their work, carefully detailed throughout, with a Meeting Room based on 'Briggflatts' in North Yorkshire, which Bidwell had personally measured. It is a sober and beautiful interior with much excellent joinery, and an intimate acoustic suitable for the chamber music recitals held by the Letchworth Music Club.

Of the more unorthodox religions, Theosophy was perhaps the most pervasive. With its emphasis on spiritual ecstasy, its belief in the coming of the World Teacher, and its worship of a new Messiah, Krishnamurti, a Holy Boy from India as the new Supreme Lord, Maitreya, the cult attracted a wide following. Miss Hope Rea became the first President of the Letchworth Theosophical Society, and assisted the building of 'Vasanta Hall', Gernon Walk, an odd little building with a flat concrete roof, designed by William Harrison Cowlishaw (1869-1957). It was opened on 1 June 1914 by the leader of Theosophy, Mrs. Annie Besant. The Christian Scientists opened a hall and schoolroom almost opposite. Dotted throughout Letchworth

68 Infants' class, Norton School, *c.*1911. The infants' teacher, Miss Edith Booth, to the right of the picture, was a cousin of Raymond Unwin.

more small churches – Baptist, Elim Tabernacle, Salvation Army, Spiritualist, and Liberal Catholic – were testimony to the broad religious tastes of the early residents. It is small wonder that John Buchan noted in his thinly disguised parody of Letchworth, 'twenty seven varieties of religious conviction including three Buddhists, a Celestial Hierarch, five latter-day Saints and about ten varieties of mystic whose names I never could remember'.[18] The Liberal Catholic Church of St Alban was built on the corner of Meadow Way and Norton Way South, a small two-cell building in Free Gothic style, set in a garden plot. The sect had broken away from the Roman Catholic Church in 1869. In the 1920s a Harpenden priest began to conduct services in a house in Lytton Avenue, and the new church was consecrated on Easter Sunday 1924. Services were based on the mass, sung in English, followed by a short healing service and laying on of hands. A teacher at the St Christopher School, Alfred Spooner, was priest in charge for over 30 years; one of his successors, Bishop Swingler, became spiritual leader of the church in Great Britain and Ireland. The Letchworth Corps of the Salvation Army held its first meeting on 26 June 1913, in the Co-operative Hall in Leys Avenue, with an open-air meeting held in Shott Lane later in the day. In 1921, a Y. M. C. A. hut from King's Cross Station, used during the First World War, was brought to Norton Way North, where the permanent building, on the corner with Nevells Road, was opened on 1 February 1936.

A Liberal Education Education was greatly prized by the pioneers.[19] Among the earliest advisers was John Russell, headmaster of the liberal King Alfred School, Hampstead. In 1905 the 'Garden City Education Council' held a public meeting to press the County Council to provide permanent school premises without delay. They also approved educational principles based on equality of opportunity for all, far-reaching at the time.

The elementary schools in Norton and Willian were inadequate and the need for central facilities was urgent. The County Council decided to go no further than a 'non-provided school', opened in November 1905 in the versatile Exhibition Road sheds. The Education Council levied a voluntary rate of 1s. 4d. in the pound, subsequently reduced to 6d. Cyril

Arthington Pease, brother of the secretary of the Fabian Society, was the first headmaster, transferring to the Norton School in 1909 but remaining in Letchworth until 1917, after accomplishing much pioneering work. Miss Edith Booth, a cousin of Raymond Unwin's, was the infant mistress. The County Council built the Norton School in 1909, on a courtyard plan, influenced by Unwin's advocacy of open-air schools. In April 1913, the Pixmore Elementary School, on School Walk, was opened. There was then a long interval before the Westbury Elementary School opened in June 1925, to serve the large local authority housing estate, in course of construction. In November 1927, the County Council agreed to build a 300-pupil co-educational grammar school on a vacant site along the western side of Town Square. Barry Parker was the architect of the low-key Georgian building, which opened on 7 October 1931.

69 The St Christopher School had its origins in the Theosophy movement, and the foundation stone was laid by Mrs Annie Besant in 1919 for the original premises built in the angle between Broadway and Spring Road (St Francis College for Girls after 1934), designed by P. Morley Horder. In 1934, the school moved to Barrington Road, occupying buildings constructed for The Letchworth School in 1909.

Private schools flourished early on. The Letchworth School was run by J. H. M. Stephenson, on advanced lines, with co-education, running from kindergarten to university preparation. It soon built purpose-designed premises by Crickmer, in Barrington Road. In 1912, Miss Cartwright opened the Letchworth Modern School for Girls in Norton Way South and there were several private preparatory schools on a domestic scale. In January 1915 a group influenced by the educational theories of Dr. Arundale took over the Letchworth School buildings, and in 1919 Mrs Annie Besant, a Theosophist leader, laid the foundation stone for a Theosophical Trust school located site between Spring Road and Broadway. Mrs. Besant herself chose the name The St Christopher School. Lyn Harris joined the staff in 1923, became headmaster in 1925, and in 1953 was succeeded by his son, Nicholas King Harris. It became one of the most progressive private schools in the country, consolidating its premises in Barrington Road in 1928, after selling its Broadway buildings, which became the St Francis College for Girls after 1934.

Evening and adult education began with gardening classes in the winter of 1904-5 at Letchworth Hall, expanding into machine construction, building construction, arts and crafts, poultry and bee keeping, singing, and sociology. In 1907, the *Letchworth Magazine* looked towards 'a Lawrence College, a Howard College and a Gorst College, sending out their men and women graduates to do champion service in science and art and commerce and industry'. The Letchworth Academy did not materialise, although efforts were made in 1914 to commemorate the first decade of the Garden City. In July 1914, a week before the outbreak of the First World War, a conference on further education was attended by the Teachers Guild, the Workers Education Association and the Letchworth 1914 Celebration Committee, under the presidency of Lord Salisbury. It was many years before Letchworth acquired its college.

Recreation and Amenities   A wide range of sports was catered for in the pioneer years.[20] Thomas Adams the Estate Manager was an outdoor man and promoted the layout of a golf course in the parkland of Letchworth Hall in 1905. Initially a modest nine-hole course, it was extended in 1911 to 18 holes. Harry Vardon, a well known professional, designed a 6,000-yard course to utilise every club in the golfer's bag and every stroke in his repertoire. Although the course length has been adjusted, it still retains its character. F.G.C. Ltd. reserved the field

70 K. and L. Hockey Club, 1919-20. The ladies' Squad appears distinctly over-dressed, or were they pioneer cheer leaders?

south of Baldock Road, where the estate had been opened, for cricket. The Letchworth Cricket Club was formed in 1907, and its earliest players included Harry Burr, F.G.C. surveyor, Harold Craske, F.G.C. secretary, H. G. Griffiths, H. Blay, H. Hankin and W.H. Sumsion. W.P. Westell, the naturalist, was a mainstay of the team while A.W. Brunt was umpire. The club took the championship of the North Herts League in 1914.

Letchworth Town Football Club was also founded in 1907, with a ground south of the Baldock Road. Local rivalries, particularly with Hitchin, Biggleswade, Baldock and Stevenage, were acute. The team won the North Herts Charity Cup in 1912, beating Hitchin 3-2, and in the same season carried off the Hitchin Hospital Cup. The Rugby Union Football Club was formed in 1925. Hockey was popular in the early years, with Edgar Simmons, the estate agent, and Allen Foxley, the architect, being particularly enthusiastic. Mabel Barry Parker was a keen defender on the ladies team. Tennis flourished, and many of the larger houses included tennis courts in their grounds. Thomas Adams and his wife were keen players. Bowls was played on private greens until a public facility was provided in Howard Park in the 1920s. An open-air swimming bath, south of Howard Park adjoining Pixmore Way, was opened on 27 June 1908. Although unheated, with primitive dressing cubicles, it quickly became popular. The 'pea soup' constitution of its water, shortly before the weekly flushing, was long remembered, as was the day when a man rushed out of his cubicle to the aid of a lady in distress, oblivious of the fact that he had removed his bathing drawers![21] The bath served the town until 1935, when the new open-air lido on Norton Common was opened.

Many factories provided their own sports facilities, and contributed to an inter-works league with Spirella and K. & L. notable leaders, while British Tab had a cup-winning cycling team. Separate boys and girls clubs were founded. 'The Girls' Club', funded by Miss Juliet Reckitt, was opened by Mrs Bertrand Russell on 12 July 1908, in a wing added at the rear of the Howard Hall. 'Swedish Drill' gymnastics and hockey became popular. 'The Boys' Club' began in a shed at the corner of Pixmore Avenue and Works Road, but eventually in 1914 was accommodated in a neat Georgian building fronting Broadway, designed by Barry Parker. Formal gymnastics were popular among boys' groups as photographs of 'human pyramids' testify!

71　The Mrs Howard Memorial Hall, built 1906. The first public building in Letchworth, designed by Parker and Unwin, the Howard Hall was similar to the Folk Hall at New Earswick and a number of smaller community buildings.

Literature and Music　'The (Mrs.) Howard (Memorial) Hall' was the focus of literary and musical life in the developing Garden City, funded by public subscriptions in memory of Lizzie Howard who had died on 7 November 1904, shortly before she was due to move to her Garden City home on Norton Way South. The hall commemorated 'her dauntless ardour and indefatigable labour' for the Garden City project. 'Her faith and enthusiasm never seemed to fail, and very many have felt the winning way she had of inspiring others', wrote Mrs. Howard Pearsall, when announcing the memorial in December 1905. The hall was to be

> A centre for the social side of the corporate life of the town, for all kinds of educational and recreative activities, and ... shall express the desire of the originators and first friends of the Garden City scheme that these new towns should bring to the country something of the life and interest and gaiety of the large towns, and do away with the dullness of country life.[22]

Designed by Parker and Unwin, the hall was boldly set at an angle, near the junction of Norton Way South and Hillshott. Its hipped roof, punctuated by picturesque dormers, was offset by a large inglenook on the north-west side, a recess off the plain hall with its exposed queen post roof. Stage and dressing facilities were very restricted. The management committee, headed by Miss M.E. Nicholson, had lofty cultural aspirations.

> You will stroll into the *Howard Hall* one wintry day and find an artist ... busy with decorating it ... You will learn that there is to be a *conversazione* that night ... or a gathering of new residents, or what not besides ... There will be a scene from one of Tolstoy's plays or an impressive recitation ... discussions upon the Liquor Question, the Unemployed, Methods of Education. Political Organisations, Arts and Crafts, Science and Civilisation and so forth.[23]

A Library opened at the hall on Whit Monday 1906, assisted by a £5 donation from Howard Pearsall.[24] By 1912 it was evident that the library, run by volunteers, was inadequate, but moves to make the Parish Council a library authority were blocked. Dr Mervyn Gilbart-Smith, the opposer, organised a book exchange scheme, run from his house in Sollershott. Although a reference library was opened at the Museum in 1920, it was not until

72 'The Cloisters', Barrington Road, designed by W. H. Cowlishaw in 1907. This view shows the double-storey loggia of 'Ladybarn', Miss Lawrence's house, at the left.

1929 that a loan collection was sent from the County Library, taken over by the Letchworth U. D. C. in January 1936, and installed in their Crickmer-designed building adjoining the Museum in January 1939. Amateur music-making was extensively supported. The First Garden City Band was formed in November 1906, by William Fenn, and has been a mainstay of musical life for 95 years. The Letchworth Philharmonic Society which gave Haydn's *Creation* at the Free Church Hall on 27 April 1906, the first of many choral works under the direction of H. Gomersall. Miss Margaret Fowles formed an orchestra, which performed at the opening of the Howard Hall and, after her death, her nephew, Dr Leonard Fowles, conducted concerts in the Pixmore Institute in 1908. Subsequently, musical life was centred on 'The Cloisters' for many years.

Miss Lawrence and 'The Cloisters'   Annie Jane Lawrence (1863-1953) became a dominant force in the social life of Letchworth. One of five children – her younger brother Frederic William (1871-1961), Baron Pethick-Lawrence later helped to promote the Letchworth Garden City Corporation legislation – Miss Lawrence settled in Letchworth in 1906. She leased an isolated three-acre plot a half mile south of the Baldock Road, and built 'The Cloisters', with a house for herself, 'Cloisters Lodge' (Ladybarn) alongside.[25]

She chose William Harrison Cowlishaw (1869-1957) as her architect. He had a craftsman's view of architecture, and numbered church needlework and pottery amongst his interests. 'The Cloisters' was unique amongst his designs and faithfully reflected the requirements of his patron, who spent £20,000 upon the project. Intended as an open-air school, building stopped in November 1907. A vast shell had been constructed, consisting of the 'cloister garth', a half oval, with large glazed bays to the north and an open colonnade to the south. There were two wings: one for kitchen and store rooms, the other with cubicles and dressing rooms leading to an oval open-air swimming bath. The outward expression of these functions was remarkable, with myriad symbolic overtones. It was rumoured that the building had appeared to Miss Lawrence in her dreams.

Approaching from Cloisters Road, built up south of the Baldock Road in the 1960s, the observer is confronted with a towering mass; the overwhelming impression must have been even more remarkable when the building stood in glorious isolation. The rich palette of materials – grey Suffolk bricks, Purbeck stone, flintwork, and vivid orange Suffolk tiles allied to the romantic massing which culminated in a soaring octagonal tower compounded the effect. The flat roof of the cloister garth had a brick balustraded walkway. Although bare blocks of stone inside and out and the gaunt brickwork and unfaced mass concrete vaults of the interior bear witness to the sudden termination of the work, enough of the symbolic artefacts were installed to indicate the overall intentions. Cowlishaw was a gifted sculptor and modelled designs for the rainwater heads – doves represented guilelessness, bats were about to start their dusk patrols, bees built up the honeycomb to provide food for the gods, and 'butterflies dancing in the empyrean'. The casement windows were to have received stained glass showing the rising of the sun; the interior walls were to have been clothed in mosaic, but sheet glass and Hall's washable distemper had to suffice.

The Cloister Garth arcade had columns of green veined Swedish marble, suggesting upward growth. Residents slept there in hammocks let down from the vaults, with men and women strictly segregated by the central hall. The arcade was provided with canvas screens to close off nocturnal breezes, but the problem of heating in winter was not solved by a series of fireplaces. In the central hall a fountain was installed around the central support to the tower, pure Art Nouveau in design. Water flowed from the dedication stone in the springing of the twin arches above, dripped into twin basins, the lower of which was divided into eight small receptacles for ceremonial hand washing, and overflowed around the cloisters in open channels – no doubt representing the dissemination of worldy wisdom. A blue-vein marble 'stream' laid at the foot of the fountain emphasised this. Communal meals were taken at a marble-faced dining table, on a raised altar-like dais, which stretched across the great bay window. The swimming bath, installed on Miss Lawrence's insistence of *mens sana in corpore sano*, was used at dawn.

Miss Lawrence dedicated the building on 27 January 1907, placing an illuminated vellum scroll, inscribed by Cowlishaw, in a glass casket which was sealed into the springer stone above the fountain. Her dedication 'To the unity, eternal reality' sought to promote the ascent 'to a full harmonious and joyful expression of life, in soul, body and social organisation'. She was inspired by J. Bruce Wallace, founder of the Alpha Union, for some years her protégé. Although deaf, Miss Lawrence had a four manual electric organ installed, with the console in the entrance hall, and the sound percolated downwards from the pipe chamber through louvres above the fountain. Bruce Wallace organised residential summer schools, and holidays for Board school teachers, leaving an indelible impression for many participants. More than 50 years later, R. W. Sorenson, Labour M.P. for Leyton, included his reminiscences of life at 'The Cloisters' in the Commons debate on the Letchworth Garden City Corporation Bill. He had gone there for a rest

> … only to be yanked out of my bunk the first day at 6 a.m. and compelled to drill on the lawn, learn the arts of pottery and weaving and to gambol to the tune of the country dance 'Rufty Tufty'.[26]

The first Alpha Summer School had been held at 'Cloisters Lodge'; its successor in 1907 took place at the partly completed 'Cloisters'. In 1908 the first residential school was held, annually until 1912. Wallace's syllabus ranged from English Literature to Psychology and Progressive Religious Thought. In 1908, Georgia Pearce, an American journalist, described Miss Lawrence, at 45 already 'white haired and elderly with a strong keen intellectual face', presiding over the activities, although hampered by growing deafness. Apart from the midday meal, eating was alfresco and, intriguingly, housework was a male province. Miss Pearce was clearly impressed by 'this 20th century temple … erected to the hallowing of humanity'.[27] The utopian delights were palpable; berobed and sandalled acolytes essaying their daily tasks, engaged in earnest discussion or simply observing the sunset or stars from the rooftop promenade, with soft organ music wafting upwards. The dream faded rather suddenly, however. Bruce Wallace married Miss Mary Tudor Pole in 1912, and 'The Cloisters' was not available for the Alpha Union Summer School, which was hosted by the town.

Frank Merry, the organist, became Warden and organised courses, including one at Easter 1913 on 'the Garden City Philosophy of Life'. After the First World War, the Letchworth

73 Esperanto Conference at 'The Cloisters', 1913. Ebenezer Howard sits to the right of the policeman, and further right is Miss Lawrence.

Adult Educational Settlement arranged academic courses at 'The Cloisters', which ceased in 1926. Miss Lawrence promoted the concept of a 'Dual Day' with morning work, a two-hour period for rest and food and a re-assembly for communal recreation, and she circulated tracts on the subject for many years. Music was an indispensable accompaniment, and she organised public concerts in the Cloister Garth, attracting audiences of one thousand. Organ recitals, band and choral concerts became mainstays of the town's cultural life. In the 1920s a band shell improved acoustic projection and the organ was enlarged. A highlight was the appearance of the London Concert Orchestra, 40 unemployed musicians brought in at Miss Lawrence's expense. The last concert was given by the Brotherhood Orchestra on the fateful Sunday, 3 September 1939, when the Second World War broke out. Craft classes and folk dancing were organised and swimming lessons for children. For many years the reward for swimming the length of the murky pool was a 'Blackbird' fountain pen, personally presented by Miss Lawrence.

She became deeply concerned over the building's future. In February 1932 she offered it free to the County Council, with an annuity of £1,000 and income from £20,000 after her death. The offer was refused. The building was commandeered and damaged during the Second World War. In 1948, aged 85, Miss Lawrence moved to St Catherine's Nursing Home. She made over 'The Cloisters' to be adapted as the North Herts Masonic Lodge, and died aged 90 on

74 Miss Lawrence at the Iceni Pottery, with Andrew Muir. In addition to education and music, Miss Lawrence was also interested in the promotion of local crafts industries.

75 The oval outdoor swimming pool at 'The Cloisters' was in great demand for swimming lessons, and the formidable Miss Lawrence used to offer a prize of a fountain pen to those who successfully swam a length of its murky water. In 1928, young ladies pose with their tunic-clad coach.

3 August 1953. The £17,500 residue of her estate formed the Lawrence Cloisters Trust. Regrettably, extensions by the Freemasons were visually insensitive, while structural problems related to the deterioration of the iron reinforcement of the concrete structure developed. Yet 'The Cloisters' was listed as a Grade II* historic building in 1979, and surely deserves to survive as a tangible link with Letchworth's golden age.

Artists in Residence   Letchworth produced its own crop of literary and artistic talent, and played host to several distinguished authors and artists. *The Letchworth Magazine*, edited by C. B. Purdom, appeared in August 1906. In January 1909, Henry Bryan Binns (d. 1923) founded *The City*, high quality and short-lived, printed by J. M. Dent.[28] The tone was set by Binns's poem, 'The City', which appeared in the first issue:

> I see a City being wrought
> Upon the rock of Living Thought

There is little doubt that the 'living thought' was Howard's Garden City concept, set out in the pages of *Tomorrow* just over a decade previously. The opening of the fourth stanza, 'Foursquare our City', was worked into a handsome processional banner by Edmund Hunter, and was proudly carried in the many street pageants in the pre-1914 pioneer period. Binns was first Chairman of the Evening School Committee, first President of the Letchworth Dramatic Society. His book *The free spirit: realisations of middle age with a note on personal expression* (1915), suggests an autobiographical retrospective of Letchworth life. A. W. Brunt, editor of

 A for the **A**rchitects buried in thought, Arranging the houses to go where they ought.

 O for the **O**ffice; how charming it looks! Who would not wish to get on to its Books?

 B for a **B**uilder, computing the cost; & the bitter remarks when a contract is lost.

D for **D**irectors who sat down to dine; We tasted their wit and they tasted our wine.

76 Garden City Alphabet, by Harold E. Hare, 1909. In this charming primer, Parker and Unwin lay out houses on a chess board under 'A'; C. F. Ball calculates his profit margins under 'B'; the Directors, including Howard at left, toast themselves in non-alcoholic wine; and the young C. B. Purdom walks to the estate office under 'O'.

The Citizen, portrayed the Garden City prolifically in verse, while Canon H.D. Rawnsley, a founder of the National Trust, John Drinkwater, and local author William Loftus Hare were diverse contributors to the poetic genre. Harold E. Hare's charming 'Garden City Alphabet' was published in *The City* in 1909, and his naive sketches and quatrains featured local scenes and personalities. Raymond Unwin appeared under 'A' for architect, the Directors of First Garden City Limited paused for non-alcoholic refreshment under 'D', and Purdom strolled casually to the Estate Office under 'O'. Local rivalries were also remembered:

'H' is for Hitchin which likes a good laugh, and gets it by walking four miles and a half.

The tone of parody was rekindled by John Betjeman in two poems.[29] 'Group life Letchworth' dwelt on the rampant individualism of a breed of children supposedly devoted to work 'each for weal of all'. 'Huxley Hall' was set in 'The Garden City café with its murals on the wall', actually Nott's 'Icknield Halls', Eastcheap. The narrator, sipping 'lime juice minus gin' dwelt on 'the deep depression' of this 'bright hygienic hell', and wondered whether the uninhibited behaviour of the children, and adults plotting each other's downfall 'in the interests of the state', were after all a confirmation that man was born in sin. Although perhaps not quite so irredeemable as Slough, Letchworth's idiosyncrasy was a natural target for Betjeman's cynicism.

A few artists settled for long periods. Edward Docker and Charles Fox commissioned houses from Baillie Scott ('Spring Wood') and Parker and Unwin ('The Den' now 'The White Cottage'). Harold Gilman (1876-1919), one of the leaders of the Camden Town group of British post-impressionist artists, came to Letchworth in 1907,[30] and in 1909 commissioned a house and studio, 100 Wilbury Road, from Parker and Unwin. Shortly after his American wife, Grace, left him, Gilman let the house to Spencer Gore (1878-1914),[31] who recorded its newness in vibrant colours, with the red tiles of the roof set against an electric blue sky, and the garden a riot of golden irises. Gore painted several Letchworth scenes including *The Road* and *Letchworth Station*, the latter showing waiting passengers set against a vivid landscape with, in the middle distance, a single white house as a token of the advancing development. A lesser-known member of the group, William Ratcliffe (1870-1955), moved to Letchworth in 1906, settling first on Westholm Green, then at No. 102 Wilbury Road with Stanley Parker.[32] He spent virtually his whole working life in Letchworth. His watercolours and oil paintings included many characteristic Letchworth scenes, painted with charm and freshness. In the 1940s Francis King (1905-2001), then art master at The St Christopher School, painted a number of Garden City scenes in a style modelled on Thomas Rowlandson, the 19th-century social caricaturist. *Garden City revels* shows a group of garden citizens paying homage to the

77 & **78** Ebenezer Howard in public life. *Above*, in May Day costume, 1912. Howard entered into the spirit of Garden City life, but sometimes looked rather self-conscious and uncomfortable. *Below*, speaking on Coronation Day, 1911. Howard speaks in front of Edmund Hunter's banner 'Foursquare our City' as part of the Coronation commemoration on the Market Place facing Leys Avenue.

great God Pan, tweedy and tubby men brandishing a rake and a cornucopia of nuts, women bearing a laurel wreath and a floral garland. It was a fitting tribute to the simple life. His *The Hitchin Bus, Station Place* was a souvenir of the war years when, under the admonition 'Is your journey really necessary?', even a trip to 'Sleepy Hollow' acquired exotic overtones. By contrast, *Letchworth Station – Scene at dusk*, has an air of mysterious half-light, pierced by the glow of gas-light.

Pageants and Plays   Pageants, masques and folk dancing were frequent events.[33] May day was celebrated with the crowning of the May Queen, and processions in which representatives of the schools, F.G.C. Ltd., the Parish Council, estate workers and Trades Unions, clubs and institutes, participated with banners held aloft. 'Arbor Days' were begun on 29 February 1908, imported from America via the 'beautiful Oldham Society'. Certificates were issued to all tree planters including Howard. The following year, H. Rider Haggard (1856-1925), novelist and enthusiast for progressive agriculture, was Guest of Honour, followed in 1910 by Walter Crane (1845-1915), the Socialist artist. After 1912 this ceremony of 'old English revels' lapsed altogether, with a passing revival to mark the Coronation of George VI in 1937. The Coronation of George V in 1911 was marked with due ceremony, with Howard speaking against a backdrop of banners, including 'Foursquare our City'. In July 1913, Miss Lawrence held a 'Battle of the Flowers' at The Cloisters, while in July 1914, a few days before the outbreak of war, a *Masque of Letchworth* brought the curtain down on such events, after three performances given by a cast of two hundred.

C. B. Purdom was the mainspring of early theatrical life in Letchworth and a founder of the dramatic society in October 1906.[34] Tolstoy's *Ivan the Fool* and Hardy's *The Three Strangers* were presented at Howard Hall on 30 and 31 January 1907. The players included Harold Hare, James Henderson, Alice Hoffman, Jack Dent, Mr and Mrs Murray Hennell, C. F. Townsend, Mr and Mrs R. P. Gossop, and W. G. Taylor. Shakespeare: *The Merchant of Venice*, *Two Gentlemen of Verona*, *Much Ado About Nothing*; and Shaw: *Candida*, *Arms and the Man*, and *You Never can Tell*, were soon staples, though plays by John Galsworthy, J. M. Synge and W. B. Yeats were also given. Purdom aimed to encourage the establishment of a Letchworth theatre, with a permanent company. He set high standards, and was not afraid of controversy. Shaw's *The Shewing-Up of Blanco Posnet* was still censored and its performance at the Pixmore Barn in August 1912 was its first by an English company. The venture folded with the outbreak of war, but Purdom revived his theatrical ambitions at Welwyn.

The Garden City Pantomimes, co-written by Purdom and Charles Lee, were long remembered.[35] The first was presented in January 1909 in 'Howard Hall' – a local satire on politicians, poets, food reformers, a Lady Bountiful and suffragettes. The second was a comic operetta—music was credited to Charles Lee, but the metre of Purdom's rhymes suggested the rhythm of Gilbert and Sullivan. The plot involved children taking over management of the Garden City Company and the Parish Council. The innocent sixth form fun can be gauged from the chorus of the Councillors of Norton.

> Sleep parishioners sleep,
> Sleep deep, innocent sheep,
> Round the fold the gaunt wolf prowls;
> Never heed his threatening howls,
> We your Council watch will keep,
> Sleep sleep parishioners sleep.

The 'gaunt wolf' was of course W.H. Gaunt, the estate manager. The spirit of the place or *genius loci* was a benevolent *djinn*, played by Percy Gossop in a get-up resembling a Burne-Jones madonna. His song, modelled on the Lord Chancellor's 'Nightmare' from *Iolanthe*, poked fun at the simple life, and took architects to task.

> When the lamps are lit and the shadows flit and a balmy breeze from Norway
> Is dodging the screen you've erected between the fireplace and the doorway
> And the rain and the sleet and the hailstones beat through every chink in the casement,
> And the plaster falls from the mouldy walls, and the damp wells up from the basement
> Perhaps you reflect that your architect was a bit too art-and-crafty
> And you wish that your lot had been cast in a cott that wasn't quite so draughty
> Ah, then is the hour when you need my power to brace and fortify you;
> For draughts and chills bring exquisite thrills when I am hovering by you.

The third pantomime, the last, was a mild skit on Aristophanes' *Lysistrata*. With the women on strike, the men of Norton undertook domestic duties. The militant suffragette leader, Miss Bunting M.P., proved to be a man in drag. Perhaps it went a little too far even for the liberal free-thinkers.

Construction of *The Picture Palace* in Eastcheap heralded mass entertainment.[36] The fire station was next door, in case of conflagration of the highly inflammable nitrate film. A domestic-style frontage masked the single level auditorium. The opening programme on 6 December 1909, six shorts including *Joan of Arc*, *Princess Nicotine* and *Foolshead Married*, was very different from the Hollywood epics which would soon fill the house. In November 1916, Miss Lawrence and the naturalist, William Percival Westell, organised Saturday afternoon shows for children – a lantern lecture on nature, and educational and travel films.

Sappho It was to be expected that the Garden City would forge a new way of life. Agitation for universal suffrage grew during the first decade of the 20th century, with the foundation of the Women's Social and Political Union by Emmeline Pankhurst (1858-1928) in 1903 coinciding with the beginning of development of the First Garden City. Middle-class women certainly played an

79 Percy Gossop as 'The Spirit of the Place', 1910. Got up like a Burne-Jones madonna, Gossop not only starred in Garden City pantomimes but he and his wife also designed the costumes and scenery.

active role in Garden City life, if they wished, but there is little evidence that working-class wives and mothers were more emancipated than their urban counterparts. Mrs. Pankhurst's elder daughter, Christabel (1880-1958), spoke at the 'Howard Hall' on 6 July 1907, on behalf of the Women's Social and Political Union. 'Women', she declared,' must have full scope for their development. ... They must be socially and politically equal with men. ... They have every right to political power ... and they mean to take it.'[37] One small benefit, already noted, was the introduction of votes for all residents in the private referenda on the alcohol issue. However, women were unable to vote in the local, or indeed national, elections, until February 1918, but women under 30 were excluded until a decade later. Women's employment was symbolised by Spirella, who offered jobs to both married and unmarried women – indeed they preferred the latter, unlike other employers in the town, who debarred married women. Even so liberal a firm as the St Edmundsbury Weavers primly stated that they felt that married women should be at home attending to their domestic duties. Until the First World War, when lack of men in key industries brought wholesale recruitment of women, advances in most aspects of life and work were more apparent than real.

As a token symbol of women's place in the new social order, a statue of Sappho, the seventh-century B.C. Greek poetess, was presented to the Garden City in January 1907, by the widow of the sculptor, Thomas Nelson Maclean (1845-94).[38] Kneeling on a plinth, clasping a lyre, the drapery clad bronze figure was first placed in Middle Street (Lytton Avenue), on the west side, facing the green, moving a few months later to the corner of Lytton Avenue

80 The Picture Palace, Eastcheap, as built in 1909 – a simple domestic building fronting a bald fletton brick hall marked the first utilitarian structure of one off the earliest cinemas in the country.

and Meadow Way, then to the lower end of Broadwater Avenue in 1914. Her final resting place, in July 1936, was in the Ball Memorial Gardens, on the site of the old open-air swimming bath. Quietly resting in the verdant surroundings, and forgotten by many, Sappho made news in May 1998, when it was discovered that she had been stolen. No trace of her subsequent whereabouts has been discovered.

The Village Named Morality Mixed feelings about the First World War might have been predicted. The night war was declared, on 4 August 1914, there was an angry debate and resounding defeat of the Socialist party's protest against Britain's entry into the fray. Later an influential minority resented the 'jingoism' of a 'great patriotic meeting' addressed by the Divisional M.P. Lord Robert Cecil, held in the Spirella Hall on 28 January 1916. The Letchworth Fellowship of International Goodwill held meetings at *The Skittles*, with speakers from the British 'Stop The War' Campaign. Some supported moves towards international conciliation, later codified in the League of Nations. In 1915, Raymond Unwin published a booklet on the subject, *The War and What After?* Controversy broke out when the 'Howard Hall' Committee refused bookings to individuals or organisations who would not undertake to desist from criticising the government's war policy.[39] Matters came to a head in November 1916 when the national papers, *The Daily Mail* and *The Daily Sketch*, attacked the Garden City as a haven for communists, with 200 jailed conscientious objectors. After all, had not Lenin, when a delegate at the Russian Social Democratic Party, held in London in May 1907, visited Letchworth?[40] Harold Armitage, editor of *The Citizen*, branded the reports as lies, and succeeded in obtaining their unreserved withdrawal.

All this provided striking raw material for the novelist John Buchan (1875-1940), famed for the derring-do yarns of his hero, and alter-ego, Richard Hannay. Buchan was invalided

81 and **82**   The First World War in Letchworth. *Above*, the Territorials depart: crowding the 'up' platform, the trainee soldiers await departure for Hertford. *Below*, the Belgian refugees arrive: the first nine families arrived as early as 25 September 1914 after the fall of Antwerp.

out of the war, and convalesced with Captain Trotter at 'Derenda Cottage' ('Rest Harrow'), Willian Way in 1915. His observations on Garden City life appeared in 1919 in *Mr Standfast*, the third Richard Hannay novel.[41] Hannay, alias 'Cornelius Brand', lodged with Mr Tancred Jimson, whose 'badly built and oddly furnished' cottage overlooked 'a pleasant Midland common' in 'Biggleswick' Garden City. The Jimsons, who studiously followed the simple life, were the expected caricatures. He, a shipping clerk in London, wore grey flannels, soft collar, orange tie and a soft black hat. His wife, Ursula, 'a large red woman with hair bleached by constant exposure to weather', was habitually clad in a 'gown, modelled on a chintz curtain'. Biggleswick itself was 'one great laboratory of thought'. Buchan-Hannay, on the look-out for fifth-columnists, described the citizens with ill-disguised contempt at jokes about the war,

83 'For the fallen', Armistice Day commemoration 1921, in front of Onslow Whiting's fine Memorial Cross.

and longed to make a man of Letchford, 'celebrated leaderwriter of *The Critic*' and 'a double-engined high-speed pacifist', by enlisting him in his batallion. The 'League of Democrats against Aggression' met in the Moot Hall, and the range of issues provided Hannay with diverse targets including Russian unrest, alternative medicine, and latent African nationalism. The climax was a meeting, addressed by John Blenkiron 'in stark defiance of the Defence of the Realm Act', which exceeded the tolerance of the audience who did not mind proving Britain wrong, but stopped short of rejoicing in the enemy. Blenkiron was an *agent provocateur*, who had come to give Hannay marching orders for further exploits of patriotic espionage. Thus ended the 'Biggleswick' interlude.

Actual events were more diverse and complex than Buchan's highly selective account. Early in the war, the army arrived for military exercises, and were annoyed to find a Garden City on a site that, on their outdated maps, appeared ideally suited. Many citizens volunteered or were called up, and the Garden City Territorials left for Hertford. The volunteer training corps drilled preparatory to forming Four Company, First Battalion, Hertfordshire Volunteer Regiment. Altogether 600 enlisted in the services. Against his better judgement, Purdom enlisted,[42] trained at Ampthill, was graded E3, but insisted on serving in France, and narrowly missed Passchendale. He was invalided out in January 1918, but took no further direct role in Letchworth affairs. Frederic Osborn was non-combatant.[43] He undertook sterling wartime work for the Howard Cottage Society, then avoided call-up by lying low in London, working daily in the British Museum Reading Room. Conscientious objectors working the land in Letchworth included Herbert Morrison (1888-1965), subsequently L.C.C. leader and a Labour Minister. Blinded in his right eye, Morrison would have been turned down, but insisted on proclaiming his pacifist principles to the Wandsworth tribunal. Employed by J. J. Kidd, a socialist market gardener who admired his principles, Morrison was digging for winter planting as the Armistice of 11 November 1918 was proclaimed by church bells and sirens. Morrison remained a good friend of the Garden City. In humanitarian terms, Letchworth's most positive contribution lay in its hospitality for Belgian refugees, the first of whom arrived on 25 September 1914. The newly developing housing area to the west of the town centre – Burnell Rise, Campers Square and Campers Road – became known as 'Little Antwerp', while their compatriots Georges Kryn and Raoul Lahy began munitions manufacture. Their story belongs in the following chapter.

For the Fallen The First World War brought to an end the era of pioneering optimism in the First Garden City. Appropriate commemoration of the sacrifice of lives assumed priority[44] as the Armistice of 11 November 1918 held firm, pending the conclusion of the

Peace Treaty at Versailles, finally signed by Germany on 28 June 1919. A Management Committee to raise funds for a £10,000 extension to Letchworth Hospital was elected on 2 June. The artist, Onslow Whiting, who subsequently designed the War Memorial in Station Place, wrote in *The Citizen* that a Universal Library should be created as 'a World Memorial to the World War'.[45] The newly created Letchworth Urban District Council decreed that Peace should officially be celebrated on Saturday 19 July. A procession headed by Spirella girls, draped in the flags of the Allies, who included Japan, set out from the factory, and progressed around the town centre. A sports day was held, with a soldiers' luncheon and tea, bonfire and fireworks, the latter organised by C. E. Foster and J. van Hooydonk.

In London, the first anniversary of the Armistice was marked by a procession along Whitehall past a temporary Cenotaph, designed by Sir Edwin Lutyens (1869-1944). A year later, this took permanent form. Letchworth had its own temporary Cenotaph for Armistice commemoration, before Onslow Whiting's fine Memorial Cross was completed in 1921. Throughout 1920, there was intensive fund raising for the hospital project. The May pageant again featured the Spirella girls, followed by a replica of Sir George Frampton's statue of Edith Cavell – the nurse who had proclaimed 'patriotism is not enough', before facing a German firing squad in Brussels, where she had remained in post long after the invasion. A garden party was held at the hospital, and folk dancing at 'The Cloisters'. Miss Lawrence wrote in *The Citizen*[46]

> Why should we ask other people to attend our sick, Letchworth as a community is large enough now to attend to its own wants. The real question remains, is everybody contributing his part to the building fund and paying his or her share.

Quite so. A generation before the introduction of the National Health Service, community healthcare tended to be conducted on a voluntary, often charitable basis. By the end of May 1920, £3,300 had been raised. The British Red Cross Society made a grant of £1,000, and Alywin Osborn Cave was appointed architect.[47] The foundation stone was laid on 8 January 1921 by Miss Edith Fox, May Queen 1920-21. A further £2,130 for equipment was raised in an Old English Fair in Howard Park, bringing the total to nearly £10,000, although the total cost was now £12,750. The opening on 15 October 1921 was officiated by H.R.H. Princess Beatrice. The new single-storey building accommodated 10 men and 10 women, with two private beds. Miss Clayton remained as matron. The hospital was taken into the National Health Service in 1948.

EIGHT

INDUSTRY AND COMMERCE

The Manufacturers' Conference   Without manufacturers willing to throw in their lot with the Garden City, the overall objective of social reform was hopelessly impractical, and the concept would have remained a minority Utopia. Industrial location was universally *laissez faire*, with no regulation of factory sites within towns, still less any attempts to direct decentralisation of population and industry. Consequently, Howard had to convince industrialists of the soundness of his ideas, hoping that a few key participants would attract others through economies of association. On 1 April 1903 a conference of manufacturers was held at the Garden City Pioneer Company's offices in Holborn, London.[1] The site selection process, discussed above in Chapter Three, was well under way. Indeed, on the following day, the Board considered reports about Chartley Castle, Staffordshire, Grendon, Warwickshire, and Burnham-on-Crouch, Essex.[2] The objective was to gauge the willingness of manufacturers to move, and the criteria they considered most important for site selection. Ralph Neville chaired the meeting. A pre-circulated checklist requested participants to rank factors including availability of labour, water transport, presence of two railway companies, healthfulness of the district, quality of agricultural land, proximity of cheap coal, a central power supply, nearness to London, and the desirability of a national conference of manufacturers. In opening, Neville highlighted the urgency of reversing the physical degeneration recently revealed in recruitment for the Anglo-Boer War. The Pioneer Company.

> wished to conduct industries under conditions which would give employers the opportunity for physical development, and the resurrection of agriculture by bringing the market to farmers' doors.[3]

The Garden City required the co-operation of manufacturers to ensure its viability:

> although of course immediate personal gain was not the object, it was not desired that the scheme should be philanthropic in the ordinary sense.[4]

He wished to learn priority criteria, recognising that

> a site could not be got that would please everybody … the company wanted such guidance as they could get in coming to the conclusion … in selecting from such sites as were available.[5]

W.H. Lever felt a desire for manufacturers to move out into the country, but a range of industries would be required to offer employment to men, women, boys and girls. Availability of river or canal transport in addition to rail, and availability of coal, would govern the type of industry willing to locate. Some key concerns might be willing to pledge a move, if they knew the general location under consideration.[6] What was the definition of 'nearness to London'? Did it mean 25-50 miles, within an hour's journey by express train? Howard Pearsall instanced the perpetual launch of new businesses in the metropolis – 'if we can tap that stream, we can fill Garden City over and over again'.[7] Lever saw the metropolis as the market for consumption. Others saw the desirability of sites 14 to 25 miles out, but doubted that such could be found at reasonable cost. The Great Eastern Railway in Essex was praised for its cheap rates for transporting produce to London – which suggested a 'homesteading' basis for initiating development.[8] F. L. Rawson emphasised the importance of a practical approach 'to show people this was not a Utopian scheme, but a thoroughly sound business scheme, going to be run on thoroughly sound, practical lines'. Mr Enock, involved with the assessment of Chartley Castle, referred to more distant sites – offices and showrooms might be in London, but works were outside, within two hours – a site between London and Manchester (as was Chartley) might be ideal.[9] This was endorsed by Howard (who unilaterally obtained an option on Chartley), cryptically stating that going beyond 50 miles from London might bring reasonable proximity to a large industrial population, such as the Midlands or the potteries of Stoke-on-Trent.

> You could not do better than be near London, but you will not be able, I feel satisfied, to secure an estate suitable for this purpose within say a radius of 40-50 miles. I quite expected that manufacturers … would with one voice say nearness to London … in my experience they mean something in the suburbs … and when it comes to a question of 30 miles it is almost as great … as going 2 or 3 times the distance.[10]

In an attempt at compromise, T. H. W. Idris reiterated that the best site would be near London, but that those on railway lines running north towards Manchester or Liverpool could be a good choice,[11] again a hint of Chartley as the choice. The conference had revealed divergent opinions on location, and possibly threw doubt on the wisdom of Chartley as the ultimate choice. The question of location had assumed a much higher priority than on the checklist, where it had figured as next to last. The Pioneer Company had found that in the London area 50 per cent of a sample of 80 industrialists expressed a willingness to consider moving to a Garden City; in the Midlands, however, only 16 out of 82 were in favour, which evidently influenced the rejection of Chartley.[12]

'Factory Sites to Let'   H. Howard Humphreys's appraisal of Letchworth Estate also considered its industrial potential.[13] He found it was 'admirably suited … just within what I may call a commercial distance of London, and the growth of self-propelled traffic [motor vehicles] will be a powerful factor in the development of your town … if a maker of automobiles can be induced to place his works upon the estate, I am certain that others would quickly follow suit'. The location of the industrial estate to the leeward of the town was also recommended and crystallised in Unwin's layout, with 135 acres south of the railway, served by Works Road, connecting via the Green Lane railway bridge to Icknield Way north of the tracks. The G.N.R. built a goods yard, and individual private sidings could be taken from the main line. The planned grouping of factories was in its infancy, but was also being pursued at Trafford Park, Manchester, alongside the ship canal. Attraction of industry to Letchworth depended upon land, labour, and infrastructure being available at competitive rates. Utilities provided by First Garden City Ltd. were first made available to the industrial estate. The ability to expand was important as cramped town centre sites were beginning to inhibit technological advances, notably the introduction of production-line processes, which worked most efficiently with an uninterrupted horizontal sequence of operations. Manufacturing, with a high value-added content, small raw material inputs, and a high skill content, to produce goods with a high ratio of value to weight, was gaining in importance. Letchworth lacked basic raw materials and was better suited to skilled manufacturing than to heavy industry. This would minimise the impact of transport costs of raw materials. However, its comparatively remote location away from a pool of skilled labour and distant from markets, was also critical. Humphreys's perceptive remarks about links with London, and the potential for skilled engineering or automotive industries, were to prove substantially correct.

Had the Company possessed adequate working capital, advance factories might have been constructed and leased out. With over £200,000 invested in infrastructure by the end of 1906, against the estate purchase price of £155,000, and share capital of £148,000, there was no room for manoeuvre.[14] However, efforts were made to attract industry, based upon the low ground rent and rates, provision of services, availability of housing and good transport facilities. Ground rents began at £25 a half-acre (0.2 ha.), with 999-year leases subject to revision every 99 years. In 1915, the annual rates were 5s. 9d. in the pound including County,

District, Parish and Poor Rates, with 4d. in the pound added for sewage disposal. Construction of standard steel-framed factories of 10,000 sq. ft. was considered, for a £400 initial payment, and the balance of £3,600 repayable over 15 years. In 1914 a six-unit tenement factory was constructed on Works Road. Land cost and rates weighed most heavily with industrialists. Benoit-Lévy, the French garden city expert, compared a 2.2 acre (0.91 ha.) London site with an annual cost of £1,740, with a 5.45 acre (2.2ha.) Letchworth site leased by the same company for only £175.[15]

Ewart and Son, manufacturers of hot water geysers, were the first lessees in 1905, but did not build their factory for five years. T. H. W. Idris, a Director of F.G.C. Ltd., opened an offshoot of his mineral water plant, and Vickers and Field, asphalt paving manufacturers, both early recruits, did not remain long. Printing and engineering were the most notable early successes. Thomas Adams added industrial promotion to duties as Company Secretary and Estate Manager. He appears to have become overstretched, and in August 1905 was replaced as Estate Manager, notwithstanding his recent success in attracting Dent's, the publishers.[16] His successor, Walter Gaunt (1874-1951), came from Trafford Park. Purdom, evidently settling old scores in an outburst of snobbery, castigated Gaunt's 'Manchester mind and accent. His ideals were within the terms of business and common sense, and he said so in an unmistakable way'.[17] He melodramatically portrayed Gaunt as a philistine, bent on destruction of idealism, as he pursued factual materialism with the single-mindedness of Mr Gradgrind in *Hard Times*. Gaunt remained Estate Manager until 1917. While some of his decisions were sometimes controversial, Gaunt undoubtedly consolidated a significant industrial base. He was unfairly parodied in the *Citizen* cartoons by Louis Weirter, who as Adams's brother-in-law continued to grind the family axe.

Printing and publishing   In 1904 a co-operative group of printers from Leicester learned of Howard's Garden City project. Initially, they had intended to rent smallholdings land, but were critical of the terms both for agricultural and industrial land. In November 1905, however, they were established as Garden City Press Ltd.[18] Bert Williams, the manager, was an idealist: all employees received a proportion of the profits, through retention of 1s. 8d. (8p) from weekly wages, and 10 per cent interest was paid out of the trading surplus. One employee had 'invested' £16 in this way, which by 1911 had accrued to £86, of which £70 represented 'interest' and 'dividend'. The Press produced many brochures published by F.G.C. Ltd. Wages were no higher than average: 35s. (£1.75p) for men for a 48-hour week, 16s. (£0.80p) for women and 7s. (£0.35p) for boy and girl employees. The company was exceptional in granting one week's paid holiday, and organised a Works Council and Education Committee. It also guaranteed the Co-partnership tenants occupancy of a number of cottages for employees. Notwithstanding its democratic organisation, there was early industrial trouble, following which three employees left to found the first successful Garden City newspaper. In 1911 the Company was reorganised on a conventional limited liability basis.

The attraction of Dent's was proof positive of the industrial viability of Letchworth. J.M. Dent and Sons were nationally renowned publishers whose cramped printing and binding works was near Bishopsgate in the East End of London.[19] They had recently produced their attractive 'classic' reprint *Everyman* Edition and it became essential for them to find new premises to increase production. Joseph Malaby Dent (1849-1926) was an employer in the tradition of Victorian altruism, concerned with the social conditions of his workforce. He met Adams at a lecture, and subsequently leased five acres (2.02 ha.) at £2,550 compared with £17,500 for a similar site in central London. Construction of the single-storey factory with its basement warehouse was begun in August 1906, and it opened a year later. It was soon in full production, with 150 employees. The workforce was critical of Garden City housing, and the firm built Temple Gardens, off Green Lane, for senior employees and their families. Social welfare included a works library and gardening club. The lack of social life, particularly music halls, prompted some employees to return to London, but most adapted.

84   Letchworth at work: Dent's printing works, folding pages for the *Everyman* Edition, *c*.1910.

Dent's elder son, Hugh, built 'Dents' Cottage' in Letchworth Lane in 1922 (designed by Bennett and Bidwell), while his younger son Jack played a leading role in many early theatrical events. Firm and family remained mainstays of the Garden City for many years.

W.H. Smith and Son were expanding rapidly as national retail newsagents and booksellers.[20] Also high quality printers and bookbinders, they were attracted to Letchworth by the potential for expansion. They and their recently-acquired associates, the Arden Press of Leamington Spa, were housed in an impressive single-storey factory, built 1906-7 at the corner of Works Road and Pixmore Avenue. Designed by Francis William Troup (1859-1941), it was one of the few early industrial buildings in Letchworth with architectural distinction. The bindery, under the control of Douglas Cockerell (1870-1945), one of the most skilled craftsmen in the field, was involved in presentation binding for parish registers and historical documents. The Arden Press was distinguished for the work of Bernard Newdigate (1869-1944),[21] best known for his restrained type style evolved in conjunction with the sculptor, Eric Gill (1882-1940), who carried out two inscriptions at 'Howgills'. In 1911 the Arden Press employed 80 men, 12 boys and 100 girls. The firm was a pioneer user of road transport for distribution to its London headquarters. Newdigate developed a special regard for the work of Morris's Kelmscott Press. He continued to work for Arden until August 1914, when he volunteered for war service and was commissioned in the Royal Warwickshires. His Garden City home was 'Astley Cottage', in The Glade. Newdigate's friend, the lettering artist and designer, Eleni Zompolides (1880-1958),[22] trained under Walter Crane at the Royal

College of Art, and settled in Letchworth in 1908, after the opening of the Arden works. She was a calligrapher and artist, and worked for Dent's in the 1920s. Smiths ceased work during the First World War, but Douglas Cockerell subsequently started a small hand bindery in Norton Way, notable for high quality tooled bindings, and hand marbled endpapers. In 1935 he bound the *Codex Sinaiaticus* for the British Museum. Other pre-1914 printers in operation included Letchworth Printers Ltd., who published *The Citizen* newspaper, and the Hayes Printing Machinery Company Ltd., pioneers of colour lithography. Their factory was destroyed by fire in 1913.

Engineering   Heatly Gresham moved from Bassingbourn near Royston, about 12 miles distant. The firm made bodies for London taxicabs. Other motor manufacturers located in Letchworth over the next few years. The estate was most suited to the industry while its products were virtually hand-built; it was an unlikely centre for mass production. Conversely, had a major company located in the town, it would have attained dominance; indeed, the Vauxhall Company nearby, at Luton and Bedford, developed into a mass manufacturer as the English branch of the American General Motors.

The Lacre Motor Co. moved from Long Acre near Covent Garden, London.[23] The firm built an impressive factory on Works Road in 1909 (architect Albert Dawkins), with a two-storey office block fronting the large production hall, regrettably demolished in the 1980s. The firm concentrated on chassis building, manufacturing neither bodywork nor engines. Labour was recruited from Bedford and Luton and an average weekly wage of 32s. (£1.60p) was paid, compared with London levels of 48-50s. (£2.40-£2.50). The discrepancy brought about an industrial dispute in 1912, and a trades-unionist employee was dismissed, allegedly for breach of conduct. The union executive requested an immediate wage rise of 4s.(20p) per week to match Luton levels, which the company rebutted by sacking the branch secretary, declaring that only non-union labour would be employed in future. The subsequent walk-out was joined by 26 non-unionists.[24] A meeting was held in Howard Park; there were allegations of police brutality, with pickets brought before the Hitchin magistrates. A national paper, *The Evening News*, publicised working conditions in Letchworth. The dispute consolidated local union activity: E. K. Simmons, secretary of the Letchworth branch of the British Socialist Party, wrote to F.G.C. Ltd.[25] urging their best endeavours

> to persuade the Lacre Company to give up an ignoble and hopeless struggle … the publicity given to the strike has already damaged the name of Letchworth. F.G.C. ought to refuse leases to firms who do not undertake to pay the standard rate of wages … The conditions of labour here are in many instances a disgrace to our town whose high aspirations as regards the general conditions of life have World wide renown … The F.G.C. cannot ignore its responsibility in the matter.

The Phoenix Motor Company moved from Finchley in 1910 to premises on Pixmore Avenue.[26] The firm began as a motor-cycle manufacturer in Holloway Road, north London, founded by a Belgian, Joseph van Hooydonk. The 11.9 h.p. Phoenix was shown at Olympia in 1912, and seven were manufactured each week, continuing until 1915, when production switched to munitions work. Hooydonk took an active role in the town's life, and provided the fireworks for the inauguration of the temporary War Memorial in 1919. Other motor companies established after the First World War will be mentioned in a later chapter. Other specialist engineering firms were also established. The Foster Instrument Company Limited, manufacturer of industrial pyrometers for furnaces, opened in Pixmore Way in 1913.[27] In response to Purdom's surveys, the founder, C. E. Foster, stressed that Garden City conditions, with the closeness of factory and home, contributed to increasing productivity. Foster's paid London wages. The only serious disadvantage lay in the need for personal contact with customers, entailing lengthy telephone calls on the infant trunk network, and additional travel time.

85   Phoenix Motor Co., *c*.1912. A range of hand-finished cars, each with a phoenix radiator mascot, awaits delivery.

Consumer Goods   The emergence of a consumer-based manufacturing sector was a 20th-century phenomenon. Expanding rapidly in south-east England in the inter-war period, a number of firms in Letchworth in this category were established before 1914. Dent's *Everyman* Edition has been mentioned. The Herz and Falk Embroidery Company was a Swiss firm, which opened in Letchworth in 1907.[28] Their labour force was largely female, but key male workers had been brought in from St Gall, and Letchworth housing conditions were stated to be a revelation, even to the Swiss. Few companies employed married women pre-1914, and the Herz and Falk employees were mainly girls, who received only 10s. (50p) for a 52½ hour week. Lloyds Ltd. began to manufacture lawn mowers in 1913. The same year D. Meredew Ltd., cabinet makers, moved out of the East End of London, where they had begun trading in 1879, specialising in the then-fashionable carved overmantels.[29] After Meredew's retirement in 1907, Fred Hard acquired the name. The move was a bold, risky venture, and Hard later recalled:

> My method was to move the families lock stock and barrel, by means of a small motor van …
> we moved 192 men, women and children … ask any one of them his opinion of the move:
> 'finest thing you ever did guv'nor'.[30]

The factory in Dunham's Lane was completed in 1914, and Ministry of Works orders dominated production during the First World War. Subsequently, traditional furniture became the staple product, expanding in the 1930s into wireless cabinets, including the famous Gordon Russell designs for Murphy, who opened a factory in Welwyn Garden City.

The Arts and Crafts movement encouraged the growth of craft workshops. A firm which allied handcraft to volume production was the St Edmundsbury Weavers.[31] Edmund Hunter (1866-1937) from Bury St Edmunds had studied art against his father's wishes. He was a skilled designer, reflecting both the influence of Morris, and his own personal interest in

Theosophy, Astrology, and Persian art. The firm was founded in Haslemere, Surrey, and moved to Letchworth in 1908. Hunter employed Spitalfields handloom weavers. His fabrics were supplied to churches and cathedrals, country houses, and even for lavish stage productions such as Beerbohm Tree's *Anthony and Cleopatra*. His Letchworth home, 'St Brighids', Sollershott West, and his factory in Birds Hill were both designed by Parker and Unwin. The factory featured concrete mullioned studio windows, a gabled tiled roof, and a domestic inglenook fireplace: Benoit-Lévy commented upon its charming aspect. The availability of electricity enabled a combination of hand and power weaving. Hunter employed four men, who earned 39s.- 47s. 6d. a week (£1.95-£2.37) and five apprentices who received 5s.-15s. (25p-75p), depending upon experience. He was exceptional in paying for two weeks' holiday and bank holidays. Hunter's wife, Dorothea, worked alongside him, but her feminist outlook did not extend to the employment of other married women in the weaving shed. The firm remained in Letchworth until the 1920s. The Iceni pottery was formed by Miss Lawrence and the architect W. H. Cowlishaw. A 'leadless' glaze was used, and the firm's products were characterised by deep green or blue colourings, simple form, and ornamented by pierced rims, the epitome of Arts and Crafts refinement.

Castle Corset The Spirella Company represented a consumer industry related to skilful marketing of female fashions in the early 20th century. It was an American concern, founded by William Wallace Kincaid (1868-1946), who used a spiral wound spring, invented by Marcus Merritt Beeman, as a substitute for whalebone in corsets. The Spirella corset played a role in women's emancipation: wearers could play tennis or ride bicycles, activities impossible in Victorian 'stays'! The firm opened temporary premises in the old 'sheds' in Nevells Road in 1910.[32] They demanded, and received, at a cost more than double that of an industrial site, a town centre site in Bridge Road, which was developed for the most imposing factory in Letchworth. Their first corsetière, Frances Wright of Hitchin, began work on 30 March 1910. Benoit-Lévy surveyed the infant company with 12 men and 48 women employees[33] – in contrast to other employers Spirella preferred married women as more expert than younger girls, who required greater training. Already the most progressive features of American social welfare were being considered. Kincaid claimed enlightened self-interest as the prime motivation for bringing the company to the Garden City.

> Letchworth … is built according to a pre-arranged plan … not more than 12 houses built upon an acre, giving every cottage a good garden … These conditions make for efficient contented progressive workmen and women. A principle of Spirella's policy has been to instil into its employees right thoughts, right methods of living, right methods of work, an appreciation of the vital needs of sunlight, of food for health and of congenial employment for happiness. The Spirella found itself in sympathy with every detail of the Garden City Movement which has found its best expression in Letchworth.[34]

The new factory was built in three phases between 1912-20. The architect, Cecil Hignett, used the commission to branch out from Parker and Unwin, and the contractor was Howard Hurst. A remarkable building resulted, dominating views northwards across the railway from the town centre, subsequently nicknamed 'Castle Corset', by Fitzwater Wray in his satirical *Sir Gadabout* saga. The three blocks enclosed a courtyard, open to Bridge Road and facing axially down Nevells Road. The workshop block nearest the railway was the first phase, built in 1912, with the central block in 1913-4, and the third block in 1919-20. The composition of the workshop blocks was dominated by four pavilions capped with Arts and Crafts hipped roofs with small upstand gables, somewhat at odds with the boldly functional treatment of the workrooms between. The pavilion windows were enormous mullioned and transomed bays, complete with leaded lights, cast in concrete. The building structure was largely reinforced concrete, exposed in beams and string courses. The structural grid was reflected in the workroom elevations, which were totally glazed between the columns. These required external

86 Spirella Gardens opening, 1931. The founder of Spirella, William Kincaid, looks somewhat bemused as A. W. Brunt declares the gardens open, whilst C. F. Ball looks on rather sternly.

hand-cleaning every three months, from precarious ladders, by the Gilley Brothers, for the princely sum of £25![35] Internally there was a reinforced concrete mezzanine gallery running the length of the workrooms. These were flat roofed, with deep exposed concrete edge beams, which acted as parapets, protecting sitting out and sun bathing areas, like the top decks of a great ocean liner. The central block was more classically treated, with the top floor containing a large social hall, complete with stage and fly tower. Its decoration included delicate Art Nouveau plasterwork. Spirella not only dominated visually, but equally provided a natural focus for the town's social life during the inter-war period.

The company supplied remarkable staff facilities.[36] The large workroom windows enabled every bench to obtain direct sunlight. Free optical testing was provided, with spectacles at wholesale prices. Bathrooms were available, and it was claimed that over 75 per cent of the workforce used them (one wonders what the other 25 per cent did!). There was a large canteen, fitness was encouraged through gymnastic classes, while a choral and orchestral society and a library catered for quieter tastes. Photographs of the 1920s show callisthenics, Greek-style formal dancing in the ballroom, with the Spirella Girls barefoot, clad in tunics, and posed as if on an antique frieze. An enclosed shed to store 350 bicycles undercover was built, and on wet evenings the firm even issued capes to employees travelling homewards without a coat. The Company recruited an army of 4,500 corsetières. The house journal, *Spirella Monthly*, urged greater and greater conquests!

> Attention! Comrades, veterans and recruits upon the firing line. The old adage advises to aim high, set a mark, point at it, shoot straight for the centre … Get on to the firing line, never mind if you miss at first for practice makes perfect. All ready, aim, fire![37]

The sales-ladies covered the length and breadth of the land, quietly selling Spirella in the intimacy of customers' homes, and achieving ever higher sales targets, with a workforce of 2,000, and daily sales of 200,000 corsets in the 1950s.[38] Mae West and Marilyn Monroe ordered Spirella products, which by the 1960s included made-to-measure swimwear and leisure wear. The company transferred brassière manufacture to Harlow New Town in the 1960s, but maintained a presence in Letchworth until 1989, by when only surgical corsets were made. Following the sharp decline in demand for firm foundations, the Spirella army headed towards the same fate as the dinosaur and the dodo. Memories kept the spirit alive and, in 1998, the First Garden City Heritage Museum mounted one of its most popular exhibitions, featuring Spirella, under the title 'Pull Yourselves Together Girls'. The training films of the 1930s need to be seen to be believed, with acres of flesh being kneaded into the encasing corsets! Today, 'Castle Corset' remains an enduring legacy of this once enormous

87 'Fashions of 1934'. Models in the latest Spirella corsetry pose as if directed by Busby Berkeley in one of the Hollywood musicals of the period.

88 This advertisement of 1950 highlights the use of the telephone to contact the local Spirella sales-ladies.

enterprise: its remarkable renaissance is recounted in Chapter Sixteen.

K. & L. and the Munitions of War The beginnings of the K. & L. factory contrasted with the popular image of Letchworth as the 'Village named Morality'.[39] In October 1914, with the German army rapidly closing in on Antwerp, Jacques Kryn, a prominent diamond merchant, fled to England with his younger brother, an engineer and car manufacturer from Liège, and his works manager, Raoul Lahy. They arrived, according to legend, with rags on their backs, and pockets full of uncut diamonds. Thousands of their countrymen had taken refuge in England, and a flourishing Belgian colony in Letchworth celebrated their National Day on 21 June 1915. Kryn suggested to an English associate, Sir Bernard Oppenheimer, that they should build a steel foundry to utilise the refugees' skills. Two cupolas and a one-ton converter were erected before Hitchin R.D.C. even received the plans! With an increasing demand for shells, tank parts, and portable bridges, the firm rapidly expanded on their Dunhams Lane site. Machine shops were enlarged and at the height of the war effort almost 3,000 Belgian refugees found employment. Munitions manufacturing was as far as possible kept secret to discourage Zeppelin raids; however, one did make its way to Hertfordshire, but discharged its bombs short of Letchworth and was eventually brought down at Cuffley. The 'village named morality' had more nearly assumed the role of Andrew Undershaft's garden city, financed from munitions profits, in Shaw's *Major Barbara*.

Co-operative Commerce Howard had envisaged company shopping to ensure wider availability of goods during the earliest years of development, a system subsequently adopted at Welwyn Garden City. Lack of capital prevented this at Letchworth. Initially, there were no shops on the estate. Hitchin traders, in particular, offered a delivery service for middle-class customers, but this was of no use to industrial workers. Consequently Bert Williams, manager of the Garden City Press, formed the Garden City Co-operative Society.[40] In 1905, with a share capital of £50 16s. 11d. (£50.84) and 95 members, he opened a single-room shop at Letchworth corner in an estate cottage. A house in Cross Street was used to serve the Cheap Cottages area. Purdom had endeavoured to interest the Co-operative Wholesale Society, but to no avail. Garden City Co-operators and Garden City Tenants built

89 K. and L. manufacture armaments for the First World War. Their millionth shell (*right*) was presented to the Minister of Munitions, David Lloyd George, later Prime Minister, remembered for his 'Homes for Heroes' pledge of November 1918.

premises in Leys Avenue in 1907, a handsome Tudor-style building designed by Parker and Unwin. Business prospered under the manager, T. L. Pearce, and in 1913 the first phase of more extensive premises in Eastcheap was opened.

The first shops were opened in Station Road, strategically located between the Birds Hill housing area and the future town centre, with access from the 'cattle creep' for shoppers from north of the tracks.[41] A general store was opened by H. Cullip, followed by Ansell's butchers, Bradshaw's ironmongery, Beddoe's confectionery and newsagents, Snowden's drapery, Smith's grocery, Martin's Garden City Dairy and Housden's cafe and druggists. All were modest buildings, with little attempt to make a visually co-ordinated shopping parade. In 1907 construction began on the south side of Leys Avenue, between the Eastcheap corner and Commerce Avenue. This block was designed by Bennett and Bidwell as a varied but unified parade, with a skilfully handled roofscape. The corner was initially occupied by the Joint City and Midland Bank, with the architects' offices above. *The Simple Life Hotel*, J. L. Wells outfitter and tailor, J. H. Green furnishers, W. B. Moss, a branch of the Hitchin grocers, and W. H. Smith followed down the hill to Commerce Avenue. Unlike Station Road, which was laid out following the straight line on Unwin's first plan, the line of Leys Avenue was subtly curved, which created a more interesting townscape. A further parade on the south side of Commerce Avenue followed in 1908-9 together with shops between the Wynd and Norton Way South, on the north side. Boot's the chemists occupied one of these, while further down towards Norton Way a distinctive block designed by Allen Foxley with triple projecting gables and ornamental plasterwork was partly occupied by Spinks' Drapers, a firm which remained for many years in the town.

At the head of Station Road and Leys Avenue, a projecting gabled block, 'The Colonnade', was built in 1909. A rather coarse design by Edgar Simmons, the estate agent who occupied one of the ground-floor shops, provided a distinctive accent, and illustrated Unwin's tech-

90 & **91**   Town centre shops. *Above*, opening of Garden City Co-operators Ltd., Leys Avenue, 1907. Now one of the principal shopping streets, Leys Avenue had not been properly made up when the store opened. *Below*, F. Nott Bakers, Eastcheap, *c.*1911. Fred Nott proudly displays his local delivery vehicles in front of his Eastcheap shop, built in 1909.

nique of using articulated building lines to achieve a varied townscape. Beyond this lay the site of the Estate Office, a somewhat utilitarian structure looking like a colonial outpost, set well back from Broadway to allow the construction of more permanent offices. Eastcheap was intended to be one of the principal shopping streets, but the development of the cottage estates east of Norton Way made Station Road and Leys Avenue more attractive for early letting. This lack of balance in the town-centre development remained for many years, until the recent Morrisons store was built to create a critical mass of commercial activity west of Broadway. Development in Eastcheap proceeded slowly. Shortly before the war Nott's, the bakers and confectioners, moved from Leys Avenue to an elegant building fronting Eastcheap, which had a distinctive series of projecting oriel windows beneath a gable. Nott's became a Letchworth institution and extended along Eastcheap in the 1920s with 'The Icknield Halls'. Opposite, on the west side, was the first phase of the Co-operative stores. The rest of the road remained undeveloped until the 1920s, save for 'The Picture Palace' and adjoining Fire Station at the south end. Broadway, too, received little development. The corner running around Station Place towards Bridge Road was developed in 1908 for Barclays Bank, an excellent Georgian-style building designed by Hugh Seebohm, with a projecting tower which linked the single-storey banking hall to the two-storey bank house. This was intended to be a symmetrical development turning from Broadway across the bridge road axis to Westcheap, a second shopping street equivalent to Eastcheap, which was never developed. The bank building did, however, establish a precedent for Georgian-style architecture along Broadway, broken in the early years only by the free Tudor-mullioned frontage of the Post Office, designed by Bennett and Bidwell in 1910.

Many of the early stores required workshops and even stables, which were provided on rear frontages facing Commerce Avenue and The Wynd. Both of these streets developed in a more or less unplanned fashion, which defied reorganisation for many years. In the early 1920s Parker prepared plans for redevelopment of The Wynd but it was more than 60 years before any significant reorganisation was achieved. The growth of shopping was marked by the existence of 30 shops by July 1907. By 1924 there were 162 shops.[42] The acute-angled site between Leys Avenue and Eastcheap was originally allocated as an open market, but the experiment was unsuccessful, and the vacant plot was developed in the early 1920s when much of the town centre was consolidated. The telephone was beginning to be recognised as an essential adjunct to commercial life, if not socially. The first Post Office telephone was installed in 1906 in The Cabin, Station Road. The exchange, with a 100-line capacity served until 1912; in 1907 there were only 33 subscribers. A new system was installed in the Broadway Post Office, and the system grew to 2,800 lines, before it was superseded by the new telephone exchange, built in Bridge Road in 1961.[43]

Newspapers and Publicity   The growth of the social, commercial and industrial life of the town brought the need for newspapers and publicity. The Garden City Press brought out a *Garden City News and Advertiser* in January 1905, with F. W. Rogers as editor and advertisement manager. It did not survive for long. However, L.A. Wheeler, Odell and Arthur William Brunt, who left the Press after industrial trouble, formed a newspaper with the encouragement of W. H. Knight who became its first, unpaid, editor. *The Citizen* (*Garden City Record and Advertising Journal*) first appeared on 22 September 1906, and its unbroken run of publication since that date has left a valuable record of the town's development and personalities.[44] The first issues were printed in Wheeler's Green Lane house. Brunt was advertisement manager, and he and a colleague delivered the paper free every Friday. 'Guaranteed weekly circulation 1,000' proclaimed the first issue, with the Latin tag *floreat urbs hortorum* (literally 'May the Garden Town flourish'). Local stores and builders advertised their services, while a Residents' Council public meeting about a licensed public house was announced at the Howard Hall.

Brunt soon became editor and 'trebled' as compositor and reporter for 32s. (£1.60) weekly. He conducted a lively paper, and his encyclopedic knowledge later formed the basis for his

Pageant of Letchworth. His tenure was not without controversy. In 1912 he wrote to the *Daily Herald* about the Lacre strike and industrial conditions, and local employers felt he had used his position to aggravate the situation. He was discharged from the paper early in 1913, to be succeeded by Harold Armitage, who skirmished with the national *Daily Sketch* and *Daily Mail* over their reporting of Letchworth as a town of cranks and cowards during the First World War. He was forced to resign in 1928 over his support of a critical theatrical review by Harold Hare.

The first *Letchworth Directory* appeared in 1907, published by Garden City Press, and F.G.C. Ltd. sponsored a pocket sized *Borough Guide* in 1908, both of which indicated the variety of businesses already trading in the town. First Garden City Limited brought out its own guides to spread knowledge of Letchworth beyond its boundaries – *Garden City in the Making* (1905), *Guide to the Garden City* (1906), and *Where shall I live?* (1907) – the latter acting as an illustrated catalogue of the Urban Cottages Exhibition. They were attractively produced, with artwork covers. Pictorial guides such as *Letchworth Garden City in Pictures* (*c.*1912), contained high quality photography, while colour lithograph posters extolling the 'Health of the Country – the Comforts of the Town' were issued before and after the First World War. Several excellent books recorded the development of the town. C. B. Purdom's *The Garden City* was published in 1913, a beautiful example of Dent's skills, with a cover illustration from an attractive view by T. Friedenson, with the gabled fronts of Silver Birch Cottages in Station Road gold blocked on the spine. Purdom provided a comprehensive account of the Garden City movement, the development of Letchworth, and with appendices contributed by Howard, Unwin, Aneurin Williams, Harold Craske, Howard Pearsall and others. Europeans were frequent visitors and *La Cité Jardin* by Georges Benoit-Lévy of the French Garden City Association appeared in 1904 with a revised edition in 1911. German interest was considerable and Berlepsch Valendas's *Die Gartenstadt Bewegung in England* of 1912 contained a thorough account of Letchworth and the Garden City movement. By the outbreak of the First World War, the Letchworth experiment was internationally renowned in town planning and housing circles, and has remained so ever since.

NINE

COMPANY, COUNCIL AND COMMUNITY

Residents Union Howard's proposed integration of the functions of landlord, development company and local authority, possibly influenced by the Fabians' municipalisation of utility services, was the weakest part of his concept, and uneasily reconciled with local democratic control through the local government structure. Local government in the 1890s was settling down to the use of the powers conferred by the 1888 legislation. While urban boroughs and city councils had built up valuable experience, there was little indication of the potential effectiveness of county councils, let alone the rural district and parish councils who had acquired limited responsibilities in rural areas. The Garden City was located in Hitchin Rural District, split between the parishes of Letchworth (67 inhabitants), Willian (176) and Norton (248). The newcomers had neither a voice in local government nor in the Company unless they were shareholders. Electoral registration had enrolled fewer than 200 voters out of a possible 1,000 by 1905. That June residents resolved to 'form a Council to watch over the interests of the residents during the development of the estate'.[1] The Residents Union was formally created at the 'sheds' on 14 July 1905 to assist in carrying out Garden City ideals. Mrs. Ebenezer Howard, Mrs. MacFadyen, Miss M. E. Nicholson, Miss F. Bates, the Rev. H. Janner, Mr. E. Docker, Raymond Unwin and Mr. R. W. Tabor were members of the first committee. The Union acted primarily as a sounding board.

As population rose, the Union generated local political interest – in January 1907 there were 144 candidates for 16 places. Residents' enfranchisement was universal at a time when women's suffrage was still controversial. Prominent local figures such as Norman MacFadyen, Henry Bryan Binns, Joseph Wicksteed, H. Clapham Lander, John T. Openshaw, T. Clarence Howard and Cyril Arthington Pease were elected. Wicksteed became Chairman, Pease and Howard secretaries. The unsatisfactory railway service, education, provision of a public library and museum, regulation of alcohol and poor relief were key concerns. The Union's influence diminished after the formation of the amalgamated Civil Parish of Letchworth in April 1908. The Poor Law was notorious for its Dickensian approach and the workhouse still represented a threat to the elderly and destitute. Consequently, 'The Guild of Help' was formed in 1906 by Edgar Wing, with the Rev. F. N. Heazell and Miss Nicholson.[2] The scheme worked through a central committee of 12, 5 district heads, and 45 helpers, on a voluntary basis. The income for August 1907-June 1908 was £54 2s. 5d., and rose to £144 7s. 2d. the next year. Only through unstinting voluntary work could such small sums be put to good use. In 1911 there were the following disbursements: Temporary loans £19; Provision of groceries £16; Clothing £15; Medicines £7; Meals for school children £6; Domestic help £8; Pensions for elderly women £1 10s; Expenses of convalescent homes £6; Subscription to National Guild of Help £1.

The Guild strove to avoid the 'Lady Bountiful' approach and was also involved in rent collecting for the Howard Cottage Society and in counselling tenants in difficulty. This was an approach advocated by Octavia Hill (1838-1912), a pioneer of social work.[3] Medical assistance was also necessary in an era long before universal health care. Mrs. H. Craske, wife of the estate accountant, founded the Letchworth Provident Dispensary, based in a house on Cross Street, and supported through weekly subscriptions. Drs. Ledward and MacFadyen were members of the Committee. It was also intended to appoint a district nurse, and ultimately to provide a cottage hospital. Nurse Webb (1881-1962) came to Letchworth in 1905. She trained at Queen Charlotte's Hospital in London before returning to serve the

92   The Letchworth Parish Council, 1908. Sir John Gorst, *front centre*, poses with the Council outside the Howard Hall. *Left to right: front row*, C. F. Ball, H. Heatly, Sir John Gorst, D. B. Cockerell, George Brown; *second row*, J. S. Lander, C. Brown, R. J. E. Underwood, H. Hurst, H. C. Lander, T. Hudson, J. T. Openshaw; *back row*, N. MacFadyen, T. C. Howard, H. Hall, F. J. Godbehear.

Garden City in 1910. In 1919 she became Staff Nurse at Spirella, retiring in 1941. In October 1914, Pixmore Farmhouse was opened as a temporary hospital, which developed into the town hospital in 1921. The Letchworth Civic Trust, formed in 1914 to promote the welfare of the town, rounds off this account of early community organisations. Through subscriptions and bequests it built up a shareholding in F.G.C. Ltd. which was later to prove a valuable lever for promoting the formation of the Letchworth Garden City Corporation.

The Parish Council   The Local Government Board approved the creation of a unified Letchworth Civil Parish, amalgamating Letchworth, Norton and Willian.[4] On 6 April 1908 the first elections were held. The following were elected: C. F. Ball, C. Brown, D. B. Cockerell, G. Cramp, F. J. Godbehear, Sir J. E. Gorst, H. Hall, H. Heatly, T. C. Howard, T. W. Hudson, H. E. Hurst, J. S. Lander, J. T. Openshaw, H. D. Pearsall, and R. J. E. Underwood. Sir John Gorst, K.C., a London barrister, was elected Chairman; George Brown became Clerk. The Council existed until the formation of the Urban District Council in 1919. In 1910, 43 candidates contested the 15 seats. Well known local figures including A. W. Brunt, H. R. Dent, Norman McFadyen, Edgar Simmons and John H. Wicksteed took seats. The Chairmen were successively Sir John Gorst (1908-9); H. Bond Holding (1909-12); Douglas B. Cockerell (1912-13); Dr. Norman MacFadyen (1914-16); Charles F. Ball (1916-19).

   Parish Councils had little power, although they were able to raise finance through rates. Friction between F.G.C. Ltd., Council and community built up, with the Company cast in a 'big brother' role, and the Council well-intentioned but lacking financial and decision-making expertise. The Garden City pantomimes and the cartoons of Louis Weirter reflected local disdain for institutions. Street lighting provoked one of the most heated arguments. The

Company had installed a few gas lanterns, designed by Parker and Unwin, mainly near road junctions, and had, of course, laid the mains. They were anxious that the Parish Council provide more general lighting. Wary of expense, the Parish Council rejected the proposition. A public meeting was called at which it was suggested that the cost of street lighting should be borne by an increase in the Company's water rate! As one of the Garden City pantomimes proclaimed, the Council was powerless 'to implore the naughty gas-man not to leave us in the dark' for after all they were 'nobodies by Act of Parliament'.

The Council reluctantly spent £2,000 making up Green Lane and Dunhams Lane, and in 1911 the County Council took over 4½ miles of roads. The R.D.C. took over refuse collection in 1909, and in 1911, at a cost of £850, the Fire Station was erected in Eastcheap, and through special donations raised by A. W. E. Bullmore, the Chief Officer (who became the U.D.C. Engineer), a fire engine was bought. Even this had been queried as some Councillors thought that ladders were unnecessary, as most houses were low enough for the residents to jump from the roofs! As for Police, Benoit-Lévy reported in 1911 that the two policemen truly had a sinecure since it would be impossible to envisage less crime than in this model settlement.[5] In 1918, however, a Magistrates Court and Police Station were built on Broadway, prompting *Punch* to state that it was up to the garden citizens to make sure that the new facilities were well used! Rates were undeniably low: for the years ending March 1909 and March 1910, only the Poor Rate was levied and this amounted to no more than 2s. 8d. and 4s. 8d. (14p and 24p) respectively. From 1910-16 this varied from 4s. 6d. to 5s. 6d. (22½p-27½p) with a street lighting rate from 1d. to 3½d. (0.4p-1½p) in the pound.[6]

Political Life   'Garden City revealed a peculiar situation politically – it had neither liberal nor conservative traditions ... quite different from the usual country town ... Garden City was to some extent the outcome of socialism, and for that reason I have myself invested in the scheme.' George Bernard Shaw thus revealed his own political inclination, which he expected to be strongly reflected in Letchworth. In the early 20th century the notion of Socialism gaining control was revolutionary, and national governments alternated between Liberals and Conservatives. Keir Hardie and the Independent Labour Party held a handful of seats, although the 'progressive' Fabians of the London County Council had spearheaded the advance of local authorities into housing and public utilities. In Letchworth the Fabians were led by the Howard Pearsalls and Raymond Unwin, prior to his departure for Hampstead. Further left were Mr. and Mrs. J. Kidd, while the Christian Socialists looked to J. Bruce Wallace. There were early arguments over whether the Socialist Society should include all shades of Socialist thought. George Bates, H. Clapham Lander and Arthur Brunt were local leaders of the Labour Party.[7] Letchworth was located in the Hitchin Constituency, traditionally a Conservative seat, but the 1906 General Election brought the Liberals to power, with T. T. Gregg as the local member. Local Liberals included W. H. Knight, editor of *The Citizen* and Dr. MacFadyen. Barry Parker was a Liberal supporter, and Thomas Adams had acted as a local Liberal party agent in the Scottish Borders.

The Conservatives organised the first political club in 1908, located between the Birds Hill housing and the town centre, with a licence, which denoted it as the 'Pub Club'. The local leader, Charles Ball the contractor, was subsequently a member of the Parish, Urban District and County Councils. Howard Hurst, another contractor, J. H. W. Stephenson and J. van Hooydonk were also prominent. Miss M. A. Nicholson, public spirited and sympathetic, was the Conservative women's leader. For many years, however, party politics held a low profile in local government, with 'Independents' or 'all parties' dominant, irrespective of their personal allegiance.

'Our Mutual Friend' – the Company   F.G.C. Ltd. inevitably attained primacy. In 1909, *The City* referred to the Company as 'Our mutual friend' but stressed the importance of local shareholders to ensure the fulfilment of the Trustee role. Greater demands were being made on F.G.C. Ltd., but subscription of capital was slow, impeding development. The period 1903-15 was, with good reason, characterised by C. B. Purdom as 'The years of struggle'.[8] Purdom and Harold Craske had control over the Company's accounts. Purdom later claimed that the 1907 valuation, by Drivers Jonas and Trustram Eve, of £379,500 for the Company's fixed assets revealed a capital surplus of £97,047 6s. 3d. The Directors were uncertain as to how to present this in the balance sheet, and it was consequently understated by charging much expenditure incidental to town development against the revenue account. This enforced greater financial caution than was strictly necessary. It was not until 1911 that the revenue account showed a profit, a mere £171, which grew to £3,034 by 1914. In 1913 a 1 per cent dividend was paid, but the outbreak of war prevented further payments. Purdom's analysis revealed an operating profit of £401 in 1904, £4,545 in 1911 and £6,017 in 1914. He privately circulated proposals for a revised accounting procedure: the unintended consequence of his tactless action was the resignation of Aneurin Williams, the F.G.C. Chairman, who had accepted personal responsibility for the slow growth of the town. Purdom also, more successfully, negotiated with the Inland Revenue over income tax on the Company's trading activities, reducing a claim from several hundred to a few pounds at a time when the tax was 1s. 0d. in the pound.

Broadway and The Town Square   In 1910 a delegation from the R.I.B.A. Town Planning Conference criticised Letchworth for lack of civic design.[9] The following year, influenced by a visit to the United States, Unwin announced 'Letchworth 1914', a project to commemorate the 10th Anniversary of the First Garden City with public buildings including a cottage hospital, public hall, boys club and institute. He also redoubled his efforts to urge completion of Town Square. At the 1912 A.G.M., Aneurin Williams declared that 'considerable attention has been given during the year to the laying out of town square'.[10] Unwin had by then prepared a definitive layout, and had convinced Gaunt that the time was ripe for positive action. In a 1913 article in *Garden Cities and Town Planning*, nominally by Gaunt, but almost certainly ghosted by Unwin, the new plan was unveiled.[11] The three-acre square was compared with Grosvenor and Belgrave Squares in London and had room for gatherings of 6,000 to 8,000 citizens. Formal planting was put in hand and the outline of the central civic and religious buildings was picked out in Lombardy poplars. They remained until February 2002, when they succumbed to the chain saw, in advance of the 'centenary' replanting scheme (see chapter 17). Alas, the buildings never progressed beyond a perspective showing their designs 'freely adapted from the works of Wren and other masters', a Baroque composition capped by cupolas and a soaring spire dominating the Broadway axis. Colonnades linked the central buildings to the simpler façades surrounding the square. A caveat lay in Gaunt's statement that the Company should not give the impression of wastefulness, to businessman and labourer alike. Letchworth at a disadvantage to Bournville and Port Sunlight, where their creators had provided ample buildings of a civic character.

A design policy was introduced for Broadway between Town Square and Station Place. The preference for the Georgian style to attain visual unity was undoubtedly influenced by Lutyens's central buildings at Hampstead Garden Suburb. Purdom, not himself an architect, felt that the Georgian style was the most out of keeping with the character of the town.[12] It appears that Parker and his staff prepared a less grandiose layout for the Town Square. The First World War postponed building on even the peripheral sites, and the Square was fitfully developed by the Museum (Parker and Unwin, 1914, first phase completed 1920), the Grammar School (Parker, 1931), and the Council Offices (Bennett and Bidwell, 1935), all conforming to the Georgian style. The Library (Crickmer, 1938) represented an uneasy interpolation of a mild 'moderne' style alongside the Museum, while later buildings on gap sites were related only by their inappropriate character for their context. Likewise along Broadway, the Estate Offices (Parker and Unwin, 1913), together with Barclays Bank (Hugh Seebohm, 1908), set the Georgian tone, matched by the Boys Club (Parker and Unwin, 1914), and the Methodist Church and Police Station.

SKETCH SHOWING LAYOUT OF
CENTRAL SQUARE LETCHWORTH

NB TO AVOID DETERMINING AT PRESENT THE DESIGN OF THE
BUILDINGS , THE WORKS OF WREN AND OTHER MASTERS HAVE
BEEN FREELY ADAPTED TO ILLUSTRATE   THE LAYOUT

93 Central Square (Town Square). A 1912 design with buildings based on 'the works of Wren and other masters'. The concept shows the influence of formal classical design, notably the work of Lutyens at the Central Square in Hampstead Garden Suburb.

Letchworth Urban District Council   As early as 1912, Sir John Gorst advocated Urban District status.[13] In April 1913 a group of Parish Council candidates, the 'Letchworth XI', demurred, arguing that Letchworth would only gain higher rates - 7s. 6d. in the pound as against 5s. 0d. (37p against 25p) - in the process. The group included Charles F. Ball, J. Van Hooydonk, Howard Hurst and Norman MacFadyen. It became increasingly evident that the economy of the Parish Council was shortsighted. Roads were neglected, street lighting was 50 per cent below the expected standard, and construction of a cemetery required under the Burial Acts was delayed. Storm water drains were urgently required, and extra housing was needed, due to the influx of munition workers and Belgian refugees. In 1917, George Brown was authorised to apply to the County Council[14] for the conversion of the parish into an Urban District Council independent of Hitchin R.D.C., comprising 'the freehold of the Letchworth Parish known as the Garden City Estate, owned by First Garden City Limited', 3,652 acres, 1 rood, 25 poles (1478 ha.). The population in 1917 stood at 10,212 (5,324 in 1911); with 2,242 houses (1,315); rateable value £60,336 (£30,406).

Letchworth U.D.C. was created in 1919, with elections for 15 Councillors on 9 April.[15] The town was not divided into wards for many years, and electors could vote for up to five candidates. There were 15 Labour, an 'All Party' 15, and several Independents to choose from. Nine 'All Party', four Labour and two Independents were elected, five of whom would retire annually. Charles F. Ball became the first Chairman and served until 1924 to be succeeded by Norman MacFadyen until 1927: both had originally strongly opposed the creation of the U.D.C. Mrs. W. H. Gaunt topped the poll with 1,014 votes. Remaining members were Miss Bartholomew, Messrs. C. F. Ball, J. van Hooydonk, H. D. Clapham, H. Bond Holding,

94 Letchworth Urban District Council, 1919. Charles Ball, the first Chairman of the U.D.C., had opposed the original move towards the new status of Letchworth.

E. H. Whiteman, W. G. 'Bill' Furmston, The Rev. H. Cubbon, C. E. Foster, Mrs. Margaret Steen, Messrs J. T. Openshaw, P. W. Bichener, J. J. Kidd and C. J. Hill. George Brown was appointed Clerk. In the early 1920s elections were hotly contested, but the new Council settled down by 1925 when *The Citizen* reported the now customary apathy with less than 50 per cent turnout.

Housing for Heroes   During the First World War the Howard Cottage Society had made valiant efforts to continue with 'Little Belgium' and the R.D.C. had also completed 110 houses, but shortage of working-class housing was acute, both locally and nationally.[16] Unwin's key role in advocating the construction of state-subsidised, local-authority owned working-class housing, based on Garden City standards, has already been noted, as has the formation of the Ministry of Health under Christopher Addison, and the open-ended financial arrangements under the 1919 Housing Act. The Letchworth U.D.C. enthusiastically pressed ahead with its housing schemes notwithstanding rapidly escalating costs and scarcity of materials.[17] There was urgent need for 600 houses; the programme under the 1919 Housing Act involved 707 houses built 1919-22. Despite high costs, the subsidies enabled the rents to be fixed at 7s. 3d.- 8s. 6d. (38-42½p) per week for a non-parlour three-bedroom house, rising to 11s. 9d.-13s. 6d. (58-67½p) per week for a parlour four-bedroom house. The schemes were designed by architects with Garden City experience – Jackmans Place by Bennett and Bidwell, Pixmore by Crickmer and Foxley; and Westbury by Aylwin Osborn Cave (1875-1935) and R. S. Bowers (1889-1943). The designs were models of their kind. In particular, Jackmans Place, north of and partly fronting the Baldock Road, enabled Bennett and Bidwell to demonstrate their skills in natural progression from Rushby Mead. The articulation of the housing and the use of gables and dormers was masterly in producing a varied yet aesthetically coordinated townscape, set off by the colour washed roughcast walls and rich red clay tiled roofs. The

95 Jackmans Place housing, 1919–21. Bennett and Bidwell updated their excellent housing designs from Rushby Mead for this pioneer Letchworth U.D.C. Council Estate.

layout involved a loop road with spur culs-de-sac, and road junctions and greens were effectively handled following the layout diagrams from Unwin's *Town Planning in Practice*. A quarter mile further west, Crickmer's site occupied the triangular area between Rushby Mead, Pixmore Way and Baldock Road. Pixmore Way was an important arterial route into the town centre, and Crickmer was content to use simple hipped roof groups similar to those at Gretna, stepped slightly back and forward, accented by 'M' gables. The Westbury scheme was on a neighbourhood scale, and pushed residential development westwards from Campers Road. The street layout approximated more to a regular grid, which Cave and Bowers relieved by small setback tapering greens.

After termination of the 1919 Act subsidies in 1922 and Addison's resignation, new terms were offered in the Housing Acts of 1923 and 1924, promoted respectively by Neville Chamberlain and John Wheatley, the first Labour Minister of Health. Housing designs were simplified to stereotypes from the Ministry *Housing Manuals*. Letchworth U.D.C. built 48 houses under the 1923 Act and 476 under the 1924 Act. Costs fell from an average of £900 for the 'Addison' Act schemes to £400 in 1924. Limited use was also made of subsidies to private builders under a supplementary 1919 Housing Act. Housing society construction virtually ceased, but under the 1923 Act the Howard Cottage Society completed Meadow Way Green and built 20 flats between Broadwater Avenue and Spring Road, the latter designed by John Tickle, a Parker and Unwin 'graduate'. By the end of 1924, 755 local authority houses had been constructed which, added to the R.D.C. housing stock of 110, gave a total of 865 or 28 per cent of the 3,064 Letchworth total. Cottage society housing accounted for 1,086 houses, or 35 per cent of the stock. It is not known what proportion of the 1,113 privately built homes were owner-occupied. In 1929-31 the Wilbury housing scheme, designed by Cecil Hignett, was built between Bedford Road and Icknield Way. The simplified designs reflected the paring down of subsidies, but the layout retained a Garden City character. The Howard Cottage Society, too, resumed construction in the 1930s, with several hundred two- and three-bedroomed cottages, and a group of elderly persons' bungalows.

Highways, Open Space and Public Health   The U.D.C. began to take over the Company's highways. F.G.C. Ltd. had allowed space for widening, and the increase in traffic made this necessary in Station Road, Works Road, Gernon Road, Commerce Avenue and Eastcheap.

96 Letchworth U.D.C. housing, Pixmore Way, 1919-21. Designed by Courtenay Crickmer, this scheme made a fine approach to the town centre.

97 Broadway, the cinder path, *c.*1923. The double lime avenue has already been planted and the road was made up shortly after this evocative photograph was taken.

Only 1¼ miles of road had been constructed during the First World War, but almost five were completed between 1919-24,[18] bringing the total to 18, rising to 26 in 1940. It was agreed that the Company would build to the Council's specification, following which the roads would be adopted and maintained at public expense. The variety of highway treatment and planting was continued, which matured into the verdure of the Garden City. Perhaps the most symbolic act was the making up of Broadway between Sollershott Circus and Town Square in 1924. The central section had remained a cinder path for bicycles and pedestrians through the war. The 100ft. reservation allowed a 24ft. carriageway, with 21ft. greenswards, 6ft. footways, and 9ft. 6in. margins. Double avenues of lime trees provided a tangible indication that Letchworth was at last acquiring a centre, after years of peripheral and lopsided development.

98 Howard Park Gardens, the paddling pool, *c*.1933. Always a popular spot for young children, photographs of the paddling pool were widely used for Garden City publicity.

Open spaces passed from Company to Council. F.G.C. Ltd. had acquired the manorial rights of the 70-acre (28.3 ha.) Norton Common, and created a furore in 1909 by posting notices 'Temporary footpaths: Sufferance only'.[19] Howard was amongst the protesters and suggested that the land be formally declared public open space. In January 1922, the Company reiterated that the Common was private property, but allowed residents to enjoy the amenities provided no damage occurred. They reserved the right to withdraw the concession at any time, however. The Council was perturbed and in June 1923 acquired a long lease for 60 acres, but the Company retained the margins for potential building sites. At this time Barry Parker prepared a plan which included boating lakes. The axial avenue was planted in accord with the original layout plan, and tennis courts, bowling greens and, in 1935, a new open-air swimming pool were provided. The U.D.C. had acquired Howard Park in 1934, and had taken over the area south of Hillshott, including the old swimming pool – now the Ball Memorial Gardens – in 1919. A bowling green and an ex-servicemen's club were established.

The 'official' definition of a Garden City included a claim that it was 'a town designed for healthy living'.[20] Infant mortality and death rates had long been accepted as a measure of the health of the population as a whole. At the time of purchase of the Letchworth Estate, the Hertfordshire County Medical Officer of Health, Dr. F. E. Fremantle, had advised the Company of the healthiness of the surrounding area. In 1912 the infant mortality rate was claimed as half that of the large industrial towns.[21] In 1912 there was an overall death rate of 95 for every 1,000 births of children dying in their first year, the lowest on record, but the Letchworth rate was 50.6 per thousand. Fremantle also claimed that the health of children had greatly improved after their arrival in Letchworth, borne out to some extent in a survey undertaken in 1919 comparing the health of groups of children in Hitchin and Letchworth. The death rate per 1,000 population also showed a significant improvement over that for England and Wales, 8.0 as compared to 13.0, with a figure of 14.1 for 95 large industrial towns including London. The national death rate was declining due to improvements in public health, and the situation in Letchworth may not have been as favourable as was claimed. In 1925, Purdom, who had enthusiastically quoted the 1912 figures in *The Garden City*, conceded that the earlier data were not sufficiently reliable. Later figures indicated a fluctuation of death rates of 5.5 per 1,000 population in 1919, rising to 8.4 in 1922 then falling to 7.4 two years later, and infant mortality rates per 1,000 births of 90 in 1919, reducing to 34.93 in 1922 and rising to 47.8 in 1924. The small population and post-war influenza epidemic accounted for the fluctuations. Purdom claimed that on the whole the high reputation for public health in Letchworth was justified. The water supply and sewage disposal facilities were comparatively new and, together with the open layout of the housing which encouraged circulation of air, assisted public health and the promotion of the benefits of 'the health of the country with the comforts of the town'.

Letchworth and Statutory Planning   Letchworth was the creation of a private landlord laying out his land as he wished. The Parker and Unwin plan was no more than a statement of intent and its land-use allocations had no statutory backing. The fundamental principle of a limited 'Town Area' within a larger agricultural belt preserved against building was entirely voluntary, and depended upon the good faith of the Company. An indication that commercialism sometimes attained primacy was given by their attitude to Norton Common. Statutory town planning made a modest beginning in 1909 when urban and borough councils were empowered to prepare schemes for land where development appeared imminent.[22] The 1919 Housing Act introduced the additional provision that any urban district or borough with a population greater than 20,000 after 1 January 1923 would be required to prepare a scheme within three years. With its 1921 population of 10,000, Letchworth U.D.C. fell outside the scope of compulsion, although co-operation with the Company over an agreed scheme based upon its master plan would have been possible, particularly given Parker's consultancy role. However, the Council did not address itself to town-planning resolutions or acquire 'interim development control' powers under the 1925 and 1932 Planning Acts. The Company made significant adjustments to the master plan, particularly in the Bedford Road area, and south of Baldock Road during the 1920s, and added almost 200 acres to the original 'town area', without any expression of concern by the Council. Statements by Sir Edgar Bonham Carter, F.G.C. Chairman, emphasised the junior position of the Council:

> The planning of the town has been carried out by F.G.C. Ltd. by means of its powers as sole owner of the estate and not by the local authority under the powers of the town planning Acts. The U.D.C. has, however, a voice in the town plan. To ensure this, the Company has deposited with the Council a 'layout' plan of the town, together with an explanatory memorandum defining user, character of building and density etc. and has agreed not to depart from the provisions of the plan without first consulting the Council.[23]

William Robert Davidge (1879-1961), an eminent planning consultant who had prepared the first advisory Hertfordshire County Plan in 1927, was retained by Letchworth U.D.C. in 1938. He recommended that the Council now consider its own scheme. Building control was largely in the hands of the Company. Unwin's bye-laws had been progressive for their date, but the 1936 Public Health Act had introduced the compulsion for every district authority to adopt model bye-laws for streets and buildings. The deposit of building plans with the Hitchin R.D.C. and Letchworth U.D.C. had been little more than a formality. It was not until after the Second World War, however, that Letchworth U.D.C. took a more positive role in statutory town planning and building control, as will be described in Chapter Thirteen.

Ten

A Living from the Land

Co-operative Cultivation   One of Howard's principal objectives was to stem the tide of rural depopulation by building up a strong rural economy. The 1890s witnessed rural stagnation and an increasing flow of labour to the Colonies, particularly Canada, Australia and New Zealand. This stimulated trade in food, which further depressed British agriculture. The wide choice of estates available to the Garden City Pioneer Company reflected this. Following his own inauspicious experience of farming in Nebraska, Howard saw the opportunity for a wide range of agricultural activities in the Garden City, 'in large farms, smallholdings, allotments, cow pastures etc; the natural competition of these various methods of agriculture tested by the willingness of occupiers to offer the highest rent to the municipality, tending to bring about the best system of husbandry'.[1] Furthermore, the existence of the developing town area would bring a ready market of 30,000 residents into being, without the disadvantage of high transportation costs. Howard's theory of substitution of higher value cash crops including fruit and vegetables for basic staples such as wheat matched the work of the economic geographer, von Thünen, who envisaged intersection of varied angled concentric demand cones indicating a tendency to grow more lucrative crops on the fringes of a settlement. Howard calculated that a community of 30,000, consuming only one third of a pint of milk a day, would account for 1,250 gallons each day, which would save the farmers £1,900 each year on railway charges. This would encourage higher rental, without increasing the price to the consumer.[2]

The Garden City Pioneer Company announced the intention of 'the provision of a broad belt of agricultural land round the town under such restrictive covenants as may secure to the inhabitants the enjoyment for all time of the combined advantages of town and country life, while the agricultural tenants may have a market for their produce brought to their doors'. How did it all work out in practice?

The Letchworth Estate and its Farms   In contrast to the detailed investigation of the suitability of the Letchworth site for industry, comparatively little seems to have been done to assess its potential for agricultural diversity.[3] Almost all of the 3,820 acres (1,546 ha.) purchased in 1903 was in agricultural use – nine farms of between 252 (102 ha.) and 842 acres (340 ha.), four smallholdings from two (0.809 ha.) to 79 acres (32 ha.), and 15 allotments on five acres. Rents were low, ranging from 8s. 6d. to £1 10s. 0d. per acre for the farms, and 16s. 0d. to £2 3s. 0d. for the smallholdings. The modest rent roll of £3,172 19s. 0d. for the whole estate averaged 16s. 8d. (83p) per acre per annum. Given this 1.6 per cent return, it is scarcely surprising that the £40 15s. 0d. average per acre purchase price had been criticised as being unduly high. The farms were neglected and poorly cultivated, with buildings in disrepair. The average weekly wage for a farm labourer was 15s. 0d. (75p), and many of the 400 inhabitants were employed elsewhere. The situation represented a classic case of rural deprivation which the Garden City movement aimed to alleviate.

The under capitalisation of First Garden City Ltd. affected the agricultural strategy as profoundly as the development of the 'town area'. However, there was no overall master plan as in the case of the latter. Even Howard had referred to his 'absence of plan' for agriculture almost as an advantage, and at Letchworth matters proceeded on an *ad hoc* basis. On completion of purchase all existing tenants were given notice to quit, and new tenancies were negotiated under which they agreed to give up possession of one tenth of their holdings in

99 Harvest Home, 1914, thresher driven by steam traction engine. The fields along what would become the central section of Broadway produced abundant crops during the First World War.

any one year, subject to compensation. The two tenants of the major part of the town area were co-operative, although the area did not come fully under company control until 1910, when it was laid to grass or farmed directly. The tenancies were rearranged, larger farms divided into holdings related to the existing homesteads, the buildings were repaired and an attempt was made to obtain more economic rents. Thomas Adams attempted to formulate a coherent farm strategy. His upbringing on a lowland Scottish farm and his experience on a 48-acre smallholding stimulated his political interest in the 'Land question'. He arranged a conference on 'Garden City in relation to agriculture' on 10 September 1904,[4] hosted by the Company, which, however, took little direct interest in it. The attraction of H. Rider Haggard (1856-1925), novelist and leader of the 'back to the land' campaign, reflected Adams's flair for publicity. Other leaders of the rural lobby attended – Constance Cochrane of the Rural Housing and Sanitation Association, J. Nugent Harris, Secretary of the Agricultural Organisation Society, and Alderman Richard Winfrey, Chairman of the South Lincolnshire Smallholdings Association. The conference presented a coherent argument for 'back to the land', based on the promotion of smallholdings.

'Back to the Land' At the conference Adams outlined his ideas for the agricultural belt. He visualised 'a just and equitable system of tenure … giving the labourer a potential interest in the land'.[5] He urged the Company to create 200 smallholdings of five acres (2 ha.) each and ample allotments for factory workers, in addition to the generous garden spaces enjoyed by each house. Local farm credit banks and co-operatives would provide capital and develop marketing skills. Cottage industries allied to agriculture would employ wives. The example of Belgium, where this system had successfully combined agricultural and industrial labour, was no doubt familiar to him. There were also to be 10 large farms of 150 acres each, with the Company providing a lead by establishing a demonstration farm, technical institute, tree nursery and research centre. The total outlay of about £10,000 was double what the Company had initially invested in maintaining the existing farming pattern. Adams went so far as to state that

> the Garden City Company will set aside a large part of its estate for smallholdings, and will secure the provision of the necessary co-operative and other facilities for making these successful. In this way it will provide an object lesson of immense value to the country.[6]

100 Garden City Agricultural Conference, 1904. H. Rider Haggard sits in the centre, with Howard and Thomas Adams immediately to his left. Near the back, on the left of the picture, are Barry Parker and Raymond Unwin.

The Company did little to put these new ideas into practice. Purdom squarely blamed the lack of capital.[6] Publicity about smallholdings had brought hundreds of applicants for land, but most lacked the capital to build their own homes. Those who could build were offered 99-year leases on ¼-acre cottage plots, with a contiguous area of agricultural land on a 21-year tenancy. In 1905 a 152-acre (61.5 ha.) smallholdings centre was established at Norton Hall Farm under the direction of E. O. Fordham, Lord Lucas, Alderman Richard Winfrey and C. R. Buxton. The Norton Cooperative Smallholdings Society paid the Company 25s. 0d. an acre and sub-let parcels up to 20 acres (8 ha.) at 35s. 0d. Twelve cottages were built in Norton village, pig sties were constructed and 10 acres planted with fruit. The experiment was not successful, neither was a bank and a smallholdings and allotments society. After Adams's replacement by Walter Gaunt, agriculture was accorded very low priority. Even Howard became irritable over Adams's continued championing of the cause in *The Garden City*. Nevertheless, in 1907, an attempt was made to include model smallholdings in the 1907 Cottage Exhibition. The guide to the Exhibition, *Where Shall I Live?*, boldly stated that the official policy was to encourage smallholdings and that 420 acres of land had already been let, to 42 tenants, giving an average holding of 10 acres.[7] Raymond Unwin prepared a grouped layout, involving a cluster of cottages fronting wedge-shaped holdings, off a lane, south of Baldock Road. This was abandoned for a more conventional layout, with the smallholding cottages widely spaced, mostly along Baldock Road. Some of the entrants were familiar from the 1905 Exhibition, Gilbert Fraser and the Concrete Machinery Co., A. H. Clough of Ringwood, and several were built by Picton and Hope. None of the smallholdings was successful in the long term, and in the 1930s the land was infilled with ribbon development. Adams's vision of 'a new race of sturdy English Yeomen … to form the bulwarks of our Empire'[8] faded, to be replaced by Howard's resignation to expediency: 'The right development of the rural area may be far more safely left with a little timely help here and there to adjust itself to new demands as they rise'. Any remaining enthusiasm for smallholdings was dampened by soil conditions. Contrary to expectation, raised by successful market gardening a few miles north in Bedfordshire, the Letchworth estate consisted largely of clay or chalk, and crops were both late and sparse.

A Small Country Living   A few hardy pioneers did overcome the difficulties, W. G. 'Bill' Furmston has already been mentioned as the genial 'Mine Host' of *The Skittles*.[9] In the early

1900s, he was a skilled craftsman and pattern maker at Doultons, the London-based sanitary engineers. Married, living in rooms with a growing family, ultimately 11 children, Furmston considered emigration to New Zealand. He learned of the Garden City project through the editor of *The Clarion*. At Whit weekend 1904 he joined a party of 200 from Ruskin College on a special excursion. Raymond Unwin met the party on the wooden plank platform and explained the scheme. He introduced C. B. Purdom, F. J. Cole, the estate forester, and the Rev. J. Bruce Wallace. They toured the estate from Willbury Camp to Norton, to Willian and Letchworth Corner, returning to the station along Spring Road. The Furmstons leased No.6 'Alpha Cottages', and convinced two of their fellow lodgers at St Pancras, Miss Revill and Miss Priestley, to follow suit – Miss Revill was in fact the first official resident of the Garden City.

The Furmstons leased a plot on Baldock Road, to build 'Pine Cottage' for £300, on a loan raised from the Co-operative Building Society. They rented 2¼ acres (0.91 ha.) on a 21-year lease, originally on behalf of a friend who failed to take it on. Bill initially commuted to London, often lodging with his mother during the week. He hired an agricultural labourer for 7d. an hour, more than double the going rate, who dug the plot and planted 400 apple trees, 400 nut trees, plums and pears. The local farmers were sceptical, chaffing at the fancy prices of Furmston's rent and his expensive hired help. His London colleagues called him 'barmy leaving a place where you have been 20 years and going down to a God-forsaken place like that'. He worked the holding less than one day a week, and sub-contracted his labourer, and estimated that he grew enough food for 40 people. Over a 25-year period he calculated that £3,000 had been spent in wages, £1,000 on seeds, plants and bushes; manure and fertilizer; greenhouse, bees, ducks and fowl; and ground rent. His family of eight lived off the produce and 'even in years when the accounts showed a money loss there was a net gain in terms of life'. There was never any large profit, merely an attempt to balance the outgoings. In 1941, the wages bill was £156, other outgoings £34, receipts £178, a loss of £12. Nevertheless he had been able to show to his own satisfaction, 'How to bring up a family of eight children, and keep a bit of Old England cultivated as it should be'.

The Furmstons were not an isolated case. Amongst Benoit-Lévy's neighbours on Wilbury Road, a Mr. Jones rented a five-acre (2 ha.) plot, at £30 per annum for his cottage plot, and £5 per annum for the remainder in the rural zone.[10] A saddler by trade, living near Epping, Jones had read Howard's book, and had brought his family, with five children ranging from 2-16 years, to Letchworth. He had built his home at a cost of £370. The produce supported his family, and provided a margin for sale. He was considering dairy farming, but did not have sufficient capital to purchase four cows. Jones had been a founder of Garden City Smallholdings. He employed two men at £1 each per week, higher than the prevailing average. He found the land too exposed for early vegetables and fruit. Early strawberries sold at 7½d. per pound, but those from Letchworth came later when the price had dropped to 2d. Potatoes were, however, an excellent money spinner, particularly if they could be saved until Christmas. He considered it would be preferable to divide the estate partly into 20-hectare farms for cereals and dairy produce, and the remainder into smallholdings for orchards, a division which suggested familiarity with Adams's plans.

A Horticultural Cornucopia   The provision of generous gardens enabled the produce to make a worthwhile contribution to the family budget.[11] Garden sizes for small cottages, and later for Council houses, varied from two to 10 poles (61 sq. yards ⅟₈₀ acre to 302.5 sq. yards – ⅟₁₆ acre). Many tenants allocated a third to grass, a third to flowers, and the remainder to vegetables. Almost all had fruit – there were about 3,500 apple, pear and plum trees. Above this, there was a demand for allotments – in 1925 there were 38 acres, giving 230 plots and, after 1945, 606 plots, by which time there were 500 members of the Allotment Cottage Garden Association.

The amount and variety of crops was remarkable. A ten-pole garden or allotment produced two dozen spring cabbages, 10 lb. broad beans, 8 lb. French beans, 20 lb. runner beans, 8 lb. carrots, 10 lb. peas, two dozen lettuces, 10 lb. Brussels sprouts, 10 lb. cauliflowers, 10 lb.

parsnips, 10 lb. beetroot, and 20 lb. onions, total 156 lb. By concentrating on a more limited range it produced three cwt. (336 lb.) potatoes, 28 lb. tomatoes, 14 lb. carrots, 14 lb. parsnips, 10 lb. turnips, 20 lb. beetroot, and 56 lb. onions, total 478 lb. Wartime restrictions, particularly the 1939-45 'Dig for Victory' Campaign, stimulated production. In 1953, an attempt was made to estimate the total volume and value of garden produce. Writing in the Jubilee Issue of *Town and Country Planning*, H. Brewer stated that there were 6,000 gardens in Letchworth. Basing his estimate on a ¼-acre (¹⁄₁₀ ha.) garden, the following produce had been grown:

> 40 lb. rhubarb 13s. 4d., eight dozen lettuces £1 12s. 0d., 16 lb. gooseberries 10s. 8d., 15 lb. redcurrants 15s. 0d., 16 lb. raspberries £1 0s. 0d., 24 lb. peas 12s. 0d., two cwt. [224 lb.] onions £3 14s. 8d., 14 lb. parsnips 4s. 8d., 7 lb. turnips 2s. 8d., two cwt. [224 lb.] apples £5 12s. 0d., 8 lb. blackcurrants 10s. 0d., 5 lb. golden plums 2s. 6d., 20 lb. Victoria plums 10s. 0d. Total 623 lb.: £15 19s. 6d.

A ten-pole (0.025 ha.) garden had produced 397 lb., worth £6 12s. 8d. Estimating an average of one third of that figure for each of the 6,000 gardens, Brewer speculated that these could produce 794,000 lb. of food with a value of £13,200. Nobody queried this and, however wide of the mark his figures may have been, there was no doubt that, particularly during and after the Second World War, many families were self sufficient for fruit and vegetables. In addition to this he recorded 32 bee keepers owning 117 hives, each contributing 30 lb. to the food pool, and more than 1,000 poultry keepers, with an average stock of six birds, each yielding 160 eggs per bird per year, in addition to a good supply of meat. Added to this 160 greenhouses might produce 120 cucumbers and 160 lb. of tomatoes each season. A veritable horticultural cornucopia!

Mixed Farming In contrast to the increasing productivity of domestic gardens, farming remained relatively static, reflecting national conditions, rather than, as had been hoped, a response to the stimulus of a ready market. Although there was some stimulus to production during the First World War, when undeveloped fields either side of Broadway were turned over to wheat, the post-war depression reached its nadir during the early 1930s. Purdom quoted rentals of 25s. 0d. to 60s. 0d. per acre in 1925, high figures which were not borne out by a report commissioned by the Company in April 1928, when they had become seriously concerned about the return from the agricultural belt.[12] Conversion to dairy farming was seen as the salvation of agricultural enterprise, through which one farmer would be able to handle more extensive holdings, enabling rationalisation into fewer, larger units. On the north, Norton Grange, Wilbury and possibly Standalone Farms would be dispensed with; on the south, Lower Farm, New Farm Baldock, Letchworth Hall and Lordship Farm, particularly if the town area was extended southwards, which eventually came to pass in the 1960s and 1970s.

Rental levels in the late 1920s were low, but it was suggested by the land agents, Hardings of St Albans, that 16s. 0d. per acre north of the railway and 21s. 0d. per acre to the south was all that was justified by conditions, a substantial reduction and more than contemplated. The Company proposed new agreements on the basis of 22s. 6d. and 25s. 0d. respectively, which the farmers queried. The rental levels had, at best, remained relatively static since 1903, when the overall average had been 16s. 8d. per acre. It was to take a more extensive changeover to dairy farming, which entailed substantial expenditure of £52,614 on cowsheds and milking parlours, and another World War, before farming became more than barely viable, and then with the assistance of government subsidies.

Agricultural Industries A variety of industries related to agriculture on the estate sprang up over the years. The Company did not establish its own research centre as recommended by Adams, but, in 1910, the Country Gentleman's Association moved to Letchworth. This was an organisation which advised landowners, and marketed and erected county cottages

101 The Co-op built its 'moderne' style creamery in 1935. Demolished in 1988, the 'Creamery Court' houses and flats now occupy its site.

and agricultural buildings. They issued a monthly magazine and annual handbook. Their publications contained early views of Letchworth and other Garden City style developments.[13] The concern leased two sites, one on Birds Hill, just west of the main industrial area, and the other on Icknield Way, to the west of Spring Road, which included extensive seed testing grounds. The propagation of cuttings was also carried out. Their chemical laboratory on Works Road was styled as a vernacular farmhouse, while on Icknield Way their handsome Tudor-style offices, reminiscent of a country house, were designed by Robert F. Johnston.

Dairies flourished early on due to the proximity of the market, even before widespread change-over to dairy farming was stimulated by the Company. Cole's Garden City Central Dairy was established in Station Road by 1907, and others operated from the farms themselves – Wilbury Farm, Letchworth Farm, Norton Grange Farm and Pixmore Farm. Between the Wars, the Bancroft Dairies of Hitchin established a branch in Station Road, while T. Squire, of Leys Avenue, was well-known locally. In the mid-1930s the Cooperative Wholesale Society built their own dairy on the newly opened Letchworth Gate. A distinctive building resulted, its blocky form and 'moderne' style rather reminiscent of a progressive pithead bath. It was designed by a Barnsley architect, C. F. Moxon. Its tower formed a focal feature on the approach to Letchworth from the Great North Road. Operations ceased in the early 1980s, and the building was demolished in 1988.

The local production of livestock brought about the need for an abattoir. The Company resisted local butchers slaughtering on their premises, and in 1925 a model abattoir was built on Works Road, capable of handling 300 head of cattle, 400 sheep and 250 calves, and more than 3,000 pigs per week. Associated with the abattoir, a processing works produced fats, fertilizers, and dried blood. The Letchworth Bacon Company diversified from sausages and pies into food and scientific, and even medical, research, and in addition opened a bakery. Among local bakers, Nott's, Leys Avenue and subsequently Eastcheap soon became dominant, to be joined by the Co-operative Society in the inter-war period.

Eleven

Garden City Comes of Age

Howard's Final Years   Within a decade of the foundation of Letchworth, Howard began to press for a second Garden City.[1] In 1910 he had the idea of developing a Garden City in memory of King Edward VII. Influenced by the success of Hampstead Garden Suburb and the subsequent town planning legislation, the Garden City Association was renamed the Garden Cities and Town Planning Association, and re-wrote its objectives to include garden suburbs and garden villages. In March 1912, the G.C.T.P.A. honoured Howard with a dinner attended by the leading figures in the emergent town planning and housing movements. In 1914, he became an Honorary Member of the newly formed Town Planning Institute, whose first President was Thomas Adams. Although wartime plans for reconstruction were based on low density suburban housing, rather than self-contained Garden Cities, the 'young lions' of the G.C.T.P.A., 'New Townsmen', C. B. Purdom, F. J. Osborn, and W. G. Taylor wrote a pamphlet on *New Towns After The War*. This advocated 100 new settlements, a milestone in progress towards state developed new towns, finally implemented after 1945.

In October 1918, Howard confided to Purdom and Osborn that he had identified the site for his second Garden City:[2] gently rolling countryside south of Digswell Viaduct on the Great Northern Railway, running through Hertfordshire from King's Cross to the North. Fourteen miles nearer to London than Letchworth, it seemed an ideal location. The Desborough Estate put a large part of the site up for auction in May 1919. Howard successfully bid for 1,500 acres (607 ha.), and even convinced the estate agent, Norman Savill, to advance him the £250 balance of the deposit. Howard, Purdom and Osborn threw in their lot with the new project – named Welwyn Garden City to distinguish it from 'Old' Welwyn, the small coaching town on the Great North Road a mile or two to the west. The settlement in 'the heights of Hertfordshire' was designated 'the First Satellite Town', in recognition of its closer proximity to London. The flotation of Second Garden City Ltd. to develop the town followed, and the preparation of an initial master plan by Crickmer, and the 'definitive' version by Louis de Soissons (1891-1962). A further parallel was a housing exhibition, the Daily Mail Ideal Home Model Village, held 1921-2. Friendly rivalry characterised relations between the two Garden Cities, but several influential pioneers, including Howard, moved to the new settlement, to a degree sapping the vitality of Letchworth.

Howard received international honours. In 1913 he was elected President of the newly formed International Garden Cities and Town Planning Federation, an internationalist body, which in the 1920s held influential conferences in Europe and the U.S.A., beginning in 1919 in war-torn Belgium. In 1925, in New York, Howard suddenly announced his intention to persuade Henry Ford to build Garden Cities. 'I'll take a taxi to Grand Central Station: there is bound to be a train to Detroit in an hour or two', was his parting comment.[3] He succeeded in meeting Ford, though with no very positive outcome. *Garden Cities of Tomorrow* was published in all major European languages.[4] The Russian translation by Aleksandr Block, published in 1911, was widely used after the 1917 Revolution, while Block, ironically, spent his exile in Welwyn Garden City.

In 1926 H.R.H. Duke of York (later George VI) was noticeably impressed by the Letchworth achievement during his Civic Week visit. In the New Year Honours for 1927, Howard received a knighthood. Not before time: according to Shaw, he had merited a Barony for the book, an earldom for Letchworth and a dukedom for Welwyn! The Minister of Health, Neville Chamberlain, visited Letchworth with Howard, and toasted his achievement in non-alcoholic wine. Time was running out, however. Howard worked on his shorthand

102 'British Tab', begun in 1920, designed by Cecil Hignett, soon developed into an enormous complex, on the north side of Icknield Way.

typewriter, the 'phonoplayer', and wrote cryptic notes for '3rd GC',[5] which would be funded by the success of his invention. In March 1928 a chest infection and stomach cancer were diagnosed. His second marriage, to Edith Annie Hayward, had not been happy. During his last illness, friends were concerned to find him lying in a neglected state on a sofa. A comfortable bed was found, and straw was laid in the road outside to muffle the sound of passing traffic. He died on 1 May. Four days later his funeral service was held at the Free Church Letchworth, and he was laid to rest in the town cemetery. The procession was filmed, and edited into views of Garden City life, Howard's lasting monument.[6] Shaw cautioned the family about expecting a fortune from the typewriter, adding that Howard was 'one of those heroic simpletons who do big things whilst our prominent worldlings are explaining why they are Utopian and impossible. And of course it is they who will make money out his work'.[7] In May 1930 a Memorial Stone was unveiled in Howard Park Letchworth. A plain brick wall in Howardsgate, Welwyn Garden City, represented his Memorial there until replaced with a handsome bronze relief plaque many years later. The G.C.T.P.A. introduced an Ebenezer Howard Memorial Medal in his memory, to be awarded for outstanding planning achievements. Appropriately both Unwin and Parker were among early recipients.

Moving into profitability   The First World War disrupted dividend payments by F.G.C. Ltd.[8] In order to meet essential development costs, the Company had, in 1915, created £50,000 second debentures, with 4½ per cent interest, as a second floating charge on the assets. In 1916 they issued 10,000 of the £5 unissued Ordinary shares as Preference shares bearing a fixed cumulative dividend of 5 per cent. In May 1920 an issue of 50,000 7 per cent gas works mortgage debenture stock was launched, to be repaid in 1925. Mortgages on the original 1903 land purchase totalled £83,934 at 4 per cent, repayable with other loans from the late 1920s. The availability of loans influenced the pace of development, while the complexity of voting powers attached to the restructured shares was to become crucial during the 1950s takeover struggles. Dividend payments were resumed: 2 per cent in 1918-21, 4 per cent in 1922, and the maximum 5 per cent in 1923, maintained thereafter. In 1923 the total capital stood at £549,141: £194,649 in Ordinary Shares, £25,160 in Preference Shares, and £329,332 from mortgages and loans. It was not until 1937, however, that clearance of dividend arrears began, and was not completed until 1946.

The financial situation of the Company drew conflicting conclusions. In 1922, C. B. Purdom again argued that development expenditure brought a greater return than reflected immediately by revenue, and its allocation to the revenue account depressed real profitability. The public utility subsidiaries had assisted overall viability, notwithstanding a miners' strike and post-war depression. Purdom disagreed with the Board's view that their disposal would enable them to concentrate upon development of the town. He laid great stress on the creation of subsidiaries at Welwyn until he was ousted in an acrimonious power struggle in 1928. The U.D.C. also pondered over the apparently poor performance of F.G.C. Ltd., which contrasted with the continued growth of the town, and their own investment in housing construction. The Council felt that the town should be transferred to them, as corporate representative of residents' interests. A Committee examined the matter, but could find no financial basis for the transfer and the matter was shelved.[9]

103 'Sir Gadabout and the Lacre Monster', cartoon by Fitzwater-Wray, c.1923. Shortly after the cartoon was drawn two key staff left Lacre to found the rival street cleansing firm, Shelvoke and Drewry.

Industrial diversity After the Great War, the ambitious Council housing schemes and the reconstruction of the sewage works helped to relieve local unemployment, but economic vitality was dependent upon regeneration of the industrial base. By 1926 this had largely been accomplished: there were 52 factories, compared with 26 in 1913. Spirella, Phoenix Motors, Heatly-Gresham and Ewarts had all extended their works post-1919, and new firms commenced operation, including several which remained key employers for 50 years. Letchworth escaped lightly from the economic slump of 1929-33. The diverse pattern of its industrial estate was examined by government – the Greater London Regional Planning Committee in 1928, and the Marley Committee on Garden Cities and Satellite Towns in 1932.

Inter-war industries continued the trend towards products with a high value to weight ratio, and a significant input of skill. The British Tabulating Machine Co. Ltd. had begun operations in Lambeth, south London in 1907. They acquired a large plot on Icknield Way in 1920, and Cecil Hignett designed their factory, partly completed the following year. The 'Tab' were leaders in the office revolution.[10] Their Hollerith machines used punched cards to record information on transactions, or census data statistics, which could be electrically sorted and classified. Employment peaked at almost 4,000. The Lacre Motor Company had gone into voluntary liquidation in 1913, following its notorious industrial dispute, but kept operational through war work. In 1919 they pioneered a mechanical road sweeper, a fearsome contraption with revolving brush beneath the driver's cab. It vanquished 'Sir Gadabout' in the cartoon-saga of 1923, but the firm left Letchworth in 1926. Two of their key staff had defected in 1922 to found Shelvoke and Drewry, a firm whose product was also related to public cleansing. Their transverse engined, tiller steered 'freighter' had semi-automatic transmission, and could carry two tons of refuse. By 1930 they had been supplied to 350 councils and exported throughout Europe and the British Empire.[11]

Phoenix Motors had undertaken government work during the war. In 1921, Joseph van Hooydonk introduced a three-litre car, retailing at over £500, followed by a 12-25 model in 1925. He confidently asserted that his only problem was to obtain land for expansion of his Pixmore Avenue factory.[12] However, the cars neither challenged quality marques such as

Daimler or Rolls Royce, nor were they competitive in the emergent mass market with Austin, Ford, Morris or Standard. Production ceased in 1928, and the factory was taken over by the Ascot Motor Company, manufacturers of motorcycles and small cars. They, too, failed and a creditors' meeting was called at the factory on 10 December 1929, while the employees milled about outside. The premises reopened as one of the first government training centres the following year. Chater-Lea was founded in London in 1890. In 1928 they moved to Icknield Way, and concentrated upon motorcycle manufacture. They supplied Automobile Association 'Scouts' until 1935, when manufacture of motorcycles ceased, although the firm continued to produce components. The Westinghouse Morse Chain Company located in Works Road in 1920 and expanded into Pixmore Avenue three years later. Their rocker joint chain drive was widely used in electric and internal combustion engines, steam and water turbines or manufacturing machinery. Allied to gear changing, the chain drive formed the basis of automatic transmission, and the firm was absorbed by Borg Warner after the Second World War.

The immediate post-war slump of 1921 sapped the viability of the K. & L. Foundry, and the 1926 General Strike caused cancellation of many of its contracts. Following voluntary liquidation, K. & L. Steel Founders and Engineers Ltd was reconstituted in 1928 within the Cohen 600 Group. By 1930, it was claimed as the best equipped steel foundry in Britain, making carbon steel castings up to eight tons for hydraulic cylinders, valves, turbine casings, cars, locomotives and wagons, bridges and cranes.[13] In 1938, its associates Jones Cranes pioneered the manufacture of a diesel driven mechanical mobile crane.

In 1930 the employment profile of the town was as follows:[14]

Engineering	1,300
Construction of vehicles	700
Body Building: Prams	280
Furniture	170
Metal Trades	400
Instrument manufacture	120
Printing and Bookbinding	550
Silk and Embroidery	120
Figure Training and other Garments	1,050
Building	600
Constructional work, Contractors etc.	140
Transport	50
Gas, Water and Electricity	140
Local Government	80
Distributive Trades, Shops, etc.	700
Other Industries, including Restaurants, Laundries, Box-making, Parachutes, etc.	500
TOTAL	6,900

Improved Communications   Between the wars, Letchworth became part of the North Hertfordshire sub-regional grouping, with Hitchin and Baldock. Improved roads brought connections with Luton, Bedford, Royston and the villages in between. In 1920 Road Motors Limited introduced six daily buses to Luton, and the National Bus Company improved internal routes. London Country Green Line buses established long-distance links with London. Cooper Blomfield owned the earliest charabancs in Letchworth, and ran day trips to Southend and Clacton, and works outings. Faced with competition the railway, from 1923 the London and North Eastern Railway (L.N.E.R.), smartened itself up. In the 1930s, new 'buffet trains' were introduced, calling at Letchworth en route to and from King's Cross to Cambridge. The fastest completed the 34-mile journey from Letchworth to King's Cross in 43 minutes, and there were 60 'up' and 'down' trains every weekday. The new rolling stock included a cocktail bar with Bauhaus-influenced tubular chrome and black leather seating.

To improve internal communication across the railway a permanent bridge was constructed to link Spirella with Station Place. Regrettably it was not the fanciful fortified bridge shown in Unwin's *Town Planning In Practice*, but a more functional triple-arched structure, designed by Barry Parker. Named in memory of Sir Ralph Neville, it was opened in May 1930 by Herbert Morrison, returning to Letchworth as Minister of Transport in Ramsay MacDonald's Labour Government. In 1927, the north-western sector of the town was replanned by Barry Parker, with Bedford Road thrust purposefully towards the junction of Wilbury Road and Stotfold Road, providing a convenient link with Bedfordshire via the Arlesey New Road. Parker had become interested in highway design both from a functional and amenity viewpoint, during his 1925 visit to the U.S.A. In 1929, his inaugural address as T.P.I. President, given in Letchworth, included slides of the landscaped parkways of Westchester County, New York.[15] He had included parkways in his master plan for Wythenshawe, the Manchester satellite. At Letchworth, links with the Great North Road, newly designated as the A1 trunk road, were poor. The 1927 *Hertfordshire Regional Planning Report* prepared by W. R. Davidge continued to recommend the diversionary route from Graveley to Willian, along Willian Way and Norton Way, rejoin-

104 The L.N.E.R. buffet trains, *c.*1935. The modernity of the interior of the buffet car, with its smart cocktail bar, was offset by the welcome reassurance of the old fashioned L.N.E.R. engine.

ing the historic Great North Road at Radwell. Whilst this by-passed Baldock, the Letchworth residential roads were hardly suitable for heavy long distance traffic. In 1931 a different solution emerged, with the construction of a gently curving landscaped road from north of Jacks Hill on the Great North Road to the Baldock Road/Pixmore Way junction, on the fringe of Letchworth. Constructed by the County Council, with a Government grant and a contribution from the Company, and opened in 1933, Letchworth Gate was designed by Barry Parker with landscaped reservations either side of the 30-foot, three-lane carriageway. Allied to extensive improvement further south, including the Welwyn and Barnet by-passes, this gave a fast connection to West End London. Keen motorists, such as Parker's daughter-in-law Barbara, were able to rival the best train times!

The Dawn of Consumerism The 1920s witnessed a rise in disposable incomes in south-east England, and demand for consumer goods and services was maintained even through the 1929-33 slump. There were 162 commercial concerns in 1925, reflecting Letchworth's expanding role as a regional shopping centre. Fifty new shops were opened between 1924-6 alone.[16] The most comprehensive development filled in the area between Station Road and Leys Avenue. Bennett and Bidwell designed the Georgian-style buildings. With the London Joint City and Midland Bank at the apex, the parades of shops stretched away either side, terminating in the entrances to an arcade framed by giant triumphal arches. Visually, the arcade interior was plain, although the octagonal centrepiece and roof light were effective.

105 The freedom of the road. A venerable taxicab poses kerbside on Letchworth Gate, the 'parkway' link to the A1, Great North Road.

Eastcheap became a major commercial street in the 1920s, when the 'Icknield Halls' were built, designed by Bennett and Bidwell in a free Queen Anne style. On the opposite side, the Co-operative Society extended in a Tudor style, designed by Leonard Gray Ekins (1877-1948) in 1921.

The local press broadcast availability of goods and services:[17] 'Advertising is the magnet' proclaimed *The Citizen* in June 1930, lending distinctly commercial overtones to Howard's concept of the irresistible force. In 1929 a free paper, *The Garden City Advertiser*, was delivered regularly to 3,600 households. It lasted ten years but was about half a century too early! Garden Citizens became increasingly fashion conscious in the '20s and '30s. In 1926 'Civic Week millinery' could be purchased from Ida in the Arcade. Parker Perry, Colonnade Buildings, had dresses for day, dinner and evening wear from 29s. 6d. (£1.49), but ladies had to journey to Hitchin for the latest lace-trimmed celanese cami-knickers, at 8s. 11d. (44p). In 1930 Lillian Reed, in the Arcade, boasted of 'Useful frocks for sports, business, home or outdoor wear. Delightful lingerie which will appeal to the woman of taste'. Spirella were omnipresent, and a 1935 advertisement commended the corsetière as 'the only intermediary between designer and client'. Permanent waves were available at the Metro Salon, Station Road, to complete a well-groomed appearance. Menswear advertising was lower in key. Peters Menswear in Eastcheap had boys' and men's flannel trousers from 8s. 11d.-21s. 0d. (44p-£1.05), and tennis flannels from 2s. 11d. (14½p). Tweed suits were available ready made at 39s. 11d. (£1.99½) from the Co-op, or made to measure from 50s. 0d. (£2.50) from Rawlinson's in Leys Avenue. Foster and Scott, in the Arcade, stocked the new 'Aquatite Raincoat'. Smokers' requisites were widely available from Fenner and Fenner or Sidney Thacker, both in Leys Avenue.

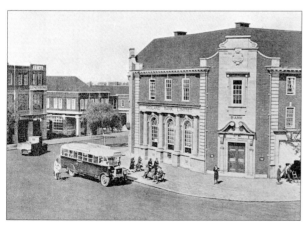

106 Station Place, early 1930s, with a Green Line coach outside the Midland Bank. The commercial centre appears remarkably traffic-free.

In 1935 the Co-op claimed patronage by two-fifths of Letchworth families for food and clothing. For the former there was severe

107 Everything for your convenience. Interior of the Co-op, *c.*1925.

competition from Moss's, and the International Stores. Price cutting of leading lines was already well established by 1930 when International offered canned peaches or apricots for 9½d. and 10½d., jellies at 3d., and blancmange powders at 1½d. and 4½d. – no doubt snapped up for Sunday tea. Fancy cakes and pastries were available at Nott's, who also offered ice cream sodas and sundaes at 6d. (2½p), and their home-made chocolates at 3s. 6d. (17½p) per pound. To cope with the effects of over eating, patent medicines were available from Russells' in Station Road or Boot's in Leys Avenue. Deliveries of the 'demon drink' were widespread; in 1935, G. B. Christie of Hitchin boasted of their supplies to Letchworth 'day in and day out' over many years. With a *frisson* of guilt, comparable with Americans visiting a 'speakeasy', Garden Citizens discreetly rang Hitchin 122 to place their orders, their hidden vices known to the telephone operator in those pre-dialling days.

Home ownership was widely canvassed. J. L. A. White developed Bedford Road in the early '30s and he offered a house for £50 deposit, legal costs of £25, and a £1 1s. 0d. (£1.05) weekly payment. Brookers fitted out the 'all electric' 'Civic House' in South View in 1926. A Revo electric cooker, daily running cost 4d. to cook for a family of four, was available for £15 15s. 5d. (£15.77) or a quarterly hire charge of 7s. 6d. (37½p) from the F.G.C. Electricity Showrooms. For lounging about in the garden, deckchairs cost 2s. 11d. (15p) from Underwoods in Leys Avenue. For home entertainment, the 'Phonos' portable gramophone, at five guineas (£5.25), was 'perfect for Summer outings, holidays, river trips and dancing'. Doubtless Charlestoning flappers annoyed their elders just as much as their 2000s counterparts with barely muted CD players. Hodgsons of Commerce Avenue offered Brown's wireless receivers, and by 1935 H.M.V. radiograms, from D. R. Stevens in Leys Avenue, were the ultimate domestic status symbol. Pianos were still popular, and relatively cheap with the elegant Gors and Kallmann overstrung baby grand at 42 guineas (£44 10s). Operatic, ballet, tap, limbering and ballroom dancing lessons were available from Diana Robinson in Nevells Road – she was no mean artist, either!

Motor cars were already being heavily promoted. In 1926, the best deal was the £165 four-seater Peugeot ('pronounce it pur-jo'), 50 m.p.h. and 60 m.p.g., and available from Exell Service Garage, Pixmore Avenue. 'Buy British and be proud of it!' proclaimed Mason's Garage, Eastcheap, established 1920. An 11.9hp Morris 'Bullnose' Cowley cost £190 and was perfect for 'carefree holidays'. Mason's also sold Humber cars and B.S.A., Rudge, Sunbeam

108 'The Effect of Matter on Mind': cartoon portrait of Barry Parker by Charles Crombie.

and Raleigh motorcycles. Their great rival, Bennett's Motor Works, opened in Station Road in 1919. Leslie Woodbridge Bennett (1894-1972) became a civic and business leader. He was a Ford main dealer and imported V8's from the USA, in addition to selling the home-built Dagenham product. Car ownership grew rapidly in Hertfordshire, faster than the national rate. In 1925 there were 14,417 motor vehicle licences issued in the County,[18] one motor vehicle for every 245 residents, which gave 562 for Letchworth. This figure rose sharply and in 1935 the U.D.C. provided the first off-street car park behind their new offices. Beyond lay the muddy patch, known as the Arena, and host to outdoor meetings and soapbox orators. Bicycles were popular, sold by Munt's, Eastcheap, where the Raleigh all-steel bicycle was available for £1 down and easy payments or £6 7s. 6d. cash (£6.37½).

Marmet prams sold widely in the 1920s, manufactured locally since 1913, with the prestige of supplying a scale miniature for Queen Mary's Dolls House in 1924. Photography had always been popular, and local pharmacists pressed the merits of the latest folding Kodaks to record Civic Week events. Locally-produced Kosmos paper was recommended for high quality prints. Among professional photographers, the Clutterbucks, with their home and studio facing the Common on Icknield Way, Brunts in Leys Avenue, and Julian and Violet Tayler at Howard Park Corner were the chief rivals. Cartoon portraits by Charles Crombie of Baldock Road were also popular, and published in the press and Civic Week Programmes.

Mass entertainment was dominated by the cinema. *The Rendezvous* opened in 1924 in the United Services Club building, but was always regarded as a ramshackle fleapit and closed in 1927. *The Picture Palace* was updated in 1924 when a new front, designed by Edgar Simmons as a triumphal arch, was added, together with a balcony to the auditorium.[19] Seats cost 4d. (2p), 8d. (4p), 1s. 2d. (6p), and 1s. 9d. (9p) for the best seats and private boxes. Charlie Chaplin's comedies were universally popular and *The Gold Rush* played to packed houses in June 1926, a welcome relaxation from Civic Week. The 'Palace Gem Orchestra' provided accompaniment. Somewhat delayed, the 'talkies' arrived on 31 March 1930, with the stentorian tones of Victor McLaglen in *King of the Khyber Rifles* booming out over the British Thomson-Houston reproducer. *Fox Movietone Follies, Applause, Mammy* with Al Jolson and *Innocents of Paris* – the debut of the elegant Maurice Chevalier – brought the delights of '100% – all talking – all singing – all dancing'

109 *The Broadway Cinema*, bathed in neon-light, advertises *Swing Time*, with Astaire and Rogers, *c.*1937.

110 The original Art Deco interior of *The Broadway*.

entertainment. A barrage of American accents counterbalanced the BBC's 'received pronunciation' and clipped vowels. By 1935, a second cinema was needed. Howard Hurst built *The Broadway* – despite its name located at the junction of Gernon Road and Eastcheap. Wilson Bidwell designed a mild Art Deco building, structurally adventurous, exploiting Hurst's enthusiasm for reinforced concrete. At night, coloured neon tubes outlined the building, and beckoned patrons towards an enchanted palace. The foyer and auditorium had striking Art Deco colour schemes by a specialist firm from the north-east. *The Broadway* was opened on Wednesday 26 August 1936 by Sir Arnold Wilson M.P.[20] He presciently declared that 'the cinema is going to stay, for it is one of the biggest influences on our lives ... I do not agree that the cinema is ruining our morals. I think it is improving them'. The black tie guests settled back for a gala screening of *Follow the Fleet* starring Fred Astaire and Ginger Rogers, which highlighted 'the wonderful acoustics of the building'.

The theatre was sporadically successful, but after the opening of the theatre at the St Christopher School (St Francis), in Broadway, there was in the late 1920s an attempt to establish a Letchworth Repertory theatre on a semi-professional basis. This was short-lived and folded in 1932. Amateur theatre flourished, however. The Letchworth Operatic Society was founded in 1921, and its first president was Barry Parker who was a skilled amateur singer. The Society was active until 1940, and concentrated on light operetta – their first production in 1923 was, appropriately, *The Arcadians*, and they also presented Gilbert and Sullivan. The Settlement Players were formed as a play-reading group in 1923 by Miss Pym, and concentrated upon Shaw, pre-1939 giving *Pygmalion*, *Major Barbara*, *Caesar and Cleopatra*, *St Joan* and *Arms and the Man*. A Drama Festival was held in 1937 with participation by the Operatic Society, Settlement Players and The Spirella Players. The following year the Y.P.F. Players were formed, out of which grew the successful St Paul's Amateur Dramatic Society (S.P.A.D.S.).

'Whit Week is Civic Week'   The official 'Coming of Age' of Letchworth was set for 17-22 May 1926, rather belated, for the estate had been opened in October 1903. An ambitious week-long programme focused on key aspects of civic and community life.[21] The main attraction was the first official Royal visit to Letchworth, by H.R.H. Duke of York (later King George VI). The General Strike in May put back the event until June. Fostering civic consciousness and community service had been a priority of the pioneers. The Letchworth Rotary Club, formed in March 1924, also stressed that Letchworth demonstrated 'How a better England can be built up'. Introducing Civic Week in *The Citizen*, Ralph Pearsall emphasised the responsibility to proclaim Howard's message widely. The principal objective was the foundation of a Civic College as a permanent tribute to Howard and his co-pioneers. The college would evolve a co-ordinated system of education from primary school to university, including adult education. Grants and endowments would overcome financial impediments. There were only four Council primary schools, and a secondary school, to be funded by the County Council, was integral with the college project. £40,000 from public donations was required above the cost of the secondary school. A site had been selected on the vacant western frontage of Town Square. Barry Parker prepared a formal classical design, with a long central block linked by colonnades to wings, one of which incorporated a theatre. In the centre a domed Hall of Memory perpetuated the names of all who had 'deserved well of their town'. Regrettably, the Civic College did not materialise. In October 1927, Councillor J. Wick raised money for planting the Town Square Gardens (renamed John F. Kennedy Gardens in 1964) and F.G.C. Ltd. promised no building in the centre for a further 25 years. Barry Parker was chosen as the architect for the Secondary School, a more utilitarian building than the elegantly proportioned classical college. The Letchworth Grammar School was opened on 7 October 1931 by the Right Hon. J. H. Whiteley, Chairman of the B.B.C.

Civic Week included lectures by eminent speakers, formal luncheons and dances, and culminated in the Civic Ball, held at the Spirella Assembly Hall, under the patronage of the Marchioness of Salisbury. The roof terrace was laid out as an Italian garden, and guests danced to Howard Aynstey's No. 1 Band until 1.30 a.m. Lesser mortals attended a 'popular dance' at the K. & L. Canteen for 1s. 6d. The town centre was decorated, under the supervision of Barry Parker, and the traders participated in a window dressing competition. The week's highlight was the Duke of York's visit on Wednesday 8 June.[22] He arrived punctually at 12.45 p.m., and, after reviewing a British Legion Guard of Honour, entered the Icknield Halls for the Civic Luncheon. After the loyal toast, the Duke rose to speak. He commended Letchworth for 'a splendid contribution … to human progress by the Garden City pioneers'. Howard had not only 'been granted the vision of this promised land; but he has also been allowed to witness its realisation'. He continued, 'the wealth of the town is in her people. Therefore I am glad to know that the conditions here, under which men and women live are so good … in conclusion I congratulate you upon the choice of a civic college as a memorial of your 21st anniversary'.

The Duke toured the town centre, Pixmore Hospital, Jackmans Place, Works Road, Green Lane, Common View and Icknield Way. He toured the Spirella factory where he was presented with a Morocco-bound album of photographs of the works. Councillor Charles F. Ball, Chairman of the U.D.C. Housing Committee, received him at the Hillbrow Estate. The Duke returned to the town centre and left Letchworth at 4.15 p.m. H.R.H. Duchess of York

111 H.R.H. The Duke of York, with Dr Norman MacFadyen, Chairman of Letchworth U.D.C. in Eastcheap, for Civic Week, 1926.

(later H.M. Queen Elizabeth the Queen Mother) had not resumed engagements following the birth of Princess Elizabeth (H.M. Queen Elizabeth II) on 21 April 1926. At least one enthusiastic Garden Citizen called out to the Duke, 'Why haven't you brought the baby?!'

Another Civic Week was held in 1935, the Silver Jubilee year of George V. Funds were raised to assist the hospital.[23] The week began with a united town service in Town Square addressed by the Dean of St Albans. On Monday 10 June the keynote theme was 'The relationship of Letchworth to the Town Planning Movement'. Herbert Morrison, leader of the L.C.C., returned to Letchworth to be presented with a ceremonial 'green belt' by Betty Hills, Miss Letchworth, to commemorate the recent resolution of the L.C.C. to acquire land for a Green Belt. Tuesday was 'Industry Day', opened by Harold Macmillan M.P., a future Conservative Prime Minister. The afternoon was enlivened by the Girls Club junior Gymnastic Display in Town Square and a folk dance festival in the evening. Unwin returned to declare 'Letchworth Points the Way' on Thursday. On Friday, 'Health Day', the new Council Offices, designed by Bennett and Bidwell, were open for inspection, and George Lionel Pepler (1882-1959), Chief Town Planning Inspector at the Ministry of Health, addressed the Sanitary Inspectors Conference at Howard Hall. *Merrie England* was staged at St Francis' Theatre that evening. 'Children's Day' brought the festivities to a close on Saturday, with a final carnival in the evening. There were no more Civic Weeks, but the Coronation of King George VI was celebrated with an elaborate historical pageant.

Twelve

WAR AND AUSTERITY

The Gathering Storm   From the appointment of Adolf Hitler as German Chancellor on 30 January 1933, the likelihood of a renewed outbreak of war gained momentum. Beginning with the harassment of Jews and their businesses in April, a wave of anti-semitism spread, with consequent emigration. The later 1930s witnessed Hitler's growing territorial demands in Eastern Europe, the growing aggression of the Fascists in Mussolini's Italy, and the ruthless crushing of the Republicans in Franco's Spain. Neville Chamberlain became Prime Minister on 28 May 1937; four months before, Hitler reiterated his demands for living space (*Lebensraum*) in eastern Europe. Hitler's 'annexation' of Austria in March 1938, and the crisis over Czechoslovakia that summer, resulted in Chamberlain's flight to Munich. Appeasement, by accepting the dismembering of Czechoslovakia, was hailed by Chamberlain as 'peace for our time'. Hitler entered Prague in triumph in March 1939, declaring Bohemia and Moravia a German 'protectorate'. If Czechoslovakia had seemed to be 'a small faraway country and a people of which we know little', the invasion acted as a catalyst for preparation at home. The Territorial Army was doubled in strength, and the Minister of Health, Walter Elliott, announced plans for the immediate evacuation of 2,500,000 children, and the delivery of 280,000 air-raid shelters. A Ministry of Supply was to be created, and conscription registers for under-21s was introduced. Chamberlain pledged, with France, to defend Poland in March 1939. Tension mounted as Hitler and Stalin signed a non-aggression pact on 23 August and, by 31 August, mobilisation for war was virtually complete. Germany invaded Poland the next morning at 5.45 a.m.

On Thursday 31 August, the great evacuation began. Parents were told to send their children to school, with a change of clothing, a toothbrush, a few personal possessions, and their gas-masks. Wearing identity labels, they were shipped off to destinations unknown. Evacuees began to arrive in Letchworth on 1 September, the first contingent at 1 p.m., shortly after the announcement of the invasion of Poland. *The Citizen* reported:

> Certainly there was some consolation that they had left the drab tenements in the grey streets
> of London for a stay in the country ... the majority of them looked upon their evacuation as
> a glorious adventure.[1]

Mothers and babies arrived on Saturday and Sunday afternoon. They milled around in the sunshine, awaiting their billets, from the Evacuation Committee, who had commandeered the Children's Library. In 2½ days the population of Letchworth swelled by over 3,000 people. There were 1,135 schoolchildren, from Islington, Tottenham, Stoke Newington and Hackney, the crowded urban districts of north and east London, whence Howard had hoped to attract Garden Citizens, plus 765 mothers with 1,102 infants, 93 L.C.C. schoolteachers, and 93 helpers. Many of them gathered round the wireless shortly after 11 a.m. on Sunday 3 September to hear Neville Chamberlain solemnly intone that no reply had been forthcoming to his ultimatum that Germany should withdraw from Poland, and consequently that Britain was at war with Germany.

The evacuees settled down to life in the Garden City. A few mothers returned immediately because they missed the *camaraderie* of city life, but most children stayed at least a year. There were reports of verminous children, horrified to find that milk came from cows. The school system required radical reorganisation, and re-opened on 19 September with a double-shift timetable – local schools from 8.45 a.m.-12.15 p.m., and evacuated schools from 1.00 p.m. –

4.30 p.m. Bexhill Down and St Mark's Schools arrived to share space with Pixmore and St Francis'. From Peacehaven, on the Sussex cliffs, the Gracie Fields Home and Orphanage came to Wilbury Turrets, and stayed until the war's end.

Iron Rations The Ministry of Food was established on 8 September 1939 to bring all aspects of food supply under government control: its best-known head, Lord Woolton, took office on 3 April 1940. Locally, the Letchworth Urban Food Control Committee[2] began the licensing of retailers, restaurants, hotels and boarding houses. Laurie Freeman became Chairman, and long-serving Town Clerk, George Brown was appointed Food Control Officer. The committee included Arthur William Brunt, Leslie Bennett and Wilson Bidwell. Ration books containing coupons for essential foods were issued, to be handed to retailers. A fixed amount was prescribed for each individual for a fixed period. The Museum Curator, Percival Westell, registered with the Co-op grocery in Eastcheap:[3] others with Moss's in Leys Avenue. Their advert showed customers with shopping baskets, gas-masks strung across their shoulders, and proclaimed

> NOW IT IS THE FASHION, For all to be on ration
> No need to count your losses, You can *still* fare well at MOSS'S.

The Citizen published weekly 'Food Facts' from the Ministry, which the prudent assembled into scrapbooks. The virtue of dried egg for pancakes and omelettes was extolled; a festive punch could be concocted from marmalade, orange squash and tea; sour-sweet cabbage with sausage meat cakes provided nourishing fare for high tea; flour soup sounded a note of desperation. At first, people were encouraged to drink more milk – consumption rose by 20 per cent during the first war-time year – then cuts in cattle feed were made and production fell away causing a revision of policy. Imports of wheat from Canada and meat from South America continued, but were affected by shipping losses. Meat rationing was introduced from March 1940. Nevertheless, the official statistics revealed a total calorie intake within one per cent of the pre-war level, and the Ministry concluded that the rationing of sugar and the virtual disappearance of sweets had improved health standards. On the debit side, fresh citrus fruits and fresh eggs were scarce as gold dust, and the refrain of a popular 1920s song 'Yes, we have no bananas' became a miserable litany until well after the end of hostilities. Entering into the Christmas spirit, the Ministry allowed an additional December 1940 ration of 4oz. sugar and 2oz. of tea! In autumn 1941, 'points' rationing was introduced, which applied to tinned food, dried fruit and some cereals. Each was given a 'point' value, in addition to a monetary price. Customers were not limited to their registered supplier. Excess demand was countered by raising the points value. Favouritism by 'under the counter' dealing, and the 'black market' sought to circumvent the restrictions, which covered 60 essential commodities. Allotments and poultry keeping had always been an adjunct to the Garden City lifestyle: now the 'dig for Victory' campaign, amateur poultry and even pig-keeping supplemented the depressingly monotonous food of factory canteens and the British Restaurant on Icknield Way. In May 1943, *The Citizen* reported that the Letchworth Police Pig Club had produced enough bacon for 22,000 rations, enough to feed the population of Letchworth for one week! In September 1942, *The Citizen* held a 'Stale Bread' competition: the results were judged by Mrs Nott, the baker's wife. Mrs A. G. Pound of 217 Icknield Way (Prize-winning cottage from 1905) submitted the winning recipe:

> Save and bake left over scraps of bread until you have 1 pound. Soak in water overnight.
> Squeeze dry and add suet, dried fruit, spice, ginger and 1 tablespoon of golden syrup dissolved
> in warm milk. Mix well, put in greased basin and boil for two hours.

Life in Letchworth regained something of the pre-1914 community spirit, as all felt and compared notes on the hardships endured, although daily conversation was inhibited by the warning, 'Careless talk costs lives'. Petrol coupons were introduced in 1940, and were not withdrawn until 1950. Many motorists simply laid up their cars for the duration. Coal rationing was introduced in July 1941. Rationing of clothing began in June 1941, and every shopkeeper was required to display the number of clothing coupons required for each item of clothing – 26 for a suit, 16 for a raincoat, seven for boots, and two for gloves. The new ration books had not been printed, and so margarine coupons were accepted as a temporary substitute! Improvisation, by using old curtains, and the illicit commandeering of parachute silk for wedding dresses, pyjamas and christening gowns, reflected local ingenuity. In March 1942, the Board of Trade decreed that hemlines would rise, and that utility cloth would be introduced. By May 1943, the Board estimated that clothes rationing, and 'make do and mend' had saved £600 million. However, the following February, clothing restrictions were lifted – men could indulge in double-breasted suits with turn-ups and lined pockets, women to pleated suits with plenty of buttons and bows. Clothing coupons were still required, however. The hated utility suits were distributed to European refugees.

The Civil Invasion Plan   In 1940, when invasion seemed inevitable, an Emergency Committee, a link in a national network, was convened.[4] It was led by Leslie Bennett, Chairman of Letchworth U.D.C. from 1940-45. He was supported by fellow Councillors Fred Nott, Robert William Tabor and Charles Sax. George Brown, the Town Clerk, was appointed A.R.P. Controller. A secret Civil Invasion Plan was drawn up for Letchworth U.D.C., as for every district throughout the country. It included the names and telephone contact numbers for the Emergency Committee, listed doctors, medical resources, fire and water appliances, and static water supplies – the latter headed by 333,000 gallons contained in Norton Common Swimming Pool. Rest centres, required in case of serious bomb damage and homelessness, or requirements to accommodate refugees, included all the church halls, and the two cinemas, with hot drinks to be provided by the Broadway café. The Civil Defence Controller would liaise with the local Military Commander on receipt of the code message 'action stations', but the latter had no legal power to issue orders to the civil authorities until the invasion had begun. Executive control by the military was limited to the following circumstances:

1. The approach of the enemy;
2. Civil population reaching state of panic which it is unlikely the civil authorities will be able to control;
3. Orders from a superior authority;
4. Request of civil authorities.[5]

Morale would be boosted by maintenance of essential services 'to the last and providing a job for everybody'. Official Ministry information bulletins would be posted around the town, supplemented by loudspeaker vans, and BBC relays (assuming that they still functioned). All food would be requisitioned, and bread and milk distributed from emergency depots. Should extreme emergency arise, on notification by the Military Commandant that the Food Officer's area is in 'imminent danger of occupation by the enemy', all available stocks were 'to be distributed as rapidly and equitably as possible to the public free of charge' and so deny their use to the enemy.

Mercifully, the call never came. Reading the document sixty years later indicates the fine balance drawn between maintaining the semblance of a civil society, and the inevitability of martial law in the event of a last ditch stand against the overwhelming forces of an invader. It serves to confirm how real the threat seemed in that far-off summer of 1940, when the line seemed barely to be held by the Battle of Britain pilots.

The Home Front   Air Raid Precautions (A.R.P.) were an essential element of civil defence. As early as 23 March 1937, a public meeting was held in the Grammar School Hall. A practice blackout was held in November 1938, with a full-scale demonstration, and recruiting

112 The Home Guard, 1940, possibly outside Town Lodge, Gernon Road. The tape across the windows was intended to minimise injury from shattered glass caused by bomb blasts. Fortunately, the Garden City sustained little damage.

of wardens on 1 May 1939. A.R.P. Officer, C.H.E. Badcock, served from April 1938 to October 1945. Late in August 1939, the Police Station in Broadway, and the Council Offices (initially the A.R.P. h.q.), were protected by sandbags. After the declaration of war, however, things were quiet. The air-raid sirens were sounded early in the morning of 6 September 1939, but nothing happened. Throughout the autumn and winter, pundits referred to 'the phoney war'. 'Anderson' air-raid shelters were distributed and erected in back gardens. A permanent A.R.P. report and control headquarters was built in Gernon Road in June 1940, at a cost of £1,221 1s. 0d.[6] There were public shelters in Town Square and on the southern fringe of Norton Common. Schools improvised shelters by adapting classrooms, on the advice of the County Education Officer.

The blackout was introduced and made compulsory. Street lights were removed, motorists were constrained to use only sidelights masked by orange acetate, and heavy blackout curtains or plywood baffles were installed on every house window. Residents were ordered to 'put out that light – your sitting room light is seen at 10,000 feet'. Commercial premises were not exempt. In August 1940, magistrates imposed a fine of £1 on Philip Kane, caretaker of the National Provincial Bank, who left a corridor light burning, to be spotted by the vigilant P.C. Sales.[7]

In the spring of 1940, with the advance of Germany into France, the War Minister, Anthony Eden, called for Local Defence Volunteers to combat a possible and expected invasion by paratroopers. Within a week 250,000 had come forward, many of them veterans of the First World War. In June 1940, as Dunkirk fell, the 4 Company, Hertfordshire Battalion, for Letchworth with Baldock, was raised under Major A. N. Gavin Jones.[8] A network of vigilant patrols, each protecting their own locality, was quickly formed. At Winston Churchill's suggestion (he had replaced Chamberlain as Prime Minister on 10 May), the force was renamed The Home Guard. Their first armaments were 100 rifles, dumped unceremoniously at Gavin Jones's Nursery. Later they learned how to make 'Molotov cocktails'. Home Guard posts ringed the roads leading to and from Letchworth: at Wilbury on the Bedford Road/ Arlesey Road; at Norton at the junction of Baldock and Stotfold Roads; at the Waterworks on Baldock Lane; on Letchworth Gate, and in Willian; and near the old isolation hospital at Rosehill on the Hitchin road. Each railway bridge was also guarded, and there were posts at the Power Station, Gasworks, Post Office, Council Offices, British Tab, and Spirella. On

113 'Bombs-a-Daisy': heavy armaments from K. and L. included this 4,000 lb personalised present from Dulcie Dudley to the Fuhrer.

3 November, the Company was inspected by the Lord Lieutenant of Hertfordshire, Viscount Hampden. By May 1943, they formed four companies of the Twelfth Hertfordshire Battalion. A Company covered Letchworth and Norton, B Company Letchworth and Willian, C Company was mobile, and D Company provided reinforcement.

The Battle of Britain of August 1940 was followed by the Blitz on London, which lasted well into spring 1941. Eighty-six bombed-out Londoners camped in the Commerce Avenue Church Rooms. Letchworth escaped lightly. On 16 October 1940, a house in Bursland sustained minor damage, and the Letchworth Gate Creamery and the K&L Factory had near-misses; casualties included a rabbit and a bird. On one occasion, a lone enemy aircraft flew low over north Letchworth but by the time Norman Dixon, on Observer Post Table 3, Wilbury Hill, had loaded his rifle, the plane had vanished. The Home Guard prepared for the worst, and were an essential component of the contingency plan in the event of invasion. Corporal Maurice Freland lived in Broadwater Avenue. His mustering plans outline the procedure.[9] The signal of invasion would be given by ringing the church bells. The Company would 'stand to' in uniform, with rifles and sten guns, and proceed to 'battle order', taking emergency rations and spare underclothing. People would be ordered to stay clear of the streets and return home. Civil panic would be quelled. The prospect of invasion receded, and on 15 November 1942 the church bells rang out to celebrate Montgomery's victory at El Alamein – Churchill's symbolic 'end of the beginning'. In November 1944, the Home Guard at Letchworth was formally stood down by Major Gavin Jones, and addressed by Leslie Bennett, U.D.C. Chairman:

> You have not faced the invader, but nevertheless there is no doubt whatever, that a keen, alert Home Guard, constantly growing, daily becoming more efficient, has played a vital part in deterring the Hun from planting his foul footsteps on this land, which is to us so dear.[10]

War Work   The armed services claimed many employees in the key factories of Letchworth, which switched to war production. In May 1940, Ernest Bevin, Churchill's Minister of Labour and National Service, took emergency powers to control banks, the munitions industry, wages, profits and conditions of work. Women became a vital part of the workforce and, in March 1941, Bevin called for 100,000 volunteers, then took measures for conscription. Locally, factories worked around the clock, with three eight-hour shifts, seven days a week. The British Restaurant served meals to night shift workers between 10 p.m. and 2 a.m. Not everyone appreciated the cuisine: in May 1944, Col. F. G. Frobisher wrote from Rowan Crescent to complain that 'too much bread resurrection pie appears to be driving a good few of the old regulars to The Crossway' (on the corner of Works Road and Norton Way North). In May 1942 *The Citizen* proclaimed

> Women are helping in the Great Arms Drive. Wages average £2-10-0 [£2.50] to £3 for a 57 hour week - some women workers make as much as £4.

114 Best-known for their municipal refuse carts, Shelvoke and Drewry turned to the production of top secret miniature submarines used for naval espionage during the Second World War.

A mother of 12, Mrs. Beatrice Theakston, was the first recruit in the War Work Exhibition in April 1942 – she had also worked in munitions during the First World War. Two of her sons were in the Army, a daughter in the W.R.N.S., another son in skilled production work, and the remainder in other industrial work. Her husband had worked 21 years at British Tab.[11] War work was heavy going, monotonous, even dangerous. The rhythm of production was boosted by broadcasting 'Music While You Work' over the Tannoy, preceded by its distinctive signature tune, 'Calling All Workers', written by Eric Coates (1886-1957). A spirit of *camaraderie* emerged, symbolised by the humour of Dulcie Dudley of K.& L., who chalked on a 4,000 lb. Bomb 'A Birthday Present to Adolf from Us'.

Training was a vital part of the scheme of things, and the Government Training Centre in the old Ascot factory on Pixmore Avenue was at full stretch. One of their more unusual assignments was the training of 50 Indian technicians in modern production methods.[12] The Settlement had arranged accommodation in 'The Peoples House' in Station Road. The architect, Barry Parker, as President of The Settlement, wrote personally to Ernest Bevin, who had masterminded the scheme, to see if the Warden, John Short, could defer his conscription. In welcoming the group to Letchworth in May 1941, U.D.C. Chairman, Leslie Bennett, declared that the objective was not solely war work, but for trainees 'to become accustomed to, and understand not only our methods of working, but also our domestic life and recreational activities'. The Secretary of State for India visited the group, and returned on 26 September, with the Royal Party, and Ernest Bevin. This was the first visit by King George VI as monarch; in 1926 he had come as Duke of York. His consort, Queen Elizabeth, had never visited the Garden City. Their first call was at the Training Centre, where they were met by a guard of honour in traditional Indian dress. Later,

115 King George VI and Queen Elizabeth visited the Letchworth Training Centre in September 1941 and met the Indian technicians. Her Majesty (later H. M. The Queen Mother) talks to Mr Mahmoud, with Ernest Bevin, Minister of Labour, in the centre of the group.

116 Leslie Irvin had demonstrated his parachute to the US Airforce in 1919, and founded his British subsidiary in 1926. Here he holds a seat-harness.

they visited the hostel in Station Road, where a large crowd pressed forward to obtain a glimpse of the royal couple. In June 1942, the Indians received certificates on completion of their course, and returned home.

Much of the industrial output was shrouded in secrecy, for the duration of the war and beyond. K.& L. Steelfounders had originated during the First World War, and had then taken a prominent role in munitions production. Following liquidation in the late 1920s, they were now part of the 600 group. Early in the war they were back in munitions work, with cast steel aerial bombs and shells in production – by the war's end they had manufactured nearly 2½ million of the latter. Paravanes and other anti-submarine equipment were also produced. Hydraulic systems for undercarriage retraction for bombers and fighters were another specialist product. Lloyds and Co. and Camco Ltd. also turned to armaments manufacture. Morse Chain concentrated on mechanical power transmission, and their chain drives were shipped to Soviet Russia, and were also used on Churchill tanks. Shelvoke and Drewry turned from dustcarts to manufacture the S.P.V. military ambulance, and also midget submarines used for naval espionage. Shortly after the war, amazed Garden Citizens inspected one displayed on the Arena. Meredew, the furniture makers, manufactured glider panels. Leslie Irvin (1895-1966) had been a film stunt man in California, and an aerial enthusiast. In 1919 he jumped from an aircraft 3,000ft above ground, with a parachute of his own invention – and landed safely with nothing more than a broken ankle – he founded his company from his hospital bed, having received an order for 300 parachutes.[13] Registered as Irving – the 'g' was added in error – the British subsidiary company began operation in Letchworth in May 1926, moving to a purpose-designed factory by Cecil Hignett in Icknield Way in 1934. The R.A.F. adopted his parachute in 1925, and by the end of the Second World War it was estimated that more than 34,000 lives had been saved by Irving 'chutes. During the war Irvin also opened a factory in India. In 1938, Spirella began to collaborate with Irving in the production of parachute canopies, which took over much of their huge building – corsets were manufactured for surgical purposes only, under strict Board of Trade control. In October 1939, a second workroom for Irving on Icknield Way, also designed by Hignett, was given priority for construction, a month after the outbreak of war. Irving safety harnesses for pilots led to the company pioneering car seat belts after the war.

Intelligence played a vital part in discovering and undermining the strategy of the enemy. It was not unexpected that the British Tabulating Machine Company, with its experience of data processing on its punched-card Hollerith machines, should have become involved in top-secret decoding.[14] German tactical orders, transmitted by short-wave radio, were encrypted by ENIGMA machines, which were reset daily. Successful code-breaking, not once, but every time, was vital. Decoding machines, called BOMBES, were the concept of Alan Turing, a mathematician from King's College, Cambridge, developed from pioneer work by Polish colleagues. British Tab formed a team, under Harold H. ('Doc') Keen, to produce an electro-mechanical decoder. The BOMBE was seven feet wide, six feet high and three feet deep, containing rotating drums, with rows of 26 contacts behind, corresponding to each letter of the alphabet. Three rows of drums matched the three wheels of the ENIGMA machine. All possible permutations were scanned until a setting was found which revealed the message: all that needed to be done was to translate from German to English, and transmit it to the Ministry *en route* to field commanders. BOMBES were made at the main British Tab factory on Icknield Way, with assembly work at Spirella. They were sent to Bletchley Park, where the first was in service in March 1940, in time to intercept invasion plans. By the war's end, 211 were in operation, at Bletchley Park, Wavendon, Adstock, Stanmore and Eastcote, operated by almost 1,700 W.R.N.S. It was not until the 1970s that the secrets were revealed.

Safe Haven The Nazi annexation of Austria, and subsequent invasion of Czechoslovakia in 1938-9, combined with the anti-semitism throughout Germany, brought many refugees; by November 1938, 11,000 refugees had settled in Britain. Some made their homes in the Garden City. As early as January 1939, two houses and a flat were acquired for 16 Czech refugees. In July 1942, Aliyah, an organisation concerned with rescuing child victims of Nazism, held a meeting at the Co-operative Hall. Ironically, there had been fears, a few months earlier, that a local hostel would have to close. 'Robingate', Barrington Road was losing 15s. per head per week. It acted as a half-way house. Its residents were permitted by the Home Office to do harvest work, and classified as Class C 'Friendly Aliens'. They moved into the community as jobs were found. By mid-1943, there were 1,500 Jews in Letchworth. They had formed the Letchworth Hebrew Congregation, 'Jeshrun', President Dr I. Epstein,[15] and in April 1941 were visited by the Chief Rabbi to the British Empire, Dr. Joseph Hertz. There was also a Hebrew Ladies' Guild. A bath, for the ritual purification of women, was added at the back of 'The Nook' in Cross Street. After the war's end, the Secretary of the Congregation, J. Richman, received permission from the Council for 'The Coppice', Garth (now Pasture) Road to be used as a hostel for children from Belsen Concentration Camp. The Austrian musicologist and composer, Hans Redlich, left voluntarily, disgusted by Nazi rule. He lodged for a while with the Barry Parkers and made a permanent home in Letchworth in 1939. He was a W.E.A. Lecturer, founded The Settlement String Orchestra, and conducted The Settlement Choral Society – a highlight was a performance of Haydn's oratorio, *The Seasons*, with nationally-known soloists. He also contributed to the work of the Hitchin Rural Music School. He became a British citizen in 1947.

Fighting Funds No scrap of paper or sliver of metal was too insignificant for 'salvage' (today's term would be recycling) for the war effort. In the Waste Paper Drive of January 1942, K. & L. lost a friendly challenge to Spirella, but offered to beat them at scrap-iron salvage. In two weeks, the boys of Pixmore School collected three sacks-full of cigarette packets and bus tickets, which it was an offence to throw away. In addition there were nationwide fundraising drives to invest in War Bonds and Loans, and National Savings, to meet the growing financial burden of armament production. Letchworth Garden City played an honourable role. Fundraising was a communal activity, with the Council a leading player, and a host of committees, some concerned with the logistics, others with social events, which could attract publicity and boost contributions.

The Battle of Britain proved the worth of the R.A.F.'s legendary Spitfire fighter. A batch of 450 had been ordered on 22 March 1940, and in August a campaign was opened to raise £5,000 to buy one in the name of *Letchworth*:[16] by December the total was complete, and a handsome souvenir brochure was issued to proclaim the achievement. Irving Air Chute and

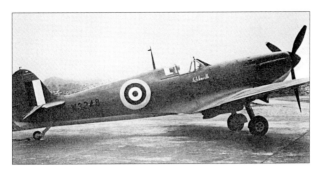

117 The Letchworth Spitfire, bearing its name with pride, as a result of local fundraising.

Spirella each donated 100 guineas, Forbes Russell gave the takings from *French without Tears*, playing at St Francis. Auctions were held at Mason's Garage in Eastcheap, a hush-hush exhibition of aerial warfare was organised at Bennett's Motor Showrooms, and schoolboys spent their pocket money inspecting the remains of a shot-down Messerschmitt Bf. 109E German fighter, displayed on the Arena. There was friendly rivalry with Hitchin and Stevenage, who also opened funds. Leslie Irvin personally took the cheque to Lord Beaverbrook, Minister of Aircraft Production. The Ministry presented the town with a commemorative plaque.

Themed fundraising weeks were organised. In February 1941, it was 'War Weapons Week' – the target of £100,000, the achievement £189,511. A troops rally and service was held at *The Broadway Cinema* on Sunday, a Civic Luncheon on Monday, with a fly-past of five bombers over the town on Tuesday and Thursday 'to show Letchworthians what their £100,000 will buy'. A mock-up of 'Hitler's coffin' stood outside the Fire Station in Eastcheap

> - the public will be privileged to drive nails into Hitler's coffin at a penny a time ... it is expected that every citizen will pay cash on the nail.[17]

Warship Week took place during 21-28 March 1942. The frigate, H.M.S. *Spey*, under construction, was adopted, and in commission on 4 May, acting as escort to Atlantic convoys and the unsuccessful landing attempt at Algiers in November 1942. The immediate target was to raise £120,000 for a corvette for coastal duties, H.M.S. *Ling*. An exhibition included a replica scale model, built by the architects Robert Bennett and Wilson Bidwell. A total of £211,880 was raised, much in the form of National Savings.[18] Tank Week, held in July 1942, was keyed to the Desert Campaign in North Africa, as General Auchinleck attempted to stem Rommel's advance – 'Aid for Auchinleck' groups were organised in every road. The target was £70,000. Kingsley Wood, Chancellor of the Exchequer, commended Letchworth's 'leading place throughout the Empire for its War Savings'.[19] In January 1943, *The Citizen* could boast that the town had saved over £1 million since the savings campaign had started. In 1943, the spotlight turned to 'Wings for Victory' – the target £150,000, the cost of 30 fighters. The star attraction was a Link Trainer:

> For half-a-crown [12½p.] (two thirds of which goes to the R.A.F. Benevolent Fund) you can experience the thrill of flying by this apparatus, as used by R.A.F. pilots as part of their training.[20]

The R.A.F. revue, *Riding High* was at St Francis' Theatre. An amazing total of £237, 534 was raised. As the focus of the war turned to the invasion and capture of enemy-held Europe, 'Salute the Soldier' Week ran from 3-10 June 1944.[21] The timing was, coincidentally, immaculate. On 4 June, Rome was liberated, and on 6 June, 'D' Day, the Normandy Landings began, highlighting the efforts to salute 'the man that must always finish off the job'. The campaign sought £150,000 to equip a base hospital, and a further £50,000 to maintain it for a year. Once again there was a round of parades, dances, exhibitions and entertainment. The initial subscriptions were slower, suggesting war fatigue, but the final Saturday saw £60,000 raised, the highest ever seen in Letchworth, and the grand total reached £246,677. As a microcosm of the national war savings effort, Letchworth demonstrated the effectiveness of setting, and meeting, targets which would be the envy of present-day fundraisers for humanitarian causes, with their emphasis on television for publicity. The media of the war-years were relatively unsophisticated, yet perhaps more acutely focused on motivating contributors.

National Service   Mobilisation of the armed forces began during spring 1939. That May, the Military Training Act came into force, and compulsory military training for men of 20-21 commenced in July. On 31 August the Army and R.A.F. reserves were called up, and the Royal Navy was mobilised. In September 1939, the National Service (Armed Forces) Act introduced compulsory military service for men of 18-41, and the various age groups were called to register by Royal Proclamation (20-22; 22-23 in October 1939: 23-27 in January 1940 and so on). As in the First World War, there were many volunteers. There were also three women's services – the Auxiliary Territorial Service (A.T.S.), The Women's Royal Naval Service (W.R.N.S.) and the Women's Auxiliary Air Force (W.A.A.F.). On the home front, the Women's Voluntary Service (W.V.S.), the Women's Land Army, and the Mechanised Transport Corp, whose employment released men for active service, and several branches of nursing, hitherto the traditional active role for women in wartime.

Local volunteers and conscripts served world-wide. *The Citizen* regularly featured pictures of local men serving in the forces, linked, when the censor allowed, to battles and honours. The paper sent Christmas parcels to locals serving in the forces, and money was raised – 750 Penguin books were sent out from the proceeds of a fun-fair. In February 1940, it was announced that three Letchworth men had served in H.M.S. *Ajax* at the time of her epic battle with the *Graf Spee*, in the mouth of the River Plate, in December 1939. On 31 May 1940, the Divisional M.P., Sir Arnold Wilson, who had volunteered for active service at 55, and was serving as an air gunner, was reported missing over France. Trooper F. W. Finney of Glebe Road was awarded the Military Medal for outstanding courage during the Dieppe raid. The Military Medal was awarded to Private Maurice Muir of the 2nd New Zealand Expeditionary Force: Mrs Muir of The Quadrant had five sons serving in the armed forces at the time. Commander B. C. Schofield won the Distinguished Service Order on a Malta convoy. In the air, one of 'the few', J.G.P. (Joce) Millard, flew Spitfires in Nos 1, 242 and 615 Squadrons. Many Letchworthians served in the Hertfordshire and Bedfordshire Regiment: they played a central part in the capture of Monte Cassino by British and Polish troops, on 12-15 May 1944, capturing 1,500 men of the crack German 4th Parachute Regiment. A few Garden Citizens served with Ord Wingate's Chindits in the Burma Campaign. At war's end it was time to count the cost – 103 Letchworth citizens dead, but many repatriated from German prison camps – *The Citizen* proudly featured 'Stalag' returnees.

Women were debarred from armed combat. Nevertheless, they played key roles in transport, communications and cryptography, for example using the Letchworth manufactured decoders at Bletchley Park. On 8 March 1942, Letchworth hosted a morale-boosting rally, which involved a parade, and a mass meeting in *The Broadway Cinema*.[22] The organisers were the W.V.S., and the event involved the British Legion, Red Cross, St John Ambulance Brigade, the Girl Guides and Women's Land Army, as well as the A.T.S., W.R.N.S., and W.A.A.F. The platform included three men, Leslie Bennett, UDC Chairman, George Brown, Chairman of the Letchworth Savings Committee, and Fred Nott, President of the War Finance Committee. Miss J. Woolacombe, Superintendent of W.R.N.S. Personnel, addressed the meeting on 'Women at War', the Marchioness of Salisbury on 'Women at Home' and Lady Davidson, M.P. for Hemel Hempstead on 'Our Country's Needs'. Interspersed were patriotic songs and community singing, led by the popular contralto, Gladys Ripley.

Mrs R. Green, the chief organiser of the Letchworth W.V.S. stated that 8 March was International Women's Day, inaugurated in New York in 1909. On 8 March 1917, the women of Leningrad had made a memorable stand for equality and freedom:

> With women of the U.S.A. and the U.S.S.R. on either side of us in this great struggle, it is only fitting that the women of Letchworth, itself a pioneer town, should hold a rally in recognition of the great part women were playing in the War efforts.

The *Citizen*'s write-up of the parade was perhaps more predictable in tone:

> How smart are these women in the services – clothes well kept, every detail of their uniform
> in perfect condition, heads erect marching in perfect union, a picture of health and a credit to
> the forces with whom they serve …

Light Relief   Initially, theatres and cinemas were closed, and the BBC resorted to interminable
popular organ concerts by Sandy Macpherson, but after a few weeks an atmosphere of
strained normality returned. On the wireless, *I.T.M.A.* (*It's That Man Again*), the smash hit
comedy programme starring Tommy Handley, offered relief from depressing, censored war
news, interspersed with stirring speeches from the Prime Minister, Winston Churchill. The
two cinemas dispensed escapism, and were packed out twice nightly. Films such as the much-
lauded *Gone with the Wind* and *Mrs. Miniver* made their perilous journey across the Atlantic –
Churchill considered the propaganda value of the latter was worth 100 warships. Noel Coward
was active in the studios, writing and starring in *In Which We Serve*, a thinly disguised version
of Lord Mountbatten's exploits in H.M.S. *Kelly*; the film also introduced John Mills and
Richard Attenborough. *The St Francis' Theatre* played host to the Forbes Russell Repertory
Company, who decamped from the Devonshire Park Theatre, Eastbourne, presumably evading
the threat of invasion.[23] They opened the 1940-1 Season with Terence Rattigan's *French
without tears*, followed by J. B. Priestley's *When we are married*, and the stage adaptation of
Dorothy Sayers's Peter Wimsey novel, *Busman's Honeymoon*. Among the cast was a young
'juvenile lead' and assistant stage manager, Patrick Macnee, later to win fame and fortune as
Steed in the television series *The Avengers*. The programmes contained a warning:

> In the event of an air raid warning patrons will be notified from the stage … Patrons wishing
> to leave are requested to do so quietly, and THE PLAY WILL CONTINUE.

During April 1941 there was Variety Week with Dorothy Squires and Billy Reid, and for the
culturally inclined a week of Lydia Kyasht's Russian Ballet. From Blackpool Tower, Bertini
and his Band brought the house down with *It's All in Fun*. The popular comedian, Tom
Walls, starred in *Canaries sometimes sing* ('Cigarettes by Abdulla'), and Ralph Lynn appeared in
the evergreen farce *Rookery Nook*. Finally, in September 1941, Donald Wolfit presented and
starred in *Hamlet* and *Richard III*. Today's theatre-lovers would find the range of entertainment astounding, particularly in the wartime context.

Much entertainment was, of course, home grown. The 3 September concert by the
Brotherhood Orchestra at The Cloisters turned out to be its last, and the building was
requisitioned by the Army in 1940. Choral societies kept going; on 9 October 1941 a full-
dress performance of Mendelssohn's *Elijah* was given at The Free Church, with soloists of
national repute, including the baritone, Roy Henderson, and 'an augmented choir and
orchestra'. On 5 June 1940, the controversial sleek new roadhouse, *The Wilbury Hotel*,
strategically located, just across the road from the Letchworth Cemetery, and outside the
Letchworth estate, opened its doors. John Edwin Bigg, a butcher from nearby Stotfold,
entreated 'many of his friends to rally round him … despite the gravity of the hour'.[24] There
would be dancing to The Wilbury Band, nightly from 8-11 p.m. Dances were popular
events in connection with the many fundraising activities. Perhaps the most exotic, and
unexpected, was the *Grand Bal-Cabaret* held on 24 April 1942 in the Icknield Halls, in aid
of the Free French.[25] The event was recorded by the B.B.C. The patron was General
Charles de Gaulle, who gave his regrets at not attending (he was represented by Lt. Colonel
de Lagatinerie) but had signed the souvenir programme in appreciation of the splendid
work for *La France Combattante*. The R.A.F Blue Star Dance Band provided the music, and
there was a full cabaret. Joan Foster had come to Letchworth in 1935, when she married
Philip Foster, whose father had founded the Foster Instrument Co. She had been educated
at the Chelsea *Lyceé*, and was recruited by Mrs Maud, a Frenchwoman, to assist with the
hospitality at the event. She remembers that many of the young French disappeared from

Letchworth soon after, presumably into the Free French armed services.

Holidays away from home were out of the question, and had only been enjoyed by the minority before the war. 'Jolly Days' were a six-week 'home town' holiday programme in August 1942.[26] There was a grand ENSA (Entertainments National Service Association – familiarly known as Every Night Something Awful!) revue at *St Francis*. Citizens could challenge Uncle Jollyday by brandishing the souvenir programme (price 2d.) to win 15s. (75p) National savings Certificates. There were 'Military Exercises' by the Home Guard and a 'bomb throwing' competition between two of its platoons, 'Water Frolics', a concert by the Welsh Guards Band, and massed community singing on the Arena.

118 Invitation (in 'Franglais') to the 'Grand Bal-Cabaret'. General de Gaulle sent his apologies.

Peace and Reconciliation Even in the darkest days of 1940, there remained those who looked towards peaceful solutions to international problems. The Letchworth Branch of the League of Nations Union had been formed in 1920, with the active involvement of the architects Barry Parker and Raymond Unwin – Parker was the first Chairman. In March 1940, a crowded meeting of the branch was addressed by Lord Lytton, who saw the war as the inevitable consequence of a lack of unity on a policy of united resistance against aggression. He felt that it was essential to begin to consider the type of settlement, which would bring a more enduring peace, for 'if we do not … we must make up our minds that war will re-occur about every thirty years'. The failure of the League of Nations to prevent the war did not remove the necessity to create and support an international organisation that would resolve disputes peacefully. The Letchworth Peace Council drew delegates from the Society of Friends, Labour Party, Co-operative Women's Guilds, The Settlement, Free Church, St Christopher School, Esperanto Society, Peace Pledge Union, Communist Party Women's Section, and General and Municipal Workers' Union. Laurie Freeman was elected Chairman. The L.P.C. saw itself as free from party politics and sectarian bias, and advised that 'the public will need to be reminded that sooner or later a peace settlement will be made … we can strive to educate a public opinion to demand and expect a better political and social order in the post-war period'. In February 1942, the Letchworth branch of the Peace Pledge Union held a meeting on 'Pacifism and Food Reform'.

President Roosevelt appears to have coined the term 'United Nations', and he declared 14 June 1942 as 'United Nations Day'. This was accepted by the British Government as a 'day of dedication to the great alliance of free nations, and one on which our people salute the united nations'. In Letchworth, a Home Guard and Civil Defence Services and British Legion parade, from Howard Park to the Arena, was held. The Rev. F. Thatcher, Rector of Letchworth, declared

> The United Nations! What a change since Dunkirk! Then we were alone, solitary, a left-in-the-lurch nation … Now we are united with a large group of nations struggling for a common purpose: to rid the world of a foul, cancerous political growth.[27]

Roosevelt reached agreement on a United Nations charter, endorsed by Britain, Russia and China, and its formation was announced in October 1944. Its inaugural meeting was held in San Francisco in April 1945, shortly before the cessation of hostilities: Roosevelt had died two weeks previously. The Letchworth branch of the United Nations Society was formed in December 1945 and, appropriately, Lord Lytton, who had encouraged international reconciliation in the dark days of 1940, became its President, shortly before his death in October 1947.

Victory Euphoria   Throughout the spring of 1945, as the allies closed on Berlin, the question was not if, but when victory in Europe would be achieved. The final surrender of the Germans occurred at 2.41 a.m. on 7 May. The next day, street parties were hastily improvised; as *The Citizen* reported, 'Beflagged Letchworth celebrates Victory'. A Thanksgiving Service was held in front of the Council Offices at noon, presided over by the new Chairman, Mrs Margaret Harvey, who reflected that 'we in this town have suffered comparatively little: may it never be said that as a result of this we have become hard of heart'. V.E. (Victory in Europe) Day, 13 May, was Children's Day, with parties held throughout the town, in Temple Gardens, Common View, Grange Road and Hallmead. All possible food was brought out, there were pony rides and fancy dress parties, with the costumes ranging from Home Guards to Russian Cossacks. That day, Flying Officer A. R. Ruttick from Ridge Avenue, who had been held prisoner of war in Germany since September 1943, was repatriated: during the succeeding weeks *The Citizen* told their stories as 'More Local Stalag Men Arrive Home'.

In August, the surrender of Japan, after the horrific impact of the atomic bombs on Hiroshima and Nagasaki, brought the worldwide conflict to a close. 'V.J. Day' was celebrated on 15 August: the new Prime Minister, Clement Attlee declared, 'The last of our enemies is laid low'. Again there were street parties, children's sports, followed by bonfires and fireworks. Spirella and the Council Offices were floodlit, and houses and streets were lit-up after long years of blackout. The following Sunday, special services of thanksgiving were held in every church. A Thanksgiving Week was held from 29 September - 6 October, with a final fundraising drive of £100,000 to be invested in National Savings[28] – 'We have a wonderful opportunity to acknowledge the debt to our fighting men. At the same time we can help in the great task of Reconstruction'. The highlight was a Victory Ball at the Icknield Halls. The thanksgiving fund reached £77,730 by the week's end. At *The Broadway*, Laurence Olivier's acclaimed Technicolor film of *Henry V* arrived on 9 October. Shot on location in Ireland, the film, with its splendid musical score by William Walton, underlined the mood of the hour. Pause for reflection showed that 197 personnel from the armed services had sacrificed their lives in the allied cause, and their names were recorded on Letchworth's Roll of Honour.[29] In due course, a tablet recording their names was added to the War Memorial in Station Place, and was ceremonially unveiled by the U.D.C. Chairman, George Woodbridge, on 11 November (Remembrance Day) 1953.

The transition to peacetime continued for several years. Fundamental changes were brought about by the Labour Government, under Clement Attlee, elected with a majority of 146 on 26 July 1945. The Hitchin Division had a Labour M.P. for the first time, Philip Asterley Jones. It was a close-run thing – Asterley Jones's majority was 340 over Major Berry, who had been returned unopposed in 1941, following the death of Sir Arnold Wilson on active service. Individual idealism and voluntary co-operation were eclipsed by public initiative as the foundations for the welfare state were laid.

The Council   Throughout the war Leslie Bennett had been U.D.C. Chairman. In 1944 he paid for a Coat of Arms from the College of Arms, which conferred civic dignity on Letchworth, and reflected links between the Garden City and the ancient manorial families. The Letters Patent described the Arms thus:

> The Arms following, that is to say, Argent three chevronels gules over all on a Chief embattled azure two roses of the first barbed and seeded proper. And for the Crest on a Wreath of the colours an owl affronty argent between two sprigs of oak vert fructed or.

The Shield is a combination of the Arms of Barrington and Montfichet, Lords of the Manor of Letchworth in the 15th and 16th centuries, represented by the red chevronels on the silver ground. The Chief (the band in blue) typifies blue sky and sun, which, with the roses, represent the Garden City. The Helmet and the Wreath are heraldic emblems. The Crest exemplifies the firm foundations upon which the Garden City is planned, and this is represented by the oak sprigs in the supporters of the Crest. The Owl, the bird of wisdom, emphasises the Motto *Prudens Futuri* ('Thoughtful for the Future').[30] In 1950, the Town Clerk, Horace Plinston, persuaded F.G.C. Ltd. to present Badges of Office to the town, formally handed over on 16 July 1951 by Sir Eric MacFadyen, F.G.C. Chairman, to Ernest Gardiner, U.D.C. Chairman.[31]

If the Arms and Regalia symbolised the past, the Council concentrated upon planning for the future. There was a concerted attempt to accelerate growth to achieve Howard's 32,000 population target, and to provide housing for Greater London overspill. Local politics became more fully aligned with national parties, particularly after the division of Letchworth into five wards in 1946. Letchworth U.D.C. attained a Labour majority, and its first female Chairman, Mrs Margaret Harvey, had been elected in April 1945. Mrs Harvey held sway until 1949, when she was succeeded by George Woodbridge. Ernest Gardiner, a Conservative, became Chairman in 1949-50, and alternated with Woodbridge over the next few years. The role of Town Clerk and Solicitor became crucial. Horace Plinston had been appointed in 1948 and readily adapted to the 'cabinet' style of administration, gaining the confidence of both parties, which was to stand the Council in good stead during the Company take-over battle.[32] The Council's housebuilding priority created arduous tasks for professional officers, notably the Surveyor, E. L. Johnson, and Housing Manager, G. W. Mulvenna.

The Company's post-war vicissitudes In the political context of 1945, the continued existence of F.G.C. Ltd. seemed anachronistic to many. Company and Council had enjoyed a cosy working relationship pre-war, but this could no longer continue. Initially, however, Company affairs resumed normality.[33] At the 1946 A.G.M. it was announced that the dividend arrears of £113,224 18s. 11d. would be paid off. In anticipation of post-war growth the issue of a further £200,000 share capital was authorised, to bring the total to £600,000, but was never implemented, possibly due to the consequences of the 1947 Town and Country Planning Act for development land. The Company's utility subsidiaries were nationalised.[34] By 1945 the power station served Biggleswade and Baldock and the surrounding Bedfordshire villages, but had not been taken into the National Grid. In 1947, its capacity was 7,500kv and in 1945 it sold 40,726,844 BTh. Units. The gasworks had supplied 200,000,000 cu. ft. in 1945, with a peak weekly demand of 5,000,000 cu. ft. – the total 1906 output! In 1947 the power station made £45,662 profit, and the gasworks £14,176, a sizeable proportion of the pre-interest revenue balance of £68,160. Compensation of £1,129,858 was agreed for the power station, £268,814 over book value. Although this enabled repayment of a bank overdraft and mortgages, a lucrative asset had been lost, and this was repeated when the gasworks was requisitioned. A degree of local loyalty disappeared. In February 1947, during a harsh winter, with fuel shortages and extensive power cuts throughout the country, the Ministry of Fuel and Power initially allowed the Letchworth Power Station to use its coal stocks, but compelled it to switch off three days later. The Garden City shivered as it faced an uncertain future, with rationing even more stringent than in wartime.

THIRTEEN

RECOVERY AND EXPANSION

Letchworth Development Corporation?   The Labour Government implemented the recommendations of Patrick Abercrombie's 1944 'Greater London Plan' for a ring of 'New Towns' around Greater London.[1] This strategy developed the concepts of Purdom and Osborn, Unwin's pioneering work on the Greater London Region, and the recommendations of the 1940 Barlow Commission Report. Abercrombie proposed 10 new towns, each of 60,000 population, to enable the rebuilding of war-damaged central London and slum clearance. The outward spread of the conurbation would be halted by a strict Green Belt policy. In April 1944, Letchworth itself began to look towards its post-war future. 'Letchworth Today and Tomorrow' was an exhibition, organised jointly by First Garden City Ltd. and Letchworth Urban District Council, held at the Grammar School in Town Square.[2] Opened by W. S. Morrison, Minister for Town and Country Planning, its objective was 'to stimulate local interest in the possibilities of a fully developed town'. In one of the associated lectures, George Lionel Pepler, Chief Technical Adviser to the Ministry, commended Letchworth's contribution to physical planning. The incoming Labour government convened a Committee of Inquiry under Lord Reith, in November 1945, to examine the logistics and principles upon which new towns 'should be established and developed as self-contained and balanced communities for work and living'.[3] As well as Frederic Osborn, the most committed of Howard's successors to state initiative in new community development, Walter Gaunt, former Letchworth Estate Manager, and then Chairman of the Hertfordshire County Planning Committee, served. With Reith as a strict taskmaster, 'terse and practical recommendations' were presented, which prepared the ground for the 1946 the New Towns Act. Designation would be pursued 'wherever the Minister is satisfied that it is expedient in the national interest to do so'. Following this there was consultation with local authorities and landowners.

The first, Stevenage New Town, strategically located between Letchworth and Welwyn, was fraught with confrontation between local and national government.[4] Lewis Silkin, Minister for Town and Country Planning, fought the matter to the House of Lords against Stevenage U.D.C. In August 1946 Silkin prevailed – Stevenage New Town was long referred to as 'Silkingrad'! Following designation, a development corporation was appointed 'to acquire, hold, manage and dispose of land ... to carry out building and other operations, to provide water, electricity, gas, sewerage ... and generally to do anything necessary or expedient for the purposes of the New Town ...',[5] in fact, embracing the complex roles of the private companies which had created both Letchworth and Welwyn Garden City. The Corporations were not local authorities, and were accountable to the Minister. They gained a reputation for remoteness. Silkin emphasised that they protected the public interest, and pressed ahead to take control of Welwyn Garden City, despite assurances that the development company would harmonise its operations with those of the public corporations.[6] Silkin demurred, and publicly declared that despite his 'greatest admiration for the pioneering work of the Welwyn Garden City Company ... [it] would not be the right instrument for continuing the task ... the Company is answerable only to its shareholders and to no one else ... only to people with financial interests ... The character of the town ... would be just what the Company would like and not what the people would like. This is opposed to any sense of democracy'. He pressed ahead with the draft Designation Order in January 1948.

That month, Letchworth U.D.C. passed a resolution requesting the Minister to create a Letchworth Development Corporation.[7] As 'the first New Town ... it would be appropriate that it should be completed before other New Towns proposed; and … land was available for 'overspill' from the London area, … the New Towns Policy was the *raison d'etre* of Letchworth's existence'. Silkin promised careful and sympathetic consideration of the matter. F.G.C. Ltd. had not been consulted and expressed their grave doubts whether such a step would be in the best interests of the town. Silkin and his Permanent Secretary, Miss Evelyn Sharp, met Company representatives on 9 June 1948. On 29 July he recalled the Council and stated that 'the Company's Board had assured him that they were anxious to play their part in completing the development of Letchworth', having undertaken to receive industry and population from London. On completion Letchworth would be conveyed to the Council, as was then envisaged with development corporations. The Company had offered two seats on the Board for ministerial nominees. Silkin accepted these assurances and informed the Council that he did not intend to appoint a development corporation, the antithesis of his action at Welwyn. He hoped that Council and Company would in future co-ordinate their activities to the mutual benefit of the town.

The U.D.C. invited F.G.C. Ltd. to nominate representatives for a joint Consultative Committee, to discuss future development and resolve differences amicably. The compulsory purchase of the Grange estate land had soured relations and, in December 1948, the Company offered to the Council, subject only to their paying legal charges, the freehold interest of Norton Common, the Ball Memorial Gardens, Town Square, Howard Park and other open spaces. This was accepted as an article of good faith of the ultimate intention to assign the whole estate. An Extraordinary General Meeting was held on 15 September 1949 to approve the resolution:

> That the stockholders approve in principle the ultimate transfer, when the development of Letchworth is substantially completed, of the Company's undertaking to the Local Authority, or other suitable public body, subject to satisfactory terms being agreed.[8]

At the same meeting there were danger signals, in resolutions to alter the Memorandum of Articles of Association to restrict the surplus to be paid to the town, after winding up the Company, to 10 per cent, on contention that development value of the estate had been nationalised through the 1947 Town and Country Planning Act. This proposition was accepted, virtually *fait accompli*, although the Chairman, Sir Eric MacFadyen, later told Horace Plinston, then U.D.C. Clerk, that, had he known the Council's feelings before the meeting, he would not have put the amendments to the vote. Plinston took Counsel's opinion but was informed that the U.D.C. had no standing to raise the matter. The ultimate community benefit was now restricted to 10 per cent. For the present, MacFadyen initiated a joint Trust, the 'Common Good Fund', into which F.G.C. Ltd. paid £14,000, and subsequent voluntary contributions, to assist the Town's voluntary organisations. It was a case of 'crumbs today' with a declining hope of 'jam tomorrow'.

Planning and Land Values The issue, as to whether land values created by planning should be retained by the owner or taken by the community in whose name the planning decision had been taken, has long remained a political shibboleth.[9] Community benefit from enhanced land values created by development was the foundation of Howard's concept. Unwin wrote extensively on the necessity to recoup a portion of the enhanced values to enable designation or purchase of amenity land and provide compensation for removal of development potential. During the Second World War the Uthwatt Committee examined the question afresh. Under the 1947 Town and Country Planning Act, land remained in private ownership, but development rights in undeveloped land were, in effect, nationalised. Development now required planning permission. If refused, no compensation was payable. Any permission granted which brought an increase in land value, or 'betterment', would be subject to a development charge. A £300,000,000 fund was created to compensate owners who could demonstrate to a Central Land Board that their land had some development value on

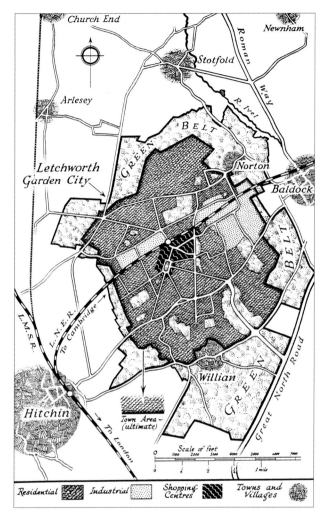

119 The Company Plan, 1946. A further expansion of the urban area, together with an industrial belt linking Letchworth almost to Baldock was envisaged.

the appointed day for the Act. The development charge was a 100 per cent levy. Locally, this halted land transactions except for public development. Resale prices were at existing use value, and the purchaser who carried out the development with planning permission had to pay the difference between purchase price and development value through the development charge.

Under the 1947 Act, the County Council, as planning authority, prepared a town map showing approved primary land use zoning for Letchworth. The draft statement was issued in 1951, and fundamental differences between the Company and Council emerged.[10] F.G.C. Ltd. claimed the right to develop the Norton Common road frontages and received compensation for loss of development value when the area was zoned for open space. The cricket ground had received residential zoning and, following refusal of planning permission, the Company successfully claimed compensation for loss of development value. The same occurred over the cycle park at the corner of Commerce Avenue, where refusal of planning permission to build shops brought £6,000 compensation for loss of development rights. By the mid-1950s, the Company had become more concerned with commercial gain than the longer term community benefit.

Letchworth and Statutory Planning The post-war era of statutory planning overlaid the landlord powers exercised by F.G.C. Ltd. Abercrombie had referred to the development potential of Letchworth in his *Greater London Plan*, and envisaged rapid population and industrial growth. He felt that the 1938 estimated population of 15,000 could be increased by 19,000, overshooting Howard's ultimate 32,000. But he considered the Company's proposed 100 per cent increase of industrial land excessive, bringing the danger of the coalescence of Letchworth with Baldock along the A505. He recommended a town boundary along a line drawn northwards from the Baldock Road pumping station to the railway,[11] a line which never really stood a chance of forming a firm boundary. The Company's post-war plan was shown diagrammatically in F. J. Osborn's newly edited re-issue of *Garden Cities of Tomorrow*, published in 1946.[12] It defined a 'Town Area – (ultimate)', with 'Green Belt' beyond, neither of which was then of statutory significance. Residential land included the Grange and Standalone estates on the north and Lordship/Manor Farm and Jackmans estates on the south, and additional areas which did not appear in the County Development Plan or any subsequent plan, including a 50-acre tract south of the Baldock Road, eventually partly developed with the North Herts Leisure Centre.

Under the 1947 Act, 145 local planning authorities were defined, with the Shire counties and County Borough Councils empowered to prepare development plans, compared with a

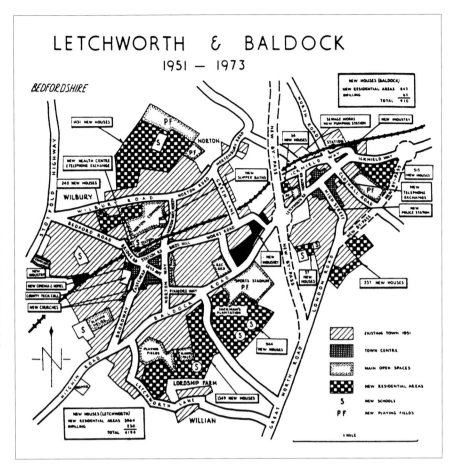

120 The County Development Plan, 1951. The plan made provision for the construction of The Grange and Jackmans Estates and showed the Baldock by-pass with a surface-level interchange for Letchworth on the A505.

potential 1,441 under the pre-war system.[13] The responsibility for forward planning for Letchworth passed to the Hertfordshire County Council, who were required to consult the districts, and could delegate development control. The County Development Plan naturally followed national policies on decentralisation and new towns,[14] and incorporated Hemel Hempstead in addition to Stevenage and Welwyn/Hatfield. The plan covered the years 1951 to 1973. In 1951 Letchworth U.D.C. covered 4,697 acres (1,900 ha.) had a population of 20,321, and £167,589 rateable value. A natural increase of population of 1,420 by 1971 was forecast, with provision for immigration of 10,259 to achieve Howard's projected 32,000 population. To provide employment maximum industrial zoning was included, ignoring Abercrombie's cautionary remarks. Public sector housing would take priority, and the Grange estate, already commenced, was to be completed by 1958-62, together with the newly zoned Jackmans estate. The Manor and Lordship Farm estates would follow in 1963-73. A total of 3,964 houses on new residential sites was envisaged, with a further 230 on infill sites. The overall population density was 13 persons per acre (5.26 per ha.) within the 2,483 acre (1,004 ha.) town area, within which were 1,698 acres (687 ha.) residential land including local shops and schools, and access roads; 273 acres (110 ha.) industrial land; 52 acres (21 ha.) shopping and town centre buildings; 34 acres (13.75 ha.) major educational facilities; and 348 acres (140 ha.) major public and private open spaces. An extension of the main shopping area, a central hotel and a sports stadium were proposed. An A1 Baldock by-pass was proposed with an interchange, presumably a traffic island, on the Baldock to Letchworth road. The omission of this access point on the subsequent A1 Motorway by-pass of the late 1960s subsequently caused problems with traffic approaching or leaving Jubilee Road, which had not been addressed by the end of the 20th century.

121 The Baptist Church, Danescroft, on the Grange Estate, 1963, by Courtenay Crickmer (in association with W. W. Knott). Crickmer had also taken a leading role in planning and designing the housing.

Easing the housing shortage Letchworth U.D.C. faced a substantial demand for housing in 1945. By 1950, 669 Council houses, 47 private houses, and 16 elderly persons bungalows by the Howard Cottage Society, had been completed. The latter, Corner Close, designed by John Tickle, grouped four angled blocks around the junction of Redhoods Way and Bedford Road, and were in the best Garden City tradition, and were the first dwellings completed under the administration of Kathleen Kaye (1912-2001), who managed Howard Cottage from 1944-67. Post-war construction had begun in June 1945 with prefabricated bungalows on the Bedford road, near the Wilbury Road junction. 'Duplex' houses were built on Icknield Way. The pace was slow, however, held up by shortages of materials, labour, and finance. There were 1,570 on the housing waiting list in 1950. 'Pre-fabs' were built off the Bedford Road and lasted for 30 years, until replaced by the Valley Road scheme. A later pre-fab development in Campfield Way and Highover Road, south of Icknield Way, was laid out to best Garden City practice, and in 2001 was under consideration for inclusion within an expanded conservation area.

The Grange Estate north of Wilbury Road had been begun pre-war when the Howard Cottage Society had built semi-detached houses along Grange Road. In 1945, Geoffrey Jellicoe, the eminent landscape architect, prepared a new layout for the 237-acre (96 ha.) site, which included areas for housing association and private development as well as 178 acres of local authority housing. The Company declined to sell the freehold and the Council made a compulsory purchase order.[15] County Council school sites had always been freehold, and were held as a precedent. Moreover, in seeking the freehold, the Council claimed it was anticipating the ultimate transfer of the whole estate. F.G.C. Ltd. maintained that this would break the integrity of the estate and opposed the order, supported by the Letchworth Manufacturers' Association, who feared a burden on the rates. A compromise was accepted under which the Company surrendered the freehold of land required for Council housing but retained the remainder. Development proceeded following Jellicoe's plan, a modified grid layout providing the customary 12 houses to the acre, giving continuity with established standards, and including generous greens and verges. The Letchworth U.D.C. panel of architects was led by Courtenay Crickmer, and included Leonard Brown, Robert Hall and John Tickle – all of whom had worked for Barry Parker in the 1930s. They updated traditional designs, using prominent gables on some housing groups. The extremity of the estate lay two miles north of the town centre, and a self-contained neighbourhood, with schools, shopping centre and playing fields, resulted. In March 1948, U.D.C. Chairman, George Woodbridge, inaugurated construction by John Mowlem and Co. Eastern Way was cut through Eastholm Green to serve the estate, leading into Gaunts Way, named after W. H. Gaunt the Estate Manager, and over to Western Way. Spread over five years of phased construction, the estate represented 'best practice' in post-war housing, comparable with the 'first generation' new town neighbourhoods. 1,431 houses were completed by the early 1960s. Appropriately, Crickmer, by then approaching 85, designed the Grange Baptist Church, in association with W. Knott, a typical building of its period, with low-pitched roofs, a cruciform traceried west window, and a 'space needle' spire, updating the traditional Hertfordshire 'spike'.

Accommodation for London overspill awaited solution of the local housing shortage. The Town Development Act of 1952 was passed by a Conservative Government, and promoted by Harold Macmillan as Minister for Housing and Local Government.[16] It encouraged 'Town development in County districts for the relief of congestion of over-population elsewhere', through local authority agreements 'by friendly negotiation and not imposed by arbitrary power'. The 'exporting' authority could contribute towards infrastructure and public service costs. Schemes in conjunction with the London County Council, which had 246,000 families prepared to move home provided jobs were available, benefited from financial and technical assistance. The farmland around the Jackmans plantation, stretching south-east along Letchworth Gate to Baldock Lane, had been added to the 'town area' and appeared in the County Development Plan. Initially set at 944 houses, an estate of 1,500 was agreed, with development to be phased over 1958-63.[17] In July 1955, agreement in principle with the L.C.C. was announced, to house a population of 5,000 with the estate conveyed to Letchworth U.D.C. after 10 years. Infrastructure grants rose from £60,000 to £105,000. The following year it was revealed that the L.C.C. would finance the £3,000,000 initial expenditure, and would be reimbursed as properties were handed over. Tenant selection would be geared to employment, with the L.C.C. endeavouring to promote industrial mobility. An Exchequer subsidy of £24 per dwelling for 60 years was available, with an additional London grant of £8 per dwelling for 10 years. Land acquisition again created friction. An extension of the industrial area, Blackhorse Road, was to be developed in conjunction with the estate. While F.G.C. Ltd. was prepared to sell residential land, it refused to part with the industrial land. The Ministry and the County Council insisted that the U.D.C. must control the land. Although comparatively remote from Jackmans, a Compulsory Purchase Order for the land was confirmed following agreement that 20 acres of K. & L. land, already zoned for industry and almost bordering the estate, would not be used for 20 years. The District Valuer's report of 7 September 1959 required the Council to pay £62,960 plus fees and legal expenses for the freehold of 212.38 acres (86 ha.), with the Jackmans land priced at £347 per acre, and the Blackhorse Road land at £465. Purchase was completed shortly before the 1959 Town and Country Planning Act restored full market value for development land transactions. The Council had benefited from the dual system whereby, under the 1954 T. & C. P. Act, land was acquired for private development at market value, but for public purposes at existing use value. A few months later the market value of Jackmans was £5,000 per acre.

Planning and design of the Jackmans Estate was undertaken by a local consortium, The Associated Architects – William Barnes, Martin Priestman and Leonard Brown. The layout introduced the principle of pedestrian and vehicular separation, based on the plan for Radburn, New Jersey, U.S.A., the 'New town for the motor age' designed by Henry Wright and Clarence Stein in 1928-9.[18] The adoption of the principles at Letchworth was reflected in the main distributor road being named Radburn Way. Subsidiary culs-de-sac were named in alphabetical sequence – Allison, Bayworth, Chatterton, Denby, Ellice … through to Vincent and Yardley. The estate had its own schools, and a shopping and community centre, with five storeys of flats above, and a circular pub – originally named *The Carousel*. The introduction of modern residential architecture to Letchworth was not an unmixed blessing and the individuality of earlier housing was replaced by a bland reflection of the government's Parker Morris housing standards. The most successful part of the estate was around Chatterton, Denby, Ellice and Fleetwood, where existing trees and hedges were retained, with footpaths leading upwards from Radburn Way. The least successful housing was a prefabricated system, built by Hawthorn Leslie, the Sunderland shipbuilders. Construction of Jackmans began in 1959, and the estate was half-completed by 1965, when the Greater London Council was created, and completed in 1973.

Private development resumed in the mid-1950s after the repeal of building licences and the restoration of market value for private development. Pleasant, if bland, semi-detached and detached houses of Longmead and Hawthorn Hill off Wilbury Road, Cloisters Road, Lawrence Avenue, Bowershott, Lordship Lane and Howard Drive, between Baldock Road and Letchworth Gate, were typical of the period.

Into the Festive 'Fifties   Although post-war austerity had not been entirely dispelled as the 'fifties began, the end of petrol rationing on 26 May 1950 seemed a portent of a bright future. It brought traffic jams and a rise in accidents as motorists tore up their coupons and headed for the coast on the Whitsun holiday weekend. Official exhortation to rejoice, allied to the post-war maxim that 'Britain can make it', came with the Festival of Britain in 1951. It commemorated the centenary of the Great Exhibition in Hyde Park, which had produced Joseph Paxton's astounding Crystal Palace. The government supremo, Herbert Morrison, Lord President of the Council, was a familiar figure in the Garden City, since his spell of compulsory work on the land as a First World War Conscientious Objector. Although the focus was on the modernist exhibition site in London, on the South Bank of the Thames, where the Royal Festival Hall survives as the tangible legacy of the event, there were pleasure gardens at Battersea Park, and a demonstration housing neighbourhood in Lansbury, in the East End. While many Letchworthians could take advantage of a day trip to town, there was an attempt to co-ordinate a national programme of related events. In Letchworth, the programme ran from May to November, with a 'Letchworth can make it' exhibition[19] – Jones Cranes had been used on the South Bank construction phase. On 30 May, the Boyd Neel String Orchestra combined with the Festival Choir in a concert of British music from Purcell to Holst. The Letchworth Film Club recorded the Festival in Letchworth. In October there was a Civic Dinner and Dance at 'The Icknield Halls'. Following a Festival Repertory season at *The St Francis' Theatre*, the Letchworth theatre groups combined for performances of *1066 and all that* from 7-10 November.[20] Kenneth Spinks directed The Settlement Players, S.P.A.D.S. (St. Paul's Amateur Dramatic Society), The Garden City Players, and The Wilbury Players, the Assistant Producer was Hugh Bidwell, and his wife, Margaret arranged the dances.

Golden Jubilee   On 1 September 1953 First Garden City Limited celebrated its Golden Jubilee. The Town and Country Planning Association brought out a special edition of *Town and Country Planning* edited by F. J. Osborn, who drew attention to the uncertainty and excitement of early development financed by 'industrialists and professional men who combined idealism with daring practicality, supported by investors willing to risk their money in an imaginative project'.[21] The ultimate vindication of Letchworth lay, he believed, in the 1946 New Towns Act, a theme brought out by others, so well entrenched was the principle of state initiative. Osborn had assembled a choice collection of articles on virtually every aspect of Letchworth life, with emphasis on pioneer memories. Reminiscence also featured in a Jubilee edition of *The Citizen*.[22]

Celebrations emphasised commerce and industry. Virtually all wartime restriction had disappeared and shopping was in full swing, with a three-guinea prize for identification of mystery articles in 63 shop-windows. The new Ford Zephyr Six was available from Bennetts, the Austin Hereford A70 from Whiteheads in Commerce Avenue, while a Daimler Conquest could be ordered from Dickinson and Adams in Eastcheap for £1,066 plus purchase tax. Television sets sold briskly from 40 guineas (£42) upwards, for this was also Coronation Year. A Jubilee Fair of Industry and Trade was held on the Arena, a muddy patch between the Co-op and the Town Hall Car Park, from 1-3 September, opened by U.D.C. Chairman

George Woodbridge. Additional attractions included 'Jubilarity' a revue by the S.P.A.D.S., a service in Howard Park, a fashion parade by Spirella, and a Letchworth display at the Museum. The opening of the first workshop block of the new North Herts Technical College, on the site west of Broadway, must have recalled the unfulfilled Civic College project.

That's Entertainment Amateur theatre continued to flourish in the 1950s. The Letchworth Arcadians were formed in 1952 and, not surprisingly, their annual programmes began with Lionel Monckton's evergreen light operetta from which they took their name. Over the years they performed many of the most popular musical shows of the century, ranging from *Chu Chin Chow* to *Hello Dolly* via *Showboat* and *Oklahoma!* The 1997 production, *The Wizard of Oz*, could be counted as a Utopian prelude to the centenary of Howard's vision, celebrated the following year. Their first President, R.S. Kellaway, was succeeded by Horace Plinston, who found the company an admirable relaxation away from the rigours of the take-over battle. The Drama Festival was revived in 1946 after the War,

122 In 1955 *The Broadway* was re-equipped to show wide screen films. Fred Astaire again did the honours at the gala re-opening.

and made its home in the Kincaid Hall, constructed from the legacy of the founder of Spirella. Kenneth Spinks and Florence Thompson were leading lights, and Hugh Bidwell (1912-84), architect son of Wilson Bidwell, became President as the Little Theatre Drama Festival evolved. The Settlement Players also broadened their repertoire, giving *Ebenezer's magnetic dream town* in 1983, to celebrate the 80th anniversary of the Garden City, and *The Killing of Sister George* in 1987. In November 2001 they gave Oscar Wilde's *An Ideal Husband*. The S.P.A.D.S. (St Paul's Amateur Dramatic Society) was founded in 1937, as the Young Fellowship Players, based on the St Paul's Church Hall. Their annual pantomimes became a Letchworth institution, held at Plinston Hall since the 1980s, where they staged *Puss in Boots* for Christmas 2001. During the 1950s, the popularity of the cinema waned with the rise of television. *The Palace* and *The Broadway* began to seem outdated: in 1955 both were refurbished to show the new wide screen CinemaScope films. Alterations to *The Broadway* were supervised by Hugh Bidwell, who had worked on the original design in his father's office. There was a gala re-opening on 12 September, again black tie and evening dress, as Fred Astaire elegantly danced his way across the giant 'curvilinear' screen, this time partnered by the endearingly waif-like Leslie Caron, in *Daddy Long Legs*. After a long, slow decline, *The Broadway* regained its glamour in the 1990s, as will be told in Chapter Sixteen.

The 1950s also witnessed the capitulation of the Garden City to the liquor trade. On 17 May 1957 there was a vote in favour of a licensed hotel with residential accommodation, public lounge, restaurant, ballroom, bars etc! This materialised a few years later as *The Broadway Hotel*, a neat if somewhat pedantic Georgian-style building designed by Sidney Clark. Construction began in 1961, and the hotel was opened on 17 October 1962, hosting a Civic Dinner to celebrate the passing of the Letchworth Garden City Corporation Act a few weeks later.

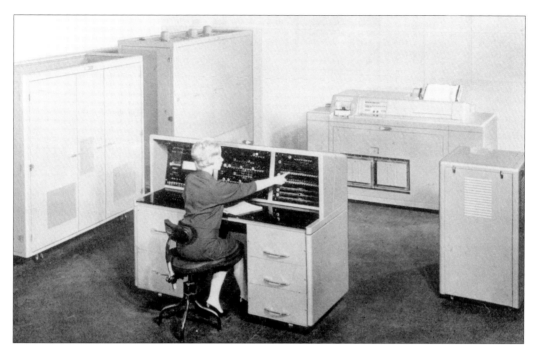

123   I.C.T. Type 1202 computer. Early computers were extremely bulky and demanded the energy resources of a miniature power station.

Full Employment   The industrial theme heralded the complete post-war industrial recovery.[23] Between 1945 and 1953, 12 new factories ranging from 3,000 to 30,000 sq. ft. were built, giving a total of 2¼ million sq. ft. industrial floorspace, with over 10,000 employees. In the 1950s many firms consolidated their operations, among them Shelvoke and Drewry and K. & L., while Spirella still retained its pre-eminence for female employment. After concentrating on traditional styles during the inter-war period, Meredew manufactured Utility furniture, and then branched out into the popular 'contemporary' style.[24] A German refugee, Alphons Loebenstein was recruited as designer in 1945. The output of modern furniture required precise manufacture, and the range was based on modular measurements. The firm also contracted to produce Heal's modular range, and later, under licence from Knoll International, manufactured the famous chromium steel-framed and leather-cushioned 'Barcelona Chair', designed by the architect Ludwig Mies van der Rohe to furnish an exhibition pavilion in 1929.

Expansion of the industrial estate eastward brought a new length of Works Road and of Jubilee Road, which led to Baldock Road. In 1955, Borg Warner, a Division of the American company manufacturing automatic transmissions and linked with Morse Chain, built a £4,000,000 factory along the entire eastern side of Jubilee Road, backing onto the reservation for the future Baldock By-Pass. They obtained contracts from many of the leading motor manufacturers and became one of the leading employers in the town. Opposite them, Armco, the English Division of a company from Ohio, U.S.A., built a major new plant which manufactured small diameter double walled steel tubing for automotive and engineering industries. 'British Tab' continued to manufacture and market 'Hollerith' accounting machines, and their punched card data recording system paved the way for computer manufacture in the late 'fifties. By 1958, they employed over 8,000, and were reconstituted as International Computers and Tabulators Ltd., in a merger with Power-Samas, evidence of the growing importance of computers for financial and administrative purposes. Early electronic computers were unwieldy, with information stored on punched cards similar to the earlier tabulators, and a control console the size of a large office desk. The firm outgrew its Icknield Way premises, and in 1963 completed a visually insensitive office block in Town Square. Through acquisition of the computer department of Ferranti in September 1963 and a merger with English Electric in 1969, they became International Computers Ltd., known locally by their initials, 'I.C.L.'.

Modern Architecture in Letchworth   Post-war architecture incorporated concrete and steel framed structures, large glazed areas, with multi-storey forms and flat roofs increasingly predominant. Housing designs were simplified by the elimination of chimneys, bay windows and non-functional ornament, with roof pitches brought down to 30 degrees or less. Traditional materials were often reduced to a veneer. Substitutes such as concrete panels or concrete tiles were widely used. Architecture lost its strong local affinity for a bland 'anywhere' character or a deliberately assertive iconoclasticism. Many new Letchworth buildings lacked a regard for their context.[25]

Educational buildings showed a remarkable visual and functional transformation.[26] In the 1940s traditional materials were scarce, and the County Architect, C. H. Aslin, was faced with an unprecedented demand for new schools in the new towns and rapidly expanding residential estates. The outcome was a lightweight system of pre-fabricated construction, with an 8ft. 3in. modular steel framework (later 3ft. 4in.; 1.0 m.), clad with precast concrete panels, extensive glazing and flat roofs. Used for primary schools, the system allowed considerable freedom of planning to form classroom groups with associated cloakroom spaces, adaptable assembly halls with generous lighting, and courtyards for outdoor teaching. At their best, the county schools were outstandingly elegant, and created an informal and high quality environment for innovative teaching. The Wilbury School off Bedford Road (1949) and the Northfields Infants School on the Grange Estate (1951) are fine examples of the system at its best. The results were not so happy in larger buildings. The Willian School on the Jackmans Estate (1963) was more impersonal, while the additions to Norton School clashed with the innovative design of the first purpose-built Garden City school. Most unfortunate of all was the North Herts College campus, with an outlook to the Town Square and a Broadway frontage following demolition of the old Methodist Church. The design was no doubt functionally based, with its combination of low rooflit workshop blocks, and two-storey and four-storey teaching blocks. The college opened in 1958 and provided long needed higher education facilities for day, evening and industrial day release courses for 5,000 students. The cost to the character of the town centre was considerable. A grouping to achieve visual enclosure for the town square frontage, or to balance the Town Hall, was studiously avoided, and the two-storey block set back from Broadway was an apologetic recognition of the street frontage. Significantly, nothing was done to link up to the well-proportioned Georgian-style Boys Club, where the blank fletton brickwork side elevation long remained a reminder of an opportunity missed. The siting of the college also removed the possibility of developing Westcheap. The site was ultimately redeveloped in 1998-9 for the new Morrisons supermarket, with the College relocated in a three-storey corner block, facing the Kennedy Gardens.

The town's first post-war commercial development showed a similar disregard for its context. 'Arena Parade', on the vacant site twixt Co-op and car park, designed in 1958 by Eric H. Davie, represented an updating of the pre-war shopping parades, sensibly planned with rear servicing to enable the pedestrianisation of Eastcheap. Visually it claimed modernity with a flat roof and brick and artificial stone cladding, and window treatment suggesting the fashionable curtain walling. It would have fitted without comment into Stevenage town centre only six miles away, but it had no affinity with Letchworth. The same was true of office blocks. The I.C.L. Offices in Town Square were designed by Trehearne Norman, Preston and Partners. Completed in 1963, the plans had been approved by the Letchworth U.D.C. after rumours of pressure from the Company. The monotonous grid of windows and blank purple brick ends above a slightly recessed ground floor represented another building

124   North Hertfordshire Technical College, officially opened 15 June 1958 occupied the land intended as 'Westcheap', to complete the town centre. It was demolished in 1998, and the site was redeveloped by Morrisons.

almost perversely determined to reject its context. A wedge-shaped office block in Station Place was equally uninspiring, while the offices in Norton Way South, on the site of the old St Michael's Church, compounded a depressing saga.

Churches were happily more individual. St Michael's developed their permanent site on Town Square between 1966-68, with a neat polygonal brick church, with windows ingeniously provided in the angles, and a roofline enlivened by a cupola and spirelet. The architect was Laurance King. Internally the church was undemonstrative, with a central altar below the cupola and a suspended crucifix, and its highlight was the excellent modern stained glass by John Hayward. The Roman Catholics also built their permanent church, St Hugh of Lincoln, facing Town Square, a pre-war design by Charles Nicholas and John Edward Dixon-Spain (1878-1955), but not built until the early 1960s, and consecrated in 1964. The setback from the frontage was a serious visual flaw, exposing the Museum's 'temporary' end as likely to remain permanent. Barry Parker had wrestled with the problem in 1938, but to no avail. Once built, the new church was a handsome traditional structure, with its walls treated as a series of receding planes, but the pale brickwork was distinctly out of harmony with the predominant red of the majority of buildings in Town Square. Nor was the design improved by the addition, in 1985, of dark grey concrete tiled pitched roofs.

A third new church was perhaps the most uncompromising in design and ultimately the most successful. A small church hall had been built at the corner of Norton Way North and Common View. In the early 1960s, St George's church was designed by Peter Bosanquet, of Brett, Boyd and Bosanquet. It ingeniously exploited the acute angle of the corner site and its change in level, with the church situated above ancillary accommodation. Externally, the building had bold geometrical form, with a low sweeping roof, complementing the vernacular forms of nearby housing. The walls were rather blandly

125 St George's Church, Norton Way North, 1963-64. This church with its soaring concrete spire remains one of the most notable modern buildings in Letchworth.

treated and might have justified a bolder, more sculptural approach. The handling of the concrete spire was very successful, formed of two angles of a triangle, which sheltered a rooflight between, and penetrated the structure to form the backdrop to the altar, with an impressive crucifix above. At the west end, a tapered concrete pier supported the circular ring of the font and the roof. A fine organ gallery concealed the main entrance a level below. The church was consecrated on 27 July 1964. It proved that 1960s archi-tecture could carry conviction and yet remain responsive to its surroundings. Regrettably, it was an exceptional achievement in Letchworth.

FOURTEEN

SAVE LETCHWORTH GARDEN CITY

Danger Signals   Post-war growth, particularly after the dismantling of the development charge, raised the overall value of the estate and made it an attractive target for speculators.[1] In 1955, the net profit reached £24,702, modest enough, triggering a substantial increase in the value of Ordinary Shares; the £1 stock jumped to 26s. 0d. (£1.30). Suspecting the possibility of a take-over, the Council requested a meeting with the Board but this was refused. A group of shareholders, fearing possible nationalisation of the estate, suggested disposal of assets, which in turn alarmed the Company, whose Board feared intense speculation to obtain the remaining developable land. The Board determined to stand firm and bring the project to completion for the benefit of shareholders as 'a substantial reward for their faith and patience during the years of growth'. The social purpose of the original development was progressively dismissed. At an Extraordinary General Meeting on 6 April 1956 Sir Eric MacFadyen pronounced that a joint stock company was 'a very inappropriate method of carrying out a social experiment'. It was also proposed to remove dividend limits, strongly opposed by the Council and the Town and Country Planning Association. Sir Eric reiterated that the assets were the property of the shareholders and that 'we have learned on good advice … that there is no binding obligation to carry out the original policy'. The Board's proxies enabled the resolutions to be passed overwhelmingly.

A Public Meeting held the following July, addressed by Lord Silkin, urged the Company to recognise their moral obligations. Horace Plinston was asked to find a way to protect and restore the community's interests. Although the Council were assured that the estate would ultimately pass to them, relations with F.G.C. Ltd. continued to be uneasy. The 10 per cent surplus for charitable purposes, following the winding up of the Company, added to the articles in 1957, was viewed by C. B. Purdom as 'knocking nails into the coffin of the Garden City, supposing it to be dead!'. Dividends rose steadily, 4½ per cent, 5 per cent, 7½ per cent – equivalent to 9 per cent, 10 per cent and 15 per cent on the original capital. In 1959, 8½ per cent was declared with a 'special dividend' of three per cent, a total of 11½ per cent representing 23 per cent on the original capital.

In January 1960, the £2 shares were divided into four 10s. 0d. (50p) shares, but voting rights remained unaltered; 20 of the new Ordinary Shares were required for one vote. The new shares immediately rose in value – 37s. 7½d. (£1.88) in May, 50s. 0d. (£2.50) in August. The following month a take-over struggle was in progress.

The Take-over   On 2 September 1960, the Raglan Property Trust made a requisition for an Extraordinary General Meeting to restructure the Company, removing the Ministerial nominations of two Board places, and urging the approval of a more swift development of the remainder of the estate, and winding up of the Company. This was a direct consequence of the final restoration of market value in land transactions. Drivers Jonas had valued the Company's assets at £1,635,000 in 1958, and the recent rise in share prices indicated a total of at least £2,000,000, compared with nominal share capital of £650,000. Raglan's Chairman and Vice Chairman, Group Captain Maurice Newnham and Brigadier Eric Flavell, stood for election to F.G.C. Ltd. Board.

This appeared to represent an attack on the town's inheritance. The Council alerted the Divisional M.P., Martin Maddan, and on 4 October 1960 met Dame Evelyn Sharp at the Ministry of Housing and Local Government. She again discounted the possibility of forming a development corporation, but suggested that the promotion of a private bill to create a non-political trustee body, in whom the estate might be vested, might be sympathetically considered. Three days later at the A.G.M., the F.G.C. Chairman emphasised that the Company wished to continue to develop the estate with regard to the green belt and other constraints, but contracts for large commercial and industrial premises, both within and beyond, would bring higher dividends. The Garden City supporters were between Scylla and Charybdis – they were fundamentally opposed to the Raglan overtures, yet F.G.C. Ltd. was also treading the entrepreneurial path. Ernest Gardiner of the Letchworth Civic Trust felt that the 'break up boys' were about to move in. Horace Plinston pointed out that the £2,250,000 Company investment should be set against the £6,500,000 spent by the Council on provision of services and property development: to a large degree the enhanced value of the estate was a reflection of the Council's investment in town development. The resolutions were defeated, and Newnham and Flavell were spurned. However, the result was a reverse rather than a defeat. The Company remained vulnerable. Plinston assessed the acquisition costs at £2,000,000, raised at 6¼ per cent, which would represent an annual charge of £128,000, and a deficit of £48,000, which with a penny rate product of £2,200 would require a 2s.0d. (10p) rate. Even if a Parliamentary Bill were successful, would ratepayers accept this?

In the midst of uncertainty there was renewed attack on 4 November 1960. Forty Lane Securities, a Raglan subsidiary controlled by Newnham, offered £1 5s. 0d. (£1.25) for each £1 of Preference Stock, which with its superior voting rights represented the cheapest way of obtaining control. Ernest Gardiner appealed to shareholders to pass their stock to the Civic Trust. A new contender entered the lists, Mrs. Amy Rose of Hotel York Ltd. Few suspected that this concern would shortly acquire the assets of the Company. Hotel York was a London-based property holding company, entirely owned or controlled by the Rose family, who

126 'Handbagging Letchworth'. Mrs Amy Rose outside the Estate office, following the takeover by her company, Hotel York Ltd.

had become directors in December 1958. Two London hotels, the *Welbeck Palace* and the *Berners*, had been sold, and Mrs Rose, a shrewd business operator, sought further investments to enhance the assets of her 'Family Trust'. On 19 November 1960, Hotel York indicated to shareholders its willingness to purchase the entire £150,000 6 per cent cumulative Preference Stock for 32s. 0d. (£1.60) for each unit, and 260,100 Ordinary Shares for 50s. 0d. (£2.50) each. Mrs. Rose undertook to ensure the integrity of the Letchworth estate although many including Plinston and Purdom doubted the veracity of this, given her propensity for lucrative asset stripping. The Board warned against acceptance of the offers, although the Company Secretary, J. D. Ritchie, was thought to be more receptive to Mrs. Rose's proposition. F.G.C. Ltd. was doubtful whether the proposed Letchworth Bill would succeed and Mrs. Rose became aware of this. She told Plinston that she could not understand opposition to her take-over bid; Plinston informed her that, whatever happened, the Council would press ahead with the Bill. His parting shot was, 'the Bill will be accepted and I do not think your Company will lose money. If I were a betting man, I'd have my usual golfing stake of 2s. 6d. (12½p) on each'.

SAVE Letchworth Garden City

PUBLIC MEETING

called by **ERNEST G. GARDINER**

THURSDAY DECEMBER 1 at 7.30 p.m.

GRAMMAR SCHOOL
Assembly Hall

127 Ernest Gardiner called for support to Save the Garden City at a meeting on 1 December 1960.

Three days later Raglan sold out to Hotel York. On 16 December, Mrs. Rose was invited to take a seat on the Board. The lady, whose abiding image among Letchworth residents is of an imposing fur-swathed presence transported to the offices in a glossy limousine, had won. She became Managing Director on 5 January 1961, with her son, Michael Balfour Rose, alongside her on the Board. At the Company Annual General Meeting, a few weeks later, Mrs. Rose and her son were re-elected over the Civic Trust candidates, Edwin Nott and Florence Thompson.

Save Letchworth Garden City! The Council had already been alerted to the dangers. On 22 November 1960, a letter was published in *The Times* and locally, signed by party leaders on the Council, which indicated unanimity in defending the ideals of Letchworth against the speculators, irrespective of political belief, through the formation of a non-political trustee body to hold and manage the assets of F.G.C. Ltd., for the benefit of the community.

While the cost of acquisition by a trustee body would be considerable, resulting in deficits in early years, the venture would ultimately prove profitable and the 'rich harvest' would be garnered. Ernest Gardiner called a 'Save Letchworth Garden City' Public Meeting for 1 December 1960 at the newly completed Grammar School Hall, attended by over five hundred. The Divisional M.P., Martin Maddan, authorised the release of a Press Statement indicating his support for the proposed Parliamentary Bill, which he believed would gain Commons approval. Lord Pethick-Lawrence and Purdom addressed the meeting. Ernest Gardiner emphasised the urgency of the situation, picturing speculators walking away 'with a profit of £1,000,000 leaving Letchworth with nothing but its name'. It was evident to Councillor Charles Sax, leader of the Labour majority, that residents were strongly behind moves to promote a Private Bill. He was concerned about the pressure on Plinston and his department, and hoped that the matter would proceed to a successful conclusion. The meeting approved a formal petition to the Minister of Housing and Local Government.

> Letchworth was the first 'New Town' and the vesting of the entirety of the land assets of a New Town in a body which is removed from the sphere of commercial gain is a principle recognised by the Government. We therefore petition the Minister … to take statutory action to secure that the Company and its lessees are protected from the activities of property speculators so that the intention of vesting the undertaking in a public body for the benefit of the community can be implemented.

The petition attracted 8,319 signatures. U.D.C. Chairman, Colin Bywaters called 20 'formal signatories' and the petition was despatched and presented to the House of Commons by Martin Maddan on 24 January 1961. A political truce was declared locally, pending resolution of the fundamental question of the future ownership of the Letchworth Estate.

The Parliamentary timetable did not permit hearings until after November 1961. Meanwhile, following the A.G.M., Mrs.Rose had *carte blanche* for action. The Board decided to obtain a new valuation, and also offered freeholds for auction. Hitherto only Church, amenity, County Council and, latterly, U.D.C. housing land had been disposed of in this manner. In July 1961, 'By order of First Garden City Ltd.', Jones, Lang, Wootton & Sons circulated a prospectus[2] offering a 10-acre (4 ha.) parcel of Howard Drive, and two-acre (0.80 ha.) plots in Cloisters Lawns and Howardswood, all with outline permission for residential development, for sale by auction on 25 July. £50,000 was obtained for the Howard Drive site, notwithstanding the Council warning that it would re-possess the land if the Bill were successful. F.G.C. Ltd. threatened a libel action against Horace Plinston. They had also discussed a population target of 60,000 with Ernest Doubleday, the County Planning Officer, suggesting that lucrative development of additional Green Belt land was envisaged. Freehold reversions were offered, and Howard's objectives appeared under attack on all fronts.

Protracted Preparation   Howard had been sceptical of Government as a vehicle for social reform. It was perhaps ironic that 'this cumbrous complex piece of machinery' (Howard's unflattering view of government procedure, excised from the published version of *Tomorrow*) should ultimately have proved the saviour of Letchworth Garden City. It was, perhaps, doubly ironic that the measure should have been presented to, and enacted by, a Conservative Government. Preparatory work and propaganda were considerable. For once, the devil did not always have the best tunes. The acrimonious A.G.M. of 16 February 1961 was linked to a leader in *The Times* which drew attention to 'A town based on principles', and concluded that 'it would indeed be a matter for dismay if purely commercial considerations were to prevail'. The Company tactics were directed towards maximum expansion, and raising the value of the estate in an effort to deter the Council. Plinston requested the Hertfordshire County Council to consider a penny rate contribution as a loan to be paid back with interest once profits materialised, on the basis that Letchworth had contributed greatly to the County's overall prosperity and rateable value. Although the County Council were sympathetic, they were wary over the principle involved, and declined support. Through the tactful fence-mending by County Alderman Claude Barker, the recorded decision expressed sympathy with the endeavours of the U.D.C. to secure the passage of the Bill.

In January 1961, the U.D.C. retained Sharpe Pritchard and Company as their Parliamentary Agents. Wentworth Pritchard took personal responsibility for the Bill. Private Bill procedure had been followed by many local authorities since the 18th century. It was initiated by deposit of the Bill on petition at the Private Bill Office for scrutiny by the Examiners. It then required a promoter to introduce it in Parliament. Geoffrey Lawrence, Q.C. was engaged as Leading Counsel, with Eric Blain as his junior. Stanley Hill was appointed as the Council's Finance Adviser. Plinston approached G. M. P. Williams, the St Albans District Valuer, to prepare a valuation of the estate. Williams had been responsible for the valuation of Welwyn Garden City when taken over by the Development Corporation, and had also valued the U.D.C. compulsory purchase of the Grange and Jackmans land.

The Council continued regular contact with Evelyn Sharp. In July 1961 she emphasised that acquisition terms and valuation methods constituted crucial points. Stanley Hill explained the distinction between a 'break up' and a 'going concern' valuation, at which the Council wished to acquire the assets. Martin Maddan suggested use of Stock Exchange value, but Dame Evelyn disagreed, and suggested that current value be used. The valuation by the District Valuer represented this basis and was also close to share price valuation. Dame Evelyn was unable to offer assistance through the Ministry, nor provide a reference to the Public Works Loan Board. On the constitutional question, Martin Maddan emphasised the proposed independence of the body from the local authority and party politics, and stated that the Minister should appoint a majority on the Board. Dame Evelyn felt that the Minister would not accept responsibility for a corporation which was not a

Government creation. In conclusion she rated the chances of success at slightly below fifty-fifty.

The U.D.C. appointed a Sub-Committee – Councillors Sax, Askew and Talbot – to take day-to-day decisions relating to the Bill, and Plinston was appointed as policy witness for the Parliamentary hearings. Maddan met his Conservative colleagues, allaying fears that the Bill might establish an undesirable precedent and represent municipalisation of a registered public company. Omens were not favourable at this stage for, unless the Bill had the co-operation of the Minister, it was regarded as a non-starter. Yet it could be pointed out that the Bill sought to protect the interests of residents and householders; if the Government were to preside over its defeat, the example would not be lost on the opposition, not least for its propaganda value. Maddan briefed Henry Brooke, Minister of Housing and Local Government, on the Bill, who indicated that he would not object in principle, but wished to be satisfied that the measure was both fair to shareholders and a viable proposition for ratepayers.

Locally, the question of additional rates loomed large. Sidney Stapleton, an 'Independent Ratepayer' candidate in the May 1961 elections, estimated a 10s. 0d. rate. Although this was wildly exaggerated, nobody knew for certain what the figure would be. The unwillingness of the County Council to assist was serious, as their penny rate was equivalent to a local rate of 2s. 3d.

On 10 October 1961 the Council met the Company, Councillors Gay, Askew, Sax, and Talbot with Mrs. Rose, and Oliver Smedley and John Rosevear, both F.G.C. Directors, the latter professionally a surveyor and compensation valuer. Presentation of the Bill was expected after the Parliamentary recess. The U.D.C. was prepared to discuss a price if the Company was prepared to implement the 1949 promise to transfer the undertaking to a local authority or public body. Smedley replied that the Board was interested in the benefit of the community only insofar as it benefited shareholders. 'I do not believe that in the changed circumstances one can expect implementation of the Ebenezer Howard ideals ... There is no sentimental Ebenezer miasma - we are a commercial company.'

Valuations were far apart - the *Evening Standard* had disclosed a U.D.C. figure of £2,000,000 whilst Smedley hinted that Cluttons' valuation for F.G.C. Ltd. would be above £3,500,000. There was no basis for a negotiated agreement. In reporting to the Council in November, Plinston had to tackle the thorny question of valuation. It was essential to avoid extravagant compensation claims, and all methods posed problems, with share valuation fluctuating in response to the Stock Market. The draft Bill had incorporated values based on 50s. 0d. (£2.50) for Ordinary Shares and 20s. 0d. (£1.00) for Preference Shares (the book value), giving a total of £2,650,000. The Council substituted 'market value as a going concern' on 16 November, and Stanley Hill calculated that a purchase price of £2.3m would, at the prevailing interest rate of 6¾ per cent, give a 1s. 3d. (7p) rate surcharge. F.G.C. Ltd. countered with Cluttons' valuation of £3,712,582. The U.D.C. considered the possibility of acquiring only the town area, excluding the 2,000-acre (809 ha.) green belt, which had acquired statutory protection through the County Development Plan. However, this would infringe the unity of the Letchworth estate, which was one of the key points in the argument. Plinston's calm grasp of detail at this stage was remarkable. In the midst of fears of escalating valuations, he inserted a clause exempting the ultimate transaction from Stamp Duty, and saved the Corporation almost £60,000 in the process.

The Views of the House   Parliamentary Standing Orders required notice of the Bill to be served on 4,000 separate interested parties, while a Book of Reference and a large-scale Plan identifying every separate interest had to be deposited before Parliament. The latter was compiled under the leadership of Plinston's deputy, Michael Kelly, using rating records as a base. The Book (virtually a new Garden City 'Domesday' survey) was deposited on 20 November 1961, the Council formally resolved to promote the Bill on 22 November, and the Bill petition was deposited a week later. Notices were published locally and in the *London Gazette*, served on all owners, lessees and occupiers, and on 4 December the Bill was deposited in the Commons

Private Bill Office, with a statement confirming compliance with Standing Orders. On 17 December there was a town meeting of electors at the Grammar School Hall. The Company forecast a 5s. 0d. (25p) rate increase and urged residents to 'Ban the Bill'. The meeting was addressed by the U.D.C. Financial Adviser, Stanley Hill, who explained the financial provisions, and was inevitably challenged by Sidney Stapleton. While risks were recognised, the overwhelming tenor of the meeting was positive and the resolution was carried: 442 for, 24 against. However, F.G.C. Ltd. obtained 100 signatures, and requisitioned a poll, held 6 January 1962, at which 3,183 were in favour and 903 against, on a low 25 per cent turnout. However, this cleared the last hurdle before presentation to Parliament. On 24 January 1962, it was deemed to have received its First Reading, through being placed on the Speaker's table.

The Bill provided for the creation of a Letchworth Garden City Corporation as a public authority,[3] with members appointed by the Minister, by the County Council, and by the U.D.C. The estate would be managed as an entity in accordance with the principles in operation until 1960. The estate would be conveyed as a whole to the new body, following which any adverse balance in revenue would be made good by the Council. After meeting all claims, any balance would be spent in favour of the community. The Company counterpetitioned, claiming a lack of justification for confiscation of private property, in the interest, not of the community, but merely that of the Council. A meeting of the Back Benchers Committee decided not to oppose the Bill. Charles Sax and Plinston met Labour M.P.s who, not surprisingly, indicated their sympathy. Plinston ensured that all parties received briefing notes on the significance of the Bill and of Letchworth itself.

The Second Reading was deferred several times, and an attempt was made by Ray Mawby, M.P. for Totnes, to defer the Second Reading by six months. However, the debate took place on 20 March. At 7.04 p.m., Lord Balniel introduced the Bill and moved the Second Reading. Dr Barnett Stross (Labour, Stoke-on-Trent) reiterated that unified ownership of Letchworth should be preserved. Ray Mawby saw the Bill as an effort to nationalise an ordinary property company. Speeches from all sides often mingled personal memories of Letchworth life with the necessity to perpetuate its founder's ideals. The Minister, Dr. Charles Hill, recommended that the Bill be examined in Select Committee. Before the Division, Martin Maddan paid tribute to Howard's ideals which had been translated into three-dimensional reality at Letchworth. He quoted Osborn, a Socialist, on the benefits of planning and unified site ownership, coupled with leaseholds, reconciling public interests with freedom of choice and enterprise. He noted that the F.G.C. Ltd. Annual Report dated 13 March 1962 stated that 'the vast majority of the present shareholders have invested in this Company to obtain maximum increase on their investment and it is the Board's policy to act in the interest of these shareholders'. He urged passage of the Bill to remove the town from the mercy of speculators and to benefit from strong management divorced from political interference. The House divided at 9.59 p.m. The Reading was carried: ayes 246, noes 13. Plinston felt he was dreaming when he heard the tellers' announcement. Conservatives such as John Biffen, John Biggs Davidson, W. F. Deedes, Charles Hill, Iain Macleod, Gerald Nabarro, Francis Pym and Geoffrey Rippon rubbed shoulders in the division lobbies with Labour stalwarts including Bessie Braddock, Fenner Brockway, James Callaghan, Barbara Castle, Judith Hart, Jennie Lee, Philip Noel-Baker and George Thomas. It was a remarkable night both for Parliament and for Letchworth.

The A.G.M. of F.G.C. Ltd. was held on 6 April 1962. Osborn and other prominent shareholders had drawn attention to inaccuracies in Mrs Rose's statements. At the meeting, Christopher Cadbury moved the rejection of the Report and Accounts, but although passed by a show of hands it was lost on a poll. Osborn moved a resolution asking the Directors to withdraw opposition to the Bill, which was carried 40 to 27 on a show of hands, but defeated 45,853 to 2,119 on a poll. Osborn's proxies from 248 shareholders, with 246,864 Ordinary and 16,312 Preference Shares, represented 20 per cent of the voting strength, but were declared invalid on a technicality.

Timing of the A.G.M. ensured further ammunition for the Examination in Select Committee. The Parties were represented by Counsel, with expert witnesses cross-examined. The Committee sat on Tuesdays, Wednesdays, Thursdays, from 11-1 and 2-4.30, commencing 2 May 1962. It comprised five Conservative and four Labour members, under the Chairmanship of Sir Samuel Storey. On behalf of the U.D.C. Geoffrey Lawrence, Q.C. presented an opening statement giving the history of the Company and its recent actions, summarising the provisions of the Bill, particularly the compensation arrangements, and claiming the overall fairness of measure. The Minister had reported favourably and, while ordinarily he was critical of compulsory purchase of private estates, there was much to be said for the ownership being a trustee for the citizens. The management arrangements appeared likely to prove satisfactory. The Minister was prepared to accept his responsibilities if the Bill were passed. This positive start was compounded by Plinston's expert testimony and astute response to cross-examination. Stanley Hill brought out the relevant financial details and revealed that investors had had ample warning of the possibility of public ownership from such an impeccable source as the *Stock Exchange Yearbook*. This noted that in September 1949 the shareholders had 'approved in principle the ultimate transfer, when development is completed, of the undertaking to public ownership subject to satisfactory terms being agreed', information provided by First Garden City Ltd! Under cross-examination he maintained that Cluttons' valuation represented asset stripping. Sir Frederic Osborn appeared and stated that Letchworth had pioneered the official British policy on decentralisation and that the protection of its integrity was of world-wide significance.

For the Company, C. P. Harvey, Q.C. challenged the claim that the Corporation brought any lasting public benefit. The U.D.C. case was pure hypocrisy for they had forced the F.G.C. Ltd. to sell the freehold of the Grange Estate. The Bill challenged the right of a company to manage its affairs in the best interests of its shareholders, and the provisions for compensation were not in accord with the Land Compensation Act 1961. Few modifications were made in Committee. On 21 May it was stated that the Bill would be addressed to the house. It received its Third Reading and passed to the Lords. F.G.C. Ltd. launched a propaganda war – a four-column tirade in the *City Press* circulating in London, headed 'Prejudice or justice – Facts for the House of Lords in the Letchworth Dispute', and petitioned the Lords against the Bill. Again the Council prepared its case thoroughly. Business followed the pattern of the Lower House and the Second Reading commenced at 6.30 p.m. on 28 June 1962. Lord Molson moved the Reading, supported by Lord Silkin, now reconciling his 1948 opinion that a public corporation was not appropriate, by stating that Sir Eric MacFadyen's undertaking that Letchworth would be run in accordance with Howard's principles had now vanished. Earl Jellicoe, on behalf of the Government, recommended the formal Reading which was unopposed. The Lords Select Committee under Lord Strang commenced on 3 July 1962. Speaking for F.G.C. Ltd., Michael Wheeler, Q.C. withdrew opposition on principle, but remained opposed to the compensation arrangements, and examination of detail continued. Clause 15 of the Bill envisaged a transaction between a willing seller and a willing buyer and was subject to close scrutiny. Much time was spent on the divergence between the U.D.C. and F.G.C. Ltd. valuations. At a late stage Wheeler attacked the 'Letchworth principles' referred to in the Bill as being vague and uncertain. Although recounted by Plinston under cross-examination, they were not to be found in the Company's Memorandum of Articles of Association which referred to Howard's book in the vaguest terms. F.G.C. Ltd. were also concerned about the definition of 'going concern'. After the Third Day the Chairman concluded that the preamble was proved without amendment and the Bill returned to the House.

The Report Stage and Third Reading on 18 July 1962 were formalities, and on 1 August 1962 the Royal Assent was given.[4] The struggle was over for the present. The Council held a special meeting on 3 August 1962 to celebrate a unique historic event, recording thanks to Martin Maddan and all concerned. A Civic Dinner was held at *The Broadway Hotel* on 8 December 1962. Bound copies of the Act were presented to Martin Maddan and Horace Plinston. Donald Howard, Mabel Barry Parker and many pioneers were present to toast the new Corporation.

128 Horace Plinston (*right*) presented with a copy of Letchworth Garden City Corporation Act by Cllr. William Askew. Plinston's deputy, Michael Kelly, arranged for the second presentation copy of the Act to be made in secret for a surprise event at the civic dinner held on 8 December 1962.

Notwithstanding the passing of the Act, First Garden City Ltd. showed a perverse determination to be awkward and the last few months passed in open warfare. In July 1962, when it was evident that the Bill would succeed, an E.G.M. was called to amend the Articles to remove the 10 per cent surplus payable to a charitable concern after winding up, which had been agreed in 1957, and a poll carried the matter with a large majority. Plinston had to obtain an injunction to restrain the Company from selling or granting new leases on several sites. On 1 January 1963 snow covered the Broadway pavements as Horace Plinston, accompanied by Laurie Freeman, entered the Estate Offices. Amy Rose had stripped out office furniture and stationery. 'What a dump' was the new Corporation's Chairman, R. A. Humbert's reaction, as he arrived to find Plinston working at a borrowed desk and chair. Four weeks later the Corporation sent a lorry to collect the furniture from one of Mrs Rose's London hotels. Post, on her insistence, was delivered to London, which meant that she saw many letters requiring the Corporation's attention.

Appointees to the Corporation were discussed with Evelyn Sharp. Colonel R. A. Humbert, a member of Welwyn Development Corporation and a St Albans-based surveyor, was appointed Chairman. The remaining members were Sir Harold Fieldhouse, Leslie Bennett, D. G. Haddow, Alderman County Councillor Claude Barker and Councillor Charles Sax. Board meetings were initially held at Welwyn Development Corporation offices to preserve confidentiality. Plinston's secondment as Solicitor and Legal Adviser to the Corporation, initially for a six-month period, was agreed. Shortly after its formal take-over of the Estate Offices, he requested Plinston to remain their Chief Officer. His deputy, Michael Kelly, was appointed Town Clerk to the U.D.C. Laurie Freeman was appointed Corporation Estate Officer.

The Letchworth Garden City Corporation Act 1962   The Act constituted the Letchworth Garden City Corporation to acquire the undertaking of First Garden City Limited, as of 1 January 1963.[4] The Preamble referred to the incorporation of the original company and its objectives 'to promote and further the distribution of the industrial population upon the land according to the lines suggested by Mr. Ebenezer Howard's book entitled *Garden Cities of Tomorrow*.'

The Act was divided into five parts. Part I dealt with interpretation and definition; Part II described the establishment and constitution of the Corporation. It comprised a Chairman and five members; the Chairman and three other members being Ministerial appointments, one County Council, and one District Council, member. The Corporation was 'to manage, to turn to account, to carry on, develop and extend the undertaking … as a public service', with powers 'to acquire, hold, manage and dispose of land … to carry out building and other operations' but was required to 'have regard to the maintenance of the undertaking … as an entity in accordance with the principles upon which Letchworth Garden City was founded' (Section 11). Part III dealt with the transfer of the undertaking, with S. 15 containing the much debated but unamended provision for a 'going concern' approach. Failing agreement, the matter would be referred to the Lands Tribunal. Part IV dealt with finance. The Corporation was empowered to borrow and to spread repayment over 60 years. S. 27 harmonised the Corporation with local authority finance. The District Council was empowered to lend to the Corporation (S. 29). Section 32 dealt with revenue disposal. After meeting all establishment charges, interest payments, repayments of borrowing, providing working capital and a reserve fund, the Corporation might apply 'any balance … to the provision of traffic facilities, lighting, drainage, markets, libraries, baths or otherwise for the embellishment of the Corporation, the provision of means of education, recreation or amusement for the people or for any other purpose which the Corporation may deem to be a requisite public service'. This provided the framework for the disbursement of Howard's legacy.

The Lands Tribunal   The difference between the Company and Corporation valuations was fundamental. In 1964 payment on account of £1,000,000 was made. The money was raised from the Shell Investment Department. This made it possible to raise 25 per cent of the figure, £250,000, from the Public Works Loan Board, which was used for development. On 2 June 1964 the Corporation applied for the compensation question to be referred to the Lands Tribunal, with hearings fixed to commence on 5 October 1965. Detailed evidence was again prepared, but the Corporation case was affected by the appointment of its leading Counsel as a High Court Judge in August 1965. By contrast, the Company's team remained intact. Shortly before the hearing commenced valuations were exchanged. Cluttons' valuation of the Company ran into 462 pages, and a second by Gerald Eve and Son grouped the assets into categories. A final figure of £3,620,951 was tabled. The Corporation's valuation showed deductions for management costs, and a profits tax was also deducted. Their offer had adjusted Williams' valuation to £2,510,000, plus professional charges and legal costs. There was thus a gap of more than £1.1m between the two parties.

The hearing lasted 77 days over a six-month period, forcing Plinston to stay in London from Mondays to Fridays, studying the daily transcripts supplied to him at 9 p.m. The Tribunal, Erskine Simes, Q.C. and John Watson, considered over 1,000,000 words of testimony. The Company's leading evidence alone took five days to present, and seven days in cross-examination. Much hinged on the fact that 'going concern' was not defined, nor were limitations placed on the term in the Act. By 10 November, after 26 days, the Corporation's Counsel, Reginald Goff, believed that it would be impossible to envisage an award lower than £2,900,000, and quite likely for it to be above £3,000,000. Counsel advised the Corporation to authorise an offer of £2,950,000 plus costs, with an absolute maximum of £3,050,000. If this were accepted, the Corporation would save substantially on legal costs. The Corporation believed that their valuation would stand up to extended cross-examination, and decided to press onwards. The case lasted a further 51 days. Stanley Hill was in the witness box for 10 days, followed by G. M. P. Williams. Under cross-examination the latter almost agreed that the Letchworth rents were those of a 'benevolent' landlord; just in time he reiterated that he had used open market values prevailing throughout North Hertfordshire. He was then taken through a gruelling 12-day examination of detail.

In December 1965, leading Counsel R. W. Goff was appointed a High Court judge. The replacement Counsel worked over the Christmas recess, only to fall ill, then a member of the tribunal succumbed to mumps. Submissions were not completed until 5 April 1966. At the final session on 27 July 1966, the Lands Tribunal made an award of £3,060,000, midpoint between the divergent figures, and close to the amount recommended the previous November. The Corporation accepted that their 'going concern' basis had been rejected, but appealed over the 'bricks and mortar' aspects, particularly the valuation placed on the Letchworth Cottages and Buildings property. Mrs. Rose had liquidated the Company on 17 March 1966, and shareholders were pressing for payment. The Liquidator accepted a figure of £3,115,000 in full settlement and, as the Corporation was liable for the Company's costs which untaxed stood at £160,000, the result was favourable, leaving £2,995,000 as the residual value. Although disappointed, Plinston must have reflected that the County Treasurer, John Alexander, had told him, 'If you can get the undertaking for £3,000,000 you will be buying a gold mine'. Mrs. Rose also expressed this opinion in a press interview.

It was ironic that the integrity of the estate should have been threatened in 1967 by the Leasehold Reform Bill, which enabled long leaseholders to acquire their freeholds. Despite lobbying, Letchworth was not excluded from the operation of the Act. The Corporation appealed to the High Court for an introduction of a Scheme of Management under section 19 of the Act, which was granted.[5] The scheme applied to all enfranchised property, with the objective of preserving the standards of amenity of the estate. It imposed covenants, which required the maintenance of the exterior of buildings and their boundary fences and hedges in good condition. Owners could not alter, extend or rebuild without written Corporation consent. This enabled continuity with the previous leasehold covenants. Many of the early Letchworth leases for residential property were of only 99-years' length. As the unexpired period shortened, and land values rose, the cost of obtaining freeholds under the legislation rose steeply. The introduction of a scheme for deferred payment provoked arguments with a Leaseholders and Freeholders Association in 1989, and this will be discussed further in the next chapter.

A final consequence concerned liability of the Garden City Corporation for Corporation Tax and Capital Gains Tax. It had been defined as a body within the Local Loans Act 1875, analogous to a local authority for the purposes of raising loans and making precepts. Under S. 66 of the Finance Act 1965, local authorities were to be exempt from Income Tax, Corporation Tax and Capital Gains Tax. The Inland Revenue did not accept this in the case of Letchworth. The matter was followed through the assessment and appeal procedure, involving a lengthy discussion of the definition of the 1875 Act and subsequent legislation. The Commissioners found in favour of the Corporation. From 1973, the Corporation was not to be liable to taxation upon revenue or capital surpluses, and later obtained exemption from Development Land Tax, and partially from the 1975 Community Land Act. The forecast of a 'gold mine' moved nearer to fulfilment.

FIFTEEN

THE OLD ORDER CHANGETH

Environmental Appraisal   During the 1960s and early 1970s the planning framework of Letchworth was reappraised.[1] In December 1965, the County Planning Officer, Ernest Doubleday, published a *Letchworth Central Area Appraisal Plan*, the first to be undertaken in a 'New Town'. Town centre planning in the early 1960s was influenced by *Traffic in Towns* by Sir Colin Buchanan, which emphasised definition of a principal road network, within which were traffic-free zones and pedestrianisation. These principles were advocated in Letchworth, which had accommodated a tenfold increase in motor traffic between 1935-65. The generous highway reservations, and absence of principal routes through the town centre, had helped to absorb the traffic without the serious pedestrian/vehicular conflicts found in Hitchin and Baldock. The gross shopping floorspace of 330,400 sq.ft. indicated an efficient use of the existing premises. Emphasis was placed on improving servicing, parking and introducing pedestrianisation. Five possible redevelopment areas were proposed, including the congested areas east and west of Commerce Avenue, and The Wynd. 'Silver Birch Cottages' in Station Road were considered to provide a poor residential environment. Development of rear servicing areas would enable pedestrianisation of Eastcheap and Leys Avenue where traffic levels were excessive. To keep pace with population growth, provision of an additional 100,000 sq.ft. gross shopping floorspace was suggested by 1973. Townscape improvements were based on a choice between 'trees or traffic'. It was suggested that the gaunt flank of the *Broadway Cinema* to Eastcheap should be screened, the Arena car park built over, and comprehensive shopping be developed between Eastcheap and Commerce Avenue. The *Appraisal* was adopted in 1967 as the basis for town centre development control.

In the late 1960s, the County Council undertook a land use/transportation study of Hitchin, Letchworth and Baldock, following American techniques which predicted vehicular movement generated by land use zones and assigned it to a highway network. *Letchworth – People and Traffic* was published in 1970. The A1(M) Baldock By-Pass, running from Corey's Mill, Stevenage to rejoin the A1 Great North Road at Radwell, had been opened in August 1967, and included an interchange with Letchworth Gate. Connections with the industrial area remained poor, with an elevated section of the by-pass running over the A505 Letchworth-Baldock Road, without connecting ramps. *People and Traffic* included a 'Willian Route' diverging from Rosehill, Hitchin, swinging round south-east of Willian, across Letchworth Gate and running north to a junction with the Baldock Road opposite Jubilee Road. Although approved in principle, it would have brought severe environmental conflicts at Willian, and was eventually dropped, in favour of a diversion from the A505 to Corey's Mill and thence via the A1(M) to Letchworth Gate, but with no new connection to the industrial area. The history of this route indicates the regional significance of traffic problems in Letchworth. The remainder of the principal network defined in the report used existing roads to sub-divide eight environmental districts from within which through-traffic would be removed. Some radical improvements were proposed and implemented, the most significant being the 'longabout' on A6141 Letchworth Gate, built 1972, in effect a short length of dual carriageway, with a pedestrian underpass, picking up access to the Lordship and Jackmans estates. Most controversial was a proposed gyratory around the Free Church at the foot of Gernon Road and Leys Avenue, partly implemented to give access to the multi-storey car park of the town centre redevelopment, in 1973.

The report also recommended the closure of many subsidiary junctions. Convenience appeared to be sacrificed to theory, and few closures were implemented.

The County Development Plan was approved in 1958, and underwent a First Review in December 1963, which worked its way through a six-month public inquiry in 1965, ministerial modifications in 1968, a second inquiry in 1969, attaining final approval in May 1971. The 1968 Town and Country Planning Act had introduced a broader brush 'structure plan' as the vehicle for strategic policies concerned with population prediction and balancing housing with employment.[2] More detailed matters were the subject of local plans. In Hertfordshire, the 1973 terminal date of the County Development Plan was extended by eight years through an informal policy statement, *Hertfordshire 1981*, to span the period until the County Structure Plan became operable. Letchworth was predicted to grow from its 30,945 population in 1971 to 36,121 by 1981, with completion of the Jackmans, Lordship and Manor Farm and Standalone Farm Estates. As the 1981 Census total of 31,559 was to show, this prediction was significantly over generous.

Enter North Hertfordshire District Council   By the 1960s local government in England represented a patchwork of authorities, essentially of late 19th-century creation. Each level had widely differing resources and responsibilities, ranging from the rural district councils, with their constituent civil parishes, urban districts, municipal and county boroughs, to shire county councils and the London County Council. The Greater London Council was created in 1965, with a second tier of Borough Councils. The 1969 Redcliffe-Maud Royal Commission recommended 58 'unitary' authorities, and three further Metropolitan areas.[3] The 1972 Local Government Act, passed by a Conservative government, adopted a different system, which retained shire counties, albeit with some boundary changes, within which district councils were created by amalgamation of the old urban and rural councils. The Hertfordshire boundary had already been adjusted with the creation of the G.L.C., and ten new District Councils were created, with effect from 1 April 1974.

In 1930, the Boundary Commission had proposed to amalgamate Letchworth with Baldock, which was huffily rejected. Now it was to be grouped not only with Baldock, but also with Hitchin, Royston, and the 33 Hitchin Rural District Council parishes, to form the new North Hertfordshire District Council, covering a broad 155 sq. mile swathe wrapped northwards around Stevenage New Town. This ended the geographic conjunction between U.D.C. and Corporation. The 31,000 Letchworth residents were absorbed into a district total of 99,500. In June 1973, 48 Councillors were elected to represent 19 wards for an initial three-year period. The first meeting of the new Council was convened on 21 June 1973. In May 1979, 25 new wards were created, represented by 50 Councillors, the number in each reflecting its population. Letchworth's five wards each had three members, giving one more overall than the 14 representing Hitchin. The old rival had been absorbed and with Letchworth made up almost two thirds of the Council. There was ample scope for both geographical as well as political loyalties to be reflected in Council decisions. The first N.H.D.C. Chairman, Bill Miller, was a Letchworth councillor, and the new authority was Labour controlled until 1976. Letchworth was chosen as the administrative centre due to the availability of a six-storey office block in Gernon Road. Modified to include a Council Chamber, and with the air conditioning omitted as an economy measure, the extensive glazing gave a dramatic demonstration of 'passive solar gain' in the sweltering summer of 1975, with internal temperatures of 120°F recorded.

Michael Kelly, the U.D.C. Clerk wondered, 'Who will mourn the passing of this U.D.C.? A few of us perhaps, particularly the survivors of the 181 Councillors … since 1919 … the hope is that in the brave new world of Local Government we shall get more of everything'.[4] In 55 years, the U.D.C. had built nearly 5,000 dwellings, 3,700 since 1945, and extensive civic facilities and public utilities. Some assets were dispersed – the Anglian Water Authority took over sewage disposal, while the County Council absorbed the library. As its farewell gesture

129 Presenting Arms, March 1974. U.D.C. Chairman Charles Sax and Corporation Chairman Robert Humbert. Michael Kelly, U.D.C. Clerk (*left*), was to become the first Chief Executive of North Hertfordshire District Council.

in March 1974, the U.D.C. passed its Coat of Arms into the safe keeping of the Garden City Corporation. Many N.H.D.C. Chief Officers were drawn from the old constituent authorities. Michael Kelly, as Chief Executive, headed the corporate management team, with Don Woolston from Hitchin U.D.C. as Solicitor, Wilfred Hammond from Hitchin R.D.C. as Secretary, Keith Sutton from Royston as Treasurer, Fred Such, the Letchworth U.D.C. Engineer and Surveyor as Technical Officer, Trevor Thompson from Hitchin as Housing Officer, and Derek Coyne from Cheshunt U.D.C. as Environmental Health Officer. N.H.D.C. became a planning authority in its own right, and Brian Hull, from the County's East Divisional Planning Office, was appointed Planning Officer. The honeymoon period was short. Residents outside Letchworth, particularly from Royston, found the new authority remote. On the first birthday of N.H.D.C., the *Letchworth Comet* declared

> Local Authority spending has never been higher, the image never lower. Of almost equal importance is the total loss of faith by individual townships in an authority which no longer represents their particular problems …'.

A harsh judgement and somewhat premature. Local Government suffered from a poor image following the 1974 reorganisation, exacerbated by the attitude of national government in the 1980s. There were gains, not least in a timely emphasis on conservation, which included the early Garden City achievements.

An Area of Special Architectural or Historic Interest Widespread dissatisfaction with comprehensive town centre redevelopment brought pressure for improved legislation to protect historic buildings and areas. The 1968 Town and Country Planning Act introduced the obligation to obtain prior consent to demolish, alter or extend buildings listed by the Minister as of special architectural or historic interest. The previous year, Duncan Sandys, a Conservative M.P., promoted and piloted the Civic Amenities Act through a Labour government. This introduced 'Conservation Areas', which the local authority had a duty to identify, designate, and to administer policies for their preservation and enhancement.[5] Although the County Council had designated Conservation Areas in Norton and Willian, no action had

XIX Early post-war prefabs in Highover Road, seen in January 2002.

XX Jackmans Estate, mid-1960s, pedestrian path between Bayworth and Chatterton, seen in June 1989.

XXI Silver Birch Cottages, Station Road, 1905–7, upon completion of restoration in 1981.

XXII Creamery Court, Letchworth Gate, 1995.

XXIII Town Centre regeneration: *The Hogshead* and 'The Colonnade', 1996.

XXIV *The Broadway Cinema*, restored externally to its Art Deco glory, 1996.

XXV 'The Goldsmith Centre', North Herts College, 1999, turns the corner from Town Square to Broadway.

XXVI Morrisons opened in July 1999, with its entrance colonnade facing Broadway to consolidate the town centre, both commercially and visually.

been taken to protect Letchworth itself, possibly due to the U.D.C.'s role in the redevelopment of Commerce Avenue. While most early Conservation Areas were largely concerned with historic towns and villages, both Hampstead Garden Suburb and Welwyn Garden City preceded the designation of Letchworth.

In 1966, publication of *The Search for Environment* by the American scholar Walter Creese focused attention on the international significance of the Garden City movement.[6] Mabel Barry Parker lived at 296 Norton Way South, the old Parker and Unwin offices, and carefully sorted her husband's papers and drawings.[7] Active in Letchworth life into her 90s, Mrs Parker moved to St Catherine's Nursing Home in 1973, following which the Corporation purchased the Norton Way building. Extended and refurbished, it opened as the First Garden City (Heritage) Museum in 1977. The Garden City lifestyle had been kept alive by the, now elderly, band of pioneers and their first generation offspring. Kenneth Johnson, then an assistant librarian, chronicled the events and personalities of Letchworth history, and for over 25 years wrote a lively column in *The Citizen*. In 1976 his *Book of Letchworth*[8] presented a kaleidoscopic view, compiled seemingly by serendipity, juxtaposing the significant with the memorably trivial. Born in Wandsworth, south London, in 1930, 'K.J.' moved to Letchworth in 1937, and was educated at The St Christopher School. He compiled a remarkable local history index, and systematically collected ephemera for the library. Never short of a *mot juste*, he described Howard's circular Garden City plan as 'just like a dartboard' in a broadcast in 2001.

N.H.D.C. inherited 31 Conservation Areas including Baldock, Hitchin and Royston, and most of the historic villages in the district. It seemed anomalous that the First Garden City was not recognised as historic. Consequently, in 1974, an extensive Conservation Area was defined, including the town centre, pioneer residential areas, and Old Letchworth, and was linked in designation to the Diamond Jubilee of the Royal Town Planning Institute, the formation of which the development of Letchworth had done much to foster.[9] This was followed by detailed research on the buildings, using early bye-law records, for reference to the Department of the Environment for listing.[10] Over 300 separate properties were included in the published list of September 1979.[11] Examples included the Spirella building, the Parker and Unwin Studio (First Garden City Heritage Museum), Baillie Scott's 'Tanglewood', 'The Cloisters', the concrete cottage at No. 158 Wilbury Road, and 'The Stanley Parker house', No. 102 Wilbury Road, all as Grade II* items. Groups such as 'Westholm', or the fine 'L' blocks in Sollershott East framing Field Lane, were Grade II. In 1977, N.H.D.C. published an illustrated Broadsheet history of Letchworth.[12] Visits proliferated. In 1976 the Town and Country Planning Association brought a major group, including Sir Frederic Osborn; in 1977 the international meeting of the Urban History Group followed. Japanese parties had an insatiable appetite for Garden City history, translated by their inscrutable and tireless interpreters.

For the 75th Anniversary of Letchworth in 1978 a major commemorative exhibition was mounted at the First Garden City (Heritage) Museum. This included Howard's desk and one of his typewriters, with his original diagrams. Hunter's fabrics, Cowlishaw's pottery and Cockerell's bookbinding represented early craft industries.[13] The exhibition was opened by Corporation Chairman Robert Humbert. Sir Frederic Osborn, aged 93, was present. Despite his frailty, he made an impromptu speech, fired by memories of the Howard Cottage Society and Letchworth life. He stressed Letchworth's continued significance for civilised living, but emphasised that its message had been least understood in the town itself. It was his last public appearance. He died in Welwyn Garden City on 1 November 1978. Sir Frederic had earlier agreed to become President of the Letchworth Garden City Society, founded on 3 May 1978, by participants in a series of lectures on Garden City history, given by the author at North Herts College. Hugh Bidwell, son of the architect Wilson Bidwell, was elected Chairman, and founder members included Horace Plinston. A quarterly *Journal*, which has brought to light myriad snippets of Garden City history, and regular lectures and outings have been part of its programme since its inception. The Society aims at fostering the ideals

130 Sir Frederic Osborn and Robert Humbert at the 75th Anniversary Exhibition. On one of his last public appearances, Sir Frederic made an impassioned speech about the significance of Letchworth.

of the founders of Letchworth, encouraging civic pride and the protection of the Garden City environment.

This latter objective was easier to achieve in theory than in practice. Although controls over property alteration were drawn both from the planning legislation and the Corporation's scheme of management, alterations continued to proliferate, particularly on smaller properties, often abetted by aggressive home improvement advertising. The sale of council houses without covenants over subsequent alterations, and N.H.D.C.'s own housing improvement policies, which were not always sensitive to Conservation Area locations, exacerbated matters. Visually unsympathetic alterations included concrete interlocking tiled roofs, metal and plastic windows. Where residential properties were unlisted, designation of a Conservation Area did not remove the householder's rights to undertake minor alterations, unless an 'Article 4 Direction' had been approved by the Secretary of State. In 1988 N.H.D.C. resolved to seek these powers. These 'minor' alterations were also seemingly beyond the scheme of management, too. Modest grants help to bridge the cost between modern substitutes and the more expensive handmade tiles and timber windows, but a significant problem remains. More on this urgent matter is contained in Chapter Sixteen.

Moving into surplus – the Howard Legacy   Section 32 of the Letchworth Garden City Corporation Act required that any balance after payment of operating expenses should be used for community benefit. In 1968 F.G.C. Ltd. had been paid off, and the Corporation's operations were moving into surplus. Although a large debt to the U.D.C. remained, a modest £1,000 was distributed as the first instalment of Howard's bequest on 11 September 1968. The Wilbury Wanderers Football Club, the Youth Club, the Guides Building Fund, the Settlement, and the Old People's Welfare Committee were beneficiaries.[14] In 1973, sale of the Standalone farmland more than wiped out the remaining debts of £3,000,000. In 1974 and 1975 balances available for distribution were £359,546 and £384,805 respectively. The time had come to look forward to spending major surpluses.[15] A town meeting held in December 1974 produced priorities for a leisure centre/swimming pool, a community hall and a day hospital. Provision was postponed due to economic uncertainty, which began with a freeze on rent reviews and mounting inflation. Matters revived in 1979 when the surplus reached £2,598,000. £502,000 had been distributed since 1974. The reconstruction of the town's industrial base again depressed the surplus, and it was also depleted by withdrawal of large tranches for the major projects. By 1988 Section 32 disbursements of £732,000 were made including £370,000 enterprise subsidies, and £140,000 grants.

The major capital expenditure was absorbed by five major projects – the First Garden City Heritage Museum, 'The Ernest Gardiner Day Hospital', North Hertfordshire Sports and Leisure Centre, 'Plinston Hall', and 'Standalone Farm Centre'. The day hospital involved lengthy discussions with the Area Health Authority. By 1982 costs had increased to a point where the Corporation withdrew its offer both to build and equip the hospital. Agreement was reached to pay for its construction, with £60,000 to be raised for essential equipment – in the event £75,000 was donated. The hospital opened in October 1984. Although privately built, equipped, and staffed, it has always catered exclusively for National Health Service patients. Twenty places were provided in a domestic scale, single-storey building off Pixmore Avenue, with a welcoming non-institutional atmosphere

131 Ernest Gardiner Day Hospital. The first matron, Mrs Jean Hyde, poses with one of her green-fingered day patients.

developed by the first matron, Mrs. Jean Hyde. The emphasis was on rehabilitation of the elderly, sick and disabled, for the most part over a six-week period. Physical and occupational therapy sessions formed all-important part of activities at the Hospital. The building was named after the former U.D.C. Chairman, who called the 'Save Letchworth' meeting in December 1960. The nearby Cottage Hospital closed in August 1988, and in spring 1989 it was announced that it would be refurbished as a hospice at a cost of £750,000, to provide 15 residential places, a day care centre and a base for two home care nurses. Public donations quickly raised over £400,000, including a donation of £100,000 by Letchworth Garden City Corporation, handed over at a reception in Plinston Hall. 'The Garden House Hospice' is now one of the foremost facilities of its kind, covering the whole North Herts District, and offering a 'hospice at home' service.

The Leisure Centre was the most ambitious Section 32 project, and was the subject of lengthy discussions with N.H.D.C., who were to be responsible for its running and maintenance, with the Corporation initially undertaking to meet up to 25 per cent of any annual deficit on running costs, up to £35,000, over the first five years. The £3.5m Leisure Centre was designed and built by package contractor, Module 2, and provided a wide range of facilities within its impersonal red brick exterior. The major attraction was the 'T'shaped combination pool, with wave-making machine and a 25 m. central section for serious swimming. In addition, a large multi-sports hall, squash courts, weight training fitness room and sauna were provided. The complex was officially opened by H.M. Queen Elizabeth II in July 1982. 'Plinston Hall' was named in memory of Horace Plinston who died in 1980. It was perhaps a surprising choice as Letchworth has never lacked such buildings, and provision of a new facility could only relegate the 'Howard Hall' still further. The 'Plinston Hall' in Town Square took the shell of the 1960s Grammar School Assembly Hall, with a new frontage block, and ancillary accommodation at the side and rear. Retractable seating was installed, and the stage was improved to allow concerts and theatrical events. Opened in June 1982, it quickly proved very popular with an estimated usage of 250,000 people in 1985.

The Best Laid Plans ... The 1970s witnessed preparation, submission and approval of the Hertfordshire County Structure Plan, and preparatory work on the North Hertfordshire District Plan.[16] Strategic planning at best involves aiming at a moving target: prediction of human activities remains notoriously inexact, however sophisticated the hardware and information technology applied. By the time of approval of the N.H.D.C. District Plan in March 1984,[17] certified, as required, as in accord with the Structure Plan, the County Planner, Geoffrey Steeley, freely admitted that few of the policies of the Structure Plan remained valid. The original planning context was the high growth rate enjoyed since 1945. The Plan aimed at securing a better balance between employment and housing, controlling the growth spiral through limiting job increases, and encouraging industrial relocation to development areas. Only Hertfordshire firms whose location met a national interest would be allowed to expand. Similar restrictions affected office development. Housing would be constructed only to match the projected natural population increase, with the hope of discouraging immigration. The Metropolitan Green Belt was extended along the A1(M) corridor northwards from Hatfield to envelop Welwyn Garden City, Stevenage, Hitchin, Letchworth and Baldock.

Preparation of the N.H.D.C. District Plan began against this background, using the 1981-91 period operable for the County Structure Plan. By the time the Draft District Plan was published for public comment in January 1981, it was evident that the Letchworth economy was undergoing a profound structural change, with widespread redundancies and closures. The detailed implications of this will be discussed in a later section, but the immediate effect on the plan preparation was a difference between the Council and Corporation as to whether the industrially zoned land north of Baldock Road should be re-allocated for housing, thus easing provision for the initial part of the plan period and meeting the obligation to identify a five-year land supply. This point was raised at the District Plan Inquiry during October-December 1982, but the point over the Baldock Road land was conceded. This increased the difficulty in meeting the requirement for housing land. Demographic analysis indicated an increasing demand for smaller dwellings in line with national trends. Letchworth was grouped in a plan policy area with Hitchin and Baldock. Although a substantial part of the requirement could be met on a large site east of Baldock, allocated in the County Development Plan, but not hitherto used, there was still a need for sites which added to the edge of Letchworth, where the District was also defining the extended Metropolitan Green Belt in detail. The additional allocations, particularly, east of Green Lane, and near Letchworth Gate on proposed school playing fields, brought protests from the Letchworth Garden City Society.[18] The Council pointed out that Howard's original land allocation had been based on the large Victorian family, and that it had subsequently been necessary to increase the town area for the Grange, Standalone, Jackmans and Lordship estates to house the anticipated 32,000 population. The modest increase in housing land was necessary to enable fulfilment of obligations. Major pressure on the perimeter of Letchworth would probably arise in the 1990s, beyond the first period of the Plan. This point was taken and the allocations were confirmed.

Recession and Recovery As already noted, Letchworth prospered through mixed manufacturing and engineering with a high value-added content. A few key firms became dominant – Spirella, Dent's, British Tab (I.C.L.), K. & L., Shelvoke and Drewry, and Borg-Warner. In the mid-1970s high inflation followed by economic recession, coinciding with

132 The Business Centre: Phase I (1985). The 'high-tech' image and slick finishes brought Garden City industrial and office buildings up-to-date.

declining demand for several Letchworth 'staples', brought widespread unemployment. Spirella production was confined to shrinking enclaves in Castle Corset. I.C.L. went through painful reorganisations and shed a large number of employees, announcing its cessation of manufacture in Letchworth in spring 1989. Borg-Warner, once a symbol of the vitality of the motor industry, suddenly closed, leaving an echoing mausoleum of 400,000 sq. ft. on a 14-acre (5.6 ha.) site. The 600 Group shut down the K. & L. Foundry, and Shelvoke and Drewry, hard hit by restrictions on local government expenditure, shed all but 10 per cent of their workforce, but later reorganised as Shelvoke Dempster, under the U.S.A. Krug International group. Unemployment had been virtually nil in the early 1970s but rose to an unprecedented 16 per cent in 1981-2.[19] Government-imposed regional controls were dismantled and local planning policies loosened. In the late 1970s a new industrial revolution, based on information technology and electronics, took place 25 miles away in the Cambridge science parks. The 'high-tech' industries blurred the distinction between office and manufacturing employment. A high quality, intensively serviced environment was required, and generated the opportunities for high skilled, high paid employment. Firms which survived the shakeout included Ogle Design who had become well known for innovative design work on cars and commercial vehicles, epitomising the importance of specialist skills, independent of the manufacturing process.

The Corporation perceived the outward ripples of the 'Cambridge effect', and sought to promote a Business Park on the 56 acres (22.6 ha.) of vacant industrial land north of Baldock Road. Andrew Egerton-Smith, appointed as Estates Manager during the 1970s, who became

Chief Executive of the Corporation in 1986, led the initiative. Once the land allocation had been reaffirmed by the District Plan, the Corporation formed a development consortium with Bride Hall, and the Pos(t)-Tel(ecommunications) Pensions Fund, in 1984. A master plan prepared by D. Y. Davies Associates stressed the importance of a landscaped park to attract new industries without the financial incentives of enterprise zones such as Corby and Peterborough. Locationally Letchworth enjoyed excellent communications, situated midway between Milton Keynes and Cambridge. The objective was to provide 1½ million sq. ft. and create 2,000 new jobs – hence the original designation Enterprise 2000. Development began with 'The Business Centre', started earlier in a refurbished building on Works Road.[20] The new headquarters was built by the Corporation, and included a business consultancy service, central boardroom and conference facilities, computer and word processing services, in a central block, with wings each housing 13 small intensively serviced units, from 713 to 1,238 sq.ft., adaptable both as office or manufacturing space. The centre was fully occupied by 1986. After a slow start, development of the remainder of the park accelerated in 1987-8. A new 65,000 ft. headquarters for Sigma Controls was opened in 1988, construction of new 18,000 sq. ft. headquarters for the Country Gentleman's Association, and for G.C.M. 600 (George Cohen Machinery Ltd.), and a backup national computer facility for Tesco began. A 'Phase 2 Business Centre' with 40,000 sq.ft. high tech space, with units between 2,300-5,000 sq.ft., was completed in June 1989. A 7.5-acre development on 'Campus 5' of the Business Park began in March 1989, to be completed in three phases and available from early 1990. Nearby, off Dunhams Lane, Wheatley Developments began work on 'Letchworth Point', with 17 varied units grouped around a courtyard with a central sculpture. The Business Park was also promoted through the County Council's 'A1 Corridor' programme as a counter magnet to the M4 corridor west of London.

Rebuilding of the older industrial area began in the 1970s, when the Letchworth power station was redeveloped with twin concrete chimney stacks which became a dominant landmark, but all too often obtruding into important Garden City views, particularly from the town centre along Station Road. Off Works Road, 'Such Close' was the first small unit development promoted by the Corporation, followed by 'Saunders Close' on the site of the old abattoir. Units became smaller – 5,000 sq.ft., to 2,500, and even 500 sq.ft. were viable. The Spirella factory was unofficially subdivided into over 100 separate occupancies. Efforts were made to refurbish existing factories. A good example of this was 'Ascot Close', south of Icknield Way, site of the old Camco factory. Its distinctively designed units in light grey brick, with bright red and blue metal cladding, were popular, marketing assisted by the gimmicky image. A major project involved the creation of the Jubilee Trading Estate from the 400,000 sq.ft. Borg-Warner complex. In contrast to 'The Business Centre', with its small but sophisticated and comparatively high rental units, 'The Jubilee Estate' was adaptable for a range of unit sizes for sale – the slogan ran 'You don't rent your home – so why rent your factory?'. One of the best industrial buildings of the 1980s was the Letchworth Roofing Co. headquarters on Works Road, by Pentangle Design, and which won a N.H.D.C. Civic Award in 1986. Its twin linked pitched roofed pavilions, with boldly overhanging roofs, gave ample scope for demonstration of craftsmanship by its owners, and its overall concept was less idiosyncratic than many of its contemporaries.

Employment training presented a challenge in the late 1970s. The Skills Training Centre was an important regional resource and the Skills Training Agency Group, of which it was a component, became the largest organisation of its type in Europe. In September 1988 the centre was expanded to include the Government's Employment Training initiative, successor to the Manpower Services Commission programmes. This was short-lived, for it closed down completely in the early 1990s. In the mid-1980s, the new business success rate in Letchworth was above 85 per cent, against a national average of 66 per cent. Between 1981-6, many firms had started, many had been rehoused, and the Business Park alone had brought more than 90 new units. The challenge of economic reconstruction appeared to have been met, but the

133 Birds Hill: 1905 housing refurbished in 1980. Sensitively landscaped, this housing remains in the rental section. The project was designed by Pentangle Design of Hitchin.

sudden closure of I.C.L. in spring 1989, with an anticipated loss of 660 jobs on two sites by September, brought a reminder of the difficulties earlier in the decade.

Home Base   Housing passed through a volatile period in the 1980s. Already in the 1970s the first major price increase cycle had caused concern over availability of homes for first-time buyers. The Council concentrated its efforts on sheltered accommodation for the elderly, but also built a few 'starter homes' for sale on the Jackmans Estate. The major private estates at Lordship Farm and Manor Park built by Wates Ltd. between 1973-9, to a layout by Shankland Cox and developed by Wates Limited, concentrated on detached executive houses. However, in 1974, 34 grouped houses priced at £10,750 each were built, a minute proportion of the 700 total for the two estates. Availability of cheap housing was concentrated on run-down areas, notably the Pixmore Estate. No moves were made to use area improvement programmes and sporadic uptake of improvement grants exacerbated the overall appearance of the area, although it was one of the major early estates, designed by Parker and Unwin.

The population of Letchworth grew more slowly than forecast – the 36,000 projection for 1981 was matched by a census return of 31,559. Smaller households multiplied – single person households by 48 per cent, and two person households by 21 per cent.[21] There was a growing mismatch between the housing stock and demographic trends, but market response was not immediate. In the late 1970s the Fearnhill Park estate, on the old school playing fields, north of Sollershott West, included luxury two-bedroom bungalows designed to attract the older residents, freeing larger houses for resale. The lack of large executive houses, Manor Park notwithstanding, worried the Corporation for the perceived attractiveness of Letchworth housing was a vital element in their Business Park strategy. In partnership with the Nationwide Housing Trust, the Corporation developed Norton Hall Farm with 24 bungalows, 30 apartments and four houses, again designed to release larger homes for resale. The units were sold to the elderly, with a buy-back provision of market value less two per cent.

The bungalows were grouped in clusters of three units around entrance patios, whilst the apartments occupied the site of the farmyard and barns, regrettably destroyed by fire before the planned conversion could take place. The Corporation had also undertaken construction of conventional sheltered housing through its Letchworth Cottages and Buildings subsidiary, including 'MacFadyen-Webb House' on the fringes of Norton Common, and 'Robert Humbert House', named after the first Corporation Chairman.

The early 1980s saw several notable refurbishment projects. 'Silver Birch Cottages', Station Road had been considered a potential redevelopment site. The Corporation acquired them and promoted full restoration of these Parker and Unwin-designed cottages. Roofs were stripped and retiled, chimneys rebuilt, and joinery replaced, revealing the visual delights of early Garden City housing. An attractive landscaped buffer area was planted along the street frontage. The refurbishment scheme, by Pentangle Design, received a N.H.D.C. Civic Commendation in 1981. The Corporation had acquired a substantial housing portfolio through Letchworth Cottages and Buildings Ltd. In 1981-2 they completely refurbished the Mansard-roofed 'Noah's Ark' cottages on Birds Hill, built as 1905 Cheap Cottages exhibits. Unlike 'Silver Birch Cottages', they remained in the rental sector, and on completion in 1981 won a N.H.D.C. Civic Award. A notable feature was the landscaped parking area, provided in place of neglected allotments in front of the buildings. Comprehensive housing improvement was also undertaken in Common View.

The Council's dwelling stock was whittled down under the 'Right to Buy' of the 1980 Housing Act. The Letchworth local authority stock stood at 4,243 in March 1989, with 413 new Council dwellings built since 1974. Between 1974-89 they had sold 1,328 dwellings, 1,143 of these since 1980.[22] Massive increases in house prices occurred in the 1980s and by 1989 little was available under £80,000, £150-175,000 was common for semi-detached properties, and £250,000 upwards for detached houses, depending on location. These rises were but a foretaste of the sharp increases which occurred a decade later. Broadway and Sollershott West with The Glade and Pasture Road/Garth Road remained the most exclusive Letchworth addresses.

The Leasehold Reform Act of 1967 introduced the right of individuals to purchase the freehold of their properties. In the early years the leasing period was either 99 or 999 years. Modern estate leases as with 'Tabbs', Icknield Way are typically 125 years. With long leases, the purchase of the freehold represented a comparatively modest amount: however, enfranchisement becomes progressively more costly as the unexpired period shortens, and is related to the value of the land. Property values rose sharply after the mid-1970s and accelerated between 1985-8, but fell back with spiralling interest rates, and slackening demand, particularly for 'first time' properties. It was estimated that a house for sale at £28,000 in 1975 might cost £250,000 in 1988. However, there was evidence in spring 1989 of reductions, sometimes of several thousand pounds, in the advertised price of Letchworth houses, while building societies were becoming reluctant to advance loans on leasehold properties with fewer than 50 years to run.

It was against this volatile market that the Corporation introduced new schemes for deferred payment for freehold purchase. The first involved cases where the property owners were over 55, and had either lived in the house for 10 years, or in the town for ten. Payment for the freehold could be deferred until the property was sold, or the leaseholder or surviving spouse died. Annual interest would be levied at a ratio four per cent below the Midland Bank average base rate or a maximum of eight per cent. A modified scheme for the under 55s required purchase by 10 annual instalments. The schemes involved freehold purchases applied for between 1 December 1988 and 31 March 1989, subsequently extended through April. Valuations followed the procedure in the 1976 Act, based upon the land value at the date of claim, and the length of the unexpired lease, and using a 'residual standing house' approach, where the value of the bricks and mortar might represent 55 per cent of the total. The levels of the valuations under the schemes provoked fierce controversy locally and were challenged by the Leaseholders and Freeholders Association, who held protest meetings and addressed the Corporation Board. Comparisons were instanced with Welwyn Garden City where freehold could be obtained for under £100. In those cases, however, 999-year leases were involved and no direct comparison was possible. With some properties having as little as 14 years left to run, the situation was seen as critical. It was claimed that valuations made in 1981 and 1985 of £3,160 and £3,613 had risen to £30,580 and £34,400 in 1989, and that the Corporation had changed its basis of valuation. This was refuted, but it was accepted that some high valuations had resulted from the correct application of the formulae – of 519 quotations made up to 2 March 1989, there were 51 between £10,000-£20,000, 12 between £20,000-£30,000 and one above £30,000. The average figure of the batch was £4,193, with a considerable number below. By May 1989 a total of 2,860 properties were enfranchised. There were then 12,570 houses in Letchworth, of which 4,243 were Council-owned. Demands for freehold quotations remained brisk, notwithstanding the controversy.

Most post-war housing, of the 1960s and 1970s, lacked the traditional Garden City architectural characteristics. In 1984 Barratt purchased the playing fields north of Letchworth Gate. The Corporation, N.H.D.C. and H.C.C. prepared a design brief which emphasised the importance of layout characteristics drawn from Rushby Mead and Unwin's *Town Planning in Practice*. The Letchworth Gate estate, developed by Barratt 1988-9, had a layout which produced well designed street pictures, while the houses used rendered walls, gables and dormers with accents of tile hanging and weatherboarding, representing a welcome revival of early Garden City designs. Even in the 1980s, the search for housing sites for allocation in the District Plan was controversial, and objections were raised to even the modest extensions of the town area in Green Lane and the development of the surplus school playing fields land between Jackmans and Letchworth Gate. A possibility not involving outward spread on to Metropolitan Green Belt land was the redevelopment of obsolete industrial land within the town area. Developed by Wheatley Homes, 'Tabbs' recycled the old I.C.L. (British Tabulating Machinery) factory site on Icknield Way. Likewise, a smaller piece of the old Shelvoke and Drewry site nearby, and, in 1988, the residential redevelopment of the former Country Gentleman's Association seed testing grounds further west in Icknield Way, regrettably bringing the demolition of its fine Tudor-style office block.

The Green Setting[23]   The Corporation inherited 2,200 acres (890 ha.) of farmland, with the 310-acre (125 ha.) Lordship Farm with its dairy herd of 85 'in hand'. In September 1963 the Board decided to take on Manor Farm, Normans Farm and Letchworth Hall Farm as well, following notice of expiry, with the milking herd based on Lordship Farm and cereal handling at Manor Farm. A farms manager, John Salwey, was appointed later to expand the farming enterprise, with the addition of Standalone Farm in 1973, Nortonbury and part of Paynes Farm in 1975. In 1976 purchase of the 230-acre (93 ha.) Grange Farm, north of the estate in Bedfordshire, was the first major increase in landholding since 1903. Additional agricultural land was later acquired at Wymondley, to the south of Letchworth. The Dairy used a 'cotel' cubicle milking parlour with 350 places, but its success was short-lived, closed down with an E.E.C. grant of £97,000, following the freezing of milk prices in 1979. Arable farming encountered similar problems of surpluses in the 1980s. Diversification, and the opening of a successful farm shop at Manor Farm, Willian, assisted a return to profitability. In 1987 a farming master plan designated Manor Farm, Willian, as the operations centre. Main crops included wheat, barley, oilseed rape, potatoes and soft fruit.

From 1979 the Corporation considered ways of enhancing the green setting and providing greater community access to the agricultural belt. A farm-landscape strategy aimed it, softening the raw edge of the town, particularly northwards to the Bedfordshire plain. Wildlife conservation areas were identified, notably the meadows of the Ivel Valley, together with key views for enhancement and replanting after the Dutch Elm disease epidemic, which killed the majority of the 1,600 mature elms on the estate. Most of the Letchworth plantations

134 Standalone Farm Visitor Centre. David Marsh and his staff with new-born lambs and 'Warrant', the Shire horse, March 1987.

were about 200 years old and followed the creation of fields under the Parliamentary Enclosures Act, and no new planting took place until the late 1970s. With the support of the Countryside Commission, 2,200 trees and 550 hedge plants were planted over three years, a prelude to a five-year programme using inaccessible field corners, filling gaps, and creating spinneys and windbreaks, involving 35,000 trees and seven miles of hedges. The Corporation and the Garden City Society collaborated on the identification of six countryside walks around the southern and eastern fringes of the estate, initiated on 3 June 1982. In the early 1970s Standalone Farm was reduced to 170 acres by the sale of land for housing development. In 1980 it was refurbished and opened as a Farm Visitor centre, intended both for school and family visits, with 2,000 visitors in its first six months, and 20,000 from April-November 1981. By 1987-8 this had risen to 80,500, including 13,500 school children. Facilities were originally centred on livestock, cows, sheep, pigs, poultry and working horses, but exhibitions of farm machinery were mounted in the farm buildings, a wildfowl area was added in 1982, followed by a forge and other rural crafts. In terms of revenue Standalone approached a break-even point by 1988-9, with 5,000 visitors over the 1989 Easter weekend.

Education 2000 In the 1970s the County Council reorganised the ten junior and four secondary schools into a comprehensive system. The old Grammar School was closed and a large new comprehensive school, 'Fearnhill', was opened on the north-western fringes of the town. Two major private schools survived. The St Christopher School enlarged their campus south of Barrington Road to include a drama studio and its properties included 'Arunside' ('Laneside' and 'Crabby Corner'), the 1904 Parker and Unwin houses, which were extended in 1985. In 1934, the St Francis School for Girls took over St Christopher's original premises and added a massive three-storey dormitory block facing Broadway. Originally run by an order of Nuns as a Roman Catholic Girls High School, its management was restructured as an Educational Trust in 1984. In that year there were 3,500 secondary pupils and 250 teachers in Letchworth.

Education 2000, a privately funded charitable trust, sought ways of promoting innovative education, and to provide school leavers with skills demanded by industry and commerce.[24] Developments in the U.S.A. had been studied. The promotion of an ex-

135 Education 2000 in action: the Japanese connection, spring 1989. Although commonplace today, this computer link-up was the first of its kind.

periment in Hertfordshire in 1987 stemmed from the innovative attitude of the education authority, with high achievement locally in both public and private schools, and the co-operation of the Corporation, who provided office accommodation for the Director of Education 2000, John Abbott, and his staff. The Corporation, through its education liaison consultant, Peter Macleod, had already assisted computer provision in junior schools and the development of a secondary school computer network. This linked with Education 2000's fourpoint objectives – community links; new technology; curriculum reappraisal; and response to the needs of young people. Staff secondments to industry were assisted, computer provision increased to a ratio of one terminal to seven pupils, with word-processing encouraged. Curriculum development stressed interdependence in place of narrow subject barriers. Finally, the decision-making and corporate ability of all pupils was to be fostered. £1.3m was raised from industry and commerce for teacher retraining and equipment. The Department of Education and Science observed the project, particularly its links with industry and its public/private sector co-operation, as they moved towards a national curriculum. In spring 1989 one of the participants, The Highfield School, joined with the Shinmei School in Tokyo on a computer link-up and live programme for Japanese television. The initiative was a pioneer of its kind, and was carried on through the 1990s by the Letchworth Garden City Heritage Foundation, as will be described in Chapter Sixteen.

Letchworth Town Centre – The 1970s and 1980s   In the late 1960s, following many comparable towns, the U.D.C. and Corporation agreed on redevelopment – of the area between Leys Avenue, Eastcheap and Gernon Road by the Laing Development Co. Ltd.[25] The existing jumble of shops and workshops was swept aside, but the line of Commerce Way was retained as the main north-south pedestrian route, with a connection to Eastcheap. The architecture, by Damond, Lock, Grabowski and Partners, reflected the current developer idioms in a mixture of low and medium rise blocks, and a six-storey office block with red brick ends and dark bronze tinted glazing. In the centre was a utilitarian tiered 400-space

136 The Central Area Shopping Centre, Commerce Way Square, built 1973-5 and refurbished in 1989. The eye-catching folly appears to be an amalgam of traditional market cross and a space probe. It disappeared after a few months.

multi-storey car park. In an attempt to relate the development to its context, tiled canopies and other cosmetic details, notably the 'lych gate' entrance from Leys Avenue, were added. The scheme also included Letchworth's first purpose-built town centre public house, *The Black Squirrel*. It was possibly coincidental that this rodent had become as scarce as then were licensed premises in the Garden City.

The precinct contained two major supermarkets, two further large units, a public hall, subsequently used for little else but bingo, above a covered market, and 34 shops ranging from national multiples to the inevitable plethora of gift and card shops. The centre was opened by H.R.H. Duke of Gloucester, himself an architect, on 22 July 1975, in European Architectural Heritage Year. His Royal Highness made no design comments! Within 15 years the precinct suffered from over intense use. In 1987-8, the then owners, Equitable Life Assurance, prepared a refurbishment scheme in conjunction with the Corporation and Council. The dull interlocking concrete block paving was replaced with more varied patterns. The tiled canopies were modified, and in the centre a tile-hung shelter was built, its form suggesting that the First Garden City was about to launch its first space probe. It transpired that this had been intended for the set-back entrance to the precinct from Leys Avenue, and it soon disappeared without trace. On the Eastcheap frontage, a glazed canopy was thrust outwards. To reduce vandalism the centre was closed at night, by ornamental gates from spring 1989, although not totally enclosed, and the multi-storey car park was modified by large-scale trelliswork to relieve its fortress-like appearance. No proposals were made to modify the office block occupied by the Council. Little short of total redevelopment could mitigate its intrusion on nearby residential areas.

The Wynd was refurbished in the early 1980s. Traffic management produced one-way circulation along Openshaw Way, from Station Road to Norton Way South, with vehicle speed restricted by 'rumble strips', and The Wynd itself was pedestrianised, reinforcing its importance in linking Leys Avenue with Station Road. Surveys had indicated a preference for smaller shops and most of the existing buildings were retained, although several were up-dated in a jokey post-modern Garden City idiom. The *pièce de resistance* was undoubtedly the small 'high tech' arcade (now 'The Gallery') with its ingenious exposed tubular steel structure, and original acid yellow and bottle green colour scheme, designed by Baldwin, Brattle and Conolly. Although it excited the wrath of the Victorian Society, its impact was muted. The forward thrusting canopy, breaking into the Station Road frontage, like the proboscis of a giant praying mantis, introduced a foreign accent of limited extent. Howard would undoubtedly have been intrigued by this small-scale updating of his 'crystal palace'. During the refurbishment of the Arena Parade in the early 1980s, a red-painted projecting arcade was installed, running around from Broadway to Eastcheap, and linked to the Co-op with an arch motif and clock. Howard himself had envisaged elegant glazed canopies like those at Victorian Southport or Harrogate, around shopping parades.

The upgrading of individual shopfronts was a means of emphasising the quality of Letchworth shopping in the face of competition from nearby superstores. The Corporation's Information Centre in Leys Avenue, where a sensitively designed traditional shopfront replaced a poor 1950s example laid the foundations for a successful policy which sought to preserve the best examples from the past, and to introduce more sensitive new designs.[26] In 1988, a fine parade of shops in Leys Avenue, designed by Allen Foxley in 1909, was sensitively restored with a projecting canopy leading into a small internal precinct. In 1986 a large new retail unit in Eastcheap, on the site of *The Palace Cinema*, revived the gables of pre-1914 shopping parades. On the approach to the town centre at Howard Park Corner a development of flats and a complex of surgeries and flats on Norton Way North consolidated a late 1980s revival of a style of architecture related to the origins of the Garden City. In 1987 a report by Conran Roche recommended improved management through a town-centre association and pedestrian priority. The latter had been on the agenda since the 1965 appraisal. Resurfacing Leys Avenue and Eastcheap with the ubiquitous block paving, the restriction of road widths, and the creation of parking bays, and raised platforms to slow traffic below 20 m.p.h., brought more comfortable conditions for pedestrians a few years later. A comprehensive town centre regeneration did not, however, get under way until the mid-late 1990s, as will be described in Chapter Sixteen.

Silver Jubilee In 1987 the Silver Jubilee of the Letchworth Garden City Corporation was celebrated. A party was held for the hardy surviving pioneers who had lived in the town between 1903-18 was organised, Standalone Farm held an Open Day and there were tours of the Garden City Corporation Enterprises. The Corporation Chairman, Sidney Melman, looked forward to 'the support of everyone who lives or works in the town making sure that Silver eventually turns to Gold'.[27] Already £7,000,000 had been paid to the town out of Section 32 surpluses, and the accounts revealed cumulative revenue surpluses of £2,540,000 for 1986/87 and £2,570,000 for 1987/88. As the spectacular jubilee firework display was held on Norton Common on 11 September 1987, lighting up the sky for miles around, it seemed that Howard's dream had been realised. Commentators as diverse as George Bernard Shaw, H.C.C. Treasurer John Alexander, and Oliver Smedley, one of the Directors of F.G.C. Ltd. who opposed the Corporation Bill in 1960-2, had viewed the revenue of the Letchworth estate as a potential gold mine. The value of the estate was increasing by leaps and bounds. The estate agents, Bidwells, had produced valuations of £41,712,000 on 31 March 1987, and £52,055,000 a year later. By contrast, the Council was feeling national governmental pressure on local government spending. This had begun in the early 1970s, with the economic crisis provoked by oil price rises, and continued through the sharp inflation of mid-decade. In

1979, the newly elected Conservative Government under Margaret Thatcher announced its intention of curbing the role of local government, and progressively reduced the rate support grant, eventually substituting the controversial individual community charge ('poll tax'), and subsequently council tax.

The Conservative Government of the 1980s was very different from its predecessor of the early 1960s, which had created the Letchworth Garden City Corporation. The dismemberment of 'Q.U.A.N.G.O.S.' (Quasi Autonomous Non-Governmental Organisations) became the order of the day. The remaining development corporations, which had built the post-war New Towns, together with the Commission for the New Towns, in which the assets of some had already been vested prior to their transfer to local control, were disbanded. The dispersal of assets to the highest bidder, in the manner attempted by First Garden City Limited, was promoted, to provide government revenue. Less immediately profitable assets were transferred to local authorities – thus in April 1983 the Welwyn Hatfield District Council received assets which excluded the most lucrative sites, the Development Corporation housing having been transferred seven years previously. Although the role of landlord and local authority were now merged, the estate was not the unified entity which had been preserved at Letchworth, while the local authority area included a second New Town at Hatfield and rural margins. The Letchworth Garden City Corporation was initially protected through its never having been absorbed into the New Towns legislative structure, but it potentially fell victim to the provisions of the Local Government Act 1972, which had created the expanded district councils including N.H.D.C. in 1974. Under Section 262 of the 1972 Act, local Acts applying to non-Metropolitan areas were to have been inoperative after 21 December 1986. The Jubilee might not have happened at all! However, in May 1986, the Department of the Environment confirmed that an order would be laid exempting the Corporation from the Provisions of S262.[28] Once again, the integrity of Letchworth had been preserved by a Government, whose politics were, on the face of it, antipathetic. However, in the early 1990s, it became evident that there would be a further fundamental change in the status of the ground landlord.

Sixteen

Proud Past ... Bright Future

Letchworth Garden City Heritage Foundation Howard's original view was that the assets of the completed town would be turned over fully to its residents. In one sense this occurred through the creation of the Corporation, yet it also had the danger, due to its constitution, of remaining remote, a point brought out in research undertaken in 1981-3 by Dr. Gillian Stamp of Brunel University.[1] A possible catalyst for the reorganisation of the Letchworth Garden City Corporation arose in June 1991. National consultation on the future structure of local government by the Secretary of State for the Environment, Michael Heseltine, brought a response from the ruling Conservative group on North Herts D.C.[2] They advocated the disbandment of the Corporation, claiming lack of accountability, and advocating transfer of the assets to the local authority. The reaction in Letchworth was critical: Andrew Egerton-Smith, Chief Executive of the Corporation, felt that the Councillors had ignored recent efforts to be open and accountable. Nevertheless, the following year, a fundamental reorganisation began. Central government wished to withdraw from its power of patronage over appointments to the Corporation Board. Locally, there was concern to retain the estate intact. The piecemeal dismemberment of the new towns, with profitable elements retained by the Commission for the New Towns, and housing passed over to the local authority, as had occurred at Welwyn Garden City, was not a commendable model. The establishment of the Corporation had, after all, been provoked by the intention of First Garden City Ltd. to dispose of its assets piecemeal.

In September 1992, it was confirmed that the Secretary of State had requested the Corporation to prepare plans to leave the public sector. The Board had explored the options, and had concluded that an Industrial and Provident Society, with charitable status, was its appropriate successor. On 15 October 1992, the Chairman, Eric Lyall addressed a residents' meeting in Plinston Hall, the first of 30 local presentations of the proposals.[3] The new body would be known as the Letchworth Garden City Heritage Foundation, and, on 27 November, a private Bill would be presented to Parliament to create it. The Rules of the Foundation would be subject to the approval of the Registrar of Friendly Societies – the draft rules would undergo a three-month consultation. Initially, there would be seven Founder-Governors; five of them General Governors, and two local authority representatives. Further Nominated Governors would be appointed in accordance with the Rules, followed by General Governors selected by the Board of Management. There would be 30 Governors overall, who would in turn appoint the Board of Management. The Foundation would receive the assets of the Corporation, and its remit would include the support of a wide range of charitable activities in Letchworth. It would manage the Garden City Estate, fulfilling one of the charitable objects – preservation of heritage and the environment – reflecting the importance of the Garden City environment. These key functions would embrace the community benefit, covenanted in Ebenezer Howard's original concept. The Bill was expected to receive Royal Assent in summer 1993, with the assets transferred to the Foundation in January 1994.

The proposals were circulated to all Letchworth residents. Comments were generally favourable: the Garden City Society emphasised that there should be safeguards to ensure that a majority of Governors should always be Letchworth residents.[4] Spring 1993 saw the Parliamentary readings, and scrutiny by Select Committee, beginning 11 May. The Letchworth Leaseholders and Freeholders' Association (who had been concerned with the escalating costs of the purchase of freeholds as 99-year leases neared reversion), and eight individuals

137 Stuart Kenny (*centre*), Director General of the Heritage Foundation, commemorates the completion of refurbishment of the railway station on 11th June 1999, with Mark Powles, Commercial Director of WAGN (*left*) and Mark Papworth of Railtrack (*right*). The station was renamed 'Letchworth Garden City', an important landmark in the campaign to restore the town's full name.

had petitioned against the Bill.[5] Among agreed amendments of the Rules were the provision of an ombudsman and a code of practice based on the Citizens' Charter. Regrettably, progress stalled, and alterations to the Bill resulted in its having to retrace its original steps. Ultimately the Lords insisted that there should be six elected Governors. The Bill passed its remaining stages, Commons and Lords, and received Royal Assent on 1 May 1995.[6] The Foundation was registered as an Industrial and Provident Society on 14 June. Vesting Day, in which the assets were to pass to the Foundation, and thus into the private sector, was set for 1 October 1995. A celebratory dinner was held at Plinston Hall the night before, to bid farewell to the Corporation and hail its successor. 'Foundation Day' featured a fun-fair and musical extravaganza in the Kennedy Gardens, inaugurated by a 180-foot bungee jump by the Director General, Stuart Kenny. That evening, Norton Common was lit up by a fireworks display and laser show with music, which entertained over 9,000 people.[7] A 'pioneers party' for residents who had settled in Letchworth before 1920 was held. The Foundation's motto, 'Proud Past … Bright Future', resulted from a competition held in schools throughout Letchworth. Thirteen-year-old Simon Lovett, a Highfield pupil, won the competition, a £100 cheque for himself, and £250 for his school.

Transition to the Foundation brought changes. Andrew Egerton-Smith resigned early in December 1994, having served the Corporation for 19 years, ten as Chief Executive. He had supervised the development of the business park, had overseen restructuring of the agricultural enterprise, and had been closely involved with the drafting and initial progress of the Heritage Foundation Bill. The new supremo, Director General of the outgoing Corporation and incoming Foundation, was Stuart Kenny, who arrived on 5 December 1994. An economist, he had entered the Civil Service in the early 1970s, working in the Department of Trade and Industry. He specialised in East-West relations and negotiated trade agreements with the Eastern bloc, in the period of *rapprochement* which heralded the thaw of centralised socialism. He then undertook aviation defence work, being closely involved in the Falklands War in 1982. He then represented the United Kingdom on, and became Chairman of, a major NATO Committee. In 1984, he was appointed to the Merseyside Task Force, convened by Michael Heseltine in the wake of the Toxteth riots. This brought direct involvement with property development and urban regeneration, which continued after his appointment as Deputy Chief Executive to the Leeds Development Corporation in 1988. Mr Kenny admits that, when approached by a head-hunter, he had not heard of Letchworth![8] After his appointment, the learning curve was steep and swift. Within three months he faced a House of Lords Committee, parrying their probing questions into 90 years of the Garden City story.

The Board reflected continuity. Eric Lyall had chaired the Corporation since October 1990: he became Chairman of the Board of Management. There were seven Founding Governors, including two local authority nominees, forming the new Board of Management. Six Governors were elected by citizens of Letchworth, and eight were nominated by the societies and organisations of Letchworth. The remaining nine were to be appointees of the Board of

Management. Each Governor held a single, non-refundable share in the Foundation, but under the Rules was specifically prohibited from profiting by the Foundation's activities. From 1997, Governors would be responsible for electing the Board of Management. This was enabled to have up to ten members, including the two local authority nominations. The period of Governorship was limited to five years for Elected Governors, and one fifth of Nominated and General Governors would retire at the end of each Financial Year. Governors would have no direct role in the Heritage Foundation, having elected the Board, which itself was non-executive. They were, however, invited to serve on the Foundation's Committees. Over the years, some have found it difficult to reconcile the fact that the Governors function primarily as an electoral college. The personal role of the Chairman of the Board of Management, who also chairs the quarterly meetings of the Governors, is an important factor in harnessing and maintaining their enthusiasm for all matters Letchworthian.

138 In the garden of the First Garden City Heritage Museum, Garden City Corporation Chairman, Eric Lyall, exchanges gifts with Fujoka Shigehiero, leader of a group of Japanese Mayors, autumn 1993. There have been many visits by Japanese city officials and planners in recent years.

The Foundation's objects are set out in Schedule 1 of the Letchworth Garden City Heritage Foundation Act 1995. It is empowered to carry on for the benefit of the local community of Letchworth:

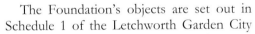

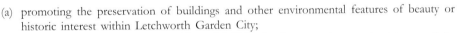

(a) promoting the preservation of buildings and other environmental features of beauty or historic interest within Letchworth Garden City;
(b) providing or assisting in the provision of facilities for the recreation or other leisure activity of the local community in the interests of social welfare with the object of improving their conditions of life;
(c) promoting the advancement of education and learning within Letchworth Garden City;
(d) promoting the relief of poverty and sickness within Letchworth Garden City;
(e) supporting any charitable organisation having an office or branch in Letchworth Garden City; and
(f) promoting any other charitable purposes for the benefit of the local community.

How these objectives have been interpreted and achieved in the first years of the Foundation's operations will be discussed below.[9] The fixed assets vested in the Foundation totalled £57.5 million, indicating how the value of the estate had grown under the Corporation's management. However, this represented a retrenchment from a peak of £67.9 million in March 1990, reflecting uncertain conditions during the recession of the early 1990s.

Garden City Housing revival During the 1990s, there was a revival of interest in the characteristics of Garden City housing. The North Hertfordshire District Local Plan was revised between 1990-3, and its Guidelines and Standards included a visual analysis of the Howard Cottage Society housing in Rushby Mead as an exemplar of best practice. The Letchworth Policies and Proposals drew attention to the characteristics of Garden City housing:

139 The Valley Road scheme updated Garden City social housing in a mixed development of 220 units, by the Howard Cottage Society, the Sanctuary Housing Association, and Woolwich Homes.

Not only do the finest of the neighbourhoods benefit from low densities, generous landscaping and hedges, but the houses are also grouped together and so relate to a sequence of outdoor spaces in an overall setting.

Furthermore, it was emphasised that

> ... the Council will expect new residential development to follow its 'Garden City Design Principles' guidelines, in order that new development in Letchworth can reflect the character of the World's First Garden City.[10]

The effectiveness of plans and policies must be judged by results. It would be unrealistic to claim that all 1990s housing fulfilled the precepts absolutely. However, there was a welcome improvement in design. On Letchworth Gate, the 1930s Creamery had been demolished in the early 1980s, but the site lay vacant while Barratts completed the St Alban Road housing. In 1992-94, Creamery Court was built, which boldly rounded off the development. The angled block turned from Letchworth Gate into Baldock Lane, with a landmark presence heralding the entry to the Garden City. Thirty houses and 18 flats were provided, with a build up of scale to the corner pavilions with tall rendered gables, standing out against the steeply pitched tiled roofs. The architects, Lawrence and Wrightson, had evidently studied examples of Garden City housing, and used familiar motifs confidently. Less dramatic, but amply fitting their context, were the new Pixmore Way flats (accessed from Pixmore Avenue), on the grounds of the former Letchworth Hospital. Developed by Matthew Homes Ltd., architects Woods Hardwick, the scheme provided 34 one- and two-bedroom flats. The pebble-dashed walls above brick recreated the 'skirt and blouse' effect used by several early Garden City architects, while the setting back and forward of the blocks created an interesting street picture, and allowed the retention of mature trees on the frontage. Given the tightly-drawn settlement boundary for Letchworth, it is not surprising that re-cycling of developed land, inelegantly termed 'brownfield sites', became an important feature of housing development in the 1990s, continuing a trend begun the previous decade with the 'Tabbs' estate on Icknield Way. Also on Icknield Way, west of Spirella, the small industrial estate, north of the railway, was progressively redeveloped with houses and flats.

The opportunity for more extensive re-development arose in Valley Road, one of the early post-war Letchworth U.D.C. estates, which included extensive pre-fab bungalows, and two-storey 'Airey' houses.[11] The latter were among the most extensively constructed industrialised component houses of the 1940s, which used a concrete post framework to which aggregate-finished concrete panels, looking like large-scale weatherboarding, were attached by copper wire. By the 1980s, these houses, of which 26,000 were built nation-wide, were suffering from fundamental structural defects, and government finance was made available for their redevelopment. The cleared Valley Road site was rebuilt be-tween 1990-92 with a social housing scheme of 220 units, including two-person bungalows, and two-, three- and four-bedroom houses. The developers were the Howard Cottage Society and the Sanctuary Housing Association, architects Hancock Associates, contractors Morrison Construction. The spaciousness of the layout, retention of trees and open spaces, picturesque composition of houses and attractive street scenes earned the scheme a Garden City Heritage Award in 1993. A 36-unit, category two elderly housing group, Tabor Court, included the 1,000th home built by the Howard Cottage Society, and the building was opened formally by Her Majesty the Queen on 30 July 1993. The Airey houses had faced Wilbury Road, and their site was redeveloped as Wilbury Chase, by

140 Her Majesty the Queen arrives for the opening of Tabor Court Sheltered Housing, 30 July 1993. This included the 1,000th home built by Howard Cottage Society. She unveiled a plaque, presented a commemorative key, and visited one of the flats.

Woolwich Homes, architects Hancock Associates, contractors Kernon Builders Ltd. It comprised 47 two- and three-bedroom houses and two-bedroom bungalows for sale. The attractive street picture along Wilbury Road, with its varied gables, represented a great improvement over the utilitarian drabness of the Aireys.

Following the withdrawal of local authorities from new rental housing, apart from special needs, such as the elderly, and the sharp rise in sale prices of existing and new houses during the 1990s, social housing became a recurrent theme in housing policies. In 1989, the Corpo-ration built 59 rental flats with 16 let under assured tenancy in Cade Close, east of Green Lane. A Methodist Nursing Home for the elderly was built nearby in 1990. The Heritage Foundation has moved away from direct housing provision and management. One of the staples of social housing in Letchworth has been Letchworth Cottages and Buildings, estab-lished in 1907. Its most extensive development was the Glebe Estate, built 1910-12 along Glebe Road and Common View, between Norton Way North and Green Lane. During the 1990s there was a phased programme of refurbishment. By 2000, L.C. and B. were generating a revenue contribution of £289,000. Concern was felt that this was not an adequate return on the investment. Moreover, two thirds of the stock had been built before 1914, and did not meet contemporary housing needs. A review was undertaken. It appeared likely that options to purchase at a discount would be offered to many tenants, and that units which

141 After the Heritage Foundation moved to Spirella, the former estate offices were refurbished, and the upper floors were converted to flats.

met present-day criteria for social housing would be retained, but brought under the management of an alternative approved Registered Social Landlord.[12]

In late March 2002, it was announced that North Herts D.C. had successfully bid for a place on the Government's annual Housing Stock transfer programme. Balloting tenants would take place during the summer, and if approved the Council's 8,700 homes could be transferred to a new partnership, non-profitmaking registered social landlord, with council and tenant representatives, to be approved by the Housing Corporation. An independent survey had revealed an immediate need for £52 million to tackle the most pressing problems, with £350 million required over the next 30 years to maintain the stock. The direct local authority role in social housing provision in the Garden City, begun over 90 years previously by Hitchin R.D.C. and massively increased by Letchworth U.D.C., might be terminated.

Town centre residential potential was significantly underused. 'Living over the shop' was widespread in the shopping parades of the 1910s-1930s, but the accommodation fell out of use post-war, and there were difficulties in separating shops from flats above. Town centre regeneration has included refurbishment of the flats above the 1960s Arena Parade, and others in Eastcheap, Leys Avenue and Station Road. The move of the Foundation to Spirella in 1998 released the old Estate Office to the solicitors, Balderston and Warren, and the upper floors were converted to eight flats, named 'Lyall Chambers', after Eric Lyall, the Foundation's recently retired Chairman. Sale of the flats, opposite the Station, was virtually instantaneous: three further flats for rent were converted in The Colonnade, above *The Hogshead* public house. In Station Road, part of the site of the former Ford dealership was redeveloped by McCarthy and Stone, for retirement flats, named 'Bennett Court', after Leslie Bennett, who had run the garage and had made a substantial contribution to civic life as U.D.C. Chairman during the Second World War.

One controversial aspect related to housing hung over the early 1990s. This was the escalating cost of freehold acquisition by leaseholders, whose original term was 99 years. The Letchworth Leaseholders and Freeholders Association and the Corporation jointly applied to the Lands Tribunal in 1991 to try to establish a correct basis for determining the terms of enfranchisement of four test cases. The Corporation had offered a concessionary scheme to assist the purchase of freeholds by elderly residents. Feelings ran high as the Association and individuals petitioned against the Heritage Foundation Bill in 1994. The Foundation began to contact all homeowners with 99-year leases, or those with a ground rent review every 99 years, to alert them to the problems, and urging consideration of freehold purchase. The dip in property values of the early 1990s had eased the situation, and by 1997, 80 per cent of the earlier leaseholders had either purchased their freeholds or were so doing. Keith Emsall, a former Corporation Board Member and District Councillor, played a leading role in the conciliation. This was as well, for property values escalated rapidly from the late 1990s. By 2001, early Garden City houses were eagerly sought, with prices in excess of £500,000 for choice examples, and a select few at £1,000,000! The insistence on low density, generous gardens, and high quality design had paid off abundantly, but raises the question as to whether a two-tier market has arrived, with the most characteristic Garden City architecture priced out of local ownership. In summer 2001, a local estate agent, Ian Elmers, reported that the average house price in Letchworth was between £130,000 and £140,000; a modern one-bedroom flat selling at £32,000 in 1995 had doubled in price, and was the cheapest property available in Letchworth.[13] A *Times* survey had shown Letchworth as the seventh most popular place to live in the country, and investors were buying houses to rent them out. First-time buyers had practically been priced out.

Town Centre Regeneration   In 1989, a survey revealed that 70 per cent of local residents spent their money outside the town, raising concern over the quality of shopping facilities. The Corporation's business consultant, Sue Cheshire, sought to bring groups of retailers into discussions at the Business Centre. Traders in The Wynd complained of lack of promotion of their refurbished precinct, and the Corporation acknowledged problems with the new 'Arcade' (now 'The Gallery'), where its most attractive feature, the coffee shop, announced impending closure. In July 1989, five North Herts Councillors buried their political differences and sought to promote the town through the Council's Town Centre sub-committee. Yet the town centre did not lack attractive features, and the refurbishment of 50 Leys Avenue, a parade of shops, won a Civic Award commendation from the Council.

The final reports of the Corporation made depressing reading, chronicling a downturn in retail confidence. Sainsbury's relocation from the shopping precinct to the business park in 1991 brought fundamental change in shopping habits and escalating vacancies of town centre shops. In Spring 1994, North Herts College applied for outline permission to redevelop its site west of Broadway as a supermarket. The freehold had been conveyed to the County Council, and the Corporation's only control lay in a restrictive covenant binding the land to educational use. Illustrative plans showed development turned away from the Broadway frontage, and controversially included a petrol filling station. Linkage with the established retail centre, east of Broadway, would become tenuous at best. Furthermore, the town would lose a valuable educational facility, as the College intended to consolidate on their other campuses. The Corporation's energies were focused on constructing the legal framework for transition to the Heritage Foundation.

On arrival in Letchworth in December 1994, Stuart Kenny focused his attention on the town centre. By February 1995, he had built on a retail strategy drawn up by Hillier Parker, by convening and chairing a Town Centre Board, to which Hugh Harper, Chairman of the Chamber of Trade, and other key local retailers were attracted. First steps to make the centre look cared for included decorative windows for empty shops. While the College site represented the key element for long-term revival, the complexity of negotiating an acceptable scheme and attracting an appropriate retailer brought other sites into the equation straight away, to create a positive commercial climate. The Corporation acquired interests in two key buildings – 'The Colonnade', facing Station Place at the head of Leys Avenue, and *The Broadway Cinema*. The former had been the Eastern Electricity showroom. It was let to Whitbread Inns, who refurbished it as a new pub-restaurant, *The Hogshead*, at a cost of £600,000.[14] The external refurbishment works were completed by the Foundation, and a 'living over the shop' scheme at Nos 1-5 Eastcheap. *The Broadway Cinema* was refurbished by a new joint company, with a major stake taken by the Heritage Foundation, in partnership with the original owners, The Letchworth Palace Ltd. After a four-month, £2-million refurbishment, returning the Art Deco exterior and foyer to their original condition, the cinema re-opened with three screens in July 1996.[15] 'The Arcade', between Leys Avenue and

142 Going ... Going ... Gone. North Herts College bites the dust in Spring 1998, clearing the site for Morrisons.

Station Road, was purchased from Refuge Assurance plc, and underwent a £600,000 refurbishment, including renewal of the glazed roof.[16] This led to the anchor unit facing Leys Avenue, long associated with Brookers, being acquired by J. D. Wetherspoon plc, for a second pub-restaurant, *The Three Magnets*. Befitting its theme, it was filled with reproduction Garden City memorabilia. Later, *The Litten Tree* (Surrey Free Inns) in the old Cakebread Robey premises in Station Road completed a threesome – suddenly a dearth of pubs became a plethora. The mid-1990s witnessed unease over personal security in town centres, particularly in the evening. The Letchworth Town Centre Partnership was awarded grant support from the Home Office to install closed circuit television cameras, and a Town Centre Manager was appointed.

Negotiations over the future of the College site proceeded. Historically, this area was planned as part of the shopping centre, containing the still-born 'Westcheap', shown on the Parker and Unwin plan to match its counterpart, Eastcheap. Slow growth, and the initial development of Station Road and Leys Avenue, had resited the commercial heart. Redevelopment of the College site would eliminate the lopsided mismatch between the paper layout and the incremental development which occurred. Stuart Kenny was convinced that the Council car park between *The Broadway Hotel* and Station Way should be added to the site, and achieved agreement to this after lengthy negotiations. The College was informed that removal of the education covenant from its site would be conditional upon agreement to retain a Letchworth presence, or pay a considerable sum to the Foundation. They chose to stay. The increased area brought an improved layout, with redesign of the supermarket to address Broadway. The Heritage Foundation, College and Council jointly marketed the site. Intense speculation arose about the potential occupier. In spring 1997 it was announced that William, Morrison Supermarkets plc were the successful bidder, lessee and developer of the 6.4-acre site. A detailed planning application submitted to North Herts D. C. showed a

143 The former Magistrates Court and the Boys Club façades were skilfully integrated with Morrisons' Broadway frontage.

70,000 sq. ft. supermarket, and 529 parking spaces. FJ Architects Ltd. designed the building, and the contractors were Shepherds Construction. North Herts College proposed a 22,000 sq. ft. corner building, with wings along Broadway, and facing Town Square.[17]

Morrisons was in scale with the old Boys Club and Magistrates Court buildings, dating from 1914 and 1915, which were retained and refurbished as a café. Morrisons were known as a regional firm, founded in Bradford in 1899. By the mid-1990s they were trading in 83 stores in Yorkshire, Lancashire, the North East and the Midlands. The Letchworth store was one of their first in the South. Work began in spring 1998 with the clearing of the 1950s college buildings. Their disappearance was unlamented. Morrisons opened in a blaze of publicity on 5 July 1999, and was soon reporting over 25,000 shoppers each week.[18] It was vital that the new supermarket should not become a 'one stop' facility. Three hours' free parking was granted to Morrisons' customers, at the Foundation's insistence, to encourage shoppers to circulate around the town centre, to benefit other retailers. The Foundation also refused the initial intent to include specialist kiosks for shoe repairs, dry-cleaning and photography, to avoid conflicts with nearby town centre traders. The College's 'Goldsmith Centre', architects Archer Boxer, was also opened, and catered for 1,200 students.

The impact of these two major developments on Letchworth town centre was immediate, bringing people back, creating a lively urban ambience, and complementing the earlier initiatives described above. In urban design terms, the visual gain was significant. The scale and design of Morrisons effectively revived the traditional street architecture, and completed the Broadway frontage. The well-mannered rusticated ground floor, brick first floor, and tiled roofs contrasted with the bolder treatment of the curved colonnaded entrances – one of them forming a focal point in the newly-created paved square, presided over by a specially commissioned bronze bust of Ebenezer Howard. If the dummy chimneystacks and cupola suggest pastiche, they also create a lively roofline. The 'Goldsmith Centre' was, perhaps, not quite so successful, as some of its window detailing appears utilitarian, while the plant room is not an enhancement of the roof. However, its scale and the bold colonnade entrance create fine townscape. Importantly, it both contrasts with and yet balances the rather Colonial/Georgian-style of the 1935 Council Offices across Broadway.

Between 1995-99, more than £50 million had been invested in the regeneration of Letchworth town centre and over 60 new shops had opened. A new Tourist Information Centre was opened in one of the corner units of 'The Arcade', facing Station Road. A new visual and performing arts centre, 'The Place', was opened above *The Three Magnets* in Leys Avenue. The Heritage Foundation's initial commitment and investment had attracted others. As the millennium approached, the sharp decline of the early 1990s had been reversed. Problems remain. The refurbished Wynd suffers from a peripheral location, as does the lower end of Leys Avenue. Questions also arose over the future of the Commerce Way precinct. This had undergone two cosmetic refurbishments, but had suffered the vacation of two major units, notably Sainsburys, the 'anchor' store. However, Iceland and Boots remained, and the family clothing multiple, Peacock's, eventually occupied part of the central unit. Woolworths also returned to Letchworth, to the centre of the precinct in summer 2000. The covered market operated 'business as usual', despite closure, in 1998, of the large hall above, used since its completion in 1974 for little but bingo. In November 1997, Hill Samuel Property Trust acquired Equitable Life's interest in the precinct, which was rebranded 'Garden Square'.[19] They had intended to refurbish it again, but no plans were made public. By November 2001, the delay was frustrating attempts to keep up the momentum of town centre regeneration; nine of the 40 units were void at that time. The owners were in discussion with the Heritage Foundation and North Herts planners over a more ambitious scheme, which included part-redevelopment and comprehensive refurbishment, which will buttress this prime retail core. Planning applications are expected during 2002.[20] While question marks will evidently hang over the future of Letchworth town centre for some years, the past few years have witnessed a remarkable transformation.

Spirella Resurrected   As the 1990s opened, 'Castle Corset' was a shadow of its former glory, suffering from a lack of maintenance, with defects evident in its pioneering concrete structure and generous glazing. Yet it remained the most monumental building in the Garden City, and symbolised a benevolent paternalist employment system that had all but vanished. Moreover, it was a Grade II* listed historic building. Proposals for an office conversion, with 'enabling' development on a cleared rear site, proved abortive.[21] Sensing that nothing would happen without its intervention, the Garden City Corporation acquired Spirella in July 1994 for £1.4 million. On his first visit, a few months later, Stuart Kenny felt that the owners should have paid the sum over to the Corporation to rid themselves of the liability! It was initially anticipated that a comprehensive refurbishment would cost £6-£7 million – the figure rose to £10 million by the end of the contract, but this included the information technology servicing and an air cooling system. The project was assisted by a £945,000 grant from English Partnerships, the government's urban regeneration agency. It was therefore essential that the conversion should add maximum value to the building, in both end use and servicing. Feasibility studies considered residential use, hotel and conferencing, and offices. As Mr Kenny recalled

> … in investment terms, offices were always going to win. That concerned me hugely because Letchworth had never been known as an office town. We had too much competition. We had Stevenage, Milton Keynes, Peterborough and Cambridge, and had we just converted to offices, we would never have let them.[22]

The solution was state-of-the-art servicing, flood cabling, and sophisticated information technology networking, available normally only to large corporations. The impressive ball-room was restored to pristine condition, including Cecil Hignett's exquisite art nouveau plasterwork, and its stained glass domes were reinstated, lighting the interior for the first time since they were 'blacked out' at the start of the Second World War. The remainder of the interior was largely simply upgraded in the spirit of the 1990s, with the retention of features which had survived the misuse of the building for decades, and some reinstatement. The sleek modern entrance hall, with its corner café, striking circular reception desk, and high-tech staircase to the first-floor meeting and conference rooms, symbolised the reincarnation of the building. Tucked away on the ground floor of the north wing is a fitness centre to assuage executive stress. Externally, the building was carefully cleaned and restored, with a new system of double-glazing closely matching the original utilitarian pattern in appearance, by Crittall Windows Ltd., who made the originals. The south-western rear corner of the building had been butchered in the 1950s, and this was rebuilt in the original style.[23] In 2001, the gardens were restored, with a fountain, replacing that originally installed in 1931 to commemorate Spirella's 21st birthday in Letchworth. Bidwells were designers and project managers, John Laing plc were the contractors, and building work was completed in August 1998, when the first 15 tenants moved in. 82,000 sq. feet of highly serviced office space had been created. The building was fully let by the end of 1999.

The official opening on 29 January 1999 was a special occasion, undertaken by H.R.H. The Prince of Wales. Known for his, often critical, views on modern architecture, Prince Charles was clearly impressed by the achievement:

> … the regeneration of the Spirella Building symbolises something very special about your willingness to invest in the future of this unique town, and is an example to others of how a magnificent building, having fallen into disuse, can be brought back to life and contribute hugely, again, to the local community.[24]

The Prince was welcomed by Eric Lyall, Chairman of the Heritage Foundation, and Stuart Kenny. He toured the building. He met a group of 'Spirella girls' in the ballroom, and representatives of three Letchworth businesses, which had been assisted by the Prince's Trust. It was his first official visit to the First Garden City: Prince Charles signed the visitors'

XXVII 'Signing in at Spirella', 29 January 1999. H.R.H. Prince Charles, with Eric Lyall, Chairman of the Letchworth Garden City Heritage Foundation.

XXVIII Commemorative plaque unveiled by His Royal Highness.

XXIX The restored Spirella Ballroom now hosts conferences and private functions.

XXX The restored Gardens, replanted in 2000-1, with the restoration of the fountain, originally unveiled in 1931.

XXXI Town Square and Broadway, with Morrisons under development, upper left.

XXXI and **XXXII** Aerial photographs taken in 1998 by Dr Takahito Saiki of Kobe Design University.

XXXII Westholm and Norton Common. The axial line of Broadway, projected across the Common, is clearly seen.

XXXIII Peter Harkness, Chairman of the Letchworth Garden City Heritage Foundation, posed on the 'high tech' staircase in Spirella, 2000, with the Board of Management. *Centre right*, Peter Harkness; *top row, left to right*, Keith Emsall, William Armitage, Lynda Needham, Paul Palmer; *front row, left to right*, Dennis Wells, Peter Jackson, Alan Scouller.

XXXIV The message of the *Design Guide* is reflected in this well designed and detailed extension of a house in Eastholm.

144   During 2001, the old 'Broadway House' office block was transformed into 'Nexus', with an eye-catching domed penthouse.

book, and was shown an earlier one, signed by his grandfather as Duke of York (later King George VI) on his inspection of Spirella in 1926. The new Spirella received many plaudits, including the prize for 'Property Innovation of the Year' at the *Property Week* Awards, in April 1999.

Close to 400 people work in Spirella. Businesses in computer software and related fields were prevalent in the tenant mix. Stevenage-based McKeown Software took 16,200 sq. ft., almost 20 per cent of the lettable floorspace: AMT Sybex, Packaging Networks, Nott Pybus and Idnet, award-winning website designers, were among other initial lettings. Commercially, as well as aesthetically, Spirella proved its success right away: rents for relets have risen by 50 per cent in three years. The demand for such accommodation had now been established in Letchworth Garden City.

At the rear of the Spirella site lay a utilitarian factory – the Bijoli works – remnant of an industrial enclave that had also included the Marmet Baby Carriage Factory. Much of this land was redeveloped for houses and flats in the early 1990s. In 1999 construction began on an offshoot, 'Spirella 2'.[25] This combined a ground-floor private nursery for under 5s, 'The

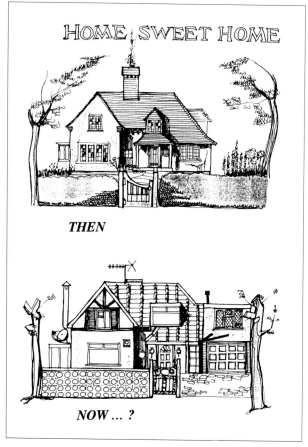

145 The Letchworth Garden City Design Guide used this cartoon to highlight the destructive impact of ill-considered 'home improvement'.

Jigsaw Nursery', with 6,000 sq. feet of office space carrying the Spirella brand. The patent coiled wire stiffening of the early corsets had been reborn in terms of state-of-the-art computer cabling.

'Broadway House', the old ICL building of the early 1960s, was by general consent one of the least admired Garden City buildings, dominating the south-east of Town Square/Kennedy Gardens with its bland, yet doleful presence. Acquired by the Heritage Foundation, an option study was undertaken by C. B. Hillier Parker, following which it was decided to retain the basic structure, with comprehensive refurbishment, inside and out, and a new name, 'Nexus'.[26] The information technology facilities matched those of Spirella, with optimal access to similar business support services. Completed in late autumn 2001, by builders Bowmer Kirkland, when the first tenants moved in, the building's 35,000 sq. ft. was 50 per cent let by January 2002. Externally, the transformation has been remarkable. No doubt some Letchworthians would have wished to see the building demolished, and the site redeveloped to a smaller scale, and intensity. The addition of a pitched roof, in deference to the traditional, domestic Garden City image, was, perhaps, the least successful feature, sitting awkwardly above the rectilinear five-storey block, when viewed across the Kennedy Gardens. The new glazing was far more elegant than the original, with the louvred sunshades giving a degree of modelling, particularly in sunlight, which was conspicuously lacking before. Most remarkable has been the transformation of the corner with Pixmore Way, with its 'high-tech' glazed entrance, and domed penthouse. This has given the building landmark presence, and adds to the variety of the Garden City skyline, when viewed from Eastcheap, or along Pixmore Way, from near or far. In 1901, Raymond Unwin had proclaimed the virtues of avenues, leading into and out of the heart of the Garden City, with 'vistas leading up to the finest buildings … giving impressions of dignity to those who come'.[27] If 'Nexus' as a whole could not aspire to this quality, its eyecatcher dome at least proved the value of Unwin's proposition, a century earlier.

Heritage Management Although much of Letchworth Garden City had been designated as a Conservation Area in 1974, followed five years later by the listing of many of its key early buildings as of special architectural or historic interest, it was evident by the late 1980s that much remained to be done to preserve its special character. The growing popularity of altering and extending residential properties, and the pressure to install double-glazing was eroding the original harmony of early Garden City houses and roads. In 1989, the Letchworth Garden City Corporation commissioned a study on conservation procedures available both to itself and to North Herts D.C.[28] One of the first fruits was the publication of a *Design Guide* to advise on principles to be observed, and features and materials to note when householders were contemplating alterations or improvements.

Many of these were 'permitted development' under planning law. A cartoon contrasted the charm of an original house with the destructive impact of ill-considered alterations. The *Guide*,[29] produced jointly with North Herts D.C., was launched in April 1991 in the Plinston Hall at a gathering of local and regional architects, designers and builders. Keith Emsall, then a Corporation Board member, praised the fact that many Letchworthians had sensitively updated their homes:

> Nevertheless, far too many residents have carried out work of such dubious quality that they have not only detracted from that particular building, but have in the process seriously damaged the appearance of whole parts of the Conservation Area.[30]

It was recognised that the cost of some materials, particularly reclaimed tiles, was significantly higher than modern mass-produced products, and, consequently, a grant scheme was introduced to help bridge the difference. A further inducement to good practice was the launching of a Heritage Award.

The *Design Guide* was circulated to all local authorities, estate agents and builders, with an explanatory leaflet delivered to all Garden City households. The North Herts District Local Plan strengthened its concern for Garden City character, but the issue of 'permitted development' remained. This would require a special Council resolution and, in the early 1990s, approval by the Secretary of State for the Environment to introduce an 'Article 4 Direction', requiring specific planning permission to be obtained for even minor alterations to domestic properties in the Letchworth Conservation Area. The matter had been looked at several times since the 1970s, and always appeared to founder on the amount of detailed survey work required, and the likely sharp increase in the number of planning applications. The introduction of a less complex legal process caused the re-examination of the issue, as will be described below. In the meantime, there was potential discrepancy between the Corporation's Scheme of Management, under which Landlord Consent was required even of minor matters, and the 'permitted development' under national planning legislation.

The Award Scheme recognised exemplars of good practice in its annual cycle.[31] In 1992, it was found that the Award-winning kitchen and garage extension at No. 45 South View, was commissioned by the daughter of the family, who had moved into this fine Crickmer-designed house in 1912. Awards were made in 1994 for matching timber replacement windows at 9 Birds Hill, in an area where U.P.V.C. was rife, and the following year for the Valley Road housing scheme. By the mid-1990s, the Awards appeared to be well established, and the Assessors' panel included Wilfred Court, long-time Architect to Hampstead Garden Suburb Trust, Roderick Gradidge of The Victorian Society, Ellen Barnes of the Letchworth Garden City Society, Keith Emsall, Chairman of the Heritage Foundation's Architectural Heritage Advisory Group, and the author. 1997 brought awards for a sensitively designed, and meticulously matched extension to a 1905 Cheap Cottage at 225 Nevells Road, and a new entrance porch on 'The Salvation Army Hall', nearby, on the corner of Norton Way North. The late 1990s brought something of a standstill. Although some worthwhile projects were submitted, there were also some, which suffered from insensitive detailing or used U.P.V.C. windows, the faults which the *Design Guide* and Award Scheme were intended to avoid. No Awards were agreed for 1999, only two Commendations, and the Award Scheme lay in abeyance in 2000 and 2001.

Following up the *Design Guide*, in 1991, the Corporation launched a Advisory Heritage Committee, which has met regularly ever since. It has reviewed the impact of the *Design Guide*, has given advice on contentious landlord consent applications, and has expressed concern about the future of key buildings such as the Mrs Howard Memorial Hall. Chaired for many years by Keith Emsall, the committee is attended by the North Herts D.C. Conservation Officers, and thus encourages discussion of the roles of both the ground landlord and planning authority in the context of issues of mutual concern. For its part, the District Council has strengthened the authority of the *Design Guide*, by officially accepting it as supplementary planning guidance. The Foundation has also revised the guide, and made it more comprehensive through the addition of extra guidance notes on extensions and hard standings.

After several incremental boundary changes in August 2001, North Herts D.C. embarked upon a comprehensive review of the Letchworth Conservation Area. Increasing the area to include previously omitted early estates such as Norton Glebe, Westbury and 'Little Belgium' was proposed and circulated for public consultation. The Architectural Heritage Advisory Group and the Letchworth Garden City Society advocated inclusion of Norton Road, the east side of Green Lane, The Meads, The Dale, the Pix Estate, parts of Hitchin Road and Baldock Road, and Willian Way. The Pix estate was included, but regrettably the other proposed areas were omitted, when the Council's Letchworth Committee considered the matter in December 2001.[32] A locally drafted 'Article 4 (2) Direction', to bring some 'permitted development' under control, at least on elements of the publicly visible façades of houses on the original 'planned estates' within the Conservation Area, was approved in January 2002. Regrettably, this only applied to roof tiles, and excluded controls over windows and doors on individual houses in many of the mature roads within the conservation area, such as Lytton Avenue, South View, Broadway and the Sollershotts. Finally, a detailed Conservation Area Character Statement was drafted, to assist planning decision-making. Clearly, the Conservation Officers, Liz Marten and Eleanor Gale, have busy times ahead. The Foundation's Architectural Heritage Advisory Group organised site visits to review the proposed boundary changes *in situ*, and warmly endorsed the Council's initiative. On 18 April 2002, International Sites and Monuments Day, a draft list of key 20th-century heritage sites, prepared by English Heritage, was published. It contained Letchworth Garden City, and its inclusion was endorsed in a *Times* leader. This represented the beginning of a discussion with ICOMOS, the International Council on Monuments and Sites, which may lead it to a more formal designation in three to four years' time.

Local appreciation of the architectural heritage of Letchworth grew during the 1990s. In 1994-5 a series of four illustrated *Heritage Trails* was published by the Garden City Corporation and its successor. These featured walks around the town centre, the Cheap Cottage area, Howard Park and Norton Way, and Howgills, Broadway and the Sollershotts. In the early 1990s, the Letchworth Garden City Society published their own trail in their *Journal*, and reissued extracts from such early classics as Brunt's *Pageant of Letchworth*, and Harold Hare's *Garden City Alphabet*. Finally, in 1998-2000, the author prepared a series of six leaflets, profiling well-known *Garden City Architects*, for publication by the Heritage Foundation. These featured Barry Parker and Raymond Unwin, Cecil Hignett, Courtenay Crickmer, Robert Bennett and Wilson Bidwell, M. H. Baillie Scott, and Geoffry Lucas.

Where Town and Country meet   The 'joyous union' of town and country had been one of the most striking aspects of Ebenezer Howard's Garden City concept. Perhaps, inevitably, the focus concentrated upon the development of the Garden City itself, and the green setting, which was after all integral to the scheme, tended to be regarded as a passive ancillary. The fact that the quality of agricultural land around Letchworth was not sufficiently high to encourage significant development of smallholdings, and that the existing agricultural tenancies were retained until land was required for development, was one factor. Another was that, from 1947, the statutory planning process specified that any departure from the existing use required specific planning permission, and the range of activities acceptable in rural areas was strictly limited. The extension of the Greater London Green Belt northwards up the A1 corridor to embrace and envelop Letchworth in the mid-1970s underscored the perception that rural areas were fundamentally detached from urban settlements. Howard's vision of interdependence between town and country became difficult to sustain. A century after *Tomorrow* appeared, efforts were being made to re-evaluate the rural belt of the Letchworth Estate, in the light of changing agricultural practices, and national attempts to improve access to the countryside.

The network of mixed farms, with its traditional pattern of fields, was superseded by more intensively mechanised 'agri-business' from the 1970s, shedding labour. Farming was increasingly geared to national and European Union controls and subsidies. The farming trading profit fluctuated between £81,000 and £121,000 between 1990-92, but the devaluation of the pound against the Green pound caused a sharp rise to £152,000 in 1993.[33] Concern over the environment was reflected in the decision to reduce the use of fertilisers and pesticides, and the receipt of a Wildlife Conservation award in 1991. Manor Farm, which operated a successful farm shop, gained a Runner Up in the Hertfordshire Farms Competition in 1994, with a special award for conservation, and the following year a Best First Time Entrant at the East of England Show. In 1995-6, the Heritage Foundation's forestry and landscape teams undertook tree planting at Radwell Manor, hedge coppicing in Willian, and the foresters restored and renewed large areas of the rural estate. A sign of the times was contract farming. By the late 1990s, the mosaic of individual farms had been consolidated into two – the Northland Estate, and Manor Farm in the south. The former was farmed by the Shaw family for nine years, and in September 1997 the contract was awarded to C.W.S. Farms. Manor or Southland remained 'in hand' under a Farm Manager and deputy. This proved very successful, with profit against turnover rising from 2.5 per cent in 1996 to 11.5 per cent in 2000, after subsidising substantially Standalone Farm educational centre. Farming is entirely arable, trading to secure maximum return, but ensuring that the land is kept in good heart. Dairy farming had been abandoned, as a result of the introduction of E.E.C. milk quotas in response to over-production. The aspiration of the rural belt feeding the Garden City, the difficulties over which were discussed in Chapter Ten, had been overtaken by modern farming practice.

Concerns over a sustainable environment in both the urban and agricultural context arose during the 1990s. Integration of conservation with farming has been mentioned above. Access was addressed by the Corporation in its designation of rural walks in the 1980s, and by the opening of Standalone Farm. What was lacking was an overall vision for the Rural Estate in relation to the Garden City. Consequently, in the run-up to the centenary of Letchworth Garden City in 2003, the Heritage Foundation launched a competition in November 1996[34] to produce an overall strategy, which took a fresh look at the rural estate. The objectives were:

(i)   Creation of a practical, attractive landscape;
(ii) Encouragement of public access and enjoyment;
(iii) Increased bio-diversity.

The proposals were required to be capable of implementation from autumn 1997, with the completion of all capital works by 2003, the centenary of Letchworth. The farmland was to be reduced in area by no more than four per cent, and there was a commitment to continue profitability. The assessors were Stuart Kenny; Sandra Hanley of Letchworth Garden City Society; David Lee of the Landscape Institute; Tom Hancock of the Town and Country Planning Association, and Simon Lyster, Director General of the Wildlife Trusts. Submissions were made on 24 March 1997 and shortlisted entrants were interviewed on 17 April. The winners were Cheltenham-based Illman Young, and Sue Illman received the £15,000 premium from Eric Lyall.[35] The winning idea was simple and effective: a 12.5-mile (18 km) circular walk, the Garden City Greenway, linking existing projects, a new resources centre, and features of rural interest, providing an attractive pathway for walkers, cyclists and horse riders. Within a few weeks detailed survey work was under way, with initial planting schemes to link existing pockets of woodland, and avenue planting along Wymondley Road, leading into Willian. The circular walk took in Radwell Meadows, where a new Country Park was established, Standalone Farm, and Willian, where the Arboretum was restored and extended, with links to Norton Pond, famed for its newts, and to Wymondley Wood, where a new educational woodland was created. The overall project had an annual capital budget of £100,000, with a maximum £1 million investment, gross of substantial governmental contributions under the Countryside Stewardship Scheme. Phased implementation was soon under way. During 1997-8 over 13.3 acres of new woodland were planted, and 1,095 yards of hedgerows were restored. The Countryside Management Service and the Foundation de-silted

Willian Pond to the benefit of coots, moorhens and frogs, who returned to their natural habitat. The following year, extensive improvements to urban woodland were made at Willian Dell, hedge-laying at Willian was completed, and a hoggin path was looped through Wymondley Wood. In 1999, a public amenity area at Radwell Meadows was completed. Matters were on course for completion of the Greenway in 2003. In the meantime, the 160-acre educational working farm at Standalone went from strength to strength, recording 101,000 visitors in its March to September 1998 season, placing it among the top farm and wildlife attractions in the East of England Tourist Board Region. Regrettably, attendance fell back in 1999, due to fears of e-coli, while 2001 was dominated by fear of the spread of foot and mouth disease to Hertfordshire, causing postponement of opening to the end of May.

146 Work on the Garden City Greenway was well under way during 2000, due for completion in 2003, to commemorate the Garden City centenary. This view shows Radwell Meadows Country Park, Nortonbury.

Enterprise Culture The ability of the Heritage Foundation to deliver its charitable objects is dependent upon its trading success. At the basis of this is the Garden City Estate itself, the Foundation's most tangible and valuable asset.[36] The Land Tribunal's Award in respect of the Estate, passed to the Garden City Corporation in 1963, was £3.06 million. The fixed assets vested in the Foundation were valued at £55 million, and by 30 September 2000 had reached £107 million. The first five years saw the Foundation investing in an ambitious capital programme, particularly in town centre regeneration. An investment of £15 million brought in about £40 million from other businesses. The operational philosophy has been to provide the initial stimulus, preferably in a highly visible form of development, achievable in the short term, *pour encourager les autres*. It has worked well. On the revenue side, the rental income was to be enhanced through covenants, with a ten-year strategy of lease acquisition. On the industrial estate, many of the early leases will shortly fall in, granted initially for 99 years, or 999 years, with a review at 99 years. In 1995-6 gross rents receivable were £4.83 million; by 1999-2000 they had risen to £6.07 million.

Until the 1980s Letchworth had a core of major employers. Successive recessions and changing industrial organisation brought about the closure of Shelvoke Dempster, Borg Warner, and I.C.L. The development of the Business Park began the transition to a modern information-technology led mix of small and medium-sized companies. Some have grown substantially – Cook U.K. in Works Road from 700 sq. ft. to 60,000 sq.ft. Their landscaped grounds are a pleasant feature along the original industrial estate road. During its first year of operation, the Heritage Foundation completed 'Iceni Court', an £850,000, 23,000 sq. ft., four-unit industrial development, which brought three new businesses to Letchworth. In 1997, work started on development of the vacant industrial land at the end of Works Road, abutting the A1. An archaeological investigation revealed nothing, but a colony of protected Common Lizards was found and relocated. SIAC Construction, a specialist in ground works and road construction, completed their new regional headquarters in 1998. The Heritage Foundation built a 15,000 sq. ft. factory, pre-let to Fermark, lingerie manufacturers, and one

147 'Factory in a Garden'. The imposing Cook U.K. building in Works Road is set off by its landscaped grounds.

of the most important employers of workers from the Asian community. All new industrial sites at 'Lacerta Court' were taken up in 1998-9, while Schottlander, suppliers to the dental industry, leased a two-acre plot, off Fifth Avenue, Business Park, for construction of a £2 million state-of-the-art research laboratory and customer training centre. At the end of Fourth Avenue, in the Business Park, 'Focus 4' provided flexible accommodation, suitable for office, research and development, or light assembly use. The three units varied from 8,700 to 13,800 sq. ft., with completion in Spring 2001. The image of all recent industrial developments has emphasised lightness and elegance. As with the town centre, the turn of the millennium witnessed a fundamental transformation. Environmental improvements in older industrial areas began in Icknield Way in February 2001, and it was hoped to proceed with Works Road as a second phase. While many of the early industrial buildings have been redeveloped, it was good to see the refurbishment of the long unoccupied Garden City Press buildings on the corner of Works Road and Pixmore Avenue under way during 1998, by Halyard properties. The Heritage Foundation's renewed investment in the industrial and business areas assisted confidence of other developers, including Wheatley Developments with their business campus off Dunhams Lane, and other developments.

Community Profile   In Summer 2001, the estimated population of Letchworth was 33,547, a substantial increase over the 1991 Census total of 32,009, which had just topped Howard's 'ideal' of 32,000.[37] Regrettably, data from the 2001 Census would not become available until August 2002. However, some trends are evident from age bands, comparing 2001 estimates with 1991 Census data (figures shown in parenthesis). 0-15, 6,866 (6,326) +7.85 per cent; 16-24 3,248 (4,238) -30.4 per cent; 25-59 15,998 (15,365) +3.9 per cent; 60-74 4,631 (3,799) +17.96 per cent; 75+ 2,801 (2,339) +16.5 per cent.

While the number of school-age children has increased, there has been a significant decline in young adults, which will work its way into the next cohort over the coming decade. The main economically active group has risen marginally, but there have been much larger rises in the two age bands covering the retired-age population, four times the overall rate of population increase. As nationally, pressure on facilities for the elderly is bound to grow.

Letchworth has become ethnically diverse, but on a small scale. In 1991, 7.7 per cent of the population was classified as non-white. This included 1,705 of Asian origin, 520 of African-Caribbean origin, and 250 Chinese or other ethnic group. The economically active

148 Director of Community Affairs, Allan Patterson, with the children of St Nicholas School in April 1999. The Heritage Foundation helped to fund their new play equipment.

population aged 16 and above totalled 16,300 in 1991, with 1,450 self-employed, 10,650 working full-time, 2,678 working part-time and 1,434 unemployed. The early 1990s were a period of economic recession, and by June 2001 there were only 235 unemployed, 1.4 per cent of the working-age population. Employment in manufacturing in 1991 accounted for 27.8 per cent of employees, with banking, commerce and other services accounting for 37 per cent, and catering and distribution 20 per cent. The decline in manufacturing continued through the 1990s, in line with county and national trends. Of employees and self-employed, 17.4 per cent were in managerial occupations, 17.4 per cent in clerical or secretarial posts, 14.8 per cent in skilled trades, 11.9 per cent were industrial plant or machine operatives. This reflected the beginning of the transition from the traditional manufacturing and service hierarchy, to computer and information technology, and financial services, which have expanded rapidly over the past decade.

In 1991, Letchworth had 12,568 households, with an average size of 2.53. 6,880, 54.75 per cent were owner-occupied, 3,960, 31.5 per cent were local authority tenure, evidence of the large council stock built from 1919-70. 904 households, 7.2 per cent, were described as Housing Association, which included social landlords such as Howard Cottage Society and Letchworth Cottages and Buildings. The private rental sector stood at 724 households, 6.15 per cent. The 3,324 pensioner-only households (1 person 1,996, 2 or more persons 1,328) represented 26.4 per cent of the total, and there were 360 lone-parent households. There were 3,582 households without a car, 5,433 with one car, 2,827 with two cars, and 645 with three or more. Not surprisingly 59.9 per cent recorded use of a car for journey to work (and another 7.6 per cent as passengers in cars), 10.3 per cent walked to work, 5.2 per cent journeyed by bus, 4.6 per cent by pedal cycle and 1.9 per cent by motor cycle. Journeys by train accounted for 6.0 per cent, although 37.8 per cent worked outside Letchworth. 3.3 per cent worked at home, a number set to rise to be reflected in the 2001 statistics.

The method of recording social class changed significantly for the 2001 Census, and the 1991 analysis is the last of its kind, based on status of occupation. Class I accounted for 7.9 per cent of population, with head of household in professional occupation; Class II, 34.8 per cent managerial and technical; Class III 11.1 per cent skilled occupation, non-manual; Class III (M) 27.8 per cent skilled occupations, manual; Class IV 14.7 per cent, partly skilled; Class V 3.7 per cent, unskilled.

Census statistics are, to a degree, an arbitrary slice through a community, frozen in time, and subject to microscopic analysis. The 1991 figures give an overall impression of a relatively affluent, predominantly middle-class, owner-occupied community. Yet here are also hints of diversity, if not of any special characteristics which would mark out the Garden Citizens from

149 Directors of the Heritage Foundation, Nexus Building penthouse, December 2001. *Left to right*, Ian Webb, Director of Finance; Alan Howard, Director of Marketing and P.R.; Stuart Kenny, Director General; Marilyn Hands, Director of Property; Allan Patterson, Secretary and Director of Community Affairs.

their peers in small towns throughout the county or across south-east England. Letchworth has always had numerous community organisations, perhaps a reflection of the pioneering spirit of the early years. Howard and his colleagues always expected his Garden City to exceed the sum of its parts, with a sense of community adding value. The return of value created through the development and administration of the Garden City was a prime obligation of its constitution. The Heritage Foundation is obliged, under its objects, to operate for the benefit of the community.[38] This is expressed in continued major support to the 'Ernest Gardiner Day Hospital', which received £247,000 in the 1999-2000 trading year, and the minibus service £71,000, and was used by over 12,500 of the Garden City's elderly and disabled. Grants and donations during the same year totalled £266,000. Since the inception of the Foundation, over £7 million has been paid out, to 30 September 2000. The range of beneficiaries has included Letchworth organisations, and also from the County and beyond, provided that they serve Letchworth residents. Promotion of religion, trade unions or political parties is excluded however, although church buildings qualified on the grounds of historic significance, thus enabling grants to be made towards the preservation of All Saints Church tower, and the bell ladder at St Nicholas Church, in 1995-6. In 1996-7 temporary accommodation for the North Herts Winter Sanctuary provided shelter for 26 people, and a grant was awarded to the North Herts soup run. £61,000 was allocated to renewing the roof of *The Settlement*, North Avenue Methodist Church Hall was awarded £40,000 towards refurbishment after damage by arson, and Letchworth Free Church Hall received £18.000, 50 per cent of the cost on a new pitched roof and guttering. In 1997-8, the largest single grant of £27,250 went to the establishment of 'The Place', a town centre visual and performing arts centre on the first floor of 18-20 Leys Avenue. In 1998-9 Letchworth Garden City Rugby Club received a £10,000 grant towards refurbishment of its clubhouse, and Arena Tavern Football Club got

£3,500. The following year Letchworth Garden City Eagles youth football club received a grant covering two thirds of their rent for their grounds off Baldock Road. Apart from the Day Hospital, many organisations providing care and assistance for the elderly or those with impaired mobility, have received funding. In winter 2000, a Shopmobility scheme began, based at the newly-opened Tourist Information Centre in Station Road, and supplied motor-ised scooters and manual wheelchairs. The Foundation is also providing a new scouts and guides building in Wymondley Woods, on the south side of the estate. If the community benefits of the Corporation era tended to be characterised by large capital projects, such as North Herts Leisure Centre or Plinston Hall, the policy of the Foundation has been to assist and enable community and other eligible groups to deliver improved services, and to im-prove their facilities.

Education has been one of the most important community activities, building upon the success of the Education 2000 initiative of the 1980s. Reformed as the Letchworth Commu-nity Education Trust, in 1995-6, an award of £200,000 ('Ebenezer II'), was made by the Foundation to provide every school in Letchworth with rapid access to the internet and a digital reference library. Individual schools have also received direct grants for various projects; for example, Hillshott School received £15,000 towards renewal of playground equipment in 1998-9. In 1997-8, a £11,335 contribution was made towards the cost of employing a Sixth Form Co-ordinator for the town's three state secondary schools. The Education Trust was wound up in September 2000, and its funds were passed to the Foundation for disbursement in accordance with the latter's charitable objects. The appointment of Alastair Stewart as the Foundation's first Education Liaison Officer was made to promote the concept of 'lifelong learning' in the Garden City, with a remit ranging from primary schools to North Herts College, including the private sector. The Winter 2001 project involved the installation of an interactive whiteboard and projector at all 16 Letchworth schools.[39] A bulk purchase was arranged, bringing the unit cost down from £4,450 to £3,350, and with a 50 per cent grant the cost to each school would be £1,720. By linking the board to individual computers group teaching and demonstrations are improved, with the possibility of interactive participation.

SEVENTEEN

BEYOND THE MILLENNIUM

Howard's Message Following Howard's death in 1928, his surviving papers were collected by Frederic Osborn, and were later deposited in the Hertfordshire County Archives. Among the hand-drawn diagrams and hand-written drafts for *Tomorrow* were sheets covered with Howard's shorthand, which had never been transcribed. In summer 2000, the local newspaper, *Hertfordshire on Sunday*, publicised efforts to decode Howard's encrypted messages. A group of seven was formed, retired shorthand users from Hitchin and Welwyn Garden City, and monthly meetings were held, led by Sue Flood, Collections Manager of Hertfordshire Archives. Progress was slow, but steady. Given his long years as a Parliamentary reporter, it was not surprising that Howard seems to have 'thought in shorthand'. Few of the papers were dated, and many appeared to be notes for lectures. Nevertheless, in the absence of any known recordings of Howard's voice, the transcriptions, painstaking and sometimes incomplete, speak powerfully and spontaneously across the intervening decades. As a Spiritualist, Howard would have relished the prospect of his words being unlocked from his shorthand at the onset of the centenary of his First Garden City.

In 'How to build a Garden City', Howard appeared to be marshalling the arguments for promotion of Garden Cities, as an element of post-1918 reconstruction, in which the 'New Townsmen', who included Osborn and C. B. Purdom, campaigned for state promotion.

> The problem of converting our old congested, overgrown, higgledy piggledy cities into true Garden Cities will present a great difficulty, but though this will be overcome when more experience has been gained ... far the simplest area to proceed is to build new towns on new and well chosen sites. Or to extend villages or small towns keeping in mind in such expansion the broad principles of them and then proceeding with great boldness of plan and purpose.[1]

After extolling the achievements of Letchworth – 'the impossible has been accomplished and already there is a population of about 14 thousand people in the town', Howard added, ' I know a really good site for the purpose I have in mind' [the Second Garden City at Welwyn]. Howard had identified the site at Welwyn, which he duly acquired at auction in 1919. In 1927, in a paper entitled 'Third Garden City', he looked back over three decades, to the foundation of the Garden City movement and Letchworth, the identification and purchase of the Welwyn site, in greater detail than published accounts, and forward to consider

> how the experience gained by myself and those associated with me ... may be brought to bear upon the problem of how can a third Garden City be started which should prove in many areas a great advance on its predecessors.[2]

He envisaged opening a Trust Fund, with a target of £2 million, all subscriptions to be invested in gilt-edged stock until the total was reached, with an undertaking to return all monies raised, if the total had not been achieved within three years. He freely admitted that 'Letchworth and Welwyn Garden City were started with a capital which was so wholly inadequate to the task ... that an enormous energy has been directed to the raising of capital'. Howard's bold plan was never put into effect. Within a few years, government inquiries examined the Garden City model, in the context of social and economic reconstruction from the Great Depression, but the Trust development agency was ultimately rejected in favour of the state development corporation. Notwithstanding his concern with the financial structure for a new experiment, Howard remained, in many respects, the 'heroic simpleton', witnessed by George Bernard Shaw. Howard dwelt upon 'How to overcome difficulties', identifying the key test:

> Will the overcoming of this difficulty add to our real and permanent well-being ... and will it add permanently to the well-being of society? ... Once sure of that never mind how great is the difficulty we should tackle it assured that even if we do not entirely succeed the effort will not be in vain. ... We should all set ourselves the task of creating a just and social order.[3]

Howard saw the task beginning with the individual, motivated by ethical behaviour in all dealings with others, and 'the spirit of devotion'. He described, with evangelistic fervour, the rebuilding of Jerusalem by Nehemiah as a parable to be followed. The Garden City had literally become the 'New Jerusalem'.

Howard's Way   What are the essential points to be drawn from Howard's work to assist the promotion of new Garden Cities?[4] Howard's original concept was based on privately sponsored development, relying on known methods of raising venture capital, using a conventional company model, with the important provision of clauses in the Articles of Association limiting dividend to five per cent. He admitted that none of the elements was original – it was their cumulative power which was significant.

1. **The idea**   The simplest and oldest ideas are best and Howard based his unique combination of proposals upon the simple fact that development of land greatly enhances its value. He turned the speculators' gain to community benefit through the original company constitution, sound at the time but, as already noted, subverted in the 1950s. However, following the latest reorganisation and the creation of the Letchworth Garden City Heritage Foundation, the quasi-public body or trust still appears to be an appropriate vehicle to harness and temper the natural inclinations of market forces to maximise their own returns.

2. **A broad appeal**   Despite the sceptics, Howard had something for everyone – co-operative and private housing, free enterprise and co-operative industry, which appealed both to Utopian idealists and practical men. Through the efforts of Adams and Neville at the Garden City Association, and subsequently industrialists and developers who were prepared to invest in the scheme, the dream was translated to reality. Today, the economic and social basis of Letchworth remains varied and viable, in an era when market forces are keenly competitive.

3. **Words and action**   Howard was determined to press for the development of a prototype and stated that it would be futile to await state action. Howard's direct action cannot be emulated today due to the complexity of regional guidance, structure and district local plans, and most of the sites considered by the Garden City Pioneer Company would now be classed as Green Belt or Rural Priority Areas. However, his determination that the book should not remain a theoretical utopia and his predilection for entrepreneurial flair is being matched in the latter-day determination of developers to succeed in building new communities. What is still required is a mechanism for harnessing developmental initiative to community benefit, as at Letchworth.

4. **Use of tried and tested methods**   Although the concept of a new ideal community sounded revolutionary, it was to be brought into being by well known techniques – the limited liability company raising capital on the security of the land, and using landlord covenants over the lessees to secure high quality of development; it resembled 'town planning' in the respect of the basis of a master plan and development control, but it differed fundamentally in that it was exercised by the landowner, and not by a local authority as a democratically elected body. Both Steeley and Hall have emphasised the existence of mechanisms which could bring about the social city. No new community, unless wholesale urban or rural enterprise zones were created, would have the ability to bypass forward planning and development control exercised through county and district council planning authorities. However, the direct landlord role retains the potential to shape development and design standards in the context of changing planning legislation.

5. **A professional approach**   The process of evaluation of various sites for the First Garden City included assessments by Adams, Unwin and other professionals, canvassing of manufacturers to learn whether they were locationally mobile, and detailed surveys of the Letchworth site, with reports on its geology, water supply and suitability for industry, before the limited competition for the layout plan was organised. Together with the complex process of land assembly, undertaken with such success as to be the envy of modern developers, the quality of professional advice was elevated to a status in community design, which it has retained ever since. However, the present tendency is to distrust the expert, with the rise of community consultation and participation in the planning process. A new balance between expert and community has been struck through the rise of 'new urbanism' in the United States, where the 'charette' process involves the service of professionals in workshops, specifically to articulate the aspirations of the community into developing the design.

6. **Persistence and pragmatism**   Howard and subsequently Adams as estate manager were not afraid to bring in others. Adams persuaded the Company to host the 1905 Cheap Cottages Exhibition, a remarkable undertaking which attracted many visitors to see 'Garden City in the making'. While some purists were offended, the publicity value was enormous at a time when the Company was overstretched through providing basic infrastructure. Likewise, Cottage Societies, the equivalent of today's Housing Societies, were encouraged to build in Letchworth at a time when the Company's finances did not permit itself building. The attraction of industrialists to a fully serviced trading estate, although borrowed from Trafford Park in Manchester, promoted the concept of a ready serviced industrial area where firms could locate and develop working relationships with each other. This concept has remained unchanged in essence, though updated in the late 20th century as the modern business park, and the networking of the information technology in the revived Spirella building. The pragmatic aspect of the implementation of the First Garden City perhaps stresses the necessity for an overall body with the ability to involve a wide range of developmental skills, rather than a house builder where the emphasis would, not unnaturally, be on building a large residential development, as exemplified in some of the new village proposals.

7. **A model for emulation**   Imitation is the sincerest form of flattery – the lesson of Letchworth, and of Hampstead Garden Suburb and Welwyn subsequently, was felt in state response through the New Towns legislation. It also created a model which was popular in the best sense as it appealed to a deep rooted desire for individual homes and gardens which the super rational high density high rise 'radiant cities' derived from Le Corbusier could never satisfy for the British. This deep seated atavistic appeal, as much a reflection of Unwin's reworking of Howard's vision as the original, helps to explain the success of the often derided suburban estates of the inter-war period which followed basic Garden City layouts and densities, but without their overall concern for community development. While the compact urban village, of which Poundbury, Dorchester, is the best known British example, may seem to be very different from the looser-knit Garden City, the concept of master-planning and spatial design shares an affinity with the best work of Parker, Unwin and de Soissons.

Garden Cities of Tomorrow   Historically, the expansion of Letchworth was examined as early as 1921 by Thomas Adams, who considered radial corridors of development fanning out from Letchworth, separated by broad agricultural wedges.[5] Possibly a rationalised form of ribbon development, the expansion of Letchworth would have joined to Baldock on the east, a virtual *fait accompli* today with only the A1(M) providing tenuous separation of the main industrial area from Baldock's western flank. The south-eastern sector within the A1(M) would be vulnerable if an improved road access were made from Letchworth Gate to the A505 to lead into the industrial area and business park. Westward, Adams saw Letchworth joined to Hitchin, which continued suburban development along the Cambridge Road has brought to within the width of the Harkness Nursery on Rosehill, immediately outside the Garden City Estate. Adams's third corridor led north-west towards Arlesey upon open land

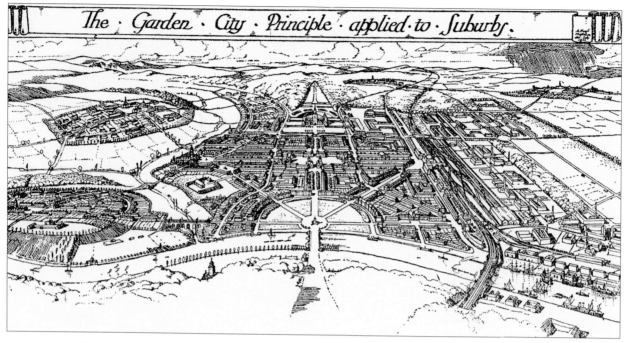

150 'The Garden City Principle applied to Suburbs', 1912. Like Howard before him, Raymond Unwin saw the expansion of the central city by satellite development, separated by 'green wedges'.

between the Stotfold Road and Arlesey Road, projecting outwards the thrust of the Bedford Road which was developed in the 1930s. This land also lay beyond the Garden City Estate and across the county boundary in Bedfordshire. Coincidentally, it included the grounds of the Fairfield Hospital, an immense Victorian mental institution closed in the 1990s. If Adams's model is rejected, an alternative proposition might be based upon Unwin's 'Garden City principle applied to suburbs'.[6] This was a reworking of Howard's diagram, showing the expansion of Adelaide, South Australia, beyond a park reservation, preserving the amenity of both the original settlement and its satellite. Unwin envisaged that planning would protect parkway belts and natural features, articulating development outwards towards detached and relatively self-contained satellites. He used this concept as the basis of one of his alternative development strategies in the 1929 *Greater London Regional Plan*.

Letchworth, as Howard's initial 'object lesson', begat an impressive lineage – Welwyn Garden City, the Greater London Regional Plan and the state-developed New Towns. By the late 1970s the New Towns Programme, in terms of massive injection of capital by Government for extensive developments on green field sites, was winding down. Milton Keynes, designated in mid-Buckinghamshire in 1967, with a multi-centred master plan by Llewellyn Davies and Walter Bor, covered an immense area with low density development and included a vast glazed shopping centre at its heart which bade fair to update Howard's Crystal Palace concept.[7] To some it appeared to be unduly consumerist and unsustainable, with its heavy reliance upon motor access, despite original minibus and light transit proposals. Building the shopping centre as the first phase of the town centre evoked Bellamy's *Boston 2000 A.D.*, rather than the co-operative harmony which underlay the earliest interpretation of Howard's vision in built form at Letchworth. Due to the energy crisis of the early 1970s, plus concern with the quality of life, conservation of natural resources and self-sufficiency began to assume primacy in discussions about the ideal form of new communities.

The Garden City Corporation always maintained close links with the Town and Country Planning Association (T.C.P.A.). In September 1975, the Corporation, in conjunction with the T.C.P.A., R.I.B.A. and R.T.P.I., organised an open ideas competition, to present ideas for 'Town and Country Tomorrow' (T.A.C.T.).[8] The themes were 'places fit to live in and how to create them', the start of a search for a contemporary Peaceful Path to Real Reform, focusing upon improvement of quality of life, conservation of energy and resources, the relevance of planned dispersal, and the application of Howard's social city concept. The assessors' panel was chaired by Brian Redhead, the journalist and broadcaster. One hundred and eighty entries were received, and exhibited not only in Letchworth, but also at T.C.P.A. in London and at the 'Habitat' Conference in Vancouver in June 1976. The professional prize winners were concerned with low energy self-sufficiency, whilst the schools entries also brought forward promising ideas, which encouraged the promotion of a Hertfordshire Schools Ideas Competition the following year. In order to develop the ideas, the T.C.P.A. convened a New Communities Committee, which examined the winners' proposals in the context of a possible development of two grid squares of Milton Keynes. Although a smaller site of 34 acres was identified, the T.C.P.A. felt this was inadequate and withdrew. In 1980, a site at Lightmoor, in Telford New Town, Shropshire was offered, where 14 families created a 'do-it-yourself' smallholding-based community.[9]

In the late 1970s the economic recession, which affected the older inner city areas and the engineering industries in addition to the traditional heavy industries of the North, called into question the policies of decentralisation and dispersal. In addition, the inner-city riots at Toxteth, Liverpool and Brixton, London in 1981, and the appointment of Michael Heseltine, Secretary of State for the Environment, as Minister with special responsibilities for the regeneration of Merseyside, removed state funding of dispersed communities from any priority. The New Town concept was applied to the reconstruction of inner-city areas, through Urban Development Corporations, in which Government funding was to be regarded as pump priming to attract private investment. The Merseyside initiative was backed through a spectacular Garden Festival in 1984, while the London Docklands Development Corporation, with its enterprise-zone status circumventing normal planning controls, controversially attracted massive City-financed office developments such as Canary Wharf and the conversion of dock buildings to expensive housing. The controversial Millennium Dome, and the less publicised but innovative Millennium Village sustainable housing, were features of ongoing Thames-side land reclamation and regeneration at the end of the 20th century. Howard himself had been concerned with the reconstruction of London, which was the subject of the final chapter of *Tomorrow*. His reactions to the form it took from the 1980s may well have been critical, although he would hardly have regarded the post-war L.C.C. and Inner Borough policies of high density, high rise housing as an unmixed blessing.

> Elsewhere new cities are being built: London must then be transformed. Elsewhere the town is invading the country: here the country must invade the town. Elsewhere cities are being built on the terms of paying low prices for the land, and then vesting such land in the new municipalities: in London the corresponding arrangements must be made or no one will consent to build … Easy comparatively it is to lay on virgin soil a plan of a magnificent city … of far greater difficulty is the problem – even if all vested interests freely effaced themselves - of rebuilding a new city on an old site.[10]

Renewed emphasis on private sector or partnership finance is also relevant. While Howard had envisaged that the L.C.C. would have taken a leading role in the redevelopment of London, his own First Garden City had been a private venture, circumscribed by its constitution to apply its surplus for the benefit of the community. Undoubtedly the Trust model, which involved private investment, would have continued to hold its attractions for him, given his pragmatic, undogmatic outlook and his suspicion of government bodies.

During the 1980s and 1990s continued debate over housing development in south-east England redirected attention to the Garden City. In 1985 the Housebuilders Consortium prepared a scheme for a 'new country town' at Tillingham Hall, Essex.[11] Although rejected by the Secretary of State, this was the first of many such proposals, and organisations such as the Town and Country Planning Association advocated a programme of planned self-contained communities. In 1988, the Secretary of State for the Environment, Nicholas Ridley, although re-affirming commitment to retention of the Metropolitan Green Belt, suggested that new villages might be built outside the present green belt, especially where developers were willing to meet infrastructure costs.[12] In January 1988 Professor Peter Hall spoke of the necessity for a positive strategic planning authority for the South East, in place of the advisory and ineffectual SERPLAN,[13] while in October 1988 Geoffrey Steeley, Hertfordshire County Planner, in the *Tenth Ebenezer Howard Memorial Lecture*, looked towards creating social city clusters.[14] That autumn H.R.H. Prince of Wales announced in his television programme 'Visions of Britain' that he proposed to build a major extension to Dorchester on Duchy of Cornwall land. This was developed as Poundbury. While attacking the harsh modernity of much 20th-century housing, he commended Letchworth for its 'humanely-designed residential areas'.[15]

Balance between economic activity and housing has been a recurrent theme in post-war planning, and has been critical in Hertfordshire, where population doubled in the half-century from 1929-79. Looking at Letchworth, the development plan process strove to maintain the equilibrium. However, the pace of economic revitalisation was essentially Corporation-led during the 1980s, using land which had been industrially allocated since the 1951 County Development Plan. Likewise, the town centre regeneration of the 1990s was the first major undertaking of the newly constituted Heritage Foundation. The North Herts Council, as planning authority, had, perhaps, a stronger control of the housing sector, through its development plan, albeit that its direct development role had receded, following completion of the large new public and sector estates in the 1970s. As the 21st century approached, what scope remained for the expansion of Letchworth and its further adaptation to the changing economic and social trends, an adjustment which had had painful and not fully resolved consequences in the past decade? Howard envisaged that the completion of the First Garden City would result in a pioneer group banding together to acquire the land for another settlement, building up to the social city. The intervening 90 years had brought about an armoury of controls on use and development of land, many based on the concepts which the planning and development of Letchworth had pioneered, and would now inhibit such direct action. Could development pressure result in peripheral expansion of Letchworth itself? Due to the Metropolitan Green Belt status of its setting, this seems unlikely and would fly in the face of Howard's concepts. Yet, it is now evident that Letchworth cannot be considered in isolation. Its earliest years saw interaction with nearby Hitchin and Baldock, and the south Bedfordshire villages beyond the Garden City Estate's rural belt. By the 1970s, the dominant A1(M) transportation corridor linked Welwyn Garden City (and Hatfield New Town), through Stevenage, to Hitchin, Letchworth and Baldock. As the first post-war New Town, Stevenage might almost be regarded as the hub of a partial 'social city' cluster across central and north Hertfordshire. It was to prevent coalescence of these settlements that the County Structure Plan extended the Metropolitan Green Belt northwards along the A1 corridor to the county boundary with Bedfordshire.[16]

Since the 1960s, Stevenage has promoted expansion, despite public and local authority opposition. Modifications to the Hertfordshire County Structure Plan, announced in 1988, confirmed removal from the Green Belt, and the housing allocation of a large site around Botany Bay Farm on the north-western outskirts of the new town, west of the A1 Motorway. This land fell partly within North Hertfordshire District. Arguments over its development raged throughout the 1990s and came to a head as the new millennium opened. The election of a Labour government in May 1997 fuelled the debate. The outgoing Conservative government had already resolved to press for the use of recycled 'brownfield' land for up to 60 per cent of new housing construction. However, the difficulty of reflecting this proportion in structure and local plans was formidable. The County Council considered that there was no alternative if housing construction totals during the plan period of the *Structure Plan Review* 1991-2011 were to be fulfilled, a stance fundamentally disputed by North Hertfordshire District Council.[17] In summer 1997, the Deputy Prime Minister, John Prescott, refused to intervene, a few weeks before he publicly reiterated the necessity to preserve greenfield land as far as possible. This paved the way for preparation of a masterplan and planning applications, by the West Stevenage Consortium of Persimmon Homes, Bryant Homes, Taywood Homes, and the Garden Village Partnership, consisting of Wilcon, Redrow and Leach Homes. Following workshops held in Stevenage, in July 2001 applications were submitted to Stevenage Borough Council for 1,000 houses within its boundary, and to North Herts Council for the 5,000 balance.[18] The package included shops, open space, community and leisure facilities, schools and employment areas. The applications were made in outline, and detailed design and siting matters could not be considered, although indicative masterplans, environmental impact statements, development and design principles, and a sustainability and landscape management statement were included. North Herts Council suspended its District Plan, which action was legally challenged by one of the consortium members. Late in 2001, a second application was received, for 3,600 houses, but the original remained tabled, with no likelihood of a decision on either until well into 2002.[19]

The period of gestation for new community development is indeed lengthy and fraught with political complexity. In the 1970s, substantial development took place at Bar Hill, north-west of Cambridge. Development of substantial science and research parks north of the city created pressure for further housing, and the 1986 *Cambridgeshire Structure Plan Review* put forward a proposal for two new communities, with major development in the A45 (now A428) corridor westward to St Neots. Eight planning applications were made and called in for public inquiry, and all were rejected: but one, Great Common Farm was accepted as having potential acceptability. A revised application was submitted, but a developer consortium submitted for a different site, north-east of Caxton on the historic Ermine Street (A1198), on the A428 midway between Cambridge and St Neots. This was approved by the planning committee in 1994. This became Cambourne and, after three years tying up legal agreements, work began on site in June 1998.[20] The masterplan was prepared by the Terry Farrell Partnership with three neighbourhoods – the 'villages' of Upper, Lower and Great Cambourne and a 50-acre business park. By December 2001, 520 of the planned 3,300 new homes had been built and occupied.[21] The Consortium – MacAlpine, Bryant, Bovis and David Wilson Homes – adopted traditional vernacular designs on a layout that was midway between the suburban cul-de-sac and the tight 'new urbanist' groupings of Poundbury.

Provision for social housing and community benefit has increasingly become a part of the private developer's responsibilities, tied to planning by legal agreements. National planning policy guidance stressed the importance of such provision, and in December 2001 it was proposed to introduce a series of 'planning tariffs',[22] which would introduce national requirements to supersede the individually negotiated legal agreements, which were often confidential until signed. Would there be a future for public or trust initiative in leading new community development? In the late 1990s, the Joseph Rowntree Trust contemplated the commemoration of the centenary of New Earswick in 2001. Following discussion with York City Council, a master-planning competition was held for a site at Osbaldwick,[23] on the eastern fringe of the city. The objective was an environmentally sustainable development, a high quality mixed tenure development, and a model for future urban extensions. The land was largely owned by York City Council, and the J. R. Trust would be the developer, with a programme of 500 houses, to be built over four to five years. Following agreement on the brief, a master-planning strategy was shaped by workshops with residents of surrounding communities. Four consultants were shortlisted and, following the Selection Board in January 2000, PRP (Phippen, Randall, Parkes) were chosen. The competition brief drew attention to the innovative Parker and Unwin layout for New Earswick, in some respects a prototype for Letchworth

Garden City. Their plan recognisably updated the layout and design of the original Parker and Unwin Garden Village.

Back to the Future   There has always been a creative tension between the 'Utopian technopolis', to which Howard's original ideas as set out in *Tomorrow* appear to be most closely related, and the artistic, Arcadian 'back to the future' concept embraced most strikingly by Raymond Unwin. Indeed, we can probably define a continuum with Howard, and his literary precursors Bellamy on one side, and Ruskin, Morris and Unwin on the other. The key question is how best to relate both to *Looking Backward* and *News from Nowhere*. The dichotomy between the two is even reflected in the Letchworth Garden City Heritage Foundation motto 'Proud Past ... Bright Future'. To borrow a line from a 1950s song 'Love and Marriage', popularised by Frank Sinatra, 'you can't have one without the other'. It is not a question of 'either ... or', but how to get the best of both worlds to enjoy 'both ... and'. The success of Letchworth Garden City as a physical and economic system is that it managed to combine the Arts and Crafts imagery of Parker and Unwin with the organisation of enlightened industrial practice, which represented an advanced system for its date. The architectural imagery represented popular idealism and, indeed, dominated housing design and layout throughout the 20th century, and was even perceptible in the alternative, futuristic concept of Le Corbusier's Radiant City. The architectural image is thus changeable, provided that underlying concepts of land tenure and commercial development are present. However, there is danger in becoming so flexible that almost any new community can be defined as a Garden City. As Steven Ward observed at a major conference held in Japan in September 2001, 'there must come a point where a development is no longer a Garden City or a Garden Suburb'. Creative tension is all well and good provided that basic principles are still discernible.

Garden City influence is discernible in two of the most internationally promoted community design concepts of the late 20th/early 21st centuries. The concepts are most identifiably linked with the term 'new urbanism' and 'sustainability'. The wider dimension of the Garden City Movement has received attention as part of an overall philosophy of new community design. The tailing-off of the British New Towns Programme, with the development of the last, Milton Keynes, from the late 1960s, resulted in a reappraisal and a focus on a smaller scale, and the revival of traditional design concepts. Beginning with the Essex County Council *Residential Design Guide* in 1973,[24] there has been a return to traditional vernacular architecture and organic grouping, with the focus once again on the street. During the 1980s, the housing development of the large builders was increasingly questioned and the low-density layouts were found to be unsuitable for the smaller houses, designed to fit the increasing number of smaller households. Furthermore, the questioning of the dominance of the car as the principal mode of transport and the generator of housing layouts, resulted in a return to a more tightly-knit form of grouping. That this was present in the earliest Garden City designs is evident from study of Unwin's layouts in Letchworth and Hampstead Garden Suburb. His seminal book, *Town Planning in Practice*, first published in 1909, has proved an inspiration for architects and planners over the past ninety years. It seems as enduring as is Howard's message from *Tomorrow*. The return to early, pre-Radburn Garden City groupings has inspired the New Urbanists in the United States, while in Britain the prime example of this approach was adopted at Poundbury, being built on the outskirts of Dorchester, on land owned by the Duchy of Cornwall.[25] Prince Charles has been critical of much modern architecture and community design. At Poundbury, he commissioned the Luxembourg urbanist Leon Krier to prepare a design, which consisted of a series of organic neighbourhoods, each equivalent to a sector of the historic core of Dorchester. Krier planned with spatial concepts which represented a combination of the diagrams found in *Town Planning in Practice*, and the theories of the Austrian urbanist Camillo Sitte, who had also heavily influenced Unwin. The architecture at Poundbury took the Dorset vernacular as its starting point. All houses faced and addressed the street, and the car was accommodated in mews courts at the rear of each group of dwellings. Furthermore, 25 per cent social housing was achieved in the first phase of development, completed in 2001. Local light industry and commercial projects were intermingled with the housing. A rich vernacular approach with a series of key buildings as landmarks has resulted. The design and layout concepts have been highly influential, although not to the taste of those who would still seek a more modern image for housing and community design.

If Poundbury represents one version of the revival of concepts which underlay Garden City planning, the emphasis on sustainability and energy conservation is a development of themes of self-sufficiency which can be traced back to the Garden City Movement at the turn of the 19th into the 20th centuries, despite recent claims to the contrary. Small sustainable communities have been developed, for example Eco-Village outside Ithaca, New York,[26] the base of Cornell University. The last tract of housing-zoned land within city limits was purchased by a housing co-operative, formed in 1992. They rejected the conventional subdivision of large plots set around curving roads. Four-fifths of the land was retained for growing produce. In the centre, the grouping of housing around a central communal hall, of the first of three to five intended neighbourhood groups, recalls the diagrams from Unwin's essays in *The Art of Building a Home*, published a century ago. The first group was completed in August 1997, and work was under way on the second in 2001. Sustainability has naturally become identified with recycling urban land, and increased densities have underlain government guidelines and key reports such as *Towards an Urban Renaissance*,[27] published in 1999, by the Task Force chaired by Richard Rogers. In it Garden Cities and Suburbs were accepted as 'innovative solutions to the urban problems at the turn of this [19th to 20th] century', but it was implied that matters had moved on. Re-appraisal of compact cities, typically the historic market towns of 30,000 population, and the urban squares of 18th- and 19th-century London, was seen as more likely to provide new paradigms. This message was underscored by the Urban and Economic Development Group [URBED] in their study, *Building the 21st Century Home; The sustainable urban neighbourhood*, which likewise felt that 'garden city inspired suburbia'[28] was an inadequate model for the new millennium. Publicity and controversy surrounding the Millennium Dome on the Greenwich Peninsula deflected attention away from the associated Millennium Village, an innovative housing scheme built on decontaminated land and taking advantage of the spectacular river-front views. The initial phase aimed at 65 per cent reduction in primary energy consumption, through the use of combined heat and power and sophisticated control systems, and 25 per cent reduction in embodied energy.[29] The phase 2A development – architect Proctor Matthews, developer Greenwich Village Ltd. – won a Sustainability Project Award in the 2001 Housing Design Awards.

At a strategic level, the Town and Country Planning Association has revived the idea of a string of new communities related to the key rail routes out of London. Their study, *Sociable Cities*, published in 1998,[30] Ebenezer Howard's centenary year, developed the concept in detail, although it has yet to find favour in the official strategic planning for South-East England, or with developers. Howard's own work has been the subject of many conferences. In 1998, the centenary of *Tomorrow* provided the theme for one such at Cornell University, New York, organised by the late Professor K. C. Parsons, and partly funded by the Clarence Stein Foundation. The papers from that conference span 'From Garden Cities to Green Cities'.[31] In September 2001, a major conference was held in Japan, at Tsukuba, the most advanced new town in the Tokyo metropolitan area, and at Kobe.[32] This attracted delegates from Europe, the United States, and all over East Asia. The Garden City concept was analysed in detail, to test its applicability to new community development for the 21st century, addressing key environmental issues and sustainability.

... Future Bright The impending centenary of Letchworth is regarded as a milestone of the Garden City Movement internationally, as well as locally. It was at the 75th Anniversary Exhibition in 1978, that the frail pioneer of the movement, Sir Frederic Osborn, reminded everyone that the significance of Letchworth had hitherto been better appreciated beyond its boundaries. Today, academics and professionals worldwide are vying to celebrate the centenary with conferences and visits. The process began with the centenary of the publication of *Tomorrow* in 1998, followed by that of the Town and Country Planning Association in 1999,[33] founded by Howard as The Garden City Association. Their efforts to secure practical demonstration of the Garden City concept are recounted in the early chapters of this book. Appropriately, in July 1999, a Garden Party was held at Spirella to commemorate the T.C.P.A. Summer 1902 witnessed the formation of the Garden City Pioneer Co., with the task of finding a suitable site, upon which to build Howard's 'ideal city made practicable'. Accordingly, in July 2002, a conference of the International Planning History Society, jointly organised by the Heritage Foundation and the University of Westminster, focusses on the achievements of the Garden City Movement, and its future, with a special session hosted at Letchworth on 12 July.[34]

In Letchworth itself, a full programme of projects and events is planned. The Foundation restored the Spirella Gardens in 2001, to enhance the setting of its landmark building. The Kennedy Gardens (Town Square) had evolved in an 'ad hoc' way, with no agreed masterplan, following the abandonment of building a Grand manner group of civic and religious buildings. Almost 90 years after they were planted, the Lombardy Poplars, outlining the block plan of the complex, had clearly exceeded their normal life-span, and many had become unsound. They succumbed to the chain saw in February 2002, and their stumps were ground out. The Cedars and Beeches were due to be removed during the Spring, to allow the ground to recover, before replanting in 2003. The Plane trees along Broadway had been cut back hard, and the beeches in Town Square had been planted too closely. The Silver Maples in the Broadway broadwalk were to be removed, with the overgrown Planes, in Winter 2002-3. Happily, the original three venerable oaks, which had helped Unwin to fix the axis of Broadway, will survive to make their contribution to the redesigned square. Considering the emphasis placed on bringing the country into the heart of the Garden City by tree planting, the original landscape designers had not done too well, in practical terms. Jointly, with North Herts D.C., the Foundation commissioned a design for new landscaping of the square, which had attained entry on the national register of Historic Parks and Gardens. Preliminary proposals by Landscape Design Associates, of Peterborough, were exhibited for public consultation in 1999. The two local organisations had provided initial funding, but major support for the £1.1 million project was sought from the Heritage Lottery Fund, and the first phase bid was approved in Spring 2001. The second phase bid followed in late Autumn 2001, and, on 19 March 2002, it was announced that a grant of £825,000 had been secured. North Herts Council, managing the scheme through their Director of Leisure and Community Development, Steve Welch, were delighted. The Council Leader, Cllr. F. John Smith recalled that he had seen the original trees flourish to maturity, when a pupil at the old Letchworth Grammar School. With work in hand from Summer 2002 to Spring 2003, it is scheduled to complete the transformation for official opening on 7 June 2003. The design for the gardens is much more open than its predecessor, with low hedges around the perimeter, and two paths parallel to the major axis of the square. By popular demand, a fountain will be located in the south-west of the gardens, but with improved technology over its predecessor, which worked intermittently in the 1970s. The centre of the square will be part-paved in natural stone, to accommodate events such as the annual Fun Day. The replacement trees will be limes, in continuity with the double avenues along Broadway to Sollershott Circus. It is intended to involve the public in tree planting, reminiscent of the Arbor Days of old.

On Saturday 3 May 2003, the 11.25 mile (18 km.) Garden City Greenway path around the Garden City Estate will open. Other projects were more tentative. The state of the 'Mrs Howard Memorial Hall' had been a cause for concern throughout the 1990s. In 1993, North Herts D.C. had proposed to relocate its museum from Town Square, and put feasibility sketches out to competition. The winning entry was developed, as the basis for Millennium Funding, but was unsuccessful. Meanwhile, the hall continued to deteriorate, while the 'Girls Club' wing became derelict, and the ugly 1960s, 'Youth Club' had been vandalised. The latter was demolished in 2000, but the remainder stands as a sad reminder that the idealism, which had built the hall by public subscription in 1905, appeared incapable of sustaining it through public finance almost a century later. Late in 2001, the Heritage Foundation was examining the possibility of acquiring the building, for restoration and development as an International Museum of Planning and Garden Cities. If successful, this would be an ideal use for the site, but could involve closure of the Heritage Museum in its historic site of the old Parker and Unwin offices. Coincidentally, this building had received its first full re-thatching, since its construction in 1907 – a testimony to the quality of the original reed thatch from Soham, near Ely, and the skill of the craftsmen.

The Diary for the centenary year will open with a commemoration of Ebenezer Howard's birthday, on 29 January 2003.[35] The main events are planned for the Summer, with a Sportathon on 29 June, using parts of the Greenway. 5-6 July will see Summer Foundation Days, with a 'classic' theme. A Civic Trust Heritage Open Day, featuring early Garden City buildings will be held on 13 and 14 September, with a Flower Festival planned for Letchworth churches. The anniversary of Foundation Day on 27 September is scheduled for a celebratory party on Norton Common. The climax will be Centenary Day, 9 October. Hopefully, the ritual of unveiling the Estate in a downpour, will not literally be recreated.

The framework of celebrations planned by the Heritage Foundation will be complemented by exhibitions. In September – October 2003, The Letchworth Museum will display the work of William Ratcliffe, long-time 'artist in residence' in the Garden City, and it is hoped to hold a sequence of exhibitions of drawings by the major Letchworth architects. The Heritage Museum will feature a sequence of exhibitions of Garden City life and development in twenty-year tranches, stepping back towards the foundation. Interwoven through the year will be events organised by Letchworth organisations. In October 2001, Allan Patterson, Director of Community Affairs of the Heritage Foundation addressed a meeting attended by 170 representatives, at Spirella, and announced that £50,000 would be available to assist centenary events.[36] A follow-up meeting on 25 April 2002 saw the launch of the centenary logo, and the first community grant award to Letchworth Chorale, to mount Elgar's oratorio, *The Dream of Gerontius*, at the Leisure Centre. Committees had been convened to co-ordinate musical, sports and walking events. Commemoration in music will be led by Nick Skinner, of the St Christopher School – the music group plans to stage many outdoor choral events, with 'Make a big noise for Letchworth' to be hosted in the Kennedy Gardens on 5 July 2003, and concerts and workshops at Letchworth venues. Among permanent mementoes of the centenary will be a wall-hanging for the Kincaid Hall at *The Settlement*. Designed by Dr Clive Schofield, it is being made by a group at *The Settlement*. At the annual town meeting on 15 May 2002, Stuart Kenny announced that the 16-month campaign to gain approval for the full name had been successful. From April 2003, the new name Letchworth Garden City will be officially used, crowning the centenary. This will end any remaining doubts as to the true significance of Ebenezer Howard's first 'object lesson', the demonstration of the ideal city made practicable, and a viable model for the new millennium.

Living Thought   Back in 1909, Henry Bryan Binns published several poems in *The City*, a high-quality and short-lived publication that celebrated the development of cultural life in Letchworth. One of these, 'The City' opened:

> I see a city being wrought, upon the rock of living thought.

There is no doubt that Binns was referring to the creation of Letchworth, the First Garden City on the bedrock of Ebenezer Howard's idealism. Indeed, Edmund Hunter, an Arts and Crafts-trained hand-loom weaver who opened his factory in Letchworth in 1908, worked the final stanza of the poem, which begins 'Four Square our city' into a handsome banner, which was proudly carried in the processions and pageants which were a feature of the pioneer days.

Ebenezer Howard was photographed in front of the banner, when he spoke to the citizens of Letchworth during the Coronation Celebrations for King George V in 1911. 'Living thought' could well be the underlying theme for the development of Letchworth Garden City, for its translation into bricks and mortar, grass and trees, from the rather mechanistic diagrams which had appeared in Howard's book, formed the bedrock upon which the First Garden City was built. Over the years, its prescription for social and sociable cities has endured, and proved capable of updating to reflect changing circumstances. Physically, Letchworth represents a seductive model for town planning. In 1909 Frederic Law Olmsted Jnr., son of the doyen of American landscape architects, visited Letchworth. He made a far-sighted assessment of its strengths and weaknesses. He found the road network of Letchworth almost too closely reminiscent of the ubiquitous grid iron of the American city but 'the number of ill-considered designs seems to be no more than is reasonably to be expected as the price of a healthy state of active experimenting'. He concluded:

> age is what Letchworth seems mainly to need; age, the growth of vegetation, and the quality of which comes from a house or a garden or a town only as the result of long-continued painstaking care in the common place work of maintenance, repair, and adaptation to use on the part of those who live in it.[37]

In the intervening period, the Garden City has attained the mellowing of Arcadia, aided by Unwin's original respect for the natural environment and subsequent high standards of planting and landscaping. From the air the sinews of the plan still stand out, revealing their strength, but clothed in a greenery which now conceals many of the errors of judgement which seemed so significant at the time of their commission. At ground level, if the overall impression now seems to be overwhelmingly suburban in character, this itself is a measure of the universal influence of Unwin's plan and policies, and the lush greenery which vividly evokes Howard's original objectives of a synthesis of town and country: the greening of the Garden City.

As the First Garden City moves towards its second century, it is evident that both the Letchworth Garden City Heritage Foundation and the North Hertfordshire District Council policy makers will need to take fundamental and probably controversial decisions. Letchworth, as the First Garden City, must surely represent more than an affluent community, benefiting comfortably from the recycling of the trading surpluses, a landmark in the museum of physical planning. The underlying principles must prove capable of flexible and pragmatic interpretation to serve the new millennium, without compromise of the core values – truly 'living thought'. Janus-like, all must look to the future by creative examination, discussion and reinterpretation of the principles upon which the First Garden City was conceived and built, and cleave to Howard's vision. In this way the spirit and vision will continue to provide the means towards future communities, of which Howard, Parker and Unwin, and the pioneers, would have been proud.

Appendix
Garden City Trees

The tree-lined roads of Letchworth have always been regarded as symbolising the Garden City concept of housing layout. Initially an attempt was made to plant a distinctive species for each road, but this was later modified after the Urban District Council took over the responsibility for highway maintenance. In more recent years there has been the problem of renewal, for many of the early specimen trees have reached the end of their life-span. Both the North Hertfordshire District Council and the Letchworth Garden City Corporation have spent large budgets on maintaining the town's arcadian character.

The following list, taken from the 1951 L.U.D.C. *Official Guide*, gives an indication of the variety of planting up to the Second World War. Some roads have subsequently been replaced with fewer species.

Road	Trees Planted	Country of Origin
Baldock Road	Sycamore	Europe
	Lime	Central and Southern Europe
Bedford Road	Schwedler Maple (Variety of Norway Maple)	Europe
Birds Hill	Round-headed Locust tree	East U.S.A.
Broadway, North	Sugar or Birdseye Maple	Canada, U.S.A.
	Silver Birch	Great Britain and Europe
	White Ash	East U.S.A.
Broadway, Middle	Small-leaved Lime	Northern Europe
Broadway, South	Manna Ash	South Europe and Asia Minor
Broughton Hill	Mountain Ash	Great Britain and Europe
Cashio Lane	Purple Plum	Central Asia
Common View	Scarlet Thorn	Europe and U.S.A.
Cowslip Hill	Silver Birch	Great Britain and Europe
The Crescent	Almond	West Asia
Cross Street	Mountain Ash	Great Britain and Europe
The Dale	Horse Chestnut	North Greece, Albania
Eastcheap	False Acacia	East U.S.A.
Field Lane	Red Horse Chestnut	Hybrid of English Horse Chestnut and American Red Buckeye
Gernon Road	Broad-leaved Lime	Europe
Glebe Road	Manna Ash	South Europe and Asia Minor
	Sycamore	Europe
	Cherry Laurel	South-East Europe and Asia Minor
Green Lane	Sycamore	Europe
Hillshott	Almond	West Asia
Hitchin Road	Norway Maple	Europe
Icknield Way East	Almond	West Asia
Icknield Way West	Double Cherry	
	Purple Plum	Central Asia
Letchworth Gate	Red Horse Chestnut	Hybrid of English Horse Chestnut and American Red Buckeye
Leys Avenue	Mountain Ash	Great Britain and Europe

Lytton Avenue	Simple-leaf Ash	England
	Manna Ash	South Europe and Asia Minor
Meadow Way	False Acacia	East U.S.A.
Nevells Road	Schwedler Maple	Europe
Norton Way North	Norway Maple	Europe
	Sycamore	Europe
Norton Way South	Horse Chestnut	North Greece, Albania
	Lime	Central and Southern Europe
Pixmore Avenue	Broad-leaved Lime	Central and Southern Europe
	Sycamore	Europe
Pixmore Way	Weeping Elm	Great Britain and Europe
	Norway Maple	Europe
Pixmore Way East	Maple	Europe
The Quadrant	Schwedler Maple	Europe
Ridge Avenue	Lombardy Poplar	Southern Europe
	Lime	Central and Southern Europe
Ridge Road	Norway Maple	Europe
Rushby Mead	Broad-leaved Lime	Central and Southern Europe
Sollershott East	Horse Chestnut	North Greece, Albania
Sollershott West	Sycamore	Europe
Souberie Avenue	Pear	Europe and North Asia
	Mountain Ash	Great Britain and Europe
	Hawthorn	Great Britain, Central Asia, Syria and North Africa
South View	Silver Birch	Great Britain and Europe
	Indian Beam	East U.S.A.
	Common Hawthorn	Great Britain, Central Asia, Syria and North Africa
	Hawthorn	
Spring Road	False Acacia	East U.S.A.
	Common Lime	Central and Southern Europe
Station Place	Lime	Central and Southern Europe
Station Road	Silver Birch	Great Britain and Europe
Town Square	Hornbeam	East England and Central Europe
	Deodar Cedar	Himalayan Mountains
	Common Beech	Great Britain
	Lombardy Poplar	Southern Europe
	Cornish Elm	Great Britain
Willian Way	Red Horse Chestnut	Hybrid of English Horse Chestnut and American Red Buckeye
Works Road	Maple	Europe
	False Acacia	East U.S.A.

NOTES

Chapter One: Coketown Rebuked

1. The quotation opens Chapter Five of Dickens's novel. The style reflects the author's concern at the harsh triumph of material values over the more humane society, reflected in the book by the circus people. Coketown was regarded as the paradigm of the Victorian industrial city; for example Mumford (1961) concludes that 'in a greater or lesser degree every city in the urban world was shaped with the characteristics of Coketown'. Ashworth (1954), Bell (1961), and Cherry (1988) all contain detailed accounts of the rise of the industrial city, and palliative measures taken to control its environmental consequences.

2. Ashworth (1954) Chs. II and III and Cherry (1988) contain useful summaries of Chadwick's pioneering work. An early and comprehensive appraisal was contained in B. W. Richardson, *The Health of the Nations: A Review of the works of Edwin Chadwick* (2 Vols.), (London, 1887).

3. Tarn (1973) provided a detailed history of the Trust movement, and charted its fusion with the Garden City movement. For a comprehensive account of the pioneering role of Henry Roberts (1803-76) in the design of working-class housing see Curl, J. S., *The Life and Work of Henry Roberts* (Chichester, Phillimore, 1983).

4. Armytage (1961) taps the rich stream of Utopianism setting the idealistic context for Owen's experimental communities. Owen's two major reports were reprinted in 1970. Owen, R., *A new view of Society*, 1813-14 (1970 Edn. Harmondsworth, Penguin Books), and *Report to the County of Lanark*, 1821 (1970 Edn. Harmondsworth, Penguin Books). Creese (1966) and Bell (1972) contain useful accounts of New Lanark.

5. Creese (1966), Bell (1972) and Tarn (1973) all include good accounts of the West Yorkshire industrial settlements.

6. Ruskin's lectures on political economy grew out of his work on architecture and art history. *Unto this last* (1862), *Sesame and the Lilies* (1865) and *The crown of wild olive* (1866) developed his views that social questions were inextricably linked with art. Morris developed overtly into a committed socialist; see Thompson, E. P. (1977).

7. Howard (1898) and Howard (1902) heading Chapter One. Mumford (1961) also used the same quotation, which vividly prophesies Garden City housing. See Cook, E. T. and Wedderburn, A., eds., *The Works of John Ruskin* (London 1903-12), Vol. 17, pp. 183-84.

8. William Morris, 'Art and Socialism: The aims and ideals of the English Socialist of Today', a lecture delivered before the Secular Society of Leicester, 23 January 1884, *Collected Works* 23, p.127.

9. Creese (1966), Darley (1975) and Tarn (1973) all include Bedford Park. For a discussion in the context of Shaw's work, see Saint, A., *Richard Norman Shaw* (New Haven and London, Yale, 1976). Life in the pioneer garden suburb is discussed in Bolsterli, M. J., *The Early Community at Bedford Park* (London, Routledge and Kegan Paul, 1977).

10. General accounts of Port Sunlight are included in Creese (1966), Darley (1975) and Tarn (1973). An excellent detailed account of the architecture and design is Hubbard and Shippobottom (1988).

11. General accounts of Bournville are included in Creese (1966), Darley (1975) and Tarn (1973). Harvey, W. A., *The Model Village and its cottages* (London, Batsford, 1906), contains a good account of the early housing by the consultant architect. For a comprehensive recent account see Harrison (1999).

12. Beevers (1988), p.17.

13. The pioneering work of the L.C.C. Architects Department in the design and construction of Council housing was described in Beattie (1980). The influence of Raymond Unwin on the design of the pioneering cottage estates was brought out; see also Unwin (1902).

Chapter Two: An Ideal City Made Practicable

1. Quoted in MacFadyen (1933), p.1. The origin of this material lies in typescript notes in Hertfordshire County Council Record Office, Howard Papers (H.C.C. D/EHo/F17). Apart from MacFadyen, the published biographical references include Moss Eccardt (1973), Fishman (1977) and Beevers (1988). The latter is by far the most comprehensive account – 'a critical biography' in the best sense.

2. H.C.C. D/EHo/F 17.

3. Beevers (1988), pp.17-18, 24. Howard cited Kropotkin's *Factories, Fields and Workshops* (1899) in *Garden Cities of Tomorrow* (1902), p.31. This work also appeared under Swan Sonnenschein's imprint.

4. Howard (1898), p.103. Chapter Ten of *Tomorrow* was titled 'A Unique Combination of Proposals'. For discussion of the major editions of *Tomorrow* see Note 14 below.

5. Purdom (1913), pp.9-14 discussed the relationship between Victoria and Hygeia, and Howard's initial concept.

6. Chadwick (1966). This account also records the exchange of ideas on urban parks between Paxton and Olmsted.

7. Armytage (1961) and Darley (1975) contain accounts of the chartist communities, the latter includes their surviving buildings.

8. Bellamy (1888), p.30.

9. MacFadyen (1933), p.20.

10. 'News from Nowhere' was originally published in serial form in *Commonweal*, Morris's Socialist League newspaper, 11 January-4 October 1890. First authorised edition London, 1891. See Morris, William, *News from Nowhere*, ed. Redmond, J. (London, Routledge, 1970). The publisher, Reeves and Turner, had also published, with Howard's

assistance, *Looking Backward* in an English edition.

11. H.C.C. D/EHo/F3. Early drafts of the material are dated 1892. The 'Master Key' diagram is in D/EHo/F1; the draft chapter in D/EHo/F3. Beevers (1988) believes that 'The Master Key' was originally intended as Howard's overall title.

12. *Ibid.*, p.6.

13. The surviving original diagrams in Howard's hand are in H.C.C. D/EHo/F 1.

14. *Tomorrow: A Peaceful Path to Real Reform* was republished by Swan Sonnenschein in 1902 in revised form as *Garden Cities of Tomorrow*, a title that has become part of the lore of community design in the 20th century. In 1946 the book was republished, edited by F. J. Osborn, with an Introductory Essay by Lewis Mumford (London, Faber and Faber). The first edition will be cited below as Howard (1898).

15. Howard (1898), p.10.

16. *Ibid.* Chapter One, 'The Town Country Magnet'. The chapter was appropriately headed with the final quatrain of Blake's 'Jerusalem', and a quotation from Ruskin's *Sesame and the Lilies* on 'the necessity of beauty'.

17. For a full discussion see Miller, M., 'The origins of the Garden City Residential Neighbourhood' in Parsons, K. C. and Schuyler, D., eds. (2002).

18. H.C.C. D/EHo/F4. The 'Crystal Way' or 'Great Victorian Way' was included in a survey of glazed arcades by Nikolaus Pevsner in *A History of Building Types* (Washington and London, Thames and Hudson, 1976), pp.262-4.

19. Howard (1898), Chapter 13, 'Social Cities', pp. 128-141. The cluster diagram of 'Slumless, Smokeless Cities' appeared on p.130. Its reduction to a fragment for the 1902 revised edition of Howard's book weakened the concept of the overall system and tended to place emphasis on *isolated* Garden Cities, without the mutual symbiosis envisioned originally.

20. Howard (1898). Chapters Two and Three dealt with Revenue from the agricultural and town land, Chapters Four and Five with Expenditure, and Chapters Six, Seven, Eight with Administration, 'Semi-Municipal Enterprise' and 'Pro-Municipal Work'.

21. *Ibid.*, pp.84-5.

22. *Ibid.*, pp.96-7.

23. Howard's intent is clear from a draft, 'Rurisville', H.C.C. D/EHo/F1, which states: 'It is usual in announcing an invention to give a clear description of its essential features (accompanied by drawings if necessary); and thirdly, if such an invention requires special instruments or appliances for its construction or working, to give a full and lucid description of such … The invention which is the subject of this book is, very fortunately, not of a value which can be protected by letters patent … Besides, the specification I am filing is a Provisional Specification, and the claims of the inventor are not set forth till the complete specification is put forward.'

Chapter Three: Utopia Limited

1. Howard collected the reviews in a scrapbook of press cuttings, now in Welwyn Garden City Central Library. The *Fabian News* verdict is quoted by Osborn in his preface to Howard (1946). Howard himself discussed the reviews in his 'Postscript' to Howard (1902), pp.161-71.

2. From the selection of 'Press Opinions' appended to Howard (1902), pp.188-91.

3. *Ibid.*, p.163.

4. *Ibid.*, p.170.

5. Lawrence, Dan H., *Bernard Shaw, Collected letters 1898-1910* (London, 1965), pp.188, 199.

6. MacFadyen (1933), p.38.

7. *Ibid.*, pp.40-3; Howard (1902), p.166.

8. Simpson (1985); Chapter Two 'Launching the First Garden City, 1901-6' contains a full account of Adams's key role.

9. Garden City Association (1901) contained a full transcript of the proceedings.

10. *Ibid.*, p.1 (title page).

11. *Ibid.*, pp.13-14.

12. *Ibid.*, pp.23-9, Neville spoke to his paper, reproduced pp.46-9, which contained the prerequisites.

13. *Ibid.*, pp.34-5.

14. Reproduced in full, *ibid.*, pp.47-74.

15. The Pressbooks are now in F.G.C.H.Mus. Burns's speech was reported in the *Morning Leader*, 6 January 1902; Adams's rejoinder appeared on 23 January.

16. Howard (1902), p.171.

17. The Company's Prospectus and a Share Application were bound into Howard (1902), pp.173-83.

18. *Ibid.*, p. 174.

19. Purdom (1913), p.29.

20. Whilst Purdom (1913) and others published partial accounts of the selection process, it can best be pieced together from the Minute Books and Correspondence of the Garden City Pioneer Company and subsequently First Garden City Ltd. These are now in F.G.C.H. Mus. When preparing the original edition, the author was indebted to the late Horace Plinston, former L.G.C. Corporation Chief Executive, for access to the correspondence for extensive study. Plinston (*c*.1980) also contains reference to the material. The sections dealing with the selection of the site and commissioning of the layout plan in the present work are based upon all original material cited above.

21. *Who was who*, 1897-1916, p. 242.

22. Letter from Waterhouse, Solicitors, 1 August 1904, Leicestershire County Record Office, 25D60/819.

23. Details given in full Bill of Sale, Walton and Lee, September 1904, Leics. CRO 25D/53/1143.

24. Ebenezer Howard letter to Aneurin Williams, 4 March 1903 (F.G.C.H.Mus.).

25. *Ibid.*; it appeared under the heading 'Books of Particulars of the following properties'.

26. Purdom, C. B., *Life over again*, London, Dent, 1951, p. 39.
27. Raymond Unwin, letter to Ebenezer Howard, 13 January 1903 (F.G.C.H.Mus.).
28. 'Garden City Pioneer Co., Manufacturers Meetings, Wednesday 1 April 1903', typescript, p.42 (F.G.C.H. Mus.).
29. John German and Son, Land Agents, Ashby-de-la-Zouch, to Ebenezer Howard, 11 April 1903 (F.G.C.H. Mus.).
30. Correspondence, Walton and Lee to John German, 12 December 1903, Leics. CRO 25D60/893. In September 1901 a valuation of £250,000 had been made.
31. Ebenezer Howard to John German and Son, 10 July 1903 (F.G.C.H. Mus.).
32. See note 22 above.
33. Bill of Sale, see note 23 above.
34. The first act of the play is set in the offices of Doyle and Broadbent, Civil Engineers, in Great George Street, Westminster. Broadbent tries to persuade Tim Haffigan who 'might be a tenth rate schoolmaster ruined by drink' to assist the Land Development Syndicate to develop in Ireland. 'John Bull's other island', pp. 405-52 in Shaw, B., *The Complete Plays of Bernard Shaw* (London, Odhams, 1934).
35. Hine (1951), p. 45.
36. Purdom (1913), pp. 29-31, Purdom (1951), p. 39, and Hare, W. L., 'A Part of Rural England', *Garden Cities and Town Planning*, 20 (6), June/July 1930, pp. 147-50.
37. *Ibid.*
38. W. A. Cadbury, letter to Ebenezer Howard, 16 July 1903 (F.G.C.H. Mus.). The Cadbury family had invested extensively in the Pioneer Company.
39. Adams to Parker, 17 July 1903 (F.G.C.H. Mus.).
40. Purdom (1913), pp.31-35.
41. Craske, H. (Company Secretary F.G.C. Ltd.), 'The Garden City Company', Appendix C in Purdom (1913), pp. 230-41; see also Purdom (1951), pp. 56-60.
42. Purdom (1913), p. 33.
43. F.G.C. Ltd., Directors' Minutes, Resolution 14, 12 November 1903 (F.G.C.H. Mus.).
44. H.C.C. D/EHo/F3.
45. *Dictionary of National Biography* (Oxford University Press, 1927).
46. Purdom, C. B., 'At the inception of Letchworth', *T.& C.P.* 21(113), September 1953, p.427; see also Purdom (1951), pp.40-2.
47. Composed on 18 March 1905, and cited in Johnson (1976), p.50.

Chapter Four: Letchford Manor

1. MacFadyen (1933), p.49.
2. *Ibid.*, p.51.
3. The topography, flora and fauna of the Garden City are described in The Letchworth Naturalists' Society, *In and Around Letchworth* (Letchworth, The Museum, 1963).
4. Johnson (1976) summarises pre-historic and pre-conquest settlement; see also Lane, W. H., 'Prehistoric and primitive man', *Coronation Booklet* (Letchworth U.D.C., 1937), pp.10-16.
5. Moss-Eccardt, J., 'An Anglo-Saxon Cemetery at Blackhorse Road, Letchworth, Hertfordshire', *Bedfordshire Archaeology Journal*, 6 (1971), pp.27-32.
6. Histories of the three parishes are summarised in Purdom (1913), Hine (1937), Hine (1951) and Johnson (1976), pp.16-41.
7. The excavations and preliminary findings were described in Matthews, K. and Burleigh, G., 'A Saxon and Early Medieval Settlement at Green Lane, Letchworth', *Hertfordshire's Past*, 26 (Spring 1989), Letchworth, pp.27-31, and North Herts. Museums, *A Saxon Site in Letchworth* (N.H.D.C., 1989).
8. The plebiscite for the name was described in Purdom (1913), p.45.
9. The most exhaustive study of Letchworth street names was compiled by Kenneth Johnson for the loose leaf Local History Index in Letchworth Library.

Chapter Five: The Layout Plan

1. The detailed material which records the commissioning of the plan is contained in the Garden City Pioneer Co. and First Garden City Ltd. records and correspondence (F.G.C.H.Mus.). Reference was made to these sources in compiling the present account.
2. Letter, 17/7/03, G.C.Pioneer Co., Correspondence (F.G.C.H.Mus.).
3. A copy of Humphreys's Report is in the F.G.C.H.Mus.
4. G. C. Pioneer Co. Engineering Committee Minutes, 12 October 1903, see Note 6 below.
5. F.G.C. Ltd., Directors' Minutes, Resolution 32, 12 October 1903. Warren wrote enthusiastically to Adams that Webb was 'absolutely the best man for preparing the scheme', 6 November 1903, F.G.C. correspondence (F.G.C.H.Mus.).
6. G. C. Pioneer Co., Engineering Committee Minutes. These were seen by the author at the Letchworth Garden City Corporation about 1980. They could not be located in F.G.C.H. Mus. with the other G. C. Pioneer Co. material, when this revision was under preparation.
7. See *Architects of Letchworth Garden City No. 6*, Miller (2000) for a biography of Lucas; also Brodie, A. (2001).
8. Sennett, A. R., *Garden Cities* (2 Vols.), (London, Bemrose, 1905). In a letter dated 18/8/03 addressed to Howard, Adams commented, 'In view of the pressure which Mr Sennett is using, and for other reasons, I think we will require to be very careful in asking professional advice with reference to the estate …', G. C. Pioneer Co, Correspondence (F.G.C.H. Mus.).
9. For biographical material on Parker and Unwin see Creese (1966), Miller (1981), (1992).
10. Allwood, R., 'George Faulkner Armitage 1849-1937', *Furniture History Review*, XXIII, pp. 67-87.

11. Recorded by Unwin in 'The Royal Gold Medal – Presentation to Sir Raymond Unwin', *J.R.I.B.A.* 3ss. 144(12), 24 April 1937, p.582.
12. Carpenter's description of Unwin in My *Days and Dreams* (London, George Allen and Unwin, 1916), pp.131-2. See also Tsuzuki, C., *Edward Carpenter 1844-1921. Prophet of Human Fellowship* (Cambridge University Press, 1980).
13. R.U. to Ethel Parker, 9 August 1981, Hitchcock Collection.
14. For discussion of the individual house designs see Miller (2000) and Hawkes, ed. (1986).
15. Barry Parker and Raymond Unwin (1901) included a paper by Unwin, 'Co-operation in Building', pp.91-108, which contained the seeds for his planning work to 1914.
16. *Ibid.*, pp.82-5.
17. 'On the Building of Houses in the Garden City', in Garden City Association (1901), pp.69, 72.
18. Unwin (1902), p.3.
19. Plans of Starbeck are in Parker Coll., F.G.C.H. Mus. Parker and Unwin published a booklet *Cottages Near a Town*, Manchester, 1903, based on their Northern Artworkers Guild exhibit. A copy is in F.G.C.H. Mus.
20. The foundation of New Earswick is described in Waddilove (1954). Accounts of the design of the early phases of cottage development are in Creese (1966), Miller (1980), (1981), (1992).
21. *Architects of Letchworth Garden City No. 4* (Miller 2000).
22. *Architects of Letchworth Garden City No. 3* (Miller 1999).
23. B. B. Moffat, R.I.B.A. Membership File, No. 1464 (L), (B.A.L.), R.I.B.A., London; also Brodie, A. (2001).
24. Raymond Unwin, 'The Planning of Garden City', Appendix B in Purdom (1913), p.228.
25. F.G.C. Ltd. Directors' Minutes, 28 January 1904 (F.G.C.H.Mus.).
26. *Ibid.*, 11 February 1904. The 'original' plan presented to the Board by Unwin is not readily identifiable. A fragmentary photoprint crudely labelled 'Mr. Unwin's Plan' (*sic*) survives in F.G.C.H. Mus., together with a modified version, drawn on linen, which was also used as the basis for the first published version.
27. The Lucas/Cranfield plan is represented by a photoprint in F.G.C.H. Mus. The Lethaby/Ricardo plan was illustrated in Adams (1934) and Purdom (1963), but is not in F.G.C.H. Mus. Its present whereabouts is unknown. Adams's letter to Ricardo dated 29 November 1910 praising the plan is in F.G.C.H. Mus.
28. A number of early sketch plans which pre-date 'The Company's Plan', as published in April 1904, have been identified by the author in F.G.C.H. Mus. See note 26 above.
29. Unwin described his plan in Appendix B, Purdom (1913), pp.222-9, and in 'Making the Plan of Letchworth', *G. C. & T.P.* 20(6), June/July 1930, pp.156-9. Whilst Mabel Barry Parker credited her late husband with a leading role in preparation of the layout plan, available contemporary evidence does not appear to corroborate this.
30. R.U. to Adams, 22 February 1904 (F.G.C.H.Mus.).
31. R.U. to Adams, 11 July 1904 (F.G.C.H.Mus.).
32. Purdom (1913), p.69 and Purdom (1951), pp.52-3.
33. Unwin Papers, UN 12 (B.A.L.) R.I.B.A. London. The published Building Regulations were included as Appendix K in Purdom (1913), pp.302-15.
34. F.G.C. Ltd., Building Committee Minutes, 6/10/04 and 20/10/04 (F.G.C.H.Mus.).
35. Purdom (1913), p.69.
36. The infrastructure was described by A. W. E. Bullmore, F.G.C. Ltd. Engineer in 'The Public Services of Garden City', Appendix D to Purdom (1913), pp.242-60. The account was updated in Chapter Five, 'The Public Services' in Purdom (1925), pp.118-28.
37. 'Appendix D', Purdom (1913), pp. 245-7.
38. In 1905 Parker and Unwin prepared a 'Plan of Present Development' for F.G.C. Ltd. This was periodically updated and reprinted. The formal centre of the town was destined to remain a paper concept until after the First World War, as will be discussed below.
39. Unwin (1909) and Purdom (1925) illustrated representative road sections showing the variety of treatment and planting.
40. The earliest Parker and Unwin drawing showing the central roundabout is dated July 1908 (F.G.C.H. Mus.); Unwin (1909) pp. 240-1 described Henard's '*carrefour à giration*'.
41. Timetables were included in all the early Garden City guides and commuting was encouraged. The railway was to play an important role in bringing visitors to Letchworth, particularly for the 1905 Cheap Cottage Exhibition (see below).
42. Bullmore, pp.249-53 in Purdom(1913).
43. *Ibid.*, pp.253-5.
44. H.C.C. D/EHo/F3. Extract from a paper given at The Mansion House, London, 11 July 1905, in which Howard described progress to date on building Letchworth.

Chapter Six: Garden City Homes

1. F.G.C. Ltd. Minute Books (F.G.C.H.Mus.).
2. Johnson (1976), p.50.
3. Accounts in Miller (1978), Miller (1979a) and Miller (1980) describe the organisation, entries and impact of the Exhibition. *The Book of the Cheap Cottage Exhibition* (London, County Gentleman and Land and Water Ltd., 1905) contained a comprehensive description of the entries (copies in F.G.C.H. Mus.). The Technical Press carried copious articles – for example see *Architectural Review, The Builder, Builder's Journal, Building News* issues over summer 1905.
4. Purdom (1913), pp.50-1.
5. UN 9/3, Unwin Papers (B.A.L.) R.I.B.A. London.
6. See *Architects of Letchworth Garden City No. 5*, Miller (2000).
7. In his autobiography, *Architect Errant* (London, Constable, 1971), Clough Williams-Ellis mentions working for his

'sort of second cousin' A. H. Clough, but does not refer to the Letchworth Cheap Cottages.

8. Brodie's system was described in detail in Moore, R., 'An early system of large panel building', *J.R.I.B.A.*, September 1969, pp.383-6.

9. *La Cité Jardin* (Benoit Lévy, 1911), pp. 94-6 names the house *Red Hawthorne*, and its residents as Mr Johnston, a retired sailor of 61, with his young wife, and three-year-old child!

10. F.G.C. Ltd. published an attractive illustrated Guide, *Where Shall I Live?*, which contained full details of the exhibits, an up-to-date progress report on the development of Letchworth, and essays by Howard, Gaunt, Unwin and others.

11. See *Architects of Letchworth Garden City No. 2*, Miller (1999).

12. For a comprehensive history of Brentham and the beginnings of Co-partnership see Reid (2001).

13. Vivian wrote about the Garden City Tenants' schemes in *Where Shall I Live?*, pp.55-7. For modern accounts see Miller (1979a), (1979b).

14. Parker and Unwin (1901), Plate 11. The scheme was illustrated in Plate 38, with a wider range of housing than was subsequently included in the Co-partners' developments. The above publication included Unwin's description of the proposals in his paper 'Co-operation in Building', pp.96-102.

15. Unwin (1906b). The event marked his emergence as a national spokesman for housing and town planning.

16. *Ibid.*, Unwin (1906a), p.111.

17. *Ibid.*, p.109.

18. Published by Garden Cities and Town Planning Association (London, 1912). See note 24 below. For a review of Scott's Letchworth work see *Architects of Letchworth Garden City No. 5*, Miller (2000); and for Scott's work overall, Haigh (1995).

19. Letchworth Cottages and Buildings Ltd. and Howard Cottage Society Ltd. are discussed in Miller (1979a), (1979b). The author had access to their archives, from which the letters from Howard to Osborn are taken.

20. Ebenezer Howard to Frederic Osborn, 13/1/13, Howard Cottage Society Archives.

21. A wide ranging study of co-operative housing was undertaken in Pearson (1987). Beevers (1988), Chapter Nine deals with Howard's interest in the subject. Howard himself wrote about the concept in 'Co-operative House-keeping, A Suggestion by Ebenezer Howard', *The Garden City 1*, NS (8) September 1906, and 'A New Outlet for Woman's Energy', *G. C. & T.P.* NS 3 (6), June 1913, pp.152-9. Purdom (1913) discussed the scheme and illustrated the plans, pp.98-103.

22. Benoit-Lévy (1911) and Purdom (1913) both contained a selection of the most progressive architect-designed houses in Letchworth. From 1974 onwards the author undertook detailed research into the buildings of Letchworth using N.H.D.C., L.G.C. Corp. and F.G.C.H. Mus. Archives. A working paper, N.H.D.C. (1976), was compiled. Biographical details of the Letchworth architects, many of them one-time Parker and Unwin assistants, were compiled using R.I.B.A. Membership Records (B.A.L.) R.I.B.A., London. Creese (1966) included a chapter on the architecture of Parker and Unwin, whilst Hawkes (1986) is based on an edited version of Parker's own essays on his architecture, originally published 1910-12 in the U.S. Arts and Crafts periodical, *The Craftsman*. For information on Letchworth Architects see Miller (1999) and Miller (2000) for series of biographical leaflets. Further biographical material in Brodie, A. (2001).

23. Unwin extensively wrote about and illustrated German medieval fortified towns, see Chapter V of *Town Planning in Practice*, Unwin (1909). Parker's photograph albums in F.G.C.H.Mus. also contain pictures of Rothenburg, a particular favourite.

24. Parker (1895) (*BN* publication), p. 108.

25. See *Architects of Letchworth Garden City No. 3*, Miller (1999).

26. Moffat, B. B., R.I.B.A. Membership File No. 1464 (L), (B.A.L.) R.I.B.A., London.

27. See *Architects of Letchworth Garden City No. 4*, Miller (2000).

28. See *Architects of Letchworth Garden City No. 3*, Miller (1999).

29. Letter from Cecil Hignett to the editor of *The Citizen*, 21/9/56.

30. See *Architects of Letchworth Garden City No. 2*, Miller (1999).

31. For an exhaustive discussion of Baillie Scott's architecture (which however omits 29 Norton Way North) see Kornwolf, J. D., *M. H. Baillie Scott and the Arts and Crafts Movement* (Baltimore, John Hopkins Press, 1972); also *Architects of Letchworth Garden City No. 5*, Miller (2000).

32. Parker spoke about his methods at a discussion on 'Control of Elevations in Practice', *J.T.P.I.* 18(7) May 1932, p.164. 'What he [Parker] got officially at Letchworth was not a hundredth part of what he got unofficially. Builders and architects came to him … and frequently he was able to make suggestions [for design improvements] … which was the most valuable part of the whole thing'. Sketches in Parker Coll. (F.G.C.H.Mus.) confirm this practice.

33. Notes on the local contractors have been compiled with the assistance of Kenneth Johnson's Local History Index, Letchworth Library.

34. Illustrated in Unwin (1909), Ill. 271, p.351.

35. Berlepsch Valendas (1912) and Benoit-Lévy (1911, first edition 1904) were perhaps the most comprehensive of the early accounts. F. L. Ackerman and Thomas Adams were responsible for the spread of the Garden City movement to U.S.A. and Canada, whilst Pavel Mizhuev and Aleksandr Block transferred the concept to Russia. International planning conferences, such as that held at the R.I.B.A. in 1910, invariably included a visit to Letchworth, preparing the ground for the foundation of the International Garden Cities and Town Planning Federation in 1913.

36. Cherry (1974), Sutcliffe (1981), and Miller (1984) deal with the emergence of planning from 19th-century bye-law and public health practice, assisted by the Garden City movement. Miller (1981a, 1981b) details Unwin's key role in the promotion of planning, whilst Swenarton (1981) concentrates on the housing-domination of planning from 1915 onwards.

37. *Town Planning in Practice* (Unwin, 1909) was simultaneously published in London and New York, a German edition appeared in 1910, and a French translation in 1922.
38. Unwin (1909), p.320.
39. The idealised layout, based on housing blocks with communal backland, stemmed from Unwin's early housing quadrangles in *The Art of Building a Home* and *Cottage Plans and Common Sense*, developed through such practical examples as his layouts at Pixmore, Letchworth, Brentham and Hampstead Garden Suburb. A discussion of its evolution is contained in Miller (1981).
40. Unwin's creative career is described in detail in Miller (1992), pp. 154-70.
41. For an overview see Swenarton (1987).

Chapter Seven: The Spirit of the Place

1. Brunt (1942), originally published as separate articles in *The Citizen*, is probably the most comprehensive guide to the early social history of Letchworth. Purdom (1951), Chapter Two 'Garden Cities' is a personal account which catches the mood of the community. Charles Lee, 'From a Letchworth Diary', pp.434-442 in *T. & C.P.* 21(113), September 1953 (The Letchworth jubilee), embellishes the past, whilst Ethel Henderson, 'Letchworth then and now', pp.457-61 in *ibid.* is naively gushing in style, evoking the essential innocence of the pioneer years. Miss Henderson later privately published an extended account as *The Ideals of Letchworth, the First Garden City*, Letchworth (*c.*1975).
2. Foreword to Brunt (1942), p.viii.
3. M. J. Pritchard, 'The First Garden City', unpub. M.A. Thesis (University of London Courtauld Institute, 1970), p.64.
4. Dorothea Hunter, letter *T.&C.P.* 21 (113), September 1953.
5. Peggy Curtice Hitchcock (née Unwin), letter to the author.
6. Carpenter described Millthorpe in *My Days and Dreams* (London, George Allen and Unwin, 1916). A more recent appraisal of Carpenter and his influence is Tsuzuki, C., *Edward Carpenter Prophet of human fellowship* (Cambridge University Press, 1980).
7. 'From a Letchworth Diary', pp.435-6.
8. Orwell, G., *The Road to Wigan Pier* (London, Gollancz, 1937). The reference to Letchworth occurs on pp.152-3 of the Penguin reprint (Harmondsworth, 1962).
9. Howard (1898), Chapter Seven, 'Semi-Municipal Enterprise – Local Option – Temperance Reform', pp.72-81.
10. Brunt (1942) and Purdom (1913), (1925), deal with the polls in detail.
11. Furmston (*c.*1940), Chapter Six, 'Landlord of *The Skittles*'.
12. Brunt (1942) contains the most comprehensive account of early religious life.
13. Hine (1951), pp. 129-30.
14. *Ibid.*, p. 130.
15. Armytage (1961) sets the Alpha Union in context with the mainstream of Utopian-religious thought.
16. Purdom describes his conversion and marriage in Purdom (1951), Chapter One. He described the interior of St Hugh with evident affection in Purdom (1913), pp.121-4.
17. Hine (1951), p. 126.
18. Buchan, John, *Mr. Standfast* (Edinburgh, 1919). The reference occurs on p.51 of the Nelson reprint (Edinburgh, 1923).
19. Brunt (1942) and *The Citizen* (Letchworth), 'Jubilee Supplement', 25 January 1963, pp.xvi-xvii, give good accounts of early education in Letchworth.
20. Brunt (1942) and 'Jubilee Supplement', pp.xiv-xv.
21. Recalled by a female pioneer at one of the author's lectures in 1978.
22. *The Garden City*, February 1905.
23. *The 'Borough' Pocket Guide to Letchworth* (Cheltenham, 1908), pp.20-2.
24. Brunt (1942) and Letchworth National Library Week Committee, *Letchworth: a town built on a book* (Letchworth, 1966).
25. Miles (1967) and Cowlishaw (1908) give detailed accounts of Miss Lawrence and the building, and subsequent history of 'The Cloisters'.
26. Quoted in Purdom (1963), pp. 71-2.
27. Miles (1967), pp.21-3.
28. F.G.C.H. Mus. Letchworth contains runs of both *Letchworth Magazine* and *The City*.
29. The poems appear on pp.69-70 and 199-200 of Betjeman, John, *Collected Poems*.
30. Connett, M., 'Harold Gilman and Letchworth', *Hertfordshire Countryside*, 39(299), March 1984, pp.21-3.
31. Strone, D., 'Two Paintings by Spencer Gore', *National Art Collection Fund News*, Jan. 1984, pp. 143-4.
32. Local History Index, Letchworth Library.
33. Brunt (1942) catalogues the early 'street theatre' in Letchworth. F.G.C.H. Mus. contains several examples of the Arbor Day Certificates, including one presented to Howard.
34. Purdom (1913), pp.135-8, Purdom (1951), pp.169-75, and Brunt (1942).
35. Purdom, Lee, Brunt, *op. cit.* Copies of the scripts are in F.G.C.H. Mus.
36. Wadowska, A., 'The oldest purpose built cinema', *Hertfordshire Countryside* 25(135), July 1970, pp.44-6.
37. *L.G.C.Soc. J.* (67), December 1996, pp. 2-3.
38. Letchworth Library Local History Index, citing 'Sappho in Letchworth', Deuchar, N. D., *G.C. &T.P.*, June-July 1930, p. 182.
39. Johnson (1976), pp.75-7, *The Citizen*, '75th Anniversary 1906-81 Souvenir Edition' (Letchworth, October 1981), p.3.
40. Armytage (1961), pp. 376-7.

41. Buchan, *op. cit.*, pp.37-61 chronicles the 'Biggleswick' interlude.
42. Purdom (1951), pp.20-30.
43. Whittick (1987) pp.22-8.
44. L.G.C.Soc. *J.* (46), June 1991, p. 9.
45. *Ibid.*
46. *The Citizen*, 21/5/20, cited in *L.G.C.Soc. J.* (55), October 1993, p. 8.
47. 'Letchworth Hospital', *L.G.C.Soc. J.* (42), June 1990, p. 8.

Chapter Eight: Industry and Commerce

1. Garden City Pioneer Co., Manufacturers Meetings, Wednesday 1 April 1903, typescript (F.G.C.H.Mus.Doc.471).
2. Garden City Pioneer Co. Board Minutes, 2 April 1903 (F.G.C.H.Mus.).
3. F.G.C.H.Mus.Doc. – 471, p. 2.
4. *Ibid.*, p.3.
5. *Ibid.*, p.4.
6. *Ibid.*, p.6.
7. *Ibid.*, p.12.
8. *Ibid.*, p.17.
9. *Ibid.*, p.25.
10. *Ibid.*, p.41.
11. *Ibid.*, p.42.
12. Plinston (1980), p.8.
13. A copy of Humphreys' Report is in F.G.C.H. Mus.
14. Purdom (1963), pp.15, 21.
15. Benoit-Lévy (1911), p. 141. The example referred to was Dent's – see note 19 below.
16. Simpson (1985), pp.36-8.
17. Purdom (1951), pp.52-4.
18. Brunt (1942), pp. 1-2, 62-3; Benoit-Lévy (1911), pp.136-8.
19. Dent, J., *The Memoirs of J. M. Dent, 1849-1926* (London, Dent, 1928), pp.127-30; Benoit-Lévy (1911), pp.140-1.
20. Benoit-Lévy (1911), pp.138-40.
21. Scruby, J., 'Bernard Newdigate', *L.G.C.Soc. J.* (64), March 1996, pp. 4-6.
22. Scruby, J., 'Eleni Zompolides', *L.G.C.Soc.J.*(65), June 1996, pp. 4-6.
23. Benoit-Lévy (1911), pp.141-3.
24. Brunt (1942), pp.65-6.
25. Plinston (1980), pp.49-50.
26. Lupton, A., 'Phoenix Motors Ltd., London and Letchworth', *L.G.C.Soc. J.*(50), June 1992, pp. 4-7.
27. Purdom (1913), p.150; Purdom (1925), pp.113-4.
28. Benoit-Lévy (1911), pp.144-5.
29. Allwood, R., 'Meredew of Letchworth: a brief history', *Furniture History*, XXXIII, 1997, pp. 305-10.
30. Hard, F., 'An Industry Moves', *T. & C.P.*, 21(113), Sept. 1953, pp.449-50.
31. Benoit-Lévy (1911), pp. 147-9, and personal information from John Hunter, grandson of Edmund Hunter.
32. Spirella Co., 'Silver Jubilee Album', F.G.C.H. Mus.
33. Benoit-Lévy (1911), pp. 149-52.
34. *Spirella Monthly*, June 1912, p.89.
35. 'Window challenge of Spirella', L.G.C.H.F. *Insight*, Christmas 1998.
36. 'Album Presented to H.R.H. Duke of York by Spirella Employees, 9 June 1926'. Duplicate Copy, F.G.C.H. Mus.
37. *Spirella Monthly*, January 1912, p.1.
38. 'Spirella memories flood back', L.G.C.H.F. *Insight*, Christmas 1998.
39. 'Letchworth's Diamond Jubilee Year', supplement to *The Citizen*, 25 January 1962, p. ix.
40. Brunt (1942), p.67.
41. *Ibid.*, pp.67-9; Henderson (*c*.1975), 'Memories of early shopkeepers'.
42. *Letchworth Garden City Directory* (Letchworth, Wheeler Odell & Co.), 1907; 'The story of a Telephone Exchange', *L.G.C.Soc.J.* (33), November 1987, pp. 5-7.
43. Purdom (1925), pp.98-103.
44. Brunt (1942), pp.8-12; *Citizen 75th Anniversary 1906-1981 Souvenir Edition*, 1 October 1981, pp.2-3.

Chapter Nine: Company, Council and Community

1. Brunt (1942), pp.26-7; Benoit-Lévy (1911), pp.187-91.
2. Benoit-Lévy (1911), p.117, and *ibid.*, pp.191-4. The latter included the detailed budget.
3. For a comprehensive biography of Octavia Hill see Darley (1996).
4. Brunt (1942), pp.27-33; Brunt dealt with the 'cost of economies' on pp.35-9.
5. Benoit-Lévy (1911), p.177.
6. Brunt (1942), p.40.
7. *Ibid.*, pp.40-7.
8. Purdom (1963), pp.15-30; Purdom (1951), pp.56-8.
9. 'The Town Planning Conference: Visit to Letchworth', *The Building News* (2910), 14 October 1910, p.539.
10. 'Letchworth's Convincing Record', *G.C. & T.P.*, 3NS(2), February 1913, pp.37-8.
11. Gaunt, W., 'The Town Square at Letchworth', *G.C. & T.P.*, 3NS(3), March 1913, pp.75-9.
12. Purdom (1913), p.70.
13. Brunt (1942), p.35; Letchworth Citizen (1963), p.iv.

14. *Ibid.*, p.iv.
15. *Ibid.*, p.iv.
16. A general history of the evolution of state aided, local authority housing is given in Swenarton (1987).
17. Letchworth U.D.C. housing programmes were discussed in Purdom (1925), pp.69-72.
18. *Ibid.*, pp. 118-23.
19. Plinston (1980), pp.66-7.
20. The Garden Cities and Town Planning Association adopted a formal definition of the term 'Garden City' in 1919: 'A Garden City is a town designed for healthy living; of a size that makes possible a full measure of social life, but not larger; surrounded by a permanent belt of rural land; the whole of the land being in public ownership or held in trust for the community'. Purdom, C. B. (ed.), *Town Theory and Practice* (London, Benn, 1921), p.34.
21. Purdom (1913), pp.176-82; Purdom (1925), pp.77-8.
22. For general histories of planning see Cherry (1974), Cherry (1988).
23. Cited in MacFadyen (1933), pp.95-6. Bonham-Carter had made similar statements in 'Garden Cities and Satellite Towns and Decentralisation', *J.T.P.I.*, November 1929, p.14. The relationship between landlord and local authority planning at Letchworth was discussed by the author in *Background Statement* No. 4 (N.H. 74), presented in evidence to the North Hertfordshire District Plan Public Local Inquiry, November 1982.

Chapter Ten: A Living from the Land
1. Howard (1898), p.17.
2. *Ibid.*, p.25.
3. Purdom (1913), Appendix F, 'Agriculture and Smallholdings in Garden City', pp.272-83 (written by H. Burr, F.G.C. Ltd. Surveyor).
4. Simpson (1985), p.24.
5. *Ibid.*, p.25.
6. First Garden City Ltd. (*c*.1906), p. 15.
7. First Garden City Ltd. (1907), p. 100.
8. Simpson (1985), p.25.
9. Furmston (*c*.1940), pp.18-20, 33-4; MacFadyen (1933), pp.91-2.
10. Benoit-Lévy (1911), pp.157-60.
11. Brewer, H., 'Home Gardens and Their Value', *T. & C.P.*, 21(113), September 1953, pp.453-5.
12. Plinston (1980), pp.60-2.
13. Country Gentleman's Association, *Artistic Country Buildings 1913-14* (Letchworth), contained a review of the Garden city Movement, and many views of Letchworth.

Chapter Eleven: Garden City Comes of Age
1. Howard's final years and achievements are recounted in Beevers (1988), Chs.11-14.
2. Purdom (1951), pp.64-8; see also Beevers (1988), Ch. 13, and for a comprehensive history of Welwyn Garden City see de Soissons (1988). A shorthand account by Howard in Hertford CRO (D/EHo/F/10/4), which appears to contain more detail than hitherto published accounts, was being transcribed in 2001-2. See Chapter Seventeen below.
3. Told by Lewis Mumford to the author, in conversation at Amenia, New York, June 1978.
4. Howard, Ebenezer (trans. L. E. Creplet), *Ville Jardins de Demain* (Paris, 1904); Howard, Ebenezer (trans. Maria Wallroth-Unterlip), *Gartenstadte in Sicht* (Jena, 1907); Howard, Ebenezer (trans. Aleksandr Block), *Goroda Budushavo* (St Petersburg, 1911); Howard, Ebenezer (trans. Dr. B. Murck and R. Svoboda), *Zatradni Mesta Budoucnosti* (Prague, 1924).
5. K. Beevers (1988), pp. 180-1; Howard (D/EHo/F/10/4), Hertford CRO.
6. The film was found in a cupboard in the projection room of *The Broadway Cinema* in the 1960s. F.G.C.H. Mus. made a video copy about 1990.
7. G. B. Shaw to A. C. Howard, 25 May 1928, HCC/EHo/F17.
8. Purdom (1925), Chapter Seven; Purdom, C. B., 'The Finance of Letchworth', *G.C. & T.P.*, 12(2), February 1922, pp.24-6.
9. Purdom (1963), p.33.
10. *I.C.T.*, International Computers and Tabulators Ltd., London, March 1960, copy in L. G. C. Lib., Local History Collection.
11. *Letchworth Official Guide* (Cheltenham, n.d., *c*.1951), p. 69.
12. L. G. C. Lib., Local History Index, and Purdom (1925).
13. Coaten, H. C., 'The Industries of Letchworth', *G.C. & T.P.* (20)6, June/July 1930, p.172.
14. *Ibid.*, p.174.
15. Parker, R. B., 'Presidential Address – Where we Stand', *J.T.P.I.*, 14 (2), November 1929, p.8.
16. Purdom (1925), Chapter Three; 'Letchworth of Today', *G.C. & T.P.*, 16(2), February 1926, p.88.
17. The following examples are culled from issues of *The Citizen* in the author's collection, and *Hullabaloo*, the 1935 Civic Week Programme.
18. *Hertfordshire Regional Planning Report 1927* (London, W. R. Davidge), pp.53, 83.
19. Wadowska, A.; see note 30 to Chapter Seven above, and local press advertisements.
20. *The Citizen*, 28/8/36.
21. *The Citizen*, 20(1026, 1027), Letchworth, 4 and 11 June 1926, Civic Week numbers: 'Letchworth's Coming of Age', *G.C. & T.P.*, 16(2), February 1926, and 16(6), July 1926.
22. *The Citizen*, 20(1027), 11 June 1926.
23. *Hullabaloo*, 'The Official Magazine of Letchworth Civic Week' (Letchworth, June 1935).

Chapter Twelve: War and Austerity

1. *The Citizen*, 8/9/39.
2. *The Citizen*, 15/9/39. L.G.C. Lib., Local History Index has copy of published notice 'Licensing of Retailers', *The Citizen*, 6/10/39.
3. Westell's Ration Book is in the collection of the F.G.C. Heritage Mus.
4. L.G.C. Lib., Ephemera 1940, Local History Collection has a copy, probably donated by Bennett.
5. *Ibid.*
6. F.G.C.H. Mus.
7. *The Citizen*, 30/8/40.
8. L.G.C. Lib., Local History Index. A map showing the posts, originally belonging to British Tab is in F.G.C.H. Mus.
9. F.G.C.H. Mus.
10. L.G.C. Lib., Ephemera 1944, Local History Collection.
11. *The Citizen*, 24/4/42. Beatrice Theakston (1878-1980) had come to Letchworth in 1907 and worked at Dent's. She had also undertaken munitions work in W.W.I. L.G.C. Lib., Local History Index.
12. The Indians' arrival was covered in *The Citizen*, 18/5/41; the Royal Visit, *The Citizen*, 26/9/41; the completion of training prior to return, *The Citizen*, 12/6/42.
13. L.G.C. Lib., Local History Index.
14. Descriptive notes, 'How Letchworth Garden City helped to win the War' (F.G.C.H. Mus.).
15. *The Citizen*, 4/4/41.
16. L.G.C. Lib., Local History Index, and copy of brochure in Ephemera, December 1940.
17. *The Citizen*, 7/2/41.
18. *The Citizen*, 5/6/42.
19. *The Citizen*, 17/7/42.
20. *The Citizen*, 28/5/43.
21. Programme for 'Salute the Soldier Week' in L.G.C. Lib., Ephemera 1944, Local History Collection.
22. *The Citizen*, 16/3/42.
23. L.G.C. Lib., Local History Collection, Ephemera 1940, 1941, 1942, Local History Index.
24. *The Citizen*, 31/5/40.
25. *The Citizen*, 24/4/42.
26. *The Citizen*, 22/8/42.
27. *The Citizen*, 19/6/42.
28. *The Citizen*, 28/9/45.
29. *The Citizen*, 13/11/53 reporting the unveiling of the tablet commemorating the fatal casualties of W.W.I.
30. In the possession of L.G.C. Corp, see below, Chapter Fourteen.
31. Plinston (1980), pp.91-2.
32. *Ibid.*, p.75.
33. Plinston (1981), pp.10-11; Purdom (1962), pp.34-9.
34. Purdom (1949), pp.137-9.

Chapter Thirteen: Recovery and Expansion

1. Abercrombie, Patrick, *Greater London Plan 1944* (London, H.M.S.O., 1945).
2. *The Citizen*, 21/4/44.
3. Ministry of Town and Country Planning, *New Towns Committee: Interim Report* (cmnd. 6759, London, H.M.S.O., 1946); *Second Interim Report* (cmnd. 6794, London, H.M.S.O., 1946); *Final Report* (cmnd. 6876, London, H.M.S.O., 1946), (Reith Reports).
4. For early history of Stevenage New Town see Purdom (1949), pp.391-4, 420-2; Mullan, Bob, *Stevenage Ltd. Aspects of the Planning and Politics of Stevenage New Town, 1945-78* (London, Routledge, 1980), pp.39-62.
5. Cullingworth, J. B., *Town and Country Planning in England and Wales* (London, George Allen and Unwin, Revised Third Edition, 1970), pp.247-8.
6. de Soissons (1988), pp.112-21.
7. Plinston (1981), pp.16-18; Purdom (1963), pp.35-6.
8. Purdom (1963), pp.37-8.
9. Cullingworth (1970), pp.147-58.
10. Purdom (1980), p.69.
11. Abercrombie (1945), para. 353, pp.140-1.
12. Howard (1946), p.105.
13. The pre-1974 structure of planning authorities was described in Cullingworth (1970), pp.43-6, 120-36.
14. Doubleday, E. H., *Hertfordshire County Development Plan Written Statement* (Hertfordshire County Council, 1951).
15. Plinston (1981), pp.11-16.
16. Cullingworth (1970), pp.254-8.
17. Plinston (1981), pp.35-8; *The Citizen*, No. 2628, Letchworth, 23 November 1956.
18. Stein, C., 'Toward New Towns for America', *Town Planning Review*, 20(3), October 1949, pp.219-29, gives the early history. As the present author discovered, Unwin was informally consulted over the original Radburn Plan, see Miller (1981b), p.528.
19. Letchworth Festival Programmes in Ephemera 1951, Local History Collection, L.G.C. Lib.
20. Programme in Ephemera 1951, Local History Collection, L.G.C. Lib.
21. *T. & C.P.* ('The Letchworth Jubilee'), 21(113), September 1953, p.400.

22. *The Citizen* ('Letchworth Jubilee Edition'), No.2459, Letchworth, 28 August 1953. The section on consumer goods and local events is drawn from this source.

23. *Letchworth. The First Garden City, Official Guide* (Cheltenham, Burrow, n.d., *c.*1951) contains a useful survey of the major industries, supplemented by *T. & C.P.* ('The Letchworth Jubilee') and *The Citizen* ('Letchworth Jubilee Edition').

24. Allwood, R., 'Meredew of Letchworth: A brief history', *Furniture History*, XXXIII, 1997, pp. 305-10.

25. The author compiled an account, including buildings constructed 1945-75, for the revision of Pevsner, N. (ed. Cherry, B.), *The Buildings of England – Hertfordshire* (Second Edition, Harmondsworth, Penguin, 1976), pp.224-34.

26. For a comprehensive and sympathetic account of the Hertfordshire Schools programme see Saint, A., *Towards a Social Architecture* (London and New Haven, Yale, 1987).

Chapter Fourteen: Save Letchworth Garden City

1. The essential accounts of the remarkable take-over struggle and its outcome are contained in three major references to which the reader is directed for a more detailed history of the period: Plinston, H., *Letchworth – A Record of Events* (typescript, F.G.C.H. Mus., Letchworth, n.d., *c.*1980); Plinston, H., *A Tale of One City* (Letchworth Garden City Corporation, 1981); Purdom, C. B., *The Letchworth Achievement* (London, Dent, 1963).

2. 'Freehold Building Land. Ripe for Development', Sale prospectus ' By order of First Garden City Ltd.', for auction 25 July 1961, by Jones Lang Wootton, Author's Collection.

3. *Letchworth Garden City Corporation*, A Bill, 10 & 11 Eliz. 2 – Session 1961-2, Author's Collection.

4. The full text of the Act is given as Appendix E to Plinston (1963).

5. *The Garden City Estate of Letchworth. Scheme of Management*, L.G.C. Corp. The Scheme was unchanged under its successor, Letchworth Garden City Heritage Foundation.

Chapter Fifteen: The Old Order Changeth

1. The key documents were: Doubleday, E. H., *Letchworth Central Area Appraisal Plan* (H.C.C., December 1965); Kitching, L. C., Such, F. H., and Leigh, J. V., *People and Traffic. A Study of Conflict and Congestion in Letchworth* (H.C.C./L.U.D.C., September 1970); Overton, D., *Hertfordshire 1981 – Policy Statement* (H.C.C., September 1972). The latter represented a continuation from the First Review of the County Development Plan, approved May 1971, which extended the time horizon of County Planning Policy from the terminal date of the County Development Plan by eight years to 1981, by which time it was anticipated that the County Structure Plan would be in operation, see below.

2. For a general review of the 1968 Act and the subsequent 'two tier' development plans see Cullingworth (1970), pp.109-117.

3. *Ibid.*, pp. 136-42 reviews the complex inter-relationship between the modification of the form of development plans and local government reorganisation.

4. Kelly, M. J., '1919-74', *Letchworth Garden City Official Guide* (Letchworth), p.6.

5. Cullingworth (1970), pp.174-8 contains a general introduction to the strengthening of historic building and conservation legislation. Department of the Environment, Planning Policy Guidance Note PPG 15, *Planning and the Historic Environment*, September 1994, contains the latest updated policy statement on preservation and enhancement of the historic built environment.

6. Creese, W. L. (1966). See also Creese (1967) for a selection of Unwin's writing on planning; Hughes, M. (ed.), *The letters of Lewis Mumford and Frederic Osborn: A transatlantic dialogue 1938-70* (Bath, Adams and Dart, 1971) contained much seminal material appraising and reinterpreting the Garden City movement.

7. Parker, C. M., 'Material available for a memoir of R. B. Parker at 296 Norton Way South', Letchworth, 1970. She noted that the catalogue had been made 'in response to a request from Lewis Mumford'. Unpub. Typescript, F.G.C.H. Mus.

8. *The Book of Letchworth*, Johnson (1976) retains its appeal as an exhaustive catalogue of incidents in the history of Letchworth, recounted in the author's characteristically idiosyncratic style. 'K.J.' has also written extensively in the local press over the past 30 years and continues to lead walks around the Garden City. The *Local History Index* in the Letchworth Library, begun by K.J., is an invaluable *Vademecum* for an Odyssey into virtually any aspect of Letchworth's history.

9. Miller (1975), pp.253-5.

10. The author compiled the research on individual sheets for each building or group to form a 'Letchworth Building Index'. This aimed at recording basic data for each building with architectural or historic significance in the development of Letchworth to 1914. A mimeographed summary in the form of a Working Paper was prepared by North Hertfordshire District Council in 1976, and used by the author as the basis of discussions with the Department of the Environment Inspectorate.

11. Department of the Environment, *List of Buildings of Special Architectural or Historic Interest. District of North Hertfordshire (Letchworth Area)*, (London, 1979).

12. North Hertfordshire District Council (Planning Officer B. G. Hull), *Letchworth Conservation Area Broadsheet*, 1977. The text and illustrations were prepared by the present author during his tenure as Principal Planning Officer (Conservation and Design) in the N.H.D.C. Planning Department.

13. For an itemised catalogue of the exhibition see Miller (1978).

14. Johnson (1976), p.118.

15. This section is based upon 'Letchworth – the past 25 years: and what next?', an account given by Andrew Egerton-Smith, L.G.C. Corp. Chief Executive, to a joint R.T.P.I. East of England Branch/ T.C.P.A. Conference held in Letchworth on 7 February 1989. Financial details and descriptions of the major projects are taken from the L.G.C. Corp., *Annual Report and Accounts* (Letchworth, 1964-95).

16. The Hertfordshire County Structure Plan was prepared under Part II of the T. & C.P. Act 1971, as amended. The

'Commencement Order' was made on 21 March 1973. A first phase of public involvement took place in spring 1973, followed by a second in winter 1973/4 on major issues, which produced heightened public support for green belt policies. A third phase of consultation on the basis of 'Planning means choosing' followed in early 1975. The District Councils which came into being on 1 April 1974 were extensively consulted; the *Hertfordshire County Structure Plan Written Statement* was published in 1976. The plan was approved in modified form by the Secretary of State, after lengthy public hearings, on 21 September 1979.

17. Preparation of the N.H.D.C. District Local Plan involved extensive work. 'Topic Studies' on related subject areas were published in 1978-9, a draft plan was published for comment over Jan.-Sept. 1981, published as a formal plan in January 1982, and examined at a Public Local Inquiry between Oct. and Dec. 1982. The Inspector's report was received in summer 1983, approving the plan with modifications. The plan was formally adopted on 6 March 1984. See N.H.D.C., *District Plan Written Statement* (Letchworth, March 1984).

18. The author was extensively examined at the Public Local Inquiry over the inclusion of sites such as the Creamery Playing Fields at Letchworth Gate. See N.H.D.C. Evidence in 'Background Statement No.4' (NH 74) and (NH 147), and the Inspector's *Report on the Public Local Inquiry*, 7 June 1983, paras. 197-253.

19. 'Letchworth – the first 25 years: and what next?', para. 12.

20. 'Helping Your Business To Succeed', *The Business Centre* (L.G.C. Corp., n.d., *c*.1985), and L.G.C. Corp *Business News*, 1984. The A1 'Corridor' project was the subject of a promotional leaflet, 'Hertfordshire's A1 – we've been in business for years', published by H.C.C. County Planning and Estates Dept. (n.d., *c*.1987).

21. N.H.D.C. *District Plan Monitoring Report, Housing*, 1983.

22. Information from N.H.D.C., Housing Department, April 1989.

23. Information on the vicissitudes of the agricultural enterprise is contained in the Corporation's *Annual Reports*. They were also summarised by Andrew Egerton-Smith in 'Letchworth – the past 25 years: and what next?'. The 'In Hand Farming Master Plan' was prepared by Bidwells in Autumn 1987. The long-distance walks are described in *Six Countryside Walks around Letchworth Garden City* (L.G.C. Corp., 1986). The Corporation publishes various brochures and information packs on the Standalone Farm Centre.

24. Education 2000 was described in the Corporation *Annual Reports* for 1986 and 1987. Briefing documents were issued to local businesses at a series of working breakfasts in spring 1987. See also 'Education 2000, Educating People for Change' (Letchworth, n.d., *c*.1988).

25. The development and its opening were illustrated in *Tenth Report and Accounts* (L.G.C. Corp., 1975). The Corporation also issued a descriptive brochure on the project. Subsequent *Annual Reports* charted progress on The Wynd and other town centre refurbishment.

26. 'Letchworth Shopfronts', prepared by Conran Roche in conjunction with L.G.C. Corp. and N.H.D.C., April 1987.

27. 'Corporation Milestone', *Insight*, 3 September 1987, L.G.C. Corp. *Insight*, published quarterly, is the Corporation's own newspaper, delivered to all Letchworth residents. Its publication has been continued by L.G.C.H.F. The estate valuations were reported in the *Annual Reports*.

28. 'Letchworth Garden City Stays in Business', Planning (670), 30 May 1986, p. 1.

Chapter Sixteen: Proud Past ... Bright Future

1. Stamp, G., *The Letchworth Garden Study* (mimeo, London, Brunel Institute of Organisation and Social Studies, July 1983).

2. *Letchworth and Baldock Herald and Post* (170), 28/6/91.

3. 'Letchworth Garden City Heritage Foundation', leaflet and L.G.C. Corp. Chairman's letter, 18/11/92.

4. *L.G.C. Soc. J.* (53), March 1993, pp. 3-4.

5. *L.G.C. Soc. J.* (54), June 1993, p. 4.

6. Letchworth Garden City Heritage Foundation Act 1995, Chapter ii, Rules of Letchworth Garden City Heritage Foundation, Registered under the Industrial and Provident Societies Act, 1965.

7. L.G.C.H.F., *Report and Accounts* to 30/9/96, p. 4.

8. L.G.C.H.F., *Insight*, March 2001, p. 3.

9. Much of the factual record of the Foundation's activities relative to its objectives is set out in its *Annual Report and Accounts*, and its quarterly newsletter *Insight*.

10. North Hertfordshire District Council, *District Local Plan No. 2, Written Statement, July 1993*, Policy 58 'Letchworth Garden City Design Principles'.

11. White (1965), pp. 182-4.

12. 'The Future of LCB', *Insight*, September 2001, p. 11.

13. 'Young can't climb on property ladder', *Hertfordshire on Sunday*, 24/6/2001, p. 2.

14. L.G.C.H.F., *Annual Report* 1996, p. 5.

15. L.G.C.H.F., *Annual Reports*, 1996, p. 5; 1997, p. 7; *Insight*, September 2001, pp. 2-3.

16. *Insight*, July 1997, pp. 1, 6-7.

17. *Insight*, May 1997, pp. 1, 6-7.

18. *Insight*, Spring 1999; L.G.C.H.F., *Annual Report and Accounts* to 30/9/99, pp. 4-5.

19. *Insight*, Summer 1999, p. 9 announced the proposed refurbishment, and *Insight*, Autumn 1999 contained a questionnaire on shopping prepared in conjunction with Garden Square.

20. At the time of finalising this text, the latest plans for the refurbishment/part redevelopment of Garden Square had not been made public. The uncertainty was aired in the local press – see *Hertfordshire on Sunday*, 11/11/01.

21. Letting Particulars, Barbican Holdings/William H. Brown, circulated November 1990.

22. Speaking in Tsukuba, Japan, at the New Garden City International Conference, organised by Kobe Design University, September 2001.

23. L.G.C.H.F., *Annual Report and Accounts* to 30/9/96, p. 6; *Annual Report and Accounts* to 30/9/98 pp. 6-7; *Insight*, Spring 1999, pp. 1-3, 6-7; Summer 1999, p. 9.

24. *Insight*, Spring 1999, p. 5.
25. L.G.C.H.F., *Annual Report and Accounts* to 30/9/99, pp. 6-7.
26. *Insight*, March 2001, pp. 1, 6-7.
27. Unwin, R., 'On building of houses in the Garden City', Garden City Association (1901), pp. 69-70.
28. Miller, M., *Letchworth Garden City. Options and incentives for the preservation of its architectural heritage*. A Report to Letchworth Garden City Corporation, December 1989.
29. *Design Guidance for residential areas in Letchworth Garden City*, 1991. Revised versions published by L.G.C.H.F., 1997 and 2001, *Insight*, June/July 2001, pp. 2-3.
30. L.G.C. Corp. Press Release, 19.4.91.
31. L.G.C. Corp. and L.G.C.H.F., *Garden City Heritage Award Reports*. The launch of the scheme was published in *Insight*, December 1991.
32. N.H.D.C., *Letchworth Committee Agendas*, 12/12/01; 23/01/02.
33. The agricultural enterprise, L.G.C. Farms Ltd. profit and loss account is shown in L.G.C.H.F., *Annual Reports*, often with a commentary on significant activities.
34. L.G.C.H.F., *Competition Brief*, 1996.
35. *Insight*, July 1997, p. 3.
36. Annual valuations of the Estate and fixed assets are contained in L.G.C.H.F., *Annual Reports*.
37. H.H.D.C., *Census Notes*, November 1993, based on OPSC small area statistics from the 1991 Census. The 2001 figures were taken from County Council estimates. The author's interpretation differs from that in *Insight*, Christmas 2001, p. 6.
38. Information from discussions with L.G.C.H.F. Chairman, Peter Harkness and Director of Community Affairs, Allan Patterson. The Foundation's *Annual Reports* contain summaries of significant awards.
39. *Insight*, September 2001, p. 10.

Chapter Seventeen: Beyond the Millennium

1. H.C.C. Archives Howard D/Eho/F2/1, 'How to build a Garden City', n.d. *c*.1918. The campaign to enlist the services of shorthand experts and code breakers was launched by *Hertfordshire on Sunday* in August and September 2000. See *H.O.S.* 3/9/00.
2. H.C.C. Archives, D/Eho/F10/4, 'Third Garden City', n.d. *c*.1927.
3. H.C.C. Archives, D/Eho/F3/48, n.d.
4. The following section is based upon the conclusions of the author's paper, given at the R.T.P.I./T.C.P.A. Conference held at the Plinston Hall, Letchworth in February 1988, with updating.
5. Adams, Thomas, 'Reserving productive areas within and around cities. A proposal to substitute agricultural wedges for zones', *Journal of the American Institute of Architects*, 9(10), 1921, pp.316-9.
6. Unwin (1912), Diagram VII, p.10; Howard (1902), Diagram 4, facing p.128. The author drew attention to the relevance of these models in the context of the problems of continued pressure for expansion of Letchworth, in Miller (1983).
7. The standard account is Bendixon and Platt (1992).
8. 'TACT', *Competition Conditions* (L.G.C. Corp., September 1975).
9. The T.C.P.A.'s attempt at 'do it yourself new towns is recounted in Hall, P. and Ward, C., *Sociable Cities: the legacy of Ebenezer Howard* (Chichester John Wiley & Sons Ltd., 1999), pp. 191-5.
10. Howard (1898), pp.148, 150.
11. As the first of the Housebuilders 'New Towns', Tillingham Hall attracted a great deal of publicity. See especially: (i) *Tillingham Hall – Outline Plan*, prepared for Consortium Developments by Conran Roche, Milton Keynes, May 1985; (ii) Shostack L. and Lock, D., 'New Towns in the South East: a planned response to a regional crisis', *The Planner (J.R.T.P.I.)*, 71(5), 1985, pp.19-22; (iii) 'Tillingham Hall – the new country town proposal', *The Planner (J.R.T.P.I.)*, pp.6-7.
12. 'Housing in Rural Areas', *A Statement by the Secretary of State for the Environment* (London, Department of the Environment, 5 July 1988).
13. Hall, P., 'The Coming Revival of Town and Country Planning', *R.S.A. Journal* (Royal Society of Arts), 136 (5302), 1988, pp.417-30.
14. Steeley, G., *The Path to Real Reform. The Tenth Ebenezer Howard Memorial Lecture*, given at Royal Society of Arts, London, 27 October 1988, L.G.C. Corp. (1988).
15. Charles (1989), pp. 138-141.
16. Hertfordshire County Council's, *County Structure Plan. Written Statement* (1976).
17. Joseph Rowntree Foundation (2001), p. 17.
18. 'Proposed development west of the A1(M)', typescript information note, North Hertfordshire District Council, July 2001.
19. *Outlook*, Community news from North Hertfordshire District Council, Winter, 2001, p. 03.
20. Joseph Rowntree Foundation (2001), pp. 10-11, 14-15.
21. *Cambourne Life*, Cambourne Project Office, n.d. *c*.2001; *Chancery Green, Cambourne*, Alfred Mc.Alpine Homes, n.d. *c*.2001.
22. A system of local tariffs imposed by planning authorities to secure development objectives of the forward planning process, including social housing, was an option put forward in *Reforming Planning Obligations: Delivering a fundamental change*, London Department of transportation and the Regions, December 2001.
23. Joseph Rowntree Foundation (2001), pp. 20-44.
24. Essex County Council, *A Design Guide for Residential Areas* (1973).
25. Krier, L. (1988); *Poundbury* (2000).
26. The author visited Eco-Village, while attending Cornell University's 'From the Garden City to Green Cities'

conference in September 1998. See also www.ecovillage.ithaca.ny.us for updated progress accounts.

27. *Towards an Urban Renaissance*, Final Report of the Urban Task Force chaired by Lord Rogers of Riverside (London, Department of the Environment, Transport and the Regions, 1999).

28. Rudlin, D. and Falk, N. (1999).

29. *Housing Design Awards 2001*, Birmingham, 2001, www.designforhomes.org/nda.

30. Hall, P. and Ward, C. (1998).

31. Parsons, K. C. and Schuyler, D. (eds) (2002).

32. The New Garden City Conference was organised by Kobe Design University, and was hosted by Tsukuba City Council (10-11/9/2001) and Kobe Design University (13-14/9/2001). A wide range of papers was presented dealing with issues of updating the Garden City to the East-Asian context, sustainability, and new urbanism. At the time of writing, January 2002, arrangements to publish the conference papers had not been made.

33. The centenary of T.C.P.A. was initiated by a book launch for *Social Cities*, Hall, P. and Ward, C. (1998), and a debate on 'Planning for people and places in the 21st century', held at the Barbican Centre, London, 9/16/98.

34. The scope of the conference was summarised in *Insight*, Summer 2000, p. 8. At the time of writing updated detailed programmes were posted on www.iphs2002.com.

35. Advance preparations for the centenary were launched in May 2000, *Insight*, Summer 2000, p.6.

36. *Insight*, Christmas 2001.

37. Olmsted (1909), p. 199.

BIBLIOGRAPHY

1. Archives
First Garden City Heritage Museum, Letchworth: Garden City Association pressbooks and correspondence, Parker Collection, plans, photographs and practice records
Hertfordshire County Council Record Office: Ebenezer Howard Papers
Hitchcock Collection: Correspondence between Raymond Unwin and Ethel Parker.
Leicester County Record Office: Papers relating to Ferrers Estate, Chartley Castle
Letchworth Garden City Corporation: First Garden City Ltd., Minute Books and correspondence
Letchworth Public Library: Local History Collection, Local History Index
North Hertfordshire District Council: Bye-law records and plans of the former Letchworth Urban District Council
Royal Institute of British Architects, British Architectural Library: Membership records and Unwin Papers
Town and Country Planning Association: Minute Books
University of Manchester: Department of Town and Country Planning, Unwin Papers, photographs and slide collection
Welwyn Garden City Library: Osborn Papers

2. Theses and Dissertations
Day, Michael, 'Sir Raymond Unwin (1863-1940) and R. Barry Parker (1867-1947): A Study and Evaluation of their contribution to the development of Site Planning Theory and Practice', unpub. M.A. Thesis, Manchester University, 1973
Miller, Mervyn, 'To Speak of Planning is to Speak of Unwin: the contribution of Sir Raymond Unwin (1863-1940) to the Evolution of British Town Planning', unpub. Ph.D. Thesis, University of Birmingham, 1981
Pritchard, Mark, 'The First Garden City', unpub. M.A. Thesis, Courtauld Institute, University of London, 1970

3. Official Publications
Local Government Board, *Manual on the Preparation of State-aided Schemes*, 1919
Local Government Board, 'Report of the Committee Appointed by the President of the Local Government Board and the Secretary for Scotland to consider questions of Building Construction in connection with the provision of dwellings for the working classes in England, Wales and Scotland and to report upon the methods for securing economy and despatch in the provision of such dwellings', Cd. 9191, 1918 (*The Tudor Walters Report*)
Ministry of Health, 'Garden Cities and Satellite Towns, Report of the Departmental Committee' (*The Marley Report*), 1935

4. Books and Articles
Abercrombie, Patrick, *Greater London Plan 1944* (London, H.M.S.O., 1945)
Adams, Thomas, *Design of Residential Areas*, Harvard City Planning Series, No.IV (Cambridge, [Mass], 1934)
Adams, Thomas, *Recent Advances in Town Planning* (London, Churchill, 1932)
Armytage, W. H. G., *Heavens Below: Utopian Experiments in England, 1560-1960* (London, Routledge and Kegan Paul, 1961)
Artistic Country Buildings 1913-14 (Letchworth, The Country Gentleman's Association Ltd., n.d. *c*.1914)
Ashworth, William, *The Genesis of Modern British Town Planning: A Study in economic and social history of the Nineteenth and Twentieth Centuries* (London, Routledge and Kegan Paul, 1954)
Atkinson, George, Raymond Unwin: founding father of the BRS, *RIBAJ*, 78 (10), Oct. 1971, pp.446-8
Aus Englischen Gartenstadten (with substantial sections by Bernard Kampfrineyer), Deutsche Gartenstadt Gesellschaft (Berlin, Renaissance-Verlag Robert Federn, 1910).
Baty-Tornikian (ed.), *Cités-jardins* (Paris, Editions Recherches/Ipraus, 2001)
Bauer, Catherine, *Modern Housing* (Boston and New York, Houghton, Mifflin Company, The Riverside Press, Cambridge, 1934)
Beattie, Susan, *A Revolution in London Housing* (London, Architectural Press, 1980)
Beevers, Robert, *The Garden City Utopia: A Critical Biography of Ebenezer Howard* (London, Macmillan, 1988)
Bell, Colin and Rose, *City Fathers: the early history of Town Planning in Britain* (London, Pelican, 1972)
Bellamy, Edward, *Looking Backward 2000-1887* (London, Wm. Reeves, 1888)
Bendixon, T. and Platt, J., *Milton Keynes: Image and reality* (Cambridge, Granta Editions, 1992)
Benoit-Lévy, Georges, *La Cité Jardin* (Paris, Editions Cité Jardins par Charles Gide, 2nd ed., 1911)
Berlepsch-Valendas, B.D.A., *Die Gartenstadtbewegung in England, ihre Entwickelung und ihr jetziger Stand* (Munchen und Berlin, Druck und Verlag von R. Oldenburg, 1912).
Birchall, Johnston, 'Co-partnership housing and the Garden City Movement', *Planning Perspectives*, 10 (1995), pp. 329-358
Bonham-Carter, Sir Edgar, 'Planning and Development of Letchworth Garden City', *T.P.R.*, January 1951, pp.362-376
'Borough' Guide, *Letchworth Garden City* (Cheltenham, Burrows, 1908)
Brodie, A., Compiler, *Directory of British Architects 1834-1914* (2 vols), British Architectural Library, Royal Institute of British Architects (London, Continuum, 2001)
Brunt, Arthur William, *Pageant of Letchworth* (Letchworth, n.d., *c*.1942)

Buder, S., *Visionaries and Planners. The Garden City Movement and the Modern Community* (New York, Oxford, Oxford University Press, 1990)

Carey, John (ed.), *The Faber Book of Utopias* (London, Faber and Faber, 1999)

Chadwick, G. F., *The Works of Sir Joseph Paxton* (London, Architectural Press, 1966)

Charles, H.R.H. Prince of Wales, *A Vision of Britain* (London, Doubleday, 1989)

Cherry, Gordon E., *Town Planning in its Social Context* (London, Leonard Hill, 1970)

Cherry, Gordon E., *The Evolution of British Town Planning* (Leighton Buzzard, Leonard Hill, 1974)

Cherry, Gordon E., *Pioneers in British Planning* (London, Architectural Press, 1981)

Cherry, Gordon, *Cities and Plans* (London, Edward Arnold, 1988)

Colquhoun, Ian, *RIBA Book of 20th century British housing* (Oxford, Butterworth, Heinemann, 1999)

Cowlishaw, W. H., 'The Cloisters, Letchworth', *A.R.*, January 1908, pp.198-207

Craske, Harold, 'Letchworth Garden City 1903-1909', *G.C.*, NS4(35), November 1909, pp.250-2

Creese, Walter L., 'Parker and Unwin: Architects of Totality', *Journal of the Society of Architectural Historians*, 22 (3), Oct. 1963, pp.161-70

Creese, Walter L., *The Search for Environment: the Garden City Before and After* (New Haven, Yale, 1966)

Creese, Walter L., *The Legacy of Raymond Unwin: a human pattern for planning* (Cambridge [Mass], M.I.T., 1976)

Culpin, Ewart G., *The Garden City Movement up to Date* (London, G.C.T.P.A., 1913 and 1914)

Culpin, Ewart G., 'The Garden City and the Manufacturer', *G.C. & T.P.*, V(2), February 1915, pp.30-8

Culpin, Ewart G., 'The Lesson of Letchworth: Garden Cities and Reconstruction', *G.C. & T.P.*, VII(4), December 1917, pp.66-71

Darley, Gillian, *Villages of Vision* (London, Architectural Press, 1975)

Day, M. G., 'The contribution of Sir Raymond Unwin (1863-1940), and R. Barry Parker (1867-1940) to the development of site planning theory and practice', in Sutcliffe, Anthony (ed.), *British Town Planning: The Formative Years* (Leicester University Press, 1981)

Deakin, Derick (ed.), *Wythenshawe. The Story of a Garden City* (Chichester, Phillimore, 1989)

Dent, J. M., *The Memoirs of J. M. Dent (1849-1926)* (London, Dent, 1928)

de Soissons, Maurice, *Welwyn Garden City: a town designed for healthy living* (Cowbridge, Publications for Companies, 1988)

Edwards, Arthur M., *The Design of Suburbia* (London, Pembridge, 1981)

Evans, Paul, 'Raymond Unwin and the Municipalisation of the Garden City' in Steadman, P. and Owers, J., *Transactions of the Martin Centre* (Cambridge, Woodhead-Faulkner, 1976)

Filler, Roger, *Welwyn Garden City* (Chichester, Phillimore, 1986)

First Garden City Ltd., *Garden City in the Making* (Garden City Press, Hitchin, 1905)

First Garden City Ltd., *Guide to Garden City* (London, n.d., c.1906)

First Garden City Ltd., *Where shall I live?*, (London, 1907)

First Garden City Ltd., *Letchworth Garden City in Pictures* (n.d., c.1912)

First Garden City Ltd., *Letchworth: Where Town and Country Meet* (Letchworth, n.d., c.1935)

Fishman, Robert, *Urban Utopias in the Twentieth Century: Ebenezer Howard, Frank Lloyd Wright and Le Corbusier* (New York, Basic Books, 1977)

Furmston, W. G., *Ancestral jottings* (Letchworth Printers Ltd., n.d., c.1940)

Garden Cities and New Towns (Hertford, Hertfordshire Publications, 1989)

Garden City Association, *Conference at Bournville ... Report of Proceedings* (London, 1901)

Garden City Association, *Garden Cities: Report of a public meeting at the Holborn Restaurant, June 2, 1902* (G.C.A., London, 1902)

Gaunt, W. H., 'The Town Square at Letchworth', *G.C. & T.P.*, 111 (3) March 1913, pp.75-9

Geddes, Patrick, *Cities in evolution. An Introduction to the Town Planning Movement and to the study of civics* (London, Williams and Norgate, 1915)

Haigh, D., *Baillie Scott. The artistic house* (London, Academy, 1995)

Hall, Peter, *Cities of Tomorrow. An intellectual history of urban planning and design in the twentieth century* (Oxford, Blackwell, 1988)

Peter Hall, 'Tomorrow for Today', *T. & C.P.*, October 1998, Special Supplement, pp. 2-3

Hall, Peter, 'The Three Magnets re-interpreted', *T.& C.P.*, October 1998, Special Supplement, pp. 6-8

Hall, Peter and Ward, Colin, *Sociable Cities. The legacy of Ebenezer Howard* (Chichester, John Wiley & Sons, 1998)

Hardy, Dennis, *From Garden Cities to New Towns. Campaigning for town and country planning, 1899-1946* (London, Spon, 1991)

Hardy, Dennis, *From New Towns to Green Politics. Campaigning for town and country planning 1946-1990* (London, Spon, 1991)

Hardy, Dennis, 'In the free air of the city', *T & C.P.*, October 1998, Special Supplement, pp. 12-13

Hardy, Dennis, *Utopian England. Community Experiments 1900-1945* (London, Spon, 2000)

Hare, William L. *et al.*, 'A Part of Rural England. North Hertfordshire before the Garden City', a series of articles commemorating the 25 years of development of Letchworth, *G.C. & T.P.*, June/July 1930, pp.147-77

Harrison, Michael, *Bournville. Model village to garden suburb* (Chichester, Phillimore, 1999)

Hawkes, D. (ed.), *Modern Country Homes in England. The Arts and Crafts Architecture of Barry Parker* (Cambridge, Cambridge University Press, 1986)

Hebbert, Michael, 'Frederic Osborn, 1885-1978', pp.177-202 in Cherry, G. E. (ed.), *Pioneers of British Planning* (London, Architectural Press, 1981)

Hebbert, Michael, 'Tomorrow never came – or did it?', *T & C.P.*, October 1998, Special Supplement, pp. 17-19

Henderson, Ethel, *The Ideals of Letchworth: The First Garden City* (private publication, Letchworth, n.d., c.1975)

Hillman, Judy, *The Bournville Hallmark. Housing people for 100 years* (Studley, Bravin Books for the Bournville Village Trust, 1994)

Hine, Reginald L., 'The Village History of England', in *Coronation Booklet* (Letchworth U.D.C., 1937)

Hine, Reginald L., *Relics of an un-common attorney* (London, J.M. Dent & Sons, 1951)

Howard, Ebenezer, *Tomorrow: A Peaceful Path to Real Reform* (London, Swan Sonnenschein, 1898)

Howard, Ebenezer, *Garden Cities of Tomorrow* (London, Swan Sonnenschein, 1902)

Howard, Ebenezer, 'The Land Question at Letchworth', *The City* (Letchworth) 1 (7), July 1909, pp. 153-7; 1 (8) August 1909, pp.177-84

Howard, Ebenezer, *Garden Cities of Tomorrow*, new edition, ed. F. J. Osborn with introduction by Lewis Mumford (London, Faber, 1946)

Hubbard, Edward and Shippobottom, Michael, *A Guide to Port Sunlight Village* (Liverpool University Press, 1988)

Jackson, Frank, *Sir Raymond Unwin: architect, planner and visionary* (London, Zwemmer, 1985)

Johnson, Kenneth, *The Book of Letchworth* (Chesham, Barracuda, 1975)

Joseph Rowntree Foundation, *Masterplanning a new community. Designs for a town extension in York* (York, 2001)

Joseph Rowntree Village Trust, *New Earswick* (York, 1912)

Kornwolf, James P., *M.H.Baillie Scott and the Arts and Crafts Movement* (Baltimore and London, John Hopkins Press, 1972)

Krier, Leon, 'Master Plan for Poundbury in Dorchester', pp. 46-55 in Papadakis, A., ed., *Prince Charles and the architectural debate*, An Architectural Design Profile (London, Academy Editions, 1989)

Lanchester, H. V., 'Letchworth Jubilee' (with contributions by Osborn, Mumford, Purdom, Feiss *et al.*), *T. & C.P.*, 21(113), Sept. 1953

Lang, Michael H., *Designing Utopia, John Ruskin's urban vision for Britain and America* (Montreal, Black Rose Books, 1999)

Letchworth Chamber of Trade, 'Letchworth: England's First Garden City' (Letchworth, n.d., *c.*1933)

Letchworth Citizen, 'Letchworth's Diamond Jubilee Year' (Letchworth, 1963)

Letchworth Civic Week Committee, 'Hullabaloo', *Civic Week Official Programme* (Letchworth, 1935)

Letchworth Garden City Corporation, *Annual Report and Accounts* (Letchworth, 1994-5)

Letchworth Garden City Corporation, *Design Guidance for residential areas in Letchworth Garden City* (Letchworth, 1991)

Letchworth Garden City Corporation/Letchworth Garden City Heritage Foundation, *Insight* (quarterly), 1977 to date

Letchworth Garden City Directory (Letchworth, Wheeler Odell, 1907)

Letchworth Garden City Heritage Foundation, *Annual Report and Accounts* (Letchworth 1995-6-to date)

The Letchworth Naturalists' Society, *In and Around Letchworth* (Letchworth, The Museum, 1963)

Letchworth Printers Ltd., *Letchworth: England's Most Progressive Garden City* (Letchworth, n.d., *c.*1923)

Letchworth Urban District Council, *Official Guide*, 1951, 1963, 1974

Lyon, T. Findlay, 'Sir Raymond Unwin 1863-1940', *J.R.I.B.A.*, 3ss 70(9), September 1963, pp.356

Malpass, P., *The Howard Cottage Society: Its origins, growth and development since 1911* (Letchworth, Howard Cottage Society, 2001)

Matthews, Keith and Burleigh, Gilbert, 'A Saxon and Early Medieval Settlement at Green Lane, Letchworth', *Hertfordshire's Past*, Spring 1989, pp.27-31

Mawson, T. H., 'The Meaning of Letchworth', a series of articles on the celebration of Letchworth's coming-of-age, *G.C. & T.P.*, 16(6), July 1926, pp.127-47

Meacham, Standish, *Regaining Paradise. Englishness and the early Garden City Movement* (New Haven and London, Yale University Press, 1999)

Miles, V. W., *The Cloisters, Letchworth* (Letchworth, Lawrence Cloisters Trust, 1967)

Miller, Mervyn, 'Letchworth Conservation Area', *T. & C.P.*, 43(5), May 1975, pp.253-5

Miller, Mervyn, 'Letchworth Revisited: Cheap Cottages from 1905', *Housing Outlook* (4), 1978, pp.10-14

Miller, Mervyn, 'Letchworth Garden City 1903-78', *Catalogue of a Commemorative Exhibition, 22 July-22 December 1978*, First Garden City Heritage Museum, Letchworth

Miller, Mervyn, 'Garden City Influence on the Evolution of Housing Policy', *Local Government Studies*, 5(6), November/December 1979, pp.5-22

Miller, Mervyn, 'The Howard Cottage Society: Pioneers of Garden City Housing', *Housing Outlook* (5), 1979, pp.13-16

Miller, Mervyn, 'In Search of the £150 Cottage', *T. & C.P.*, 49(2), February 1980, pp.48-50

Miller, Mervyn, 'Raymond Unwin, 1863-1940', pp.72-102 in Cherry, G. E. (ed.), *Pioneers in British Planning* (Architectural Press, 1981)

Miller, Mervyn, 'Letchworth Garden City – Eighty Years On', *Built Environment*, 9(3/4), 1983, pp.167-184

Miller, Mervyn, 'The Roots of Planning', *The Planner (J.(R).T.P.I.)*, 70(9), September 1984, pp.11-15 (1984)

Miller, Mervyn, 'The elusive green Background: Raymond Unwin and the Greater London Regional Plan', *Planning Perspectives*, 4(1), January 1989, pp.15-44

Miller, Mervyn, *Raymond Unwin: Garden Cities and Town Planning* (Leicester University Press, 1992)

Miller, Mervyn and Gray, A. Stuart, *Hampstead Garden Suburb* (Chichester, Phillimore, 1992)

Miller, Mervyn, *Letchworth Garden City (The Archive Photograph Series)* (Stroud, Chalford, 1995)

Miller, Mervyn, 'The art of building a home: the design continuum of Parker and Unwin', pp. 180-193 in Burman, Peter (ed.), *Architecture 1900* (Shaftesbury, Donhead, 1998)

Miller, Mervyn, 'Letchworth Garden City – dream and reality', *T & C.P.*, October 1998, Special Supplement, pp. 20-23

Miller, Mervyn, *One man's vision. Key diagrams published in Ebenezer Howard's Tomorrow* (Commentary on slide set of Howard's diagrams, Hertford, Hertfordshire County Council, 1999)

Miller, Mervyn, *Architects of Letchworth Garden City: No.1 Barry Parker and Raymond Unwin; No.2 C. M. Crickmer; No.3 Cecil Hignett; No.4 Robert Bennett and Wilson Bidwell; No.5 M.H. Baillie Scott; No.6 Geoffry Lucas* (Letchworth, Letchworth Garden City Heritage Foundation, 1999 (Nos.1-3), 2000 (Nos.4-6)

Morris, William, *News from Nowhere* (London, Reeves and Turner, 1891)

Morton, A. L. (ed.), *Political writings of William Morris* (London, Lawrence and Wishart, 1979)

Moss-Eccardt, John, *Ebenezer Howard* (Aylesbury, Shire, 1973)

Mumford, Lewis, *The City in History* (London, Secker and Warburg, 1961)

MacFadyen, Dugald, *Sir Ebenezer Howard and the Town Planning Movement* (Manchester University Press, 1933)

Nettlefold, J. S., 'Ideals and Results and Letchworth', *G.C. & T.P.*, 3(4), April 1913, pp.89-91

New Townsmen, *New Towns After War* (London, Dent, 1918)

North Hertfordshire District Council (M. K. Miller), 'Letchworth Buildings Index', Working Paper, 1976

North Hertfordshire District Council, 'Letchworth, Baldock and District Guide', 1976

North Hertfordshire District Council, 'Letchworth Conservation Area Broadsheet', 1977

North Hertfordshire District Council, *District Local Plan No.2, Written Statement, July 1993* (Letchworth N.H.D.C., 1993)

Olmsted, Frederick Law (Jr.), 'Through American Spectacles', *G.C. & T.P.*, NS 4(34), May 1909, pp. 198-200

Osborn, F. J., *Green-Belt Cities: The British Contribution* (London, Faber and Faber, 1946)

Parker, Barry, 'Our Homes', *B.N.*, 19/26 July 1895, private offprint, Buxton, 1895

Parker, Barry, 'On the Planning of a Small House', *The City* (Letchworth), 1 (6), June 1909, pp.139-44

Parker, Barry, 'Presidential Address: Where We Stand', *J.T.P.I.*, 16(1), November 1929, pp.1-10

Parker, Barry, 'Site Planning As Exemplified at New Earswick', *T.P.R.*, 27(2), February 1937, pp.79-102

Parker, Barry, 'Memoir of Sir Raymond Unwin', *J.R.I.B.A.*, 15 July 1940

Parker, Barry, 'The Life and Work of Sir Raymond Unwin', 26 (5), *J.T.P.L.*, August 1940, pp.161-2

Parker, Barry and Unwin, Raymond, *The Art of Building a Home* (London, Longmans, 1901)

Parker, Barry and Unwin, Raymond, 'Cottages Near a Town', *Catalogue of the Northern Artworkers Guild Exhibition* (Manchester, H.C.D. Chorlton, 1903), pp.34-43

Parsons, K. C. and Schuyler, D. (eds.), *From the Garden City to Green Cities* (Baltimore, John Hopkins Press, 2002)

Pearson, Lynn F., *The Architectural and Social History of Cooperative Living* (London, Macmillan, 1987)

Pepper, Simon, 'Introduction: The Garden City Legacy', *A.R.*, 163 (976), June 1978, pp.321-324

Pevsner, N. (rev. Cherry, B.), *The Buildings of England: Hertfordshire* (Harmondsworth, Penguin, 1977)

Plinston, Horace, 'Letchworth: A Record of Events', unpub. typescript, First Garden City Heritage Museum, Letchworth, n.d., *c*.1980

Plinston, Horace, *A Tale of One City* (Letchworth Garden City Corporation, 1981)

Poundbury (Dorchester, Duchy of Cornwall, n.d. *c*.2000)

Purdom, C. B., *The Garden City* (Dent, 1913)

Purdom, C. B., *Garden Cities and Satellite Towns* (Dent, 1925, Rev. 1949)

Purdom, C. B., *The Building of Satellite Towns* (London, Dent, New Edition 1949)

Purdom, C. B., *Life Over Again* (London, Dent, 1951)

Purdom, C. B., *The Letchworth Achievement* (London, Dent, 1963)

Purdom, C. B., 'Unwin and the Garden City Movement', *T. & C.P.*, 21 (11), November 1963, pp.429-33

Reid, Aileen, *Brentham. A history of the pioneer garden suburb, 1901-2001* (London, Brentham Heritage Society, 2001)

Rodgers, David T., *Atlantic Crossings. Special policies in a progressive age* (Cambridge, Mass., Becknap Press of Harvard University Press, 1998)

Rook, Tony, *Welwyn Garden City Past* (Chichester, Phillimore, 2001)

Rudlin, D. and Falk, N., *Building the 21st Century Home. The sustainable urban neighbourhood* (London, Architectural Press, 1999)

Sennett, A. R., *Garden Cities in Theory and Practice* (London, Bemrose, 1905)

Simpson, Michael, 'Thomas Adams, 1871-1940', pp.19-45 in Cherry, G. E. (ed.), *Pioneers in British Planning* (Architectural Press, 1981)

Simpson, Michael, *Thomas Adams and the Modern Planning Movement* (London, Mansell, 1985)

'Sir Freshwater Spray' (Fitzwater-Wray, William), *How Sir Gadabout came to Garden City* (Letchworth (reprint from *The Worker*), 1922)

Steeley, Geoffrey, 'The path to real reform', *T & C.P.*, October 1998, Special Supplement, pp. 14-16

Stein, Clarence S., *Toward new towns for America* (Liverpool University Press, 1951)

Sutcliffe, Anthony (ed.), *British Town Planning: The Formative Years* (Leicester University Press, 1981)

Swenarton, Mark, *Homes Fit for Heroes* (London, Heinemann Educational Books Ltd., 1987)

Swenarton, Mark, *Artisans and architects. The Ruskinian tradition in architectural thought* (London, Macmillan Press, 1989)

Tarn, J. N., *Five per cent Philanthropy: An Account of Housing in Urban Areas, 1850-1914* (Cambridge University Press, 1973)

Taylor, Nicholas, *The Village in the City* (Temple Smith, London, 1973)

Thomas, Ray, 'Howardian economics and the future of London', *T & C.P.*, October 1998, Special Supplement, pp. 9-11

Thompson, E. P., *William Morris: Romantic to Revolutionary* (Revised Edition, London, Merlin, 1977)

Towards an Urban Renaissance, Final Report of the Urban Task Force, chaired by Lord Rogers of Riverside (London, Department of the Environment, Transportation and the Regions, 1999)

Unwin, Raymond, 'On the Building of Houses in the Garden City', *The Garden City Conference at Bournville … Report of Proceedings*, G.C.A. (London, 1901), pp.69-74

Unwin, Raymond, 'Cottage Plans and Common Sense', *Fabian Tract No.109* (Fabian Society, London, 1902)

Unwin, Raymond, 'The Cheap Cottage: What is really needed', *G.C.*, 1(4), July 1906, pp.55-7, (1906a)

Unwin, Raymond, 'The Planning of the Residential Districts of Towns', (i) Transactions of the Seventh International Congress of Architects, R.I.B.A., London, pp.417-25; (ii) *The Builder*, 91 (3311), 21 July 1906, pp.99-100 (1906b)

Unwin, Raymond, *Town Planning in Practice* (London, T. Fisher Unwin, 1909)

Unwin, Raymond, *Nothing Gained by Overcrowding: How the Garden City type of development may benefit both owner and occupier* (London, G.C.T.P.A., 1912)

Unwin, Raymond, 'The Planning of Garden City', Appendix B in Purdom (1913)

Unwin, Raymond, 'Making the Plan of Letchworth', *G.C. & T.P.*, 20(6), June/July 1930, pp.156-9

Waddilove, L. E., *One Man's Vision: The Story of the Joseph Rowntree Trust* (London, Allen and Unwin, 1954)

Ward, Colin, 'Howard, Kropotkin and the decentralist vision'. *T. & C.P.*, October 1998, Special Supplement, pp. 4-5

Ward, Stephen V. (ed.), *The Garden City. Past, Present and Future* (London, Spon, 1992).

Ward, Stephen, 'The Garden City as a global project', *T & C.P.*, October 1998, Special Supplement, pp. 28-32

White, R. B., *Prefabrication. A History of its development in Great Britain*, National Building Studies Special Report 36, Ministry of Technology Building Research Station, London, H.M.S.O., 1965

Whittick, Arnold, *F.J.O. – Practical Idealist. A biography of F. J. Osborn* (London, Town and Country Planning Association, 1987)

INDEX